WITHDRAWN

W9-ACT-511

3 3013

F
3444
.F55

Fisher, Lillian

Last Inca Revolt,
1780-1783

DATE DUE

BRADNER LIBRARY
SCHOOLCRAFT COLLEGE
LIVONIA, MICHIGAN 48152

THE CIVILIZATION OF THE AMERICAN INDIAN SERIES

The Last Inca Revolt, 1780–1783

THE
LAST
INCA
REVOLT

1780-1783

By Lillian Estelle Fisher

UNIVERSITY OF OKLAHOMA PRESS : NORMAN

By Lillian Estelle Fisher

Viceregal Administration in the Spanish American Colonies
    (Berkeley, 1926)
The Intendant System in Spanish America (Berkeley, 1929)
The Background of the Revolution for Mexican Independence
    (Boston, 1934)
Champion of Reform, Manuel Abad y Queipo (New York, 1955)
The Last Inca Revolt, 1780–1783 (Norman, 1966)

Library of Congress Catalog Card Number: 65-11237

Copyright 1966 by the University of Oklahoma Press, Publishing Division
of the University. Composed and printed at Norman, Oklahoma, U.S.A.,
by the University of Oklahoma Press. First edition.

In memory of Professor Herbert A. Allison

Preface

THE PURPOSE OF THIS WORK is to relate the dramatic and tragic story of the last Inca revolt (1780–83). The long-suffering Indians were finally aroused from centuries of lethargy and decided to get rid of the burdensome Spanish oppressions. Certain Creoles (Spaniards born in America) and mestizos (mixed-bloods), who were dissatisfied with the political, economic, social, and even religious conditions, urged them to start a revolution, and in many cases aided them secretly or openly.

Little has been written concerning the importance and extent of this uprising in South America. It stretched from Tucumán to Colombia and Venezuela through Peru, Bolivia, northwestern Argentina, and part of Ecuador, covering a larger territory than that of our war for independence on the North American continent, our Civil War, or most of the European conflicts preceding the world wars. It was the greatest Indian revolt in the Americas and fully taxed the resources of Spain and the genius of military officials to put it down.

It is difficult to find a cause more righteous than that of the Indians, bowed down by years of oppression, from which no relief could be obtained through legitimate channels. Few causes have had as noble and upright a leader as José Gabriel Túpac Amaru, who tried all of the means at his command to remove the abuses suffered by his people. Only as a last resort did he take to arms. The bloodiest and cruelest part of the revolution came after his death when his brother and his generals took charge. They were infuriated by the Inca's death and showed no mercy to the Spaniards, whom they were determined to exterminate.

The Indians failed because of the superiority of Spanish arms, yet no man of the colonial period contributed more to the well-being of Peru than the martyred Inca, whose demands for justice and reforms at last reached the royal ears in consequence of the rebellion. The King was greatly alarmed; therefore, a new regime to reform the decadent and abusive administration and thereby enable Spain to hold its vast American possessions for another half a century was inaugurated, in Peru and other Spanish colonies of the New World.

This work is based largely upon primary source material obtained in the Biblioteca and Archivo Nacional of Lima, the Archives of the Indies in Spain, the Bancroft Library, the University of California Library, and the Library of Congress. The abbreviation AGI is employed for Archivo General de Indias and B. L. for Bancroft Library. Spanish words are italicized only at first use. For the sake of brevity, long titles of documents and books are abbreviated after the first citation, and the place and date of publication will be found in the bibliography.

I am especially indebted to Professor Herbert Ingram Priestley, former director of the Bancroft Library and now deceased, for obtaining for me copies of the manuscripts from the Biblioteca and Archivo Nacional of Lima used in this work. These copies are now deposited in the Bancroft Library.

LILLIAN ESTELLE FISHER

Berkeley, California
January 29, 1966

Table of Contents

List of Illustrations, Maps

MAPS

The Last Inca Revolt, 1780–1783

Background of Revolt

ALMOST FROM THE VERY MOMENT that Francisco Pizarro and his men set foot on Peruvian soil on the second voyage in 1532, the Spaniards dealt treacherously with the Incas and showed no respect for their high civilization—a situation that was to exist for almost three centuries. Following the Spaniards' journey to Cajamarca, during which they were received hospitably by the inhabitants, Pizarro sought an interview with the Inca Atahualpa, who had recently overthrown his half-brother Huascar and had taken over the Inca empire. In the course of the meeting the Spaniards seized Atahualpa and fired on his followers because he refused to accept Christianity and threw a Bible on the ground with the assertion that his God in the sky watched over his people. And although Atahualpa collected approximately $17,500,000 in gold (at present values) as ransom, he was ordered strangled to death on the grounds that he had murdered Huascar, that he practiced idolatry and polygamy, and that he was plotting against the Spaniards. With the death of Atahualpa—whatever his cruelties and personal defects—came the dissolution of the Inca empire.

The Spaniards soon conquered the capital, Cuzco, and chose a new Inca, Túpac Hualpa, as the nominal ruler of the eight to ten million Incas. He, in turn, was slain, by dissidents among his own people. Manco Capac, a brother of Huascar, then became the sovereign and allied himself with Pizarro; but soon realizing that the conquerors were greedy and could not be trusted, he rebelled and besieged Cuzco for five months in 1536. When he found himself unable to sustain the siege in the face of the Spanish cavalry, he harassed the invaders from his stronghold in the Vilcamayo Valley.[1]

By now the Spaniards had fallen to quarreling among them-

---

[1] Sebastián Lorente, *Historia de la conquista del Peru,* 198–202, 207, 226–28, 275ff.

3

selves, with the result that two factions were formed—one led by Diego Almagro and one consisting of the forces loyal to Pizarro. The Almagro faction "crowned" Manco's brother Paullo, who appeared to be popular among the Indians and able to draw supporters away from Manco. Converted to Christianity, Paullo was regarded as a means for effective transition to Spanish control, but was unable to pacify Manco. When the Pizarro faction conquered Almagro's followers in 1538, Paullo easily transferred his allegiance.

After Manco was killed in 1545 by Spanish refugees, the Vilcabamba succession devolved upon his son, Sayri Túpac. Paullo was asked to negotiate with his nephew, the rival Inca, who proved to be far more amenable than Manco to Hispanization. Sayri Túpac promised to surrender to the Spaniards during the following summer, but, because of Paullo's death in 1549, the schism did not end. The Spaniards, however, were tolerant of the Vilcabamba state as long as it offered no more than moderate interference in colonial affairs. Finally Sayri Túpac was persuaded by his aunts, who had married Spanish men, to leave his state (in 1558) to be baptized with a Christian name. He lived on his estate in the Yucay Valley, dying suddenly in 1560.

His elder half-brother, Titu Cusi, an illegitimate son of Manco, succeeded him. Although Titu Cusi had allowed his sons to be baptized and had spent a brief period in Cuzco, he was never brought into colonial life. His death in 1571 was followed by the accession of the youth Túpac Amaru I and by a period of warfare in which a number of missionaries and envoys were killed. Friar Diego de Ortíz and his assistant, Martín Pando, for example, were put to death when the former was unable to restore Titu Cusi's health during his last illness. The Indians then told Túpac Amaru that the Viceroy was sending spies, and when Alilano de Anaya tried to conciliate the Inca, he, too, was killed. Viceroy Francisco de Toledo therefore decided to conquer the separatist state of five hundred persons. He beheaded Túpac Amaru I in 1571, although many influential citizens asked that he be spared. Túpac Amaru

4

was a regal figure who maintained his dignity to the last moment and died nobly. Toledo then opened the state to Spanish settlers.[2]

The Indians and the Spaniards always mingled—at all levels. Princesses and beautiful girls were given to the invaders, who accepted them willingly. The mother of Pizarro's children, Francisco, Gonzalo, and Francesca, was Princess Inés Huayllas, a sister of Atahualpa. After Pizarro's death she married Francisco de Ampuro, and the children, except for Gonzalo who had died young, were taken to Spain, where they married Spanish relatives.[3] It was thought that in this manner the hostile elements could be assimilated rather than destroyed. A similar idea had been suggested to Manco during his rebellion. One of his generals said that the native armies would enter Los Reyes, kill all the Spanish men, seize the women, and, with them as wives, create a strong new generation for an imperial state. As the Spaniards had put many native women to death in order to bring the rebels to terms, the Incas were probably forced to adopt this policy.[4]

Throughout the early years of the Conquest, many political governors countenanced official murder of the Incas as a means of getting rid of them, but other Spaniards advocated protection of the Indians and their rulers, favoring the establishment of the *encomienda* system. Under this system the Indians living on the lands given to the Spaniards were assigned to them as laborers for one generation (a period which later was extended to even four generations). Thus the natives were subordinated yet protected by the colonial government. On the encomiendas a kind of tyrannical local government, with native officials, was formed; and the *encomendero,* the owner of the encomienda, readily accepted the system. The result was a disorganized and tentative leadership which fostered corruption. Civil wars and native uprisings pro-

[2] Charles Gibson, *The Inca Concept of Sovereignty and the Spanish Administration in Peru,* 72–84; Arthur Franklin Zimmerman, *Francisco de Toledo, Fifth Viceroy of Peru, 1569–1581,* 109–18.

[3] *Documents from Early Peru: The Pizarros and Almagros, 1531–1578* (Harkness Collection, Library of Congress), 232.

[4] "Relación del sitio del Cuzco," *Colección de libros españoles raros ó curiosos,* XIII, 43–44, 52, 79–80.

vided the Spaniards an excuse to enslave the Incas, exploiting the large resources of human labor in mining and other economic activities with an energy that was never effectively controlled.[5] As a result, the Indian population was cut in half in the thirty years following the Conquest.[6]

Despite the debasement of their people, members of the Inca royal family managed to acquire a fairly good education from the missionaries, continued to receive honors, and did not hesitate to insist upon special privileges from the Spanish crown. To some of them the viceroy paid respect at the king's command. Then, under Viceroy Toledo (viceroy, 1569–81) historians declared that the whole Inca class consisted of usurpers and tyrants. This concept had justified the Viceroy's conquest of the Vilcabamba state and his recognition of local leaders as the only legitimate leaders. In Toledo's administration the transition to Spanish control became complete.[7]

Toledo brought many of the Indians into *reducciones* or villages. The Incas were settled in a large village, called San Francisco de la Victoria, where a garrison of fifty men was kept. In and near Cuzco some 21,000 Indians were gathered together in forty reducciones. Formerly they had lived in 309 villages. Other reducciones were established in other locations, but did not extend over the whole viceroyalty.[8] Toledo appointed Baltazar de la Cruz general protector of the Indians, permitting him to take charge of important lawsuits which the *corregidores* (chief provincial administrative officials and judges) and local judges could not decide and to defend the Indians before the *audiencia*. All petitions to the protector must be presented through the local judges, who were forbidden to accept gifts, contracts, or bribes. The Viceroy also codified a series of laws for the government of the Incas. He tried to stop exploitation of Indian workmen and to insure that they should be treated like human beings and free subjects. His laws

[5] Gibson, *op. cit.*, 13–14, 88–92; Ruben Vargas Ugarte, *Historia del Peru*, 72–75.
[6] See George Kubler, "The Quechua in the Colonial World," *Handbook of South American Indians*, II, 334ff.
[7] Gibson, *op. cit.*, 112–15.
[8] Zimmerman, *op. cit.*, 118–22.

6

were wise, aiming not to destroy tribal life but to preserve it and give legal status to tribal chiefs. Toledo's legislation thus gave the king and the viceroy control of a group of minor functionaries who were largely responsible for peace and the well-being of the natives, whose condition they were charged to alleviate. Unfortunately, however, abuses crept into the administrative system and numbers of Spaniards evaded the laws.[9]

As time passed, the condition of the subject race worsened, until by 1780 Peru was a land of oppression. Under the mercantilistic economic system of Europe, the Incas were exploited entirely for the benefit of the foreigners, who were considered the elect. Because Spanish officials believed that the Indians would not work voluntarily, they were brought under a system of forced labor called the *mita*. The Indians were assigned to mines, factories, large estates, and public works in the cities known as *mitas de la plaza*. In fact, everybody above the natives in the social scale exacted from them some form of personal service despite laws forbidding such exploitation. According to law, one-seventh of the tribute-paying Indians were subject to forced labor for eighteen weeks of the year, after which they were to be allowed to return to their homes and others employed. Theoretically, following completion of their term of service, natives would be free until their turn came again seven years later. In actual fact, the law was ignored and many Indians remained away from their homes for years. Of course, during this time their lands and cattle were neglected, and greedy officials often took advantage of their families to gain their possessions.[10]

Although the law provided that Indians might not be transported farther than two leagues from their homes, in 1777 some thirty thousand were brought from thirty to three hundred leagues to work in the mines at Potosí and Huancavelica. And, despite royal decrees of 1619 and 1752 requiring that their traveling expenses be paid, this was not done. Since any of the fourteen hun-

[9] *Ibid.,* 213–15, 225, 285–86.

[10] Ricardo Beltrán y Rózpide, *Colección de las memorias ó relaciones que escribieron los virreyes del Perú acerca del estado en que dejaban las cosas generales del reino,* I, art. 51, p. 241.

7

dred mines in Peru remaining idle for a year and a day could become the property of whoever worked it, it was necessary to fill the labor quota, and most mines were operated by Indians drafted by force.[11] Some were even kidnaped.[12]

If the natives in a community could not pay their cacique for exemption from the mita, they started out for the mines in a great procession. Those going from Chucuito to Potosí numbered two thousand with their families, and, including servants and followers, totaled seven thousand persons. Each man took eight or ten llamas and a number of alpacas for meat. The wealthiest *mitayos* (draftees) were accompanied by thirty or forty llamas to carry their supplies. Thus the three-hundred-mile journey to Potosí lasted two months and involved the movement of thirty thousand to fifty thousand animals.[13] Such a migration naturally interfered with the economic stability of and social conditions in Chucuito.

The Indians arrived at the mines already worn out from their travels, and there many additional hardships awaited them. They were often forced to work day and night. Only on Sundays could they leave the mines, and sometimes even then they were forced to work all day. From their meager wage of four reales a day, eight pesos a year were deducted for tribute and fines. Moreover, if an Indian lived to the end of his service, he was usually deeply indebted to the proprietor of the mine and was not permitted to leave until his debt was paid. Scarcely one native out of five survived, since the altitude, fatigue, fumes, lack of proper nourishment, and generally unhealthy conditions took rapid toll. Each year 12,000 natives were taken to Potosí alone, and it is estimated that during the colonial period 8,085,000 perished in the mines.[14]

11 *Ibid.*, I, art. 5, pp. 219–20.

12 *Memorias de los virreyes que han gobernado el Peru*, IV, 90–91, 107.

13 Kubler, *op. cit.*, II, 372.

14 Bando de Diego Túpac Amaru, Azángaro, August 29, 1781 (published in Boleslao Lewin, *Túpac Amaru el rebelde su época, sus luchas y su influencia en el continente*, 472); José Gabriel Túpac Amaru al visitador José Antonio de Areche, Tinta, March 5, 1781, in Manuel Odriozola, *Documentos históricos del Peru en las épocas del coloniaje después de la conquista y de independencia hasta la presente*, I, 148–49, 222–23 (hereafter cited as Odriozola, *Documentos*).

8

While the church and high officials recognized the evils of the mita, they tolerated it for economic reasons.

As the population decreased, it often became impossible to supply a sufficient number of men for the mita, but appeals to the authorities came to nought. In 1768, Marcos Túpac Amaru, uncle of José Gabriel Túpac Amaru, the leader of the Inca revolt in 1780, made such an appeal for the province of Tinta. The mita captain in Potosí had taken some mules from Surimana, which belonged to Marcos, as a penalty for failure to provide the required number of men. The corregidor did nothing to help him recover them, although the law forbade economic penalties against caciques for inability to fill the mita quota.[15]

The Incas also suffered great hardships in the *obrajes,* or factories, where different kinds of woolen and cotton cloth and blankets were manufactured. Here, too, they worked under the mita system and in order to pay their debts. They associated with criminals sent to work in the factories as punishment. Locked in the buildings as in a prison, they labored from dawn until dusk. If they did not finish their appointed tasks or made mistakes, the laborers were whipped or fettered or tortured. Any loss of time had to be made up at the end of the year. Because of lack of sanitation and ventilation, along with the half-rotten food provided for them, many Indians died before their debts were paid. Some of those who survived did not leave the factories for forty years.[16] When viceroys sent inspectors to the factories, the owners frequently furnished false reports or tried to bribe them; if the inspectors proved to be honest, their lives were threatened and often they fled before making the inspection.[17] It is not surprising, therefore, that Visitador Antonio de Areche said that the mita was a great

[15] Representación de los caciques del año 1768. Quoted in Manuel de Mendiburu, *Diccionario histórico-biográfico del Peru,* VIII, 117; Francisco A. Loayza, ed., *Los pequeños grandes libros de historia Americana,* Serie I, Vol. VIII, 10–11.

[16] Auto de Xal, Túpac Amaru, Azángaro, October 7, 1781. MS copy in the Bancroft Library (hereafter designated B. L.).

[17] Jorge Juan and Antonio de Ulloa, *Noticias secretas de America,* 275–79, 281–83, 289–91.

evil which should be abolished if the decrease in population were to be checked and the civilization of the Indians advanced.[18]

Conditions were no better for the Incas classified as *yanaconas,* persons bound to personal service, who were at the mercy of the *hacendados,* or estate owners. In fact, conditions were much worse than in the sixteenth century, when these Indians had a few privileges and some were fairly prosperous.[19] By the eighteenth century the number of yanaconas had greatly increased. They had become tribute-paying workers and were usually indebted to the encomenderos, who tried to get as many workers as possible by offering the Indians small gifts to enter their service. In the hot lands the yanaconas labored from two o'clock in the morning until dark cultivating cacao and sugar cane. In the more arid regions they cared for the cattle in return for a little food and clothing, for small plots of land assigned to them for cultivation, and for having their tribute paid, or for eighteen pesos a year. Lost time had to be made up on Sundays, and they were charged for any cattle that died or went astray.[20]

The corregidores, in their role as collectors of tribute, also imposed exacting burdens upon the Indians. They made up the tribute payers' register, usually in two sets. One, which was made public, conformed to the law; the other, kept by the official for himself, actually served for the collection. The latter included all Indians, even those officially exempted from paying tribute. The corregidor demanded tribute from all alike, retaining for himself all money that remained after the government had been paid its legal amount. Since the Indians were careless about keeping receipts, the corregidor frequently collected more than once from an individual. When an Indian could not pay his taxes, members of his family had to find the money somewhere or everything they had would be confiscated.[21]

[18] Carta de Areche al ministro de Indias, Lima, September 23, 1777 (published in Luis Antonio Eguiguren, *Guerra separatista del Perú 1777–1780,* 11–12).

[19] Juan Matienzo, *Gobierno del Perú. Carta escrita en el siglo XVI,* 17–21.

[20] Odriozola, *Documentos,* I, 146; Lorente, *Historia del Perú bajo los Borbones, 1700–1821,* 176.

[21] Informe de Diego Túpac Amaru, Azángaro, October 18, 1781, in Odriozola, *Documentos,* I, 219–21.

Fines levied by corregidores provided additional economic hardships for many natives. Unscrupulous men determined to make fortunes in the colonies imposed fines upon all classes, often without just cause and in violation of the law. Each official received annually fines totaling six hundred to one thousand pesos, depending upon his avarice and the wealth of the province. He usually handed over to the receiver of those funds about one hundred pesos and kept the rest. When public buildings were constructed or repaired, he compelled provincials to help pay for them. He put the Indians to work making brick, transporting lime, sand, and stone, and finishing woodwork for the small wage of a little coca or one real a day; yet he charged the treasury for all the labor and kept the money.[22]

In addition, corregidores appropriated the best pieces of land for themselves and took water rights away from the Indians. Ever since the Conquest Spaniards had put their cattle on common pasture lands and crowded out the natives, who had only a few cattle by comparison. Even the king's efforts to make the Spaniards pay damages to the Indians failed.[23]

Corregidores had a monopoly on trade in their districts—another means of acquiring wealth. They endeavored to prevent the Indians from engaging in their usual occupations and took them into their employ, giving them a wage barely sufficient for their support. The officials, indeed, reaped all the profit and did not even remit the tribute; and as long as it remained unpaid, laborers could not leave their work. The natives had no redress for such grievances because the corregidor had almost absolute control in his province.[24]

Each corregidor controlled what was called the *repartimiento* of merchandise in his district. This monopoly on the distribution of goods had nothing to do with the system of the same name applied to Indian laborers distributed to the conquerors with the

[22] Representación de los naturales del Peru al rey, Peru, December 4, 1781. MS copy in B. L.

[23] Representación hecha por el licenciado Francisco Falcón en concilio provincial sobre los daños y molestias que se hacen á los Indios, in Loayza, *op. cit.*, Serie I, Vol. X, 128–31.

[24] Bernard Moses, *South America on the Eve of Independence*, 170.

land; yet all documents call it a *repartimiento,* no doubt to distinguish it from the myriad financial monopolies. Its purpose was to furnish the natives with European goods. Since merchants did not penetrate the interior of the country for a long time after the Conquest, corregidores were given the privilege of introducing at reasonable prices articles suited to each district. Unfortunately, the institution soon became a means of wholesale robbery.

A new corregidor always brought merchandise to distribute to the natives. His first act upon arriving in his province was to take a census of the Indians. Then he selected an article for every Indian and fixed the price arbitrarily. The unfortunate Indians had no choice in the matter, being forced to buy almost anything— damaged goods, sick and dying mules, inferior merchandise at double or triple the price of sound items. They were compelled to purchase razors when they had no beards, silk stockings, books, mirrors, ribbons, velvet, silk, cambric, and blue powder for their hair.[25] Shortly before the Inca revolt, Beltazar de Arandia, corregidor of Chicas, found in the storehouse of his predecessor, Francisco García de Prado, some surprising items for sale to people supposed to be illiterate. Among them were eleven volumes of *The Christian Year,* six books of the Dominicans, two of *Spiritual Discoveries,* and two of the *Economic Dictionary.* Other books dealt with the instruction of youth, manners in the drawing room, and spiritual matters.[26]

When the distribution of merchandise was finished, the corregidor gave the cacique an inventory of the articles delivered to each person. Then came a time of great anguish for the cacique and the Indians when they realized the quantity, quality, and price of the goods. They protested that they were poor, but the official hurried off to the next village to make a similar distribution.

Payment for goods fell due at the same time as the tribute, and the same penalty was exacted for failure to meet either. When the corregidor returned to collect the debt, he took more goods with

[25] Informe de Diego Túpac Amaru, Azángaro, October 18, 1781, in Odriozola, *Documentos,* I, 218–19; Auto de Diego Túpac Amaru, Azángaro, October 17, 1781. MS copy in B. L.

[26] Carlos Correa Luna, *Don Baltazar de Arandia,* 186–87.

him, and this time allowed the natives to select what they wanted.[27] José Gabriel Túpac Amaru said that at first the Indians were allowed to take merchandise voluntarily at a fair price, but soon goods from Castile were collected in large quantities and the price of even an ordinary article, worth two or three pesos, mounted to ten or twelve. A knife of most inferior quality, costing one real, was sold for one peso.[28] The corregidor thus often made 100 per cent profit on the goods he sold instead of the normal 4 per cent. Sometimes he inflicted three repartimientos upon the natives during his term of five years and reaped huge profits. It was common for profits to total 60,000 pesos, and sometimes they reached 200,000 to 300,000 pesos.[29] Perhaps the corregidor's inadequate salary tempted him to remunerate himself in this manner.

It is no wonder that José Gabriel Túpac Amaru did not believe that there were any honest corregidores. He said that, if the Indians had been given a reasonable time to pay for the articles of the repartimiento, it might have been endured somehow. But when payment could not be made, the corregidores seized the Indians, their wives, children, and livestock, thereby depriving them of freedom of employment. Men were forced to abandon their families, with the result that the female members were forced into prostitution; thus public concubinage, so destructive to society, spread. Moreover, when there was no chance for the man to work, the tribute fell into arrears and the king was deprived of his revenue.[30]

Corregidores carried whips to aid them in collecting the tribute or debts from the repartimiento, threw the natives who could not pay into prison, seized everything they had, and even knocked down their houses.[31] In the valleys of Urubamba, Limantambo,

[27] Juan and Ulloa, *op. cit.*, 240–45.

[28] Carta escrita por José Gabriel Túpac Amaru al visitador D. Jose Antonio de Areche, Tinta, March 5, 1781, in Odriozola, *Documentos*, I, 146–47.

[29] Memorias relativas á la sublevación del cacique de Tungasuca José Gabriel Túpac Amaru sus consequencias y fin de esta extraordinario suceso suyo acaecimiento empezó el año de 1780. MS copy in B. L.

[30] Carta escrita por José Gabriel Túpac Amaru al visitador D. José Antonio de Areche, Tinta, March 5, 1781, in Odriozola, *Documentos*, I, 146–48.

[31] Bando de Diego Túpac Amaru, Azángaro, August 29, 1781, in Lewin, *op. cit.*, 471–72.

Oropesa, and Calca the corregidores collected the grain raised by the Indians, carried on trade with it, raised the price, and gave scant measure. In the provinces around Lake Titicaca they did the same with the sheep taken from the natives.[32] They forced 60,000 Indians to become domestic servants because they could not pay their debts.[33]

The Incas protested in vain against the abuses arising from the repartimiento. If they appealed to the corregidores, those officials usually did not understand their speech. Even the least petition had to be written. As this cost money, the Indians often spent more to have petitions drawn up in legal form than they asked for in the first place. Even the priests did not understand their pleas for relief and handed them over to assistants, who, fearing retaliation from higher authorities, did not dare do anything for them.[34] Diego Túpac Amaru said that when the aggrieved natives had recourse to the higher authorities and complained of the powerful, they got their heads cut off.[35] Thus the objections of the Indians to fiscal burdens and to the repartimiento were a direct cause of the Inca Revolt.

The natives were oppressed even by their own caciques, who often worked for the encomenderos and were hard task masters. Many assumed powers within their own communities equal to those of the Inca emperor and failed to observe the ethical provisions of colonial legislation.[36] They compelled their people to serve them, to take care of their cattle, to make long journeys to sell their products for a little coca or a peso, to work for Spaniards, and to do all kinds of labor. To enforce their will, caciques often kept the Indians' blankets until the work was done. Such caciques remained in office because they flattered the corregidores and their

[32] Representación de los naturales del Peru al rey, Peru, December 4, 1781. MS copy in B. L.

[33] John Miller, *Memorias del General Miller al servicio de la república del Peru,* I, 56.

[34] Deán Antonio González Pavón, "Causas de la sublevación indigena (Documento inédito de año de 1788)," in Loayza, *op. cit.,* Serie I, Vol. X, 76–77.

[35] Informe de Diego Túpac Amaru, Azángaro, October 18, 1781, in Odriozola, *Documentos,* I, 220–21.

[36] Kubler, *op. cit.,* II 364, 366, 375–76.

assistants.[37] They were some conscientious caciques, also, like José Gabriel Túpac Amaru, who tried to provide for the needy under their charge.

Customs collectors and their assistants also took advantage of the Indians, paying no attention to the book of rates. They collected taxes for everything they could and raised the rates as much as 100 per cent. Oils, wines, and brandies were not permitted to be taken directly to the customhouses, but had to be placed in the guards' offices and kept there from four to eight days. During that time there was a leakage of a number of gallons on account of dishonest domestics. Meanwhile, from day to day the price went down. If the Incas insisted on promptness, the guards insulted them and delayed still longer.[38] Diego Túpac Amaru declared that only the air was free.[39] To halt the stealing by customs officials, Bishop Moscoso suggested that they should receive a fixed salary and that a treasury offiicial should live in the customhouse.[40]

Unfortunately, a number of priests, who should have been protectors of the Indians, also became their oppressors. Some of the priests seemed to invent various fiestas in honor of the saints for their personal profit. On those occasions they raked in all the money and products they could and delayed church services until all the fees were collected. A priest in the province of Quito is said to have collected annually more than 200 sheep, 6,000 chickens, 4,000 guinea pigs, and 50,000 eggs. By such procedure he increased his salary of seven or eight hundred pesos to five or six thousand pesos.[41] Priests charged so much for baptism that many Indians did not bring their children to them; and burial fees became so exorbitant that Pope Paul V had to issue a decree against them. In the bishopric of Cuzco certain priests were named heirs of an Indian's property and received two hundred pesos besides as a burial fee, though the children of the deceased had to be put

[37] Loayza, *op. cit.*, Serie I, Vol. X, 155–61.
[38] Representación de los naturales del Peru, Peru, December 4, 1781., MS copy in B. L.
[39] Bando de Diego Túpac Amaru, Azángaro, August 29, 1781, in Lewin, *op. cit.*, 471.
[40] Loayza, *op. cit.*, Serie I, Vol. V, 128–29.
[41] Juan and Ulloa, *op. cit.*, 335–38.

in an orphanage.[42] Marriage fees were as high as thirty pesos; therefore, many people preferred to live in sin rather than to marry. Finally the king abolished payment for the sacraments and church services, but the law was not strictly enforced.[43]

José Gabriel Túpac Amaru accused certain priests of supporting their families from church funds and of spending the money of the poor in extravagant living.[44] Even bishops did not always fulfill the duties of their high calling and failed to inspect the different parts of their bishoprics to see that the Indians were well instructed in Christianity. The bishoprics were very large, and some people believed that they should be divided to insure more efficient administration.[45] Bishop Moscoso was subject to criticism because of his irregular conduct; and an *expediente* (bundle of papers) of one hundred pages in the Archives of the Indies deals with a scandal in which he was involved.[46] Such a man likely did not exert himself unduly to improve conditions among the Indians.

The restlessness and dissatisfaction of the Creoles and their opposition to the Europeans could not help but affect the Indians. The Creoles introduced many forbidden books into Peru, and if the works of the French philosophers were not actually read by the natives, their contents were so widely discussed that they heard about them. (Certain Peruvian writers hold that the Indians read more than is commonly believed.) Both Indians and Creoles witnessed the arrival of scientific expeditions and came into contact with persons from Europe who had been influenced by the new liberal tendencies. There were also prominent men living in Peru who had very advanced ideas. Chief among them were Pedro Peralta Barnuevo Rocha y Benavides of Lima, a devotee of physical and natural science, Eusebio Llano Zapata, who was the author of many articles on nature, and Ignacio de Castro of Cuzco.[47] Professor José Baquíjano was even bold enough to work against scho-

[42] Philip Ainsworth Means, *Fall of the Inca Empire and the Spanish Rule in Peru, 1530–1780*, 199.
[43] Valentín Abecia, *Historia de Chuquisaca*, 164.
[44] Odriozola, *Documentos*, I, 127, 152.
[45] Auto de Xal, Túpac Amaru, Azángaro, October 1, 1781. MS copy in B. L.
[46] Loayza, *op. cit.*, Serie I, Vol. III, 154, 190–92, 244–45.
[47] Daniel Valcárcel, *La rebelión de Túpac Amaru*, 19.

lasticism in the University of San Marcos. He was president of the Society of Lovers of the Country and aided its scientific propaganda by means of articles in the *Peruvian Mercury*. He had brought with him from Europe a library which included the works of the French philosophers, and he lamented the intellectual backwardness of Peru.[48] The Creoles, and even the Indians, influenced by the ideas of such men, could no longer overlook the economic backwardness in their country and its governmental corruption.

After the Conquest there had been great confusion in Spanish administration. Certain viceroys—Toledo, for example—brought order and some efficiency, but it did not last. Reforms were badly needed in the eighteenth century when weak kings grew careless in the choice of viceroys and high colonial officials. Gubernatorial functions had also become so complicated that viceroys had to depend largely upon secretaries and minor officials, many of whom were corrupt and did as they pleased.[49]

Viceroys took their time putting royal decrees into effect, no matter whether they applied to the Indians or to important governmental matters. When a decree came to Lima that Indians were not to be detained on the small plantations, the audiencia protested that the harvest was approaching. The viceroy therefore did not enforce the measure, reporting to the king that the judges had hindered him in doing so.[50] Of the 734 royal orders sent to Viceroy Manuel Guirior, who governed Peru just before the Inca Revolt, eighteen orders and eleven decrees were not obeyed.[51]

Governors and ministers of justice lacked experience and were deplorably corrupt. The Incas could not hope to obtain justice from them, for justice was often sold to the highest bidder and the judges divided the spoils.[52] This procedure was quite a contrast to an old

[48] Felipe Barreda Laos, *Vida intelectual del virreinato del Peru*, 317–21.

[49] Carta de Don Josef Antonio de Areche á Don Fernando Marqués de la Plata, Lima, February 1, 1783, AGI, 111–1–8, Audiencia de Lima. MS copy in B. L.

[50] *Colección de documentos inéditos relativos al descubrimiento, conquista y organización de las antiguas posesiones españoles de América y Oceanía*, IV, 422–23. (hereafter cited as *Colección de documentos inéditos*).

[51] Informe del alcalde de corte de la audiencia de Lima, Don Fernando Marqués de la Plata, Lima, December 22, 1783, AGI, 111–1–9, Audiencia de Lima. MS copy in B. L.

[52] Juan and Ulloa, *op. cit.*, 432–33, 464, 466–68, 473–74.

17

Inca law which provided that judges who secretly received gifts from litigants would be regarded as thieves and punished with death.[53]

The corregidores, who governed the fifty *corregimientos* (provinces) into which Peru was divided, bought their posts at a high price and often resorted to all kinds of dishonesty. They wanted to make up their expenditures and accumulate a fortune; thus few governed for the benefit of the Indians.[54] In the administration of justice they favored the powerful and the persons who came with gifts. They neglected the cases of the poor and of the Indians, who were burdened with increasing expenses from lawyers' fees and journeys to the places where the corregidores and their assistants resided. If the natives asked to have their cases handled promptly, they were punished and imprisoned. Officials considered the Indians little more than beasts of burden or instruments for the rapid increase of their own fortunes; instead of protectors, they became oppressors.[55]

Finally learning of the corruption in the courts, in the treasury, and among public officials, King Charles III appointed José Antonio de Areche, a councilor of the Indies and a man of inflexible character, *visitador-general* to remedy the situation. This post gave Areche practically the same powers as the viceroy. He was to check dishonesty in connection with revenues, establish just taxes, obtain punctual collection, and see that the laws were obeyed.[56] The inquisitorial character of the visitation made it unpopular; moreover, Viceroy Manuel Guirior did not welcome it because it weakened his authority. The Viceroy was a cultured but somewhat irresponsible pleasure seeker who was surrounded by corrupt assistants. At first he pretended to co-operate with Areche and received him favorably, but he turned against him when the visitador began to enforce

[53] Paul Radin, *The Indians of South America*, 269.

[54] *Memorias relativas á la sublevación del cacique de Tungasuca José Gabriel Túpac Amaru.* MS copy in B. L.

[55] *Representación de los naturales del Peru al rey*, Peru, December 4, 1781. MS copy in B. L.

[56] *Carta de Don Josef Antonio de Areche á Don Fernando Marqués de la Plata*, Lima, February 1, 1783, AGI, 111–1–8, Audiencia de Lima. MS copy in B. L.

the laws and make reforms in the treasury which affected his friends and dependents. Areche also reaped the unpopularity of a royal measure, passed shortly before his arrival, to increase the *alcabala* (sales tax) from 4 to 6 per cent, but to abolish the 3 per cent *avería*, or convoy dues on silver from America.[57] Areche arrived in time to receive the blame when collection of the tax began.

After the Viceroy refused to co-operate with him and opposed his financial measures, the visitador lost his temper and made complaints against Guirior to the crown. He declared that the Viceroy was extravagant, that he had deceived the King, that the orders he sent out in the monarch's name were false, that his measures had caused an uprising in Arequipa, and that he had held a celebration which he called his coronation.[58] These accusations prompted the King to recall Guirior and appoint another viceroy.

Areche's taxes caused great hardships among the natives, many of whom were poor. He used harsh methods to collect the tribute and the alcabala, the latter from Indians formerly exempted. He considerably increased the number of tribute payers by his plan of registering them. The increase may have resulted from the correction of defects in earlier registers caused by natives hiding from the tax, or it may have been that more Indians were included among the taxpayers than the law required. Areche ordered that all men of mixed blood should be included in a new general tax list when previously only full-blood Indians had been subject to the tribute. The result was that the contribution of the Indians was raised by 1,000,000 pesos annually and the funds received by the treasury mounted to 4,000,000 pesos in 1778 and to 5,838,852 the next year, leaving a balance of 1,614,208 pesos after all debts were paid.[59] These measures were not appreciated in Peru; many people later attributed the Inca Revolt to them and to Areche's quarrel with

[57] Carta de Don Antonio de Areche á Don José de Gálvez, Lima, February 5, 1783, num. 485, AGI, 111–1–8, Audiencia de Lima. MS copy in B. L.

[58] Informe del alcalde de corte de la audiencia de Lima, Don Fernando Marqués de la Plata, Lima, December 22, 1783, AGI, 111–1–9, Audiencia de Lima. MS copy in B. L.

[59] Copia de carta escrita á un Sr. ministro de Madrid por un vecino del Cuzco, Cuzco, September 1, 1782, signed "B. L. M.," pp. 146–51. MS copy in B. L.

Viceroy Guirior. Even the arrival of a new viceroy, Agustín de Jáuregui, did not help the situation since the difficulty of tax collection and opposition to the visitador's measures continued. People and institutions that could have afforded to pay higher taxes refused to do so or paid grudgingly.[60]

From this account it can be seen that under the economic, social, intellectual, and political conditions existing in Peru in the eighteenth century much dissatisfaction was developing among the Creoles and the Indians. The energetic reforms of the early Bourbons in Spain had not yet reached America; therefore the corruptness of viceroys, judges, and minor officials continued without interference. The Laws of the Indies, that monument to the colonial genius of Spain, were disregarded. Weakness of viceregal administration, maladministration of justice, increased taxes, and the irritations resulting from Visitador Areche's activities all added to the discontent. Areche himself prophesied the coming revolt when he said:

> The lack of righteous judges, the mita of the Indians, and provincial commerce have made a corpse of this America. Corregidores are interested only in themselves. . . . How near everything is to ruin, if these terrible abuses are not corrected, for they have been going on a long time. The Indians are very near their tragic end unless a remedy is taken.[61]

In fact, from the middle of the eighteenth century the natives had been throwing off their lethargy and trying to assert their rights by means of revolts, which had greatly increased in number. Some of these—like the fourteen-year rebellion of Juan Santos, the uprising in Arequipa when the customhouse was established, and the Farfán conspiracy in Cuzco—were quite serious. In his *Memoria*, Guirior gave a detailed account of disturbances in fourteen provinces, including the assassination of corregidores in three of them, yet he did not seem to expect the explosion that was to break out in 1780. When redress could not be obtained for oppressions and

---

[60] Carta de Don Josef Antonio de Areche á Don Fernando Marqués de la Plata, Lima, February 1, 1783, AGI, 111-1-8, Audiencia de Lima. MS copy in B. L.
[61] Antonio de Cánovas del Castillo, *Historia general de España,* V, 420.

political corruption still flourished, mestizo and Indian leaders, urged on by certain Creoles, began to consider another rebellion. Only a spark was needed to cause the discontent to burst into a great conflagration.

CHAPTER II

José Gabriel Túpac Amaru, Friend of the Oppressed

JOSÉ GABRIEL CONDORCANQUI, who took the name of his early ancestors and aspired to relieve the oppressions suffered by his people, was an unusual man. He was of noble descent, intelligent, fairly well educated, and brave, but he lacked the essential qualities to regenerate the people and restore their empire. Instead of trying to gain the co-operation of the Spanish Americans, who had common interests and some of the same grievances, he allied himself only with his own people. The former would have added strength to his cause with their wealth and military equipment, while the Indians were inexperienced, undisciplined, and short of arms. It is not likely that the Inca intended to break the bonds with Spain, for in all his proclamations he spoke highly of the King and his just laws and declared his loyalty to him; nor did he intend to abolish Spanish institutions and restore Inca culture. He worked for reforms and struck at the powerful families long entrenched in public life. Naturally, such procedure met great opposition among the Spaniards. As a last resort, when the sons of Spain failed to make economic, political, financial, and social reforms, he unfurled the banner of revolt.

The heritage of José Gabriel was of the best. He was the son of Cacique Miguel Condorcanqui and his wife, Rosa Noguera, and a descendant of the Inca kings. An ancestor was Sayri Túpac, the Inca who was baptized with the Christian name of Diego and persuaded to take up his residence in Cuzco, where many of his kinsmen lived, and who died at Yucay in 1560. Tradition says that Viceroy Hurtado Mendoza recognized him as lord of Yucay and marquis of Oropesa, but this is not true. His daughter, Princess Beatriz Clara, later married Martín García Oñez de Loyola, captain-general of Chile; and in 1616, Lorenza, their daughter, was created marquesa of Oropesa and Yucay. Lorenza was thus the first person to use the title that was handed down to her descendants. About 1624, she married Juan Henríquez de Borja, son of St. Francis of Borja and grandson of the Duke of Gandia, and bore him two sons and a daughter. All of her children held responsible positions in Spain and married into important families.

José Gabriel Condorcanqui was one of her descendants through Juana Pilcohuaco, a granddaughter of Manco Inca and a natural (meaning begotten as opposed to adopted) daughter of Felipe Túpac Amaru I, who was put to death by Viceroy Toledo. Juana was the sister of Doña Beatriz Clara and a second cousin of María de Loyola and Melchor Carlos Loyola. When the authorities forced Felipe Túpac Amaru to go to Cuzco, he took his daughters, Juana and Magdalena, with him. After his death the two girls were protected by the Archibishop of Lima, Gerónimo de Loaysa. Magdalena soon died, without issue, and Juana was reared in the home of Teresa Ordóñez. When Doña Teresa died, Juana went to live with a relative of her patroness, Feliciana de Silva, wife of Captain Manuel Criado de Castilla, who was also corregidor of the Cuzco Province.

Juana married Diego Felipe Condorcanqui, cacique of Surimana and Tungasuca. As she was very poor, she appealed to the Viceroy, the Marquis of Cañete, for alms. By a decree of October 19, 1592, he gave her a small piece of land in the vicinity of Cuzco that had belonged to her father and recognized her as the legitimate daughter of Felipe Túpac Amaru. She had five children, and especially for their sake she wanted to obtain information about her genealogy. In 1609 the corregidor of Cuzco collected this information from certain trustworthy witnesses, who all said that Juana was the last Inca's natural (not adopted) daughter. At the same time, through the protector of the Indians, Francisco de Vilela, she asked the corregidor for the right to apply to the Viceroy for money and land to maintain herself according to her position as a descendant of the Inca. Viceroy Esquilache granted her request in 1618, gave the land needed, and recognized her nobility. She and her children were to enjoy all the exemptions that the laws allowed to royal Incas. Moreover, the next year the Viceroy presented Juana and her daughter, Agueda, with two Indian servants. Later, on September 16, 1635, the Count of Chinchón confirmed these rights and gave Juana's husband the lands which Viceroy Luis de Velasco had granted to the corregidor of Canas and Canchis in 1602.

Only Blas, the grandfather of José Gabriel Túpac Amaru, survived from Juana's children. He inherited the caciqueship of the town Surimana in the province of Canas and Canchis, as well as his mother's lands. He married Francisca Torres, and their children were Bartolomé, Sebastián, Agustín Túpac Amaru, and Juana Pilcohuaco, to whom he gave her grandmother's name. The oldest son, Bartolomé, in 1687 received confirmation of the family's lands and rights, along with another statement verifying that he was descended directly from Felipe Túpac Amaru. Moreover, by a decree of October 19, 1699, the Count of Monclova permitted him to carry a sword and dagger, a privilege allowed only to noblemen. On August 23, 1701, the cacique showed the confirmation to Bernardo Prado de Figueroa, corregidor of Cuzco, asking him to inform the higher government of the contents; and this was done. He also showed it to the new corregidor of Cuzco, Esequivel Paraba y Navia, Marquis del Valle Umbroso, on June 26, 1715, and asked him to observe his nobility, which would give him the right to be one of the twenty-four noble Indian electors who chose the royal *alférez*. He was accordingly appointed elector and voted in the election of that year.

Bartolomé died without heirs, and his brother, Sebastián, who married Catalina del Camino, then succeeded to the caciqueship. Their children were Miguel, Marcos, Manuela, and Antonia. Miguel was the father of Clemente and José Gabriel Túpac Amaru through his first marriage to Rosa Noguera. It was thus that the noblest blood of Peru and Spain flowed in José Gabriel Condorcanqui's veins.[1] When his mother died, his father married Ventura

---

[1] "Genealogia de Túpac Amaru por José Gabriel Túpac Amaru (Documento Inédito del año 1777)," in Loayza, *op. cit.*, Serie I, Vol. X, 12–17, 41; Philip Ainsworth Means, "The Rebellion of Túpac Amaru II, 1780–1781," *Hispanic American Historical Review*, Vol. II, No. 1 (February, 1919), 5–6; Hakluyt Society, *History of the Incas*, Ser. II, No. XXII, pp. *xviii–xix;* Odriozola, *Documentos*, I, ii.

Monjarras; and in 1747 a half brother was born, who was named Juan Bautista.[2]

José Gabriel and another half brother, Diego, perhaps of illegitimate birth, whom some writers incorrectly call his cousin, frequently testified in proclamations and writings to their nobility. They knew that in 1544 a coat of arms had been granted by King Charles III to the Inca royal family. It consisted of a sun in full glory, an eagle displayed between a rainbow and two serpents, with a castle at the base.

High Spanish officials did not like the honors which this famous family possessed. Viceroy Esquilache in 1618 perceived the danger of allowing a member of the direct line of the Incas, especially with the title of Oropesa, to hold jurisdiction in Peru. Therefore he wrote a report concerning the claim of heirs to the marquisate of Oropesa which pointed out that the estates under the title were the richest and best in Peru and were located near Cuzco, where the memory of the Incas was most respected. He added that many descendants of the Incas were still living, subject to no tribute and no personal service, and that, moreover, some were very rich and powerful. He recommended to the Council of the Indies that all claimants to the marquisate be compelled to live in Spain and be paid for their estates, but his advice was not heeded.[3]

José Gabriel was born in 1742 at Tinta in the province of the same name, sometimes called Canas and Canchis. It was located in the picturesque Vilcamayo Valley south of Lima and about twenty leagues south of Cuzco. The boy was baptized at Tungasuca, the birthplace of his father. His childhood was spent in an exceedingly mountainous and beautiful tract of country. The Vilcamayo River flowed through a rich and productive valley containing towns and villages. Beyond the valley were mountains, with ravines that led to lofty highlands, and in the far distance were the snow-crowned peaks of the Andes.

[2] Valcárcel, *La rebelión de Túpac Amaru,* 22.

[3] Loayza, *Cuarenta años de cautivario (Memorias del Inca Juan Bautista Túpac Amaru), op. cit.,* Serie I, Vol. I, 30 n. Brothers not conceived in legitimate matrimony were often called cousins, and it is still the custom to do so in certain hill towns. Sir Clements R. Markham, *Travels in Peru and India,* 137–38.

When Manco Inca escaped from the Spaniards in 1536, he took refuge in the large Vilcamayo Valley, as has been related. There he established his court, evidently knowing that the valley was the richest region in all Peru. The Sun Temple, the Convent of Virgins, and other Inca institutions at Cuzco were transferred to this mountain fastness. There the Incas maintained their independence for thirty-five years.[4]

José Gabriel had a better education than most Indian boys since he was the son of a chief of considerable wealth and influence. He received his early instruction from two ecclesiastics, Father López, priest of Pampamarca, a native of Panama and a talented man, and Father Rodríguez, priest of Yanaoca, a native of Guayaquil. His father died when he was quite young, but his uncles, Marcos Condorcanqui and José Noguera, who were his guardians and the pro tempore caciques, tried to give him the best education possible. At ten years of age he went to study in the Jesuit College of San Francisco de Borja at Cuzco, founded by Viceroy Esquilache in 1619 for Indian boys of noble birth. A manuscript in the Library of Osuna says that José Gabriel Túpac Amaru "is a capable man and doctor in both laws because he attended the College of Principe for caciques' sons" near Lima, but it is not certain that this is so. The fact that even his enemies spoke of his culture, however, may favor the accuracy of this report.

The Inca youth won the approval of his teachers for his ability. He read Latin readily, spoke Spanish correctly, and his native language, Quechua, with peculiar grace.[5] His education was advanced compared to that of other natives. He believed in education and sent his own sons to college in Cuzco.[6]

At the age of sixteen, José Gabriel married Micaela Bastidas Puyucahua, a pure-blood Spaniard. She was a native of Pampa-

[4] Sir Clements R. Markham, A History of Peru, 194–95; Hakluyt Society, op. cit., Ser. II, No. XXII, pp. xxi–xxii, 230–32; Valcárcel, La rebelión de Túpac Amaru, 26; "Genealogia de Túpac Amaru por José Gabriel Túpac Amaru," in Loayza, op. cit., Serie I, Vol. X, 55n.

[5] Loayza, op. cit., Serie I, Vol. III, 172–73n.; Markham, A History of Peru, 194–95; Valcárcel, La rebelión de Túpac Amaru, 23.

[6] Memorándum escrito en el Cuzco, February 15 de 1835 (MS copy in B. L.); Markham, Travels in Peru and India, 135.

marca and a very beautiful girl of a good family who lived in Abancay not far from Cuzco.[7] From this marriage there were three children—Hipólito, born in 1761, Mariano in 1763, and Fernando in 1770. José Gabriel could easily support his family because, after his oldest brother, Clemente, died, he inherited the office of cacique of Tungasuca, Pampamarca, and other places. On October 25, 1776, he paid Corregidor Pedro Muñoz de Arjona a visit and asked that his right to the office be respected. The papers concerning his genealogy, baptism, and marriage were examined, and he was granted the caciqueship, which would be handed down to his heirs.[8]

It was a responsible position. He governed the Indians and collected tribute for the Spanish corregidor. He appreciated the efficient Inca system of government and the few local officials who still existed. Under the Incas there had been in Cuzco a council of four judges called *apocunas,* each of whom governed one part of the empire. Below them were the *hunos,* lords over ten thousand Indians; still other officials governed five thousand natives; and lower officers supervised one thousand. The apocunas and hunos were appointed by the Inca on their merit, but if their sons proved to be capable, sometimes they might succeed their fathers. Certain judges were spies, whose duties appeared to be similar to those of visitadores, and their positions were not inheritable. Each province had a great lord over it.

José Gabriel made use of this system as much as possible, since the people respected it. He was assisted by two native officials, the *picha-pachaca,* in charge of five hundred Indians, and the *pachaca,* in charge of one hundred.[9] Those offices, like the caciqueship, were handed down from father to son. Their possessors enjoyed certain privileges, for example, a fixed salary and immunity to arrest for serious offenses.

[7] Confesión de Micaela Bastidas, Cuzco, April 22, 1781, in Loayza, *op. cit.,* Serie I, Vol. IX, 108.

[8] "Genealogía de Túpac Amaru," in Loayza, *op. cit.,* Serie I, Vol. X, 17–18; Markham, *A History of Peru,* 195.

[9] Francisco Falcón, "Representatión hecha en el concilio provincial sobre los daños y molestias que hacen a los Indios," in Loayza, *op. cit.,* Serie I, Vol. X, 134–36.

José Gabriel was not the only important Inca at that time. Other caciques were also members of the royal family, men of considerable wealth who had much influence with their countrymen. They were exempt from payment of tribute and from giving personal service. They were permitted to wear the costume that had distinguished nobles at the Inca court. This consisted of a tunic called an *uncu*, a rich mantle or cloak of black velvet, and the *yacolla*, intended as a sign of mourning for the fall of their ancient rulers. Members of the Inca family added as an emblem of nobility a sort of coronet, called the *mascaipacha*, from which hung a red fringe of alpaca wool. The native people kept pictures of their Inca rulers in their houses and observed periodical festivities in memory of their beloved sovereigns. On those occasions plays were acted to the accompaniment of mournful music.

All those customs were left unchanged by Viceroy Toledo, although he had taken very strict measures to suppress the Incas. For instance, he decreed that any Indian who married an idolatrous woman would be given one hundred lashes, the punishment most offensive to the Indians. They were not permitted to take surnames from the names of birds, beasts, serpents, or rivers, though this was an ancient custom. No Indian who had been punished for idolatry, for taking part in infidel rites, or for dancing the dance called *arihua* might be appointed to any office.[10]

José Gabriel, who cherished many of the old Inca customs, made a striking appearance; he also had a pleasant and amiable countenance and unassuming manners. On one occasion he said that he was only a poor rustic and did not need the learning of priests to discharge his obligations.[11] He is described by Pablo Astete, who knew him well, as being five feet eight inches tall, well proportioned, sinewy, and robust, with a handsome Indian face, a slightly aquiline nose, and large, vivacious, penetrating black

[10] Markham, *Travels in Peru and India*, 120–22; Markham, *A History of Peru*, 195; Del Solar, *op. cit.*, 51.
[11] Carta de José Gabriel Túpac Amaru á Gregorio Mariano Sánchez, un padre, Cocotoy, November 12, 1780, in Odriozola, *Documentos*, I, 124; Pedro de Angelis, *Documentos para la historia de la sublevación de José Gabriel Túpac Amaru, cacique de la provincia de Tinta*, 16 (hereafter cited as Angelis, *Documentos*).

eyes. His countenance was intelligent, kind, and animated, his skin very white for an Indian, but not as white as a Spaniard's. He was majestic in appearance, and his natural severity was often relieved by his smile. Further,

> His address was dignified and courteous toward superiors and equals; but in his intercourse with the aborigines, by whom he was profoundly venerated, there was a sedateness not inconsistent with his claims to the diadem of the Incas. In mind he was enterprising, cool, and persevering. He was thoughtful and at times his passions were violent. He was frank and agreeable with his friends, but did not have many intimate ones. Yet he was esteemed by all classes of society. He did not commit excesses, although the occasions for vengeance were frequent.

People remembered the generosity with which he rewarded a medicine man who accompanied him from Lima to Tungasuca.

José Gabriel maintained that he was a Christian through baptism and would not profane the temples of God, whom he adored. Neither would he offend priests. He made such declarations in practically all his edicts; and despite the fact that one writer said he did so to cover up his depraved purposes, no case has been found in which he ever treated ecclesiastics cruelly, as did some of his generals.[12] Even priests spoke well of him. Vicente Jaras, the priest from Livitaca, said:

> Túpac Amaru is not an Indian idiot, as it is believed in this city. I am not acquainted with him, but I know he is sufficiently capable. He is generous to the people who follow him and even to travelers. He pretends to be pious and even tries to persuade people to think that heaven favors him.[13]

[12] Carta de José Gabriel Túpac Amaru al obispo del Cuzco, Tungasuca, December 12, 1780, in Odriozola, *Documentos*, I, 125; Memorándum escrito en el Cuzco, February 15, de 1835, num. 2494. MS copy in B. L. Relación de los pasages acaecidos en esta ciudad del Cuzco con motivo de la rebelión causada por el indio José Gabriel Túpac Amaru cacique del pueblo de Tungasuca anexo de la doctrina de Pampamarca sita en la provincia de Tinto, Cuzco, December 3, 1789, p. 66. MS copy in B. L. Markham, *A History of Peru*, 195–96; Carlos Wiesse, *Historia del Peru*, 148.

[13] Loayza, *La verdad desnuda, op. cit.*, Serie I, Vol. III, 172.

José Gabriel lived like a Spanish nobleman. In Cuzco, he usually wore a long coat and knee-breeches of black velvet, a ruffled shirt, a waistcoat of gold tissue worth seventy or eighty *duros* (dollars), embroidered linen, silk stockings, gold buckles at his knees and on his shoes, and a Spanish beaver hat valued at twenty-five duros. He kept his hair curled in ringlets that extended nearly down to his waist.[14]

Later, after his rebellion broke out, he modified his costume somewhat. When he rode into the town of Azángaro on a white horse, he was dressed in a blue velvet suit adorned with gold. His riding cloak was also of velvet of the same color, trimmed with scarlet cloth and gold thread, and was rounded at the corners like a cape. He wore a three-cornered hat. Over his suit he wore the *uncu* of his ancestors, in the shape of a bishop's rochet, without sleeves and richly embroidered. Around his neck hung a gold chain to which a large golden sun was attached, the insigne of his princely ancestors. He carried a gray blunderbuss, with a mouth the size of an orange, a pistol, and a sword.[15] On another occasion, in addition to his arms, he carried two slings made of silk crossed upon the shoulders, like the ribbons worn by knights of the military orders, and he had a third fastened to his girdle. He wore a cocked hat, with a plume on the side and on the crown a little cross of grass, called *chilligua*.[16]

Túpac Amaru was, according to Indian standards, a very wealthy man. His principal income came from transporting to Potosí, Lima, and other places quicksilver and merchandise on the backs of the 350 mules which he had inherited. His Spanish enemies called him the "muleteer cacique." Always attended by a small retinue, he traveled over a large portion of Peru; therefore,

[14] Mendiburu, *Diccionario,* VIII, 109–10.

[15] Odriozola, *Documentos,* I, 119; Mendiburu, *Diccionario,* VIII, 131.

[16] Relación de los hechos mas notables acaecidos en la sublevación general fraguada en los reynos del Peru, por el Indio José Gabriel Túpac Amaru, gobr. del pueblo de Tungasuca en la provincia de Tinta . . . desde el año 1780 hasta el de 1782. MS copy in B. L. *Revista de archivos y bibliotecas nacionales (Peruanas),* Año III, Vol. V, 158–59. See also Del Solar, *op. cit.,* 62.

he was in close touch with the people and conditions in all parts of the country.[17]

José Gabriel also had a large cacao estate near San Gaván in the province of Caravaya, thirteen thousand feet above sea level. Caravaya was a narrow strip of lofty tableland and forest-covered tropical valleys in the midst of the snowy range of the eastern Andes. The amount of income derived from his estate is unknown, but he must have had considerable influence there since the people took part in his rebellion. After his death, his brother, Diego Cristóbal, said that this estate was to be granted as a rightful inheritance to Mariano Túpac Amaru since it had belonged to the youth's father.[18]

Ambition beset José Gabriel, who traveled to Lima in 1770 to establish his claim to the marquisate of Oropesa, granted by the king of Spain to the Inca royal family. He wanted to prove his right to the marquisate against the claim of Vicente José García, who had gone to court to try to prove in his wife's name descent from the Inca kings.

The audiencia acknowledged José Gabriel's right to the marquisate. Its *fiscal*, Sarafín Leytan y Mola, paid him many compliments for his nobility and royal blood and declared him to be the heir to the marquisate since he was eighth in lineal descent from Manco Inca and of the direct line of Túpac Amaru I. The fiscal's statement was withheld from official publication, however, and so not everything was definitely settled before José Gabriel returned to his province.

The Inca seemed changed when he came home. Some persons believed that the compliments which he had received in Lima had gone to his head. Before his visit to Lima he had been humble and devout, but now he gave added attention to his style of living. He dropped his name, Condorcanqui, and took that of his ancestor,

---

[17] Memorándum escrito en el Cuzco, Febrero 15 de 1835, num. 2494, Buenos Aires; Del Solar, *op. cit.*, 52.

[18] Informe de Diego Túpac Amaru, Azángaro, October 18, 1781, in Odriozola, *Documentos*, I, 225; Markham, *Travels in Peru and India*, 206–208.

Túpac Amaru.[19] The name was sometimes spelled "Tupamaro," a corruption of two words in the Quechua language, "Túpac" and "Amaru," meaning shining serpent, or a person highly endowed with the gifts of nature, and was especially venerated by the Indians.[20]

José Gabriel tried to live up to this name and wanted his family to respect it. His domestic circle was rather large. It consisted of his wife, three sons, his half brother, Diego Cristóbal Túpac Amaru, Marcela Castro, Diego's mother, and his nephew, Andrés Mendagure, son of Pedro Mendagure and Cecilia Túpac Amaru, his half sister.[21] One of his best friends, who often visited in his home, was Antonio Valdés, priest of Sicuani. This churchman knew the Quechua language perfectly and had translated into Spanish and prepared for the stage the ancient Inca drama of Ollantay, which was acted frequently at Tungasuca before José Gabriel, who cherished the traditions of his people.[22] Other priests from neighboring villages and families of equal rank with the Túpac Amarus were received as guests in the Inca home.

In addition to being a good host, José Gabriel was conscientious, showed tact and moderation, and aided Indians in distress. He even paid tribute of the poor and supported whole families who had been ruined financially. A resident of Lima said: "For the most part Túpac Araru has governed himself not with that stolidness which we attribute to people of his class. The measures of which he has availed himself to carry out his plans prove some talent in him."[23] In fact, he administered his district so well that he was

[19] Relación de los pasages acaecidos en esta ciudad del Cuzco . . . , Cuzco, December 3, 1780, p. 65. MS copy in B. L. Lewin, *op. cit.,* 187–88. Markham, *A History of Peru,* 196; Markham, *Travels in Peru and India,* 137; Del Solar, *op. cit.,* 54, 57–58.

[20] Odriozola, *Documentos,* I, 1; Del Solar, *op. cit.,* 53.

[21] Memorandum escrito en el Cuzco, Febrero 15 de 1835, num. 2494, Buenos Aires; Mendiburu, *Diccionario,* VIII, 109; Moses, *op. cit.,* 204; Loayza, *Cuarenta años de cautivero, op. cit.,* Serie I, Vol. I, p. 30.

[22] Markham, *Travels in Peru and India,* 138.

[23] Memorándum escrito en el Cuzco, Febrero 15 de 1835, num. 2494, Buenos Aires; Copia de una carta escrita por un sujeto residente en Lima con referencia á las noticias que han comunicado del Cuzco, Lima, December 23, 1780. MS copy in B. L. Markham, *A History of Peru,* 196.

praised by Pedro Muñoz de Arjona, then corregidor of the province, who distinguished him above all other caciques.

In January, 1777, José Gabriel again appeared in Lima, this time to defend his interests against Diego Felipe Betancour, who was trying to usurp the caciqueship. José Gabriel again submitted to the audiencia a document to prove his direct descent from the Incas—his genealogy, dated 1777 and later found in the Archives of the Indies at Seville. He contended that Betancour was an imposter whose claim was based on false information supplied by his mother, Manuela.

According to José Gabriel, in 1683 this Manuela had appeared before Pedro Balvin, corregidor of Cuzco, who had helped her draw up documents stating that she was single, that her name was Túpac Amaru, that her father was Lucas Túpac Amaru, cacique of Surimana, and that she herself came from Surimana in the province of Quispicanchis. Herein lay the first misrepresentations, for the town was located in the province of Canas and Canchis and there was no such person as Lucas Túpac Amaru. Furthermore, said José Gabriel, his ancestors had been the only caciques of Surimana. He also questioned the reliability of Manuela's witnesses, one being ninety-four years old and another an Indian from Cuzco, Marcos Yanqui Rimachi by name, whose testimony was based on hearsay alone. On such evidence, however, the corregidor had declared Manuela and her brothers exempt from personal service, although he ordered them to consult the royal government regarding the payment of tribute. From this last order it seemed obvious that they were tribute-paying Indians, and did not belong to the nobility.

Without making further investigation, Viceroy Monclova, on July 10, 1690, had ordered the justices in Cuzco to guard for Manuela and her decendants all the privileges and honors granted by the royal decree. The fact remained, however, that she had not been mentioned in any of the decrees. Then, the next year, she complained that because she was a native, the justices had ignored the honor due to her house. She also asked permission to put up the royal coat of arms on her dwelling, although she did not present royal authorization to do so. The corregidor of Cuzco finally said that he had seen the titles giving her this right—that the queen had granted the favor to Juan Tito Túpac Amaru, son of Felipe Túpac Amaru, so that he could sit in the cabildo. This information seemed to prove that Manuela was a descendant of Juan Tito Túpac Amaru, and no further investigation was made.

Now, in 1777, José Gabriel contended that if the higher authorities had investigated the matter, they would have found that the royal decrees said nothing about Juan Tito Túpac Amaru, whose very existence was doubtful. He pointed out that one document had been issued in favor of Alonso Tito Atauchi (1544) and the other for Felipe Túpac Yupanqui (1545), and that since Manuela had not asked to be declared a descendant of Juan Tito, the corregidor had no right to trace her lineage to him. Moreover, the unknown Juan Tito was not the last Inca lord.

Betancour then presented the so-called royal decrees to the government, with the claim that he was Manuela's son, and asked that all the privileges included in the documents be reserved to him. José Gabriel replied that the spuriousness of Betancour's documents could be proved by comparing them with the genuine decree concerning Alonso Tito Atauchi. Manuela, he said, obviously did not know about it when she gave her information in 1683 or doubtless she would have based her claim on it. Neither did she know that in 1544 Felipe Túpac Amaru, the direct descendant of Manco Inca, had not yet been born and that he had been beheaded when still a young boy. All in all, therefore, he could not have had any descendants in 1544.

The proof which José Gabriel offered—and which showed that he was a fairly good historian—evidently angered Betancour's lawyer, Vicente García, who now set out to slander him. He tried to accuse the Inca of an impropriety in a wineshop, but José Gabriel said that he had never entered such a place because he considered such an act beneath him. The lawyer then accused him of putting up the royal arms over his house and asked for an order to make him take them down. José Gabriel replied that he had not used the arms, although he had a right to do so. García then tried to spread a rumor that José Gabriel was the son of a foreigner. José Gabriel did not answer this charge because he did not know about it. The lawyer also had maliciously removed José Gabriel's baptismal certificate from the priest's record book.

The Inca, however, submitted another baptismal certificate, which had figured in his petition for succession to the caciqueship. (According to this document he was thirty-eight years old when the revolt broke out, instead of forty, as some people have believed.) He insisted that the audiencia compel the lawyer to produce all the original documents on which Betancour's claim was based so that they could be compared with the ones he himself had submitted. That this was not done appears evident from the fact that in 1780 José Gabriel returned again to Lima and presented to the audiencia a duplicate of his 1777 statement. The case had evidently not been decided to his satisfaction, and no document has been found which shows that the audiencia ever recognized his title of marquis of Oropesa.[24]

While José Gabriel remained in Lima in 1777 waiting for the audiencia to disapprove of Betancour's claims, he attended philosophical discussions held at the University of San Marcos. On July 22, and again three months later, he also tried to obtain relief for the Indians working under the mita. He represented his own caciqueship and the *ayullus* of Yllaygua, Yanaoca, and Chicnaygua, belonging to the towns of Tanaoca and Yanaoca in the province of Tinta. The caciques of those towns had given him power on October 4, 1777, before José Palacios, a clerk of Cuzco, to present their petitions concerning the mita of the Viceroy.

Túpac Amaru faithfully performed his mission and clearly set forth the abuses under the mita system. He informed the Viceroy of the hardships the Indians suffered in traveling two hundred or more leagues to reach Potosí to work under the mita. He cited the difficulty of providing the fifteen Indians required for the mita since the native population had decreased, and claimed that he was compelled to use strangers to fill his quota for fear of incurring the penalty inflicted earlier on his uncle, Marcos Túpac Amaru, for

[24] "Genealogia de Túpac Amaru," in Loayza, *op. cit.*, Serie I, Vol. X, 1–6, 19–59, and 55n.

failure to provide the requisite number of workers. He told the Viceroy that Indians sent out "venturing" to find new deposits of metals and pick them out of the mountains were given no more time to perform their tasks than if the metals were ready for loading. In other words, work that could scarcely be done in three days had to be finished in one day. He also said that mine operators preferred mitayos to other laborers because they could treat them like slaves. "It is not sensible that the natives suffer bad treatment under the mita," he added, "when they are considered so useful and necessary."

He cited certain chapters of the ordinance book concerning personal service by the Indians to remind the executive that the King did not want them to suffer from the mita. In chapter ten the sovereign expressed the desire that they be relieved as much as possible and that Negroes or voluntary day laborers be provided for the mines. In chapter fourteen he provided for adequate wages to be paid punctually and for taking care of workers' health; in four and eight he ordered that towns be built near the mines, so that workers would not have to be brought so far. In chapter eighteen he definitely stated that caciques who sent in the second mita Indians who had served in the first would be punished. José Gabriel asked the Viceroy to see that such laws were obeyed and to reduce the number of natives required for the mita.[25] The collector of revenues, Juan José Lemos, agreed with José Gabriel concerning the abuses of the mita, and calling attention to the increasing number of natives who had died in the service of the mita of Potosí, declared that it would exterminate them.[26]

Visitador Areche did not think that the Inca had sent satisfactory proofs of his statements. He said that the King had appointed Jorge Escovedo, a minister of the Audiencia of Charcas, to supervise the corregimiento of Potosí and the Indian mitayos. He did agree that the natives should be allowed traveling expenses, should be treated justly, and should not be brought great distances

[25] Unedited letter of José Gabriel Túpac Amaru to the Viceroy, published in Eguiguren, *op. cit.*, 8, 14–19.

[26] Loayza, *Preliminarios del incendio, op. cit.*, Serie I, Vol. XIII, 9–12, 21–28.

to the mines, but he did not think that the mita, despite its evils, could be abolished. He advised an investigation and wrote himself to the superintendent of the mita giving him the Indians' reasons for wanting to free themselves from the system. The superintendent replied that he had paid the Indians for their journey to the mines and denied that they were badly treated. He was the wrong man to ask for such information, since he wanted the system continued. Areche advised Túpac Amaru to go home and await the measures which the superintendent of the mita would institute to remove its abuses. When the Marquis of Soto Florida gave him the same advice, at the end of May, 1778, José Gabriel returned to Pampamarca, where he waited in vain.[27]

The cacique now tried to cultivate the friendship of Spanish priests and officials, never losing an opportunity to impress upon them the wretched condition of the Indians. His earnest appeals for help had some results, since the priests Manuel Arroyo and Ignacio Castro, Agustín de Gurruchatequi, bishop of Cuzco, Francisco Campos, bishop of La Paz, and the Bishop of Arequipa preached frequently against the inhuman treatment of the Indians. They even sent José Gabriel's petitions to Spain with Ventura Santalices, governor of La Paz, who was devoted to the Indians' cause. The Governor persuaded the Spanish authorities to listen to him and even obtained a seat in the Council of the Indies, but he died suddenly in Spain, perhaps from poison.

Blas Túpac Amaru, an uncle of José Gabriel, also worked for the worthy cause. He lived in Potosí and knew at first hand about the suffering of the Indians in the mines. Aided by his nephew, he made such energetic remonstrances against the evils in Peru that he, too, was summoned to Spain, where he was promised many concessions. José Gabriel said that the King appointed his uncle perpetual defender of the natives of Potosí, with a good salary, and gave him power to act against the corrupt government of the corregidores, the abuses of customs collectors, the mita of Potosí, and other burdens suffered by the natives. Blas was thought

---

[27] Letter of Areche concerning the mita, Lima, September 23, 1777, in Eguiguren, *op. cit.*, 12, 13; Loayza, *Preliminarios del incendio, op. cit.*, Serie I, Vol. XIII, 19–21.

to have been murdered at sea on his way home because it was feared that he was carrying dispatches to remove the abuses. José Gabriel then declared that the King had given him the same commission which his uncle had obtained. He should have known that while the sovereign probably promised to solve the problem, he would hardly give a descendant of the Incas such important dispatches. The clergy and other persons working for the natives thus succeeded only in obtaining momentary relief in the small district where their influence was felt.[28]

One of the greatest obstacles to reform as well as one of the cruelest oppressors of the Indians was Antonio de Arriaga, a European Spaniard and military man who in 1776 was appointed corregidor of the province of Tinta. He is usually described as unscrupulous and greedy and is credited with providing the immediate cause of the revolt of 1780. Yet on one occasion (June 28, 1780) Visitador Areche warned him to pay stricter attention to the collection of tribute, to keep exact lists of taxpayers, to arrest persons who did not pay their taxes, and to seize their goods. This does not look as if Arriaga was quite as greedy as represented. If he had been greedier, there would have been no uncollected taxes. He replied (July 22) that, if there was any laxness, it was due to his failing health.[29] Arriaga, however, was ably assisted by members of his family, whom the people disliked. His brother Miguel, as a functionary of the royal treasury, was the man who had finally collected, no doubt harshly, the new taxes in the province of Tinta. His nephew, Eusebio Balza, had been sergeant of militias in Tucumán and came to Tinta to perform the same duties. He also served as corregidor when his uncle was absent.

At first Arriaga and Túpac Amaru seemed friendly. When Simón

[28] Bando de Josef Gabriel Túpac Amaru, Inca, in Vicente de Ballivián y Roxas, *Archivo Boliviano. Colección de documentos relativos á la historia de Bolivia, durante la época colonial*, 242–44; Gregorio Funes, *Ensayo de la historia civil de Buenos Aires: Tucumán y Paraguay*, 234–35; Markham, *A History of Peru*, 193–94; Manuel Ordóñez López and Luis Crespo, *Bosquejo de la historia de Bolivia*, 113; V. M. Carrió, *Crónicas Americanas*, 78.

[29] Carta de José Antonio de Areche al Antonio de Arriaga, Lima, June 28, 1780. MS copy in B. L. Carta de José Antonio de Arriaga al visitador Jospe Antonio de Areche, Cuzco, July 22, 1780, in Loayza, *op. cit.*, Serie I, Vol. III, 249–50.

Jiménez Villalba, archdean of the diocese of Cuzco, asked the Inca for a loan of two thousand pesos which José Gabriel did not have, the latter borrowed it from Arriaga. On March 15, 1780, he wrote the corregidor that he would pay this amount plus some three hundred pesos which the customhouse of Tungasuca still owed him from the alcabala. On the twenty-second he wrote again, saying that he had heard that the meat in Tungasuca was tasteless, and he was therefore sending Arriaga, as a sign of affection, a little bull and six lambs to roast.[30] It is not known what ended this friendship, but ended it was, and the corregidor became the cacique's bitter enemy. Each act of kindness, each recognition, each visit which José Gabriel received, and everything he did was considered a usurpation of rights that belonged to the corregidor alone. It is certain that the official was jealous of the Inca. On one occasion he called him the "fraudulent Indian." This hurt and angered Túpac Amaru, who remarked to certain friends, "Very soon the corregidor will pay me for this insult."

Legally the corregidor was the cacique's superior. Arriaga assumed that this meant that he could be absolute ruler in his district over all classes of people.[31] His bad spirit and haughtiness naturally caused much hostility. It was reported that he beat his collectors and knocked them down when they refused to obey him, and that he treated seculars, priests, and persons of all classes in a similar manner, saying that he could depend only on first-rank grandees of Spain for assistance. He disregarded the laws and even dared to impose three repartimientos upon the people, each one amounting to about 150,000 pesos.[32] According to José Gabriel, he collected 300,000 pesos when the book of rates for five years showed 112,000 pesos as the legal amount allowed. At his death Arriaga left a fortune of 50,000 pesos.[33]

[30] Túpac Amaru al corregidor Don Arriaga, Tungasuca, March 15, 1780. MS copy in B. L. Carta de José Gabriel Túpac Amaru á Don Antonio de Arriaga, Tungasuca, March 22, 1780, in Loayza, *La verdad desnuda*, Serie I, Vol. III, 48–49.

[31] Memorándum escrito en Cuzco, February 15 de 1835, num. 2494, Biblioteca Nacional, Buenos Aires; Valcárcel, *La rebelión de Túpac Amaru*, 33.

[32] Miller, *op. cit.*, I, 68.

[33] Carta escrita por D. José Gabriel Túpac Amaru al visitador D. José Antonio de Areche, Tinta, March 5, 1781, in Odriozola, *Documentos*, I, 147; Valcárcel, *La rebelión de Túpac Amaru*, 33.

Arriaga was also on bad terms with the church. The enmity between him and Bishop Moscoso y Peralta antedated the corregidor's arrival in Tinta. While serving as temporary governor of Tucumán, Arriaga had exercised the functions of vice-patron of the church. This meant that he had the right to fill vacancies from a list of three names submitted to him by the bishop. Moscoso, who was bishop of Tucumán at the time, resented the governor's making changes in his list and appointing men not on it. The two were polite to each other; therefore the feud did not break into the open until six months after Moscoso became bishop of Cuzco and Arriaga corregidor of Tinta. The prelate then accused Arriaga of intoxication and of being especially grasping. On the other hand, Arriaga said that the Bishop was too fond of worldly pleasures.

Their worst quarrel occurred over the question of secular and church jurisdiction in the town of Yauri. The Bishop of Cuzco appointed Vicente de la Puente, a mulatto and a man of scandalous conduct though priest of Coporaque, to investigate a disturbance in Yauri. Puente soon got into trouble with the inhabitants, who complained again and again of his behavior and disregarded his authority. When investigation was made, it was alleged that Puente and Juan José Palomino, administrator of ecclesiastical livings, had incited sedition in Yauri on April 13 and 27. At that time Puente had tried to enter the house of the priest, Justo Martínez, by force, while the parishioners resisted. Palomino profaned the sanctuary by dragging out of it a wounded Indian, Francisco Aguilar, whom he tied to the tail of a horse, evidently on Puente's orders. When Father Martínez complained to the Bishop, Puente was removed and Faustino del Rivero, an ecclesiastic from Cuzco, was appointed to succeed him.

Rivero was no peacemaker. He soon imprisoned three suspected criminals and insisted upon the arrest of the citizens who had resisted church authority. The corregidor finally issued an order for the imprisonment of Jacinto Mesa, Alejo Trujillo, Manuel Álvarez, Francisco Aguilar, José Mamani, and others, and kept them in the prison at Tinta from May 31 to July 7, 1780. Arriaga thought this measure would restore harmony, but Rivero wanted

40

the Bishop's commissioner to take their confessions and send them to Cuzco. When the confessions were heard, Mesa grew irritated and demanded his right to be tried by a civil court, thus angering the ecclesiastical commissioner. Then the corregidor suspended the confession, sent word to the Bishop to abstain entirely in the matter, and set the prisoners free under bond, whereupon the Bishop ordered him to send them to Cuzco under penalty of excommunication.

The corregidor pointed out to the Bishop that the prisoners were under secular, not church, jurisdiction. He sent two communications to the Viceroy by his nephew, Balza, in which he explained the disagreement with the Bishop, but when he refused to hand over the prisoners, the provisor, Juan Antonio Tristán, excommunicated him on July 27 for protecting sacrilegious natives.

Arriaga was deeply hurt and asked to be absolved, but the provisor refused. The corregidor then went to the *cabildo*, the justice, and magistrates of Cuzco to see if anything could be done. Bishop Moscoso reported that he tried to re-establish good relations, but Arriaga answered him haughtily and would agree to nothing except to let the matter take its course in the Audiencia of Lima. On August 17, the audiencia judges asked the provisor to lift the ban of excommunication, but he again refused to do so. For more than two months the corregidor suffered the penalty of the church. A second order from the audiencia the provisor had to obey.

Tension still existed, for the church court was hostile and found means to annoy the corregidor. The last of September the provisor ordered Francisco Álvarez, serving temporarily as priest of Coporaque, to consume the sacraments, close the church, send the keys to Cuzco, and remove all priests from the town. This caused commotion among the Indians and hatred for the provisor and the priest. Arriaga, alarmed, hastened to Coporaque to keep the priest from carrying out the order.

The real source of the trouble with the Bishop lay in Arriaga's secretly informing the Viceroy, through his nephew, that Moscoso was involved in the Farfán conspiracy and the Inca uprising—thus practically signing his own death warrant. The prelate's nephew,

José Antonio Borda, who happened to be at the viceregal palace and was a friend of Visitador Areche, discovered what had happened and lost no time in telling his uncle of Arriaga's accusation, after which Bishop Moscoso made new complaints to higher authorities about Arriaga. Of course, almost everybody took the word of a bishop. Areche would not even grant Balza an audience and refused to give any credence to the accusation.[34] It was thought that the Bishop began plotting to get rid of Arriaga after this incident.

He first removed the priests, Justo and Antonio Martínez, intimate friends of the corregidor, from the *doctrinas* of Sicuani and Yauri. Had they remained in their parishes, it is likely they could have prevented the execution of Arriaga. But, as matters stood, Túpac Amaru no doubt thought that he could proceed against the corregidor in the name of human and divine laws.

Some people in Peru believed that Túpac Amaru's uprising resulted from the rivalry over jurisdiction between the Bishop of Cuzco and the corregidor of Tinta. They said that the prelate was an ignorant, spiteful, greedy man who thought only of acquiring wealth, that he appropriated church revenues in the belief that he had a perfect right to control them, and that he even kept the money allotted for repair of churches, as was the case in the parish of Maranganí. The church of that town had no roof, and when Bishop Moscoso visited there in 1779, he ordered services to be discontinued during the rainy season. He pretended to be interested in repairing the building and took the four thousand pesos collected by the priest, Martínez, for that purpose. After three years, the church still lacked a roof.

Moscoso, however, was sometimes represented in different light. In the *Gaceta de Madrid* of June 15, 1781, he was said to be very honorable and generous, yet this was not the case. Even the visitador mentioned him among those vassals who offered the King their possessions for the war against Great Britain, but, when that conflict broke out, funds of the royal treasury had to be used. The

---

[34] Representación dirigida al rey por Don Miguel de Arriaga y Don Eusebio Balza de Verganza con fecha de 24 de Diciembre 1780, in Loayza, *La verdad desnuda, op. cit.,* Serie I, Vol. III, 31–45, 67–88, 108–10. Cánovas del Castillo, *op. cit.,* V, 421–22, 425–31; Valcárcel, *La rebelión de Túpac Amaru,* 34–37.

Bishop evidently did not use his great wealth to help individuals or worthy causes, as would be expected. A citizen of Cuzco said:

> As soon as Señor Moscoso arrived in this neighborhood the tranquility and peace, which it enjoyed, perished, because under the hyprocritical zeal of discharging his duties he has not done another thing but clink chains and draw blood on account of his passions . . . . He abhorrs the Europeans extremely, takes vengeance upon various inhabitants for despicable motives, and maintains relations with persons of the other sex, not of good fame, causing serious scandal to the city. The first high office he obtained was in Arequipa and in that city he began to show insubordination. . . . He says he has no superior in the land but the Pope.[35]

Since the man who made this statement was evidently a friend of the corregidor at Tinta, it is probably exaggerated.

Rumors also spread that the Bishop had carried on secret correspondence with José Gabriel Túpac Amaru. It was said that an Indian of Pampamarca or Tungasuca, who arrived in Cuzco the day before Arriaga's death with letters for Antonio Martínez, formerly priest of Sicuani, stated in the presence of various persons that Túpac Amaru had imprisoned the corregidor by order of the Bishop. A number of people believed this report.[36]

At any rate, the plot leading toward rebellion deepened when Puente was removed from his parish and went to Cuzco. He may have stopped at Tungasuca on the way and lodged at Túpac Amaru's house, where he no doubt denounced the corregidor. Then the two men must have discussed in detail the plans for revolt. Balza said that before this time the Bishop was not so bitter toward his uncle, as his anger concerned only competence of jurisdiction, but that afterwards he hated him furiously. Balza also claimed that the corregidor had no enemies in Cuzco except the Bishop and the ecclesiastical judges. He declared further that, after Arriaga's death, Bernardo de la Madrid, a European, wrote him from Lima that the Bishop had been an enemy of his uncle, had carried on

---

[35] Copia de la carta escrita á un Sor. ministro de Madrid por un vecino del Cuzco, Cuzco, September 1, 1782, signed "B. L. M.," pp. 136–44. MS copy in B. L.
[36] *Ibid.*, 144–45, 170.

correspondence with Túpac Amaru, and was responsible for the corregidor's death.[37]

Jiménez Villalba also said that he had obtained information from Tiburcio Landa, governor of Paucartambo, in April, 1780, that Bishop Moscoso had a connection with José Gabriel's rebellion. Villalba therefore had urged Arriaga to arrest the Inca, since there was no doubt of his being a rebel. A number of persons in Cuzco also thought that Arriaga should arrest Túpac Amaru. Because he did not, he had to die. After the tragedy the Archdean talked with the Bishop and was convinced of his complicity. He relayed his conviction to both Viceroy Guirior and Visitador Areche, but they did nothing about it. Later both José Gabriel and Diego Túpac Amaru blamed the Bishop for the whole incident.[38]

The immediate plot, against the corregidor, was carried out on November 4, 1780, when the priest of Yanaoca, Rodríguez de Ávila, José Gabriel's old tutor, celebrated the King's birthday at his home. The corregidor, the cacique, and other guests were present. During the feast Túpac Amaru excused himself and left early under the pretext that he expected guests from Cuzco. Then, with ten or twelve mestizos, he waited in ambush, for the corregidor to pass along the road leading to Tinta. In a little while Arriaga appeared, accompanied by his secretary and two Negroes, who followed farther behind. A lasso swung out, landed around the official's neck, and pulled him off his mule. He and his little retinue were all made prisoners. They were taken to a cave and kept there until midnight, when the cacique conducted them silently to Tungasuca.[39]

The Inca then forced Arriaga to sign a letter directed to the treasurer ordering that official to send immediately to Tungasuca all the funds in the treasury to organize an expedition to defend

[37] Representación de Don Eusebio Balza dirigida desde el Cuzco al supremo consejo de Indias en 8 de Septiembre de 1781, in Loayza, *op. cit.*, Serie I, Vol. III, 86–90.

[38] Carta de Simón Jiménez Villalba al Señor Don Benito de Mata Linares, Cuzco, June 18, 1784; Loayza, *La verdad desnuda, op. cit.*, Serie I, Vol. III, 195–202.

[39] Relación de los pasages acaecidos en esta ciudad del Cuzco . . . , Cuzco, December 3, 1780, pp. 67–68. MS copy in B. L. Del Solar, *op. cit.*, 66; Lorente, 180–81; Del Solar *op. cit.*, 64–66.

the port of Aranta against a feared invasion of English pirates. It was believed in some quarters that the signature was forged by Arriaga's clerk. However that may be, the letter had the desired result. Twenty-two thousand pesos of tribute money, four thousand to six thousand pesos belonging to the corregidor, one hundred marks of silver, jewels, ingots of gold, baggage, seventy-five muskets, horses, and mules were received. Lorente says that twenty-six thousand pesos, seven hundred marks of wrought silver, some pounds of gold, two hundred mules, supplies, and luxurious furniture were collected. Orders were then issued through the prisoner to towns in the province for all Spaniards, mestizos, and Indians to come to Tungasuca to organize a force to combat the pirates, supposed to have already landed. A considerable number of men soon assembled. With another similarly signed letter Túpac Amaru summoned Bernardo de la Madrid, an intimate friend of the corregidor, who was in the workshop of Pomacanche, one league distant, and Figueroa Gallego, owner of the mill of Quepococha, who happened to be in Tinta building three bridges. When they arrived, he imprisoned them along with Francisco Cisneros, the corregidor's lieutenant collector, in his house.[40]

A kind of trial was permitted for Arriaga. Three witnesses were heard; then the death sentence was pronounced. The corregidor's nephew said that the sentence had been ordered by Bishop Moscoso. Whether the accusation was true or not, the Bishop made no effort to save Arriaga, although he resided only fourteen leagues away; moreover, he did not report his death to the Viceroy until November 17, ten days after the event.

Túpac Amaru decided to ask Antonio López de Sora, his former teacher, to inform the prisoner of his fate and to hear his confession.[41] This priest had been one of the guests of the priest of Yanaoca, and after he returned to his parish, he heard from Vejara-

[40] Copia de una carta escrita por un sugeto residente en Lima con referencia á las noticias que se han comunicado del Cuzco, Lima, December 23, 1780. MS copy in B. L. Relación de los pasages acaecidos en esta ciudad del Cuzco . . . , Cuzco, December 3, 1780, pp. 67–68. MS copy in B. L. Del Solar, *op. cit.*, 66; Lorente, *Historia de la conquista del Peru*, 181–82; Markham, *A History of Peru*, 197–98.

[41] Loayza, *Estado del Peru, op. cit.*, Serie I, Vol. V, 147. Valcárcel, *La rebelión de Túpac Amaru*, 45.

no, his assistant, that the corregidor was at Tungasuca. Then Túpac Amaru came to the priest's house, said that he had a sick man for him to confess, and finally revealed the person's identity. The priest went to Tungasuca (November 8), where he was taken to a small room in which the corregidor sat shackled. When he asked what had happened, Arriaga related the story of his seizure. Then the priest handed him a picture of Christ and told him that he was to be put to death.

When the corregidor entreated the priest to intercede for him, the churchman hastened to Túpac Amaru, who informed him that he had an order from a higher authority to put the official to death. López returned to the prisoner to report that there was no hope for him, yet Arriaga insisted upon another application. The priest sought the cacique again and, convinced that he did not have an order for Arriaga's death, asked to see the order. The cacique answered that it had been sent to Lampa so that the corregidores of Lampa, Azángaro, and Carabaya might also be seized and tried. Boleslao Lewin maintains that tales about supposed royal decrees for their benefit were constantly being circulated among the Indians and that José Gabriel decided to use them for his purpose. Later, in his letter to Visitador Areche, the Inca confessed that he did not have any such order, and his brother Diego confirmed his statement.

Next morning Arriaga insisted upon seeing Túpac Amaru, who was finally summoned. The Inca said it was too late to do anything because he had had the order for his execution since October 26. When the hour came, on November 10, for the execution, Arriaga walked fearlessly to the gallows in the chief plaza of Tungasuca, where his executioners took away his staff of office and put on him the habit of the Order of Mercy. At the foot of the gallows, he asked Túpac Amaru's pardon for having called him the "fraudulent Indian." Three rows of men with weapons surrounded the plaza to prevent any attempt to rescue the prisoner.

In the process of hanging the corregidor, the braided leather rope broke. Then the condemned man and the executioner, a Zambo shoemaker of the town, Antonio Oblitas, who had been

CHIEF CENTER OF THE INCA REVOLT
(Modern boundaries shown)

the victim's former slave, fell down to the ground together. Assistants brought another rope, put it around Arriaga's neck, and forced him to go up to the gallows again. Several men pulled the rope, while two others and the executioner hung on to the feet of the unfortunate man until he was dead.

The following day the funeral was held with great solemnity. Even Túpac Amaru and his chief collaborators attended, but they certainly did not mourn. The body was then buried in the church at Tungasuca.[42] At that time it was believed that Túpac Amaru had Chief Sergeant Juan Antonio de Figueroa and Bernardo de la Madrid in prison awaiting execution, but they were not put to death.[43]

Arriaga's nephew now defended him against the Bishop's charge of drunkenness. Moscoso had said that the corregidor had brought thirty thousand bottles of spirits from Spain. Balza maintained that his uncle needed this liquor to entertain his friends. He added that Moscoso should have known this, for when he passed through the province of Tinta in 1779 after his appointment as bishop of Cuzco, Arriaga gave him a fine reception that cost four thousand pesos, providing Spanish wine and excellent food, and asked no priest or any other person to contribute one cent toward the reception.[44]

Balza became angry when he was held liable for his uncle's debts and made a bitter complaint against Bishop Moscoso to the higher authorities. This was merely one phase of the struggle between Europeans and Creoles, for Moscoso was a Creole born in

[42] Relación de los pasages acaecidos en esta ciudad del Cuzco . . . , Cuzco, December 3, 1780, pp. 68–70; Cánovas del Castillo, op. cit., V, 435, 436–37n.; Lorente, Historia de la conquista del Peru, 181. Another writer stated that while Arriaga was preparing for death, he sent a message to Túpac Amaru asking pardon for calling him the "fraudulent Indian." Memorándum escrito en Cuzco, Februaro 15 de 1835. Biblioteca Nacional, Buenos Aires, Sección Manuscritos, num. 2492. Cited by Lewin, op. cit., 188; Valcárcel, La rebelión de Túpac Amaru, 45.

[43] Copia de una carta escrita por un sugeto residente en Lima con referencia á las noticias que han comunicado del Cuzco, Lima, December 23, 1780, p. 97. MS copy in B. L.

[44] Representación de Don Eusebio Balza dirigida desde el Cuzco al supremo consejo de Indias en 8 de Septiembre de 1781, in Loayza, La verdad desnuda, op cit., Serie I, Vol. III, 86–90, 92–94, 138.

48

Arequipa, whereas Arriaga and Balza were Peninsular Spaniards.[45] The Arriaga family must have been disgruntled when the Viceroy appointed Francisco Salcedo to be corregidor of Tinta after the execution of Antonio de Arriaga, although he had promised the position to Miguel Arriaga, the dead man's brother.[46]

Bishop Moscoso did not immediately inform the people of Cuzco of the corregidor's death; yet on the same day that Arriaga was executed (November 10), he told Joaquín Valcárcel, chief sergeant of the army, and José de Lagos, administrator of tobacco, about it. As the news could not have reached the Bishop until the twelfth, he must have had secret information of what would happen from Túpac Amaru.[47] A citizen of Cuzco said that more than two months afterwards Moscoso told the people of the official's death in the presence of the inspector-general and other persons, when his great hatred of Arriaga was expressed by accusations of drunkenness, robbery, and other sins.[48] A document in the Archives of the Indies in Seville contains the statement that Moscoso wrote to Túpac Amaru thanking him for Arriaga's death. A witness heard José Gabriel's wife say that her husband had been placed in great danger only to please the Bishop. And Túpac Amaru himself said, in a letter of January 3, 1781, to the cabildo of Cuzco, that the corregidor was executed because he opposed the church. Who but the clergy and the Bishop would have persuaded him that Arriaga was working against the church? It will probably never be known for sure whether or not Moscoso helped to bring the revolution about, although certain documents indicate that he was sympathetic toward it.[49] Strangely, no investigation was made of the corregidor's death, yet the King had given Visitador Areche broad powers of investigation.[50]

Immediately after Arriaga's execution Túpac Amaru addressed the assembled multitude in the Quechua language. Mounted on a

---

[45] Valcárcel, *La rebelión de Túpac Amaru*, 32, 37.

[46] *Ibid.*, 90.

[47] Loayza, *La verdad desnuda, op. cit.*, Serie I, Vol. III, 94–95.

[48] Copia de carta escrita á un Sor. ministro de Madrid por un vecino del Cuzco, Cuzco, September 1, 1782, signed "B. L. M." MS copy in B. L.

[49] Loayza, *La verdad desnuda, op. cit.*, Serie I, Vol. III, 95; Vol. IX, pp. 45–46n.

[50] *Ibid.*, Serie I, Vol. III, 105.

fiery charger and attired in the princely costume of his ancestors, he carried a banner bearing his coat of arms.[51] At this time, however, he did not say anything about his royal descent, but merely explained why the corregidor had been put to death and promised to free the people from oppression by abolishing the mita, the repartimientos, the alcabalas, and other taxes. He declared that he did not intend to do anything against the King or the church, but would kill the corregidores and *chapetones* who tyrannized over the people. He added that this could not be done unless the Indians aided him with all their forces, for otherwise he would be hanged for attempting to help them.

After this speech he distributed among the crowd the silver pillaged from the corregidor, giving the Indians two reales each and the Spaniards four. Then a great shout was raised to proclaim Túpac Amaru "Liberator of the Country," and all the people offered to obey him and sacrifice their lives in his cause. The corregidor's nephew later claimed that the Inca had stolen 22,000 pesos from Arriaga and that, if the silver and jewels were counted, the total would amount to 50,000 pesos. Furthermore, said Balza, his uncle still owed 16,000 pesos for one-third of the tribute of the town of San Juan for 1780, which could not be collected while he was under excommunication.[52]

José Gabriel soon began to appoint officials and collect arms. He obtained about one hundred guns from the corregidor's supplies, collected others in Tinta, and accepted many from friendly Spaniards and mestizos. He also ordered some guns, powder, and shot made. It was thought that his wife, his brother Diego, and a son helped to inspire him, since they believed in a certain prophecy engraved on a stone in a temple of Cuzco, which said that, after the ruin of the kingdom, the Incas would regain possession through the aid of a people called the English.[53] Although some

---

[51] Markham, *Travels in Peru and India*, 141.

[52] Loayza, *La verdad desnuda, op. cit.*, Serie I, Vol. III, 111.

[53] Copia de una carta escrita por un sugeto residente en Lima con referencia á las noticias que han comunicado del Cuzco, Lima, December 23, 1780, p. 98. MS copy in B. L. Angelis, *Documentos*, 4; Relación de los pasages acaecidos en esta ciudad de Cuzco . . . , Cuzco, December 3, 1780, pp. 70–72. MS copy in B. L.

Indians may have heard of the American Revolution in North America, it probably had no influence upon Túpac Amaru's uprising.

Alexander von Humboldt believed that the immediate cause of the rebellion was Túpac Amaru's desire to avenge the outrage he had received from the courts when they did not declare him a descendant of the royal Incas.[54] Romulo Cúneo Vidal, on the other hand, contended that he was too well informed to count much on his indirect descent through the female line and that his position of cacique and occupation of muleteer did not amount to much, either. Other men had better claims than he to royal descent. Among them was Mateo García Pumacagua, cacique of Chincheros, who traced his ancestry from King Túpac Yupanqui. Antonio and Gabriel Ugarte, whom Túpac Amaru called cousins, were also descendants of the royal Incas. On one occasion José Gabriel thought of giving Antonio, the youngest, boldest, and most hostile of the Ugartes toward the Spaniards, the *mascaipacha,* or Inca crown. On November 22, 1780, he called on those cousins to aid his rebellion by imprisoning the corregidor and the armed men in Cuzco when he approached with his army. The cousins, of Spanish descent born in Peru and commanding royalist troops in that city, would have been a great help to him.

When the rebellion began, at dawn a lampoon was put on the wall of a house in Tinta, which said, "Prepare, Ugarte, for we wish to crown you!" A certain cacique of Quispicanchis offered to put twenty thousand Indians under the order of Antonio Ugarte to exterminate the Spaniards; thus there were probably other claimants to the rights of the Incas. Vidal maintained that the Indians followed Túpac Amaru more to have him throw off the oppressive yoke than to place him on the throne of his ancestors.[55]

Regardless of ramifications, José Gabriel Túpac Amaru was the mainspring of the revolution. In the province of Chayanta his friends the Catari brothers were already under arms. In Potosí he could count on the wretched mestizos, who believed they would

---

[54] Alexander von Humboldt, *Ensayo político sobre Nueva España,* I, 215.

[55] Loayza, *La verdad desnuda, op. cit.,* Serie I, Vol. III, 189–90. Del Solar, *op. cit.,* 137, 144–47.

be included among the tribute payers; and others low in the social order would make no effort to defend the colonial government that had treated them so harshly. With the church also arrayed against Corregidor Arriaga of Tinta, the time seemed ripe for action. The corregidor's execution provided the spark that lighted the fire of the greatest and most extensive Indian revolution on the American continents.

CHAPTER III

Uprising of the Catari Brothers

EVEN BEFORE 1780 abuses by Joaquín Alós in the province of Chayanta, to which he had been appointed corregidor in 1778, had prompted a serious insurrection, which prepared the way for Tupac Amaru's revolt. A native of Cataluña, Alós, like other corregidores, had outraged the Indians with the repartimiento and other tricks to gain wealth. In one year he had not only increased and repeated the monopoly, but also tried to establish a monopoly on the sale of coca, *aguardiente,* and other items and to profit from the mines. The natives, angered by his activities, threatened to put him to death. When he asked the Audiencia of La Plata for aid, the judges merely advised him to treat the Indians kindly and avoid uprisings.[1]

Alós first took note of the restlessness of the Indians when he attempted to collect for repartimiento articles in certain areas. The Indians refused to pay the full assessment, and finally compromised by agreeing to pay half. The cause of dissatisfaction was obvious. The corregidor had obtained about 400,000 pesos from the repartimiento, not including what his assistants, Luis Núñez and Lucas Billafán, had received, when the legal limit was 150,000 pesos. Not only were many Indians left destitute, but also they had been required to take articles which they did not want—breviaries, books for mass, chasubles, and caps of doctors of divinity.[2] Alós tried to quiet them with promises, but at the same time took the precaution of calling out militiamen to guard himself.

[1] Instrucción de lo acaecido con Don Joaquin de Alós en la provincia de Chayanta, Buenos Aires, March 6, 1781, in Odriozola, *Documentos, I,* 298–300; Carta de Juan de Vertíz al José de Gálvez, March 15, 1781, num. 458 reservada (published in Lewin, *op. cit.,* 435–36). According to Juan del Pino Manrique, Chayanta had 54,639 inhabitants, but Cosme Bueno gives 36,000. Angelis, *Documentos,* II, p. iii; Odriozola, *Documentos,* III, 122.

[2] Representación de Tomás Catari de 12 de Noviembre de 1780, AGN, Buenos Aires, División colonia, Sección gobierno, Tribunales, Leg. 124 (cited by Lewin, *op. cit.,* 129).

A revolt had been brewing as early as 1777, when Blas Bernal, a mestizo friend of Corregidor Usarinqui and governor of the Indian town of Macha, had whipped Tomás Catari, an Indian he considered of low rank, and imprisoned him for one month following a complaint from Bernal's mistress that Catari would not let her sheep into his fold. In retaliation the Indian and a friend, Isidro Acho, went to the treasury officials of Potosí and accused Bernal of using two tax lists, thereby stealing 487 pesos of the tribute money in the town of Macha. Catari also claimed that he was the legitimate cacique by right of inheritance.[3]

Joaquín Dulón, guardian of the royal treasury in Potosí, heard the charges, and on February 4, 1778, drew up a recommendation to the corregidor of Chayanta, Nicolás Usarinqui, that Catari and Acho be appointed to collect the tribute instead of Bernal. He gave the Indians a copy of the dispatch for the corregidor along with another statement for the approval of the judges of the Audiencia of La Plata.[4]

Pleased with the results of his journey, Catari showed the dispatch to Usarinqui and later to Alós, his successor. Both disregarded it, and the latter imprisoned Catari and Acho and put them in the stocks. Somehow Catari was able to get word to the protector of the natives in Potosí, who persuaded the corregidor to free the two men and let them perform their duties as collectors of tribute. Alós kept only the first part of the bargain, however, and, at the end of April, Catari again appealed to the protector. When the treasury officials of Potosí ordered the corregidor on May 1 to explain why he had not obeyed their orders, Alós replied that he feared an uprising. At the same time he told Catari and Acho to present the necessary bonds to hold the position. This was done, but Alós now protested that the bonds, although they amounted to 1,700 pesos, were insufficient. He threatened, moreover, to im-

[3] Petición de Tomás Catari al virrey, de los primeros días de enero de 1779 (published in Lewin, *op. cit.*, 453–54); Relación de los hechos mas notables acaecidos en la sublevación general por el Indio José Gabriel Túpac Amaru . . . , 3–5. MS copy in B. L. Confesión de Nicolás Catari, La Plata, April 10, 1781, in Odriozola, *Documentos*, I, 332; Ordóñez López and Crespo, *op. cit.*, 111.

[4] Petición de Tomás Catari al virrey, de los primeros días de enero de 1779 (published in Lewin, *op. cit.*, 452–53).

54

prison, whip, and banish the two Indians if they appealed to the courts again.[5]

Tomás Catari then decided to go to Buenos Aires to seek justice from the Viceroy. Taking Tomás Acho, son of Isidro Acho of Macha, with him, he traveled the six hundred leagues to Buenos Aires on foot, arriving at the end of 1778 almost naked. On December 4, he repeated his charges before Viceroy José de Vertíz, with the protector of the natives, Juan de Samudio, acting as interpreter. He denounced Blas Bernal as a thief who stole tribute money and declared that his own rightful position had been taken away from him. He could not bring substantiating documents, he said, because they had been seized by the corregidor.

There is evidence that Catari found friends in Buenos Aires since he was given prompt attention and an order was issued for him to be restored to the governorship if he had a right to it. The Viceroy's decree was submitted to the audiencia in February, but the matter was delayed because documentary evidence was lacking. On April 19, the judges ordered Corregidor Alós to produce the documents. Meantime, Catari had gone to La Plata to try to hasten implementation of the Viceroy's orders. He could do little, however, since one of the judges was absent, another was engaged in a criminal procedure, and the audiencia insisted upon seeing his documents.[6]

Returning to his province, Catari claimed that in Buenos Aires he had obtained more than he asked for. His brother Nicolás declared that he had brought an order from the Viceroy to take action against Bernal and another order concerning tribute. Tomás tried to put the measures into effect. Appointing Marcos Mamani collector, he began to collect tribute and told the Indians to ignore Bernal. Catari's aggressive actions led the corregidor to believe that he was plotting against him, and so he removed the treasury

[5] *Ibid.,* 453.

[6] Representación hecha al rey por D. Tomás Catari, Paracrani, October 13, 1780, in Odriozola, *Documentos,* I, 289–90; Oficio del virrey de Buenos Aires, Juan José de Vertíz á José de Gálvez, Buenos Aires, October 24, 1780, *ibid.,* I, 296; Dictamen del fiscal de la audiencia de Charcas del Abril de 1779 (published in Lewin, *op. cit.,* 455–56); Petición del protector de naturales, del 4 de Diciembre de 1778, *ibid.,* 462.

officials of Potosí and increased the number of his soldiers to enforce the repartimiento. On May 18, 1779, he arrested Catari, Acho, and four other Indians, putting them in the custody of Bernal, who was to take them to the maximum security prison in Aullagas.

The next day, when the Indians heard what had happened, they hastened to Bernal's home to demand Catari's freedom, but Bernal had fled. At one o'clock in the morning forty of them passed the hacienda of Bernal's son-in-law, Antonio Ribota, who fired a gun to frighten them and caused a skirmish, after which the Indians took him along with them.

During the disturbance the Indians of Ocuri freed the prisoners, and Tomás went home claiming to be the tribute collector. The corregidor did not arrest Tomás again immediately for he hastened to his estate of Pacrani and aided the Indians of Majipicha in the collection of the tribute.[7] This caused the cacique governor of the district, Ignacio Burogoa, to protest to the corregidor because the natives would not pay the tribute to him, preferring to give it to Catari.[8] The new collector in the doctrina of Guaicoma also informed Alós that Catari had visited there accompanied by many Indians and had informed the people that he was now the cacique. Catari soon had the whole district in an uproar by declaring that only three reales should be paid on each third of the tribute and that he would undertake the collection. Accompanied by Santos Yupura, he then journeyed to Potosí with the money.

Meantime, Alós relayed all the complaints of Bernal, Burogoa, and others against Catari to the Audiencia of La Plata, and on June 12 he issued an order to arrest Tomás. The audiencia was pretending to carry out the Viceroy's commands, but Alós had not yet sent the documents concerning Catari's case and had no inten-

---

[7] Relación de los hechos mas notables en la sublevación general . . . , 5. MS copy in B. L. Confesión de Nicolás Catari, La Plata, April 10, 1781, in Odriozola, *Documentos*, I, 323. The confession of Nicolás is also in Angelis, *Documentos*, 238ff. Informe de Alós al presidente de la audiencia de 29 de Junio de 1779, AGN, Buenos Aires, Tribunales, Leg. 171, exp. 29 (published in Lewin, *op. cit.*, 459–60); Informe de Alós al presidente de la audiencia de 20 de Junio de 1780, *loc. cit.*, Leg. 181, exp. 79, in Lewin, *op. cit.*, 463.

[8] Denuncia de Ignacio Burogoa contra Tomás Catari, AGN, Buenos Aires, Tribunales, Leg. 181, exp. 29 (published in Lewin, *op. cit.*, 458).

tion of sending them. As a result, on May 30, 1781, as on several other occasions, Viceroy Vertíz had complained to the Minister of the Indies that the judges did not perform their duties, that most of them worked for Alós, and that they had delayed the Catari case for more than a month.[9]

During his sojourn in Potosí, Catari was arrested again under the warrant issued by Alós and kept in prison for almost four months. On December 12, 1779, he appealed to the audiencia for an impartial investigation. The judges again ordered the corregidor to submit the documents and to let Catari be tried with the assistance of the protector of the natives, but Alós, who had friends in the corrupt audiencia, did not obey. Fearing that the Indians of Macha would liberate their chief, Alós ordered him transferred to the custody of Florencio Lupa, cacique of Moscari. But the Indians got wind of the plan and acted quickly, freeing Catari while he was being taken through Pocoata at night.

Catari, apparently still having faith in legal procedures, went to La Plata (also called Chuquisaca) to explain his position to the audiencia. He presented his case in writing, but on June 10, 1780, was arrested and held incommunicado. Ten days later Corregidor Alós informed the president of the audiencia that the Indians had attacked Antonio Ribota in reprisal and that the natives of Chayanta had allied themselves with inhabitants of the province of Paria, where a number of years before Governor Lanquipacha had been killed. In fact, four provinces were now allied with Chayanta.[10]

After Catari's third arrest, the corregidor could not keep the Indians from persecuting Bernal. More than one hundred of them sacked his possessions and demanded that his governorship be conferred upon Catari. Bernal fled to the town of San Pedro and hid, and the corregidor appointed another tribute collector. When

[9] Decreto de Alós de 12 de Junio de 1779 ordenando la prisión de Tomás Catari, AGN, Buenos Aires, Criminales, Leg. 181, exp. 28 (published in Lewin, *op. cit.*, 459); Informe de Alós al presidente de la audiencia de 29 de Junio de 1779, *loc. cit.*, Leg. 171, exp. 29, *ibid.*, 459–60; Carta de Juan de Vertíz al José de Gálvez, March 15, 1781, num. 458 reservada, *ibid.*, 435–36.

[10] Carta de Tomás Catari al fiscal protector general de la primer mitad de Junio de 1779, AGN, Buenos Aires, Tribunales, Leg. 181, exp. 29 (published in Lewin, *op. cit.*, 457). See also *ibid.*, pp. 165–67.

rumors that Bernal was dead and that Catari was responsible reached the Indians, they searched diligently for the cacique. When at last they found him, they handed him over to the corregidor in the hope of obtaining Catari's freedom. Then, when this freedom was not granted, they beheaded Bernal and proclaimed Catari "governor and benefactor of the people," after which they returned peacefully to their homes.

When the Audiencia of La Plata heard of Bernal's death, it sent an order for Catari to be taken to Potosí and charges drawn up against him.[11] He was accused of rebellion; and, according to Victor Santa Cruz, it was the mention of the word "rebellion" that now gave the Indians the idea of rising against their oppressors.[12] From his prison Catari appealed to the president of the audiencia to send him from Potosí to the royal prison in La Plata so that his case might be tried more quickly.[13]

Alarmed by the imprisonment of their chief, the Indians began to assemble once more. After informing the corregidor that certain priests had ruined the province, they made a number of requests: removal of certain Spanish and mestizo officials, reduction of the sum to be paid for the repartimiento articles, and freedom for Catari. Alós promised to remit the repartimiento money in the town of Pocoata at the time of making up the tribute lists and collecting men for the mita of Cerro Rico at Potosí,[14] the usual date of which was St. Bartholomew's Day, which in 1780 fell on August 24. As the Indians generally got drunk on this occasion, it was feared that

[11] Informe de Alós al presidente de la audiencia de 29 de Junio de 1779, AGN, Buenos Aires, Leg. 171, exp. 29, in Lewin, *op. cit.*, 459.; Informe de Alós á la audiencia de 7 de Septiembre de 1779, AGN, Buenos Aires, Tribunales, Leg. 181, exp. 29, *ibid.*, 460–61; Relación de los hechos mas notables acaecidos en la sublevación general . . . , 5–6. MS copy in B. L. Confesión de Nicolás Catari, La Plata, April 10, 1781, in Odriozola, *Documentos* I, 324; Confesión de Dámaso Catari, La Plata, April 1, 1781, *ibid.*, I, 308. The confession of Dámaso Catari is also in Angelis, *Documentos*, I, 116ff.

[12] Victor Santa Cruz, *Historia colonial de la Paz*, 106.

[13] Petición de Tomás Catari, dirigida al presidente de la audiencia el 12 de Diciembre de 1779, AGN, Buenos Aires, Tribunales, Leg. 181, exp. 29, in Lewin, *op. cit.*, 460–61.

[14] Representación hecha al rey por Tomás Catari, Paracrani, October 13, 1780, in Odriozola, *Documentos*, I, 290.

they might become belligerent now on account of Catari's imprisonment.

They came earlier and in larger numbers than usual, for they had been summoned secretly. The corregidor hastily mobilized the militias of Aullagas, Pintatora, Chayanta, and Sacaca, and between two and three hundred soldiers arrived at Pocoata on August 23. The surprised natives resented such an unusual measure.

The Indians in Guancarani, one league from Pocoata, were so incensed that the corregidor sent two priests, Roque Burgos and Agustín Arzadúm, to calm them. The priests returned to report that the natives demanded Catari's release and reduction of the tribute to twelve reales in return for peace, but the corregidor had no intention of acceding to the demands. However, hostilities did not break out the next day as had been expected.[15]

Anger was seething under the surface. On the morning of August 25, the Indians boldly entered the corregidor's house and freed an Indian prisoner. By afternoon, however, they were restrained, the mitayos were assigned to the mines, and the taxpayers' register was made in an orderly manner. Afterwards the inhabitants returned to their homes, but Alós still kept his guards on duty. When he and his assistants started to return home on the twenty-sixth, they found all the countryside and mountain ridges covered with scores of Indians, who shouted and played martial musical instruments. The greatly outnumbered Spaniards were terrified and retreated to Pocoata, where Alós ordered the soldiers to surround his house.

At eleven o'clock in the morning Dámaso Catari arrived with a petition asking that his brother Tomás be handed over to him. This surprised the Spaniards. When Dámaso saw that they hesitated to answer his request, he calmly said, "Kill me soon that I may go to the sun to give my orders and arrangements! For me and mine to be saved is to die tomorrow." After various confer-

---

[15] Andrés Lamas, *Colección de memorias y documentos para la historia y geografía de los pueblos del Río de la Plata*, I, 362 (hereafter cited as *Colección . . . de los pueblos del Río de la Plata*); Representación de Tomás Catari virrey del 12 de Noviembre de 1780, AGN, Buenos Aires, División colonia, Sección gobierno, Tribunales, Leg. 124, exp. 3, in Lewin, *op. cit.*, 465.

ences, the petition was given to José Benavides, a lawyer from the Audiencia of La Plata, who, not knowing what else to do, ordered Tomás freed. Dámaso came out boldly and had scarcely joined his followers when a shot was heard at Camareta, which was the signal for the attack.[16] This is the Spanish version of the beginning of the uprising.

The account of the revolt given by the three Catari brothers is quite different. Nicolás said that he went to Pocoata on August 26 to visit his brother Tomás. He did not take part in the ensuing revolt, although he knew it had been planned by Governor Sebastián Colque. He also knew that the people were going to demand that the repartimiento be reduced to twelve pesos on a mule and proportionately on other things, and the tribute to half; indeed, they pretended to have an order to this effect from the audiencia. Nicolás also stated that the commune did not start the uprising, but that the corregidor was ready to resist the Indians with soldiers. Two requests were prepared for Alós to free Tomás, whom he had offered to take out of prison for that day. Dámaso went to the official first with one of the petitions asking for the prisoner, who he had learned from Pedro Caypa was in the house. The corregidor answered that it was not in his power to free him. When Tomás Acho presented the other petition, Caypa, governor of Pocoata, said scornfully, "Enter and take Catari!" This he said in the presence of Alós, who discharged a pistol and killed Acho. When the Indians outside heard the shots, they threw stones. Then the soldiers took up arms to defend the plaza.[17] Tomás Catari's account corroborates this report,[18] and Dámaso's story was similar.[19] Although the accounts vary, it is clear that the insurrection was caused by the corregidor's refusal to free Tomás Catari.

[16] Relación de los hechos mas notables acaecidos en la sublevación general . . . , 6–9. MS copy in B. L. Instrucción de lo acaecido con D. Joaquín Alós . . . , in Angelis, *Documentos,* 210–11.

[17] Confesión de Nicolás Catari, La Plata, April 10, 1781, in Odriozola, *Documentos,* I, 321–22.

[18] Representación hecha al rey por Tomás Catari, Paracrani, October 13, 1780, in Odriozola, *Documentos,* I, 291.

[19] Confesión de Dámaso Catari, La Plata, April 1, 1781, in Odriozola, *Documentos,* I, 305–306.

When a hostile multitude approached the town at half-past twelve, the corregidor asked Caypa to see if he could calm the storm. Fifteen of the corregidor's men occupied the middle of the plaza when Caypa appeared with the bugle-horns and foot soldiers. The attack soon began, and the Spaniards were thrown into confusion by the rain of stones and the violence of the Indians. Alós, seeing that resistance was useless, gave orders to flee. He broke through the multitude on a swift horse and came out into the country, but was caught and made a prisoner. Other persons escaped from the skirmish by taking refuge in the church and closing the doors, but twenty-eight of the corregidor's party were killed. Among them was Dr. Benavides, the corregidor's assessor; and even before he died, the Indians cut out his tongue. The clerk, Mateo Teles, had his hand cut off and then was killed. Cayetano de Uriondo, a native of La Plata, escaped among the corpses heaped in the plaza. He had received seven serious wounds on his head, but the priest, Miguel Fuentes, took him to his house and healed him. According to Tomás Catari, three hundred Indians were killed. The natives occupied the plaza and put to death all persons who remained there. When they heard that the corregidor had been imprisoned, they quieted down somewhat.

Next day they tried to make peace treaties and asked that arms be surrendered to the priest and that he give them money. When the refugees came out of the church, the Indians robbed them even of their clothes. Dressed in the choir vestments and protected by the priests, the refugees journeyed on foot to Aullagas, seven leagues away.

Meantime, the insurgents arrived at Macha, where they encountered no resistance, for the few Spanish inhabitants either hid or fled and left them in possession of the town. The news of the rebellion soon spread to neighboring towns, where adherents were won over.

The corregidor was suffering many hardships. His captors made him walk barefooted over almost impassable trails to reach the highest part of the mountain. One of the guards finally let him wear his shoes, as he had been robbed of everything. Reaching the mountain top, the natives shut him up in a hut. There he suffered great mental anguish, for the Indians discussed in his presence where they would put him to death. They forced him to sign orders to imprison people still hostile to them and even an order to decrease the repartimiento. Through his worries and anxieties, the official was soon reduced to skin and bones.

Some of the Indians thought there was sufficient reason to put the corregidor to death and take vengeance upon the Spaniards.[20] Alós had caused many Indians to be killed, yet his enemies spared his life because they hoped to exchange him for their own leader. They also spared the Europeans who sought refuge in the church even though those same people had destroyed many Indians. The natives took all the wounded to Dr. José de Ulloa to be cured, restored all plunder, gave the tribute money to their priest, and did not profane sacred places.[21] This is the Indian version.

Miguel Arzadúm, priest of Chayrapata, and his assistant, Mariano de la Vega, decided to try to rescue Alós. When they came to the place where he was staying, the Indians would not permit them to speak to him, but the priest managed to persuade them to take him to Macha. When they arrived at a little inn near the town, they shut him up again. Arzadúm continued to negotiate for his release, telling the Indians that Catari would soon be free. The priest even went to La Plata and reported to the audiencia. After a conference lasting until midnight, the members decided to release Catari and give him the caciqueship of one of the communities of Macha so that he might go with the priest to calm the rebels. At last a letter reached Vega, who attended Alós constantly, reporting that Catari had been freed and that the priest Gregorio de Merlos had arranged to have him conducted to Ocuri.

When the Indians were informed of this, they planned to give their leader a hearty welcome into the town. After a tiresome journey, Catari, accompanied by Merlos, arrived at Macha on August

[20] Relación de los hechos mas notables acaecidos en la sublevación general . . . , 9–12. MS copy in B. L. *Revista de Archivos y Bibliotecas (Peruanas)*, Año 1900, Vol. V, 146, 149; Santa Cruz, *op. cit.*, 107.

[21] Representación hecha al rey por D. Tomás Catari, Paracrani, October 13, 1780, in Odriozola, *Documentos*, I, 291–92.

30. As soon as the Indians saw him, they threw themselves before their hero's mule to kiss his feet. Surrounded by the crowd, he then went to his home, where feasts were held. Catari soon made himself master of the situation. He issued a secret order that Florencio Lupa, the agent of the corregidor who had imprisoned him, should be removed from his position. He also gave orders for the corregidor to be set free. Some priests, including Merlos, accompanied Alós. When they reached Macha, Catari accompanied them to Ocuri, and from there returned home again.[22]

The priest of Macha persuaded the Indians to ask the corregidor's pardon and kiss his hand; this must have been a bitter pill for them to swallow, but they did it. Even the Indians who had seized followers of the corregidor brought them to the priest's house.[23]

No punishment was meted out to the corregidor and his lieutenant, Luis Núñez, except that they had to restore what they had taken and were sent to La Plata, where they were well treated. Viceroy Vertíz proclaimed Alós free from all charges, declaring that he was a credit to the King and merited compensation for his injuries. This was indeed a travesty of justice. (Later, in 1785, when the former corregidor was on his way from La Plata to Buenos Aires, the authorities intercepted him at Tucumán to serve against the insurgents who were attempting to invade Jujuy. He hastened to overtake the troop of veteran soldiers going to Peru and caused it to arrive in time to avoid the loss of the fort on the Río Negro and the fall of Jujuy.[24] For this service he became governor of Paraguay and of Valparaiso the next year. He served as brigadier in Chile when the war for independence broke out, and in 1810 swore obe-

[22] Relación de los hechos mas notables acaecidos en la sublevación general . . . , 12–14. MS copy in B. L. *Revista de Archivos y Bibliotecas (Peruanas),* Año 1900, Vol. V, 363; Oficio de Merlos á Vertíz, del 14 de Noviembre de 1780, AGN, Buenos Aires, División colonia, Sección gobierno, Tribunales, Leg. 124, exp. 3 (published in Lewin, *op. cit.,* 424–25); Representación de Tomás Catari al virrey del 12 de Noviembre de 1780, *ibid.,* 465–66.

[23] Representación hecha al rey por D. Tomás Catari, October 13, 1780, in Odriozola, *Documentos,* I, 293–94.

[24] Vertíz informe á Gálvez que al corregidor de Chayanta Joaquín Alós, resultó indemne de los cargos que se le formaron, AGN, Buenos Aires (Correspondencia Vertíz-Gálvez, 1783), in Lewin, *op. cit.,* 484.

dience to the *Junta* of Santiago, while at the same time he approved the royalist cause. He later journeyed to Lima and died there from old age.)

Spanish officials assured the Indians that Alós and Núñez would never return to Chayanta again and that a sympathetic chief justice would be appointed. Estevén Amescaray was chosen, but he refused to accept the post. The audiencia then selected Manuel de Valenzuela, who went out to quell the uprising and perform his duties. He found that the Spaniards, the mestizos, and even the caciques had fled from the province of Chayanta and that Alós, whose life had been spared almost miraculously, had the boldness to charge him more than 150,000 pesos which still remained due from the repartimiento. When the new official refused to pay, Alós tried to prejudice the audiencia against him and asked for some one of his own faction to be the chief justice. He persisted until Domingo Angeles, a man satisfactory to him, was appointed.[25]

The Indians, however, refused to accept Angeles because he was their former corregidor's friend. Nevertheless, he journeyed to the town of Ocuri, where he overheard a conversation concerning a conspiracy against him. He hastened back to his home, saying that his life was in danger. The audiencia then appointed Juan Antonio Acuña, who was corregidor of Yamparaes and known for his hatred of the natives and his friendship for Alós. Catari immediately asked that he be removed. The Indians were polite to the new official and did not hinder his journey, but Acuña noticed their restlessness, soon left the valley, and finally arrived in Aullagas.[26]

On October 5, when Alós' assistant Juan Gelli, protected by a habit of the Order of St. Francis, arrived in La Plata, the audiencia learned that Lupa had been imprisoned. The judges issued an order for him to be brought to La Plata, but before it could be

[25] Instrucción de lo acaecido con Don Joaquín de Alós en la provincia de Chayanta, Buenos Aires, March 6, 1781, in Odriozola, *Documentos,* I, 298–300; Angelis, *Documentos,* 211–12.

[26] Relación de los hechos mas notables acaecidos en la sublevación general . . . , 27–28. MS copy in B. L.

received the Indians had put him to death. They hated Lupa because he had acted as an intermediary between the corregidor and the people and had helped enrich the officials. He had collected half a real a year from every Indian for his service in defending their cause. He was also a tool of the judges of the audiencia and had become wealthy. When it was learned definitely that the revolters intended to kill Lupa, Tomás Catari and the priest had tried to prevent their doing so. The priest had kept Lupa at his residence as long as possible, but when he went home, two Indians from Moscari dragged him out of his house, whipped him with thorns, and beheaded him. The priest recovered the body and buried it. The next day it was falsely reported that Tomás Catari had given the order to execute Lupa. In truth, after Lupa had been put to death, Tomás had asked that the guilty be punished.[27]

The priest Merlos succeeded in freeing Marcos Soto, cacique of the town of Chayanta, Juan Movillo, collector of the alcabala of the same town, and the son of the cacique and his three dependents at Sacaca—all of them, like Lupa, under sentence of death. The priest also persuaded the Indians not to attack Chuquisaca (La Plata) and Aullagas, where they intended to kill the Spaniards, and to hand over to him the full amount of the tribute.[28] Nicolás Catari also claimed that his brother Tomás took part in freeing Soto because he did not approve such acts of violence.[29]

Tomás Catari used his freedom to declare the tribute decreased and the mita, the repartimiento, and other taxes extinguished. He sent to the Viceroy and the King a long report of the grievances of the Indians; in it he blamed Alós for all that had happened and

[27] Representación hecha al rey por D. Tomás Catari, Paracrani, October 13, 1780, in Odriozola, *Documentos*, I, 249; Relación de los hechos mas notables acaecidos en la sublevación general . . . , 14–15; Confesión de D. Dámaso Catari, La Plata, April 1, 1781, in Odriozola, *op. cit.*, I, 307; Documento anónimo sobre el papel desempeñado por Florencio Lupa, Biblioteca Nacional, Buenos Aires, Sección manuscritos, num. 2158, in Lewin, *op. cit.*, 470.

[28] Oficio de Merlos á Vertíz, del 14 de Noviembre de 1780, AGN, Buenos Aires, División colonia, Sección gobierno, Tribunales, Leg. 124, exp. 3 (published in Lewin, *op. cit.*, 425–26).

[29] Confesión de Nicolás Catari, La Plata, April 10, 1781, in Odriozola, *Documentos*, I, 325.

asked pardon for the insurgents.[30] Apparently he never tired of sending useless petitions to Viceroy Vertíz in legal fashion. On November 12, 1780, he asked that either Juan Bautista de Ormachea or Manuel de Valenzuela be appointed chief justice of Chayanta, and Isidro Serrano protector of the natives. He accused all the priests, except Merlos, of working with the corregidor and neglecting their parishioners. He also complained bitterly of the audiencia for not answering his petitions. A month later he heard that Serrano had been arrested by the audiencia and would be put to death by its order.[31] Dámaso Catari said that Tomás even intended to go to Buenos Aires to protest against the evils resulting from certain of the viceroy's measures. Although Catari's actions were mild, it was noticed that under an apparent quietness there was a general drawing together of people from the most remote provinces and that a rebellion was in the making.

Secret correspondence was also carried on with Túpac Amaru, but it is difficult to estimate the closeness of the relationship. Dámaso declared that Tomás rejoiced to learn that King Túpac Amaru favored the people and had said that the government would be changed. It seems that the Inca had sent edicts to the provinces to offer the inhabitants protection, to treat them kindly, to consider the Indians and Creoles friends, and to order Europeans beheaded. As the Indians wanted a native king, Tomás intended to wait until Túpac Amaru had completed the conquest of the city of La Plata, and then he would join him. The people of Chayanta expected the Inca to get rid of their burdensome taxes, of the repartimientos, and of the *diezmos,* and to make them peaceful owners of their lands and the products they raised. Catari repeatedly said that Túpac Amaru belonged to the same country as they did, that he served them with zeal, and that, when he saw their misery, he would soon alleviate it.[32]

[30] Representación de Tomás Catari al virrey del 12 de Noviembre de 1780, AGN, Buenos Aires, División colonia, Sección gobierno, Tribunales, Leg. 124, exp. 3, in Lewin, *op. cit.,* 465–68.

[31] Representación de Tomás Catari al virrey del 12 de Noviembre de 1780, in Lewin, *op. cit.,* 468.

[32] Odriozola, *Documentos,* I, 308 (second page 308, as the number is repeated),

Nicolás Catari also maintained that there was communication with the Inca leader of Peru. An Indian from Challapata in the province of Paria arrived the second week of Lent, reporting that the conquests of his king, Túpac Amaru, were far advanced and that he was approaching Oruro. At the same time an edict of the Inca came from the region of Tinquipaya, and an Indian from Paria, Miguel Michela, went to Pocoata to publish it, but the priest seized the paper. This was the only notice the Cataris had from Túpac Amaru, but Dámaso sent two boys from Macha with a letter to Oruro to learn more about him. This had happened during the tense situation when the people feared that the corregidor had deceived them by failing to free Tomás Catari at Pocoata. They therefore desired to recognize and obey the Inca, whom they believed had already been crowned.[33] Dámaso must have had some kind of answer to his letter, for he said that the Indians who united with the Creoles had assured him that they had killed all the chapetones of Oruro, where they awaited Túpac Amaru. They also told him, he said, that the Inca was near with eight thousand Creoles and six thousand Indians, who came to kill all the European Spaniards they found.[34]

The number of Creoles may have been slightly exaggerated. Although Túpac Amaru used in his army all the Creoles he could win to his cause, there is no way to know how many there were. Most documents are silent on this matter. Moreover, as a number of them were written by Spanish sympathizers, they represent the Creoles who helped the Indian cause for selfish reasons and as traitors. Undoubtedly there were some disinterested men among them who really favored and worked for the Inca's cause. The majority of Creoles, however, seemed indifferent to the Indian revolts.

Soon Tomás Catari and some of his followers passed through the plantation of Rosario while he was collecting the tribute. The owner, Manuel Álvarez Villarroel, colonel of the militia of La

---

314; Relación de los hechos mas notables acaecidos en la sublevación general . . . , 26–27. MS copy in B. L.

[33] Confesión de Nicolás Catari, La Plata, April 10, 1781, in Odriozola, *Documentos*, I, 329–30.

[34] Angelis, *Documentos*, 223.

Plata, arrested him. When Alós had been in prison, he had issued an order for the arrest of Tomás as soon as he was freed; and now Villarroel obeyed. Ignacio Flores, whom Viceroy Vertíz appointed to take action against Villarroel for imprisoning the Indian without a viceregal decree, claimed that the Colonel had received secret orders from the audiencia to take Catari. Shortly after Catari's arrest, his clerk, Isidro Serrano, was captured in the same region and documents were obtained concerning the assembling of the Indians. This time the people of Chayanta could not free the prisoners, although the priest proved to be a sincere friend of Tomás, had him brought to his house, and asked to have him protected. Villarroel handed the prisoners over to the chief justice, Acuña, who planned to get rid of them quickly by taking them to La Plata. Reinforced by six or eight soldiers, he undertook this journey by night on January 15, 1781. He did not seem to realize that he had in his keeping the most revered leader of the Indians.

Acuña and his prisoners left Poloto after they had rested there all day. When they ascended the precipitous and rocky hill of Chataquila, near the town of Quilaquila in the province of Yamparaes, four leagues from La Plata, they suddenly spied a troop of Indians in front of them. Apparently Villarroel, who was with the party, pushed Catari over the precipice, although the Spanish version declared that the Indians killed him, which certainly seems unlikely in view of the fact that they had come to free him. The natives then threw stones from above and in a short time killed Acuña, Serrano, and other men; only a few escaped, and all the papers were lost.[35]

When Merlos heard the sad news, he foresaw great danger to the province. He eulogized Tomás Catari as a man of gentle heart and good intentions who favored the Spaniards, greatly loved the King, and had reprimanded the people for their faults and urged them to be peaceful. He declared that the Indian had not

[35] Relación de los hechos mas notables acaecidos en la sublevación general . . . , 27–29; Confesión de Nicolás Catari, La Plata, April 10, 1781, in Odriozola, *Documentos,* I, 324–25; AGN, Buenos Aires, Criminales, Leg. 21, exp. 17 (cited by Lewin *op. cit.,* 171, 174–75); Carta de Flores á Vertíz de 15 de Abril de 1781, AGN, Montevideo, Fondo documental, in Lewin, *op. cit.,* 469.

caused the uprising in Chayanta and had maintained no relations with Túpac Amaru.[36] In fact, Catari was killed before definitely declaring the rebellion in the viceroyalty of La Plata because he was waiting for Túpac Amaru's armies to arrive.

Catari did not act alone. Although he was shrewd and not necessarily ignorant, except of the Spanish language, he was only a poor Indian. In spite of his poverty, funds were at his disposal. He was able to hire Isidro Serrano as his clerk in Macha, Lucero in La Plata, and another man named Juan Peláez; all were persons of some education who knew Spanish. There must have been some kind of organization back of Catari since he found influential friends in all the cities where he personally made complaints to the government.[37] After his death legends about his resurrection spread in Chayanta and the neighboring provinces which kept the natives stirred up.[38]

His brother, Dámaso, now assumed leadership of the revolt. Both he and Nicolás were infuriated by their brother's death and called upon the people of the neighboring provinces for help. Nicolás invited the Indians of Moromoro, Pintatora, Sorcopoco, Ayguari, Guadalupe, Chacani, Autoras, and Trigo-Guasi to join them. In a few days they came in great numbers and stationed themselves on the hills, thus terrifying the inhabitants. This mob shortly attacked Colonel Villarroel in the district of Aullagas, where he owned mines, and sacked and burned his house. When jumping a wall in an attempt to escape, Villarroel had the misfortune to break his leg, yet he did not give up, but remained in a mine which had access to the hill of Gallofa. A supposedly loyal peon betrayed him and handed him over to the Indians. They took him out to the plain near a ravine, maltreated him, and, after various

[36] AGN, Buenos Aires, División colonia, Sección gobierno, Tribunales, Leg. 124, exp. 3, and *ibid.*, Sección criminales, Leg. 21, exp. 17 (cited by Lewin, *op. cit.*, 102–103).

[37] Correspondencia Vertíz-Gálvez, 1783, num. 686, AGN, Buenos Aires, in Lewin, *op. cit.*, 484.

[38] Oficio de Merlos á Vertíz del 15 de Febrero de 1781, La Plata, February 15, 1781, AGN, Buenos Aires, División colonia, Sección gobierno, Tribunales, Leg. 124, exp. 3, in Lewin, *op. cit.*, 427–29. Confesión de Dámaso Catari, La Plata, April 1, 1781, in Odriozola, *Documentos*, I, 307–308.

charges, killed him because he had captured Tomás Catari prior to Catari's last journey toward La Plata. Then they went to the plantations of Palca and Rosario, where the dead man had interests, took five thousand pesos and all the supplies they could find, and divided them among themselves.[39]

When the Indians sacked Aullagas, it was Nicolás who distributed the wrought and stamped silver. As Dámaso had been absent on account of illness when Villarroel was killed, he received nothing. Later the Indians gave him three hundred of the five thousand pesos taken from a convoy sent to Potosí. Nicolás received one hundred pesos, and the remainder was divided among the men who took part in the struggle.[40]

After Villarroel's death, the insurgents withdrew to the town of Macha. From there the Catari brothers summoned many Indians living in the more distant provinces. Accompanied by the widow of Tomás Catari and by many governors, leaders, and *alcaldes,* the multitude of raging Indians started for Macha. They were armed with slings, sticks having sharp edges, wooden weapons edged with lead, called *macanas,* and knives. They began their march with robbery, burning, and the destruction of all persons who refused to follow them. When they arrived at the town of Ocuri, the priest came out of the church with the Sacrament in his hands, but they did not show the least respect and kept their caps on. In Macha they profaned the sanctuary by forcibly taking Governor Pascual Chura out of it and killing him because he would not follow them.[41]

Now they did not even show respect for Merlos. He said that on three occasions Dámaso Catari had entered his home to insult him and threatened to kill him if he did not leave his parish and take his assistant, Mariano de la Vega, with him. Dámaso believed that the two men had been responsible for the imprisonment and

[39] Relación de los hechos mas notables acaecidos en la sublevación general . . . , 29–30. MS copy in B. L. *Revista de Archivos y Bibliotecas (Peruanas),* Año 1900, Vol. V, 161.

[40] Confesión de Dámaso Catari, La Plata, April 1, 1781, in Odriozola, *op. cit.,* I, 307–308.

[41] Relación de los hechos mas notables acaecidos en la sublevación general . . . , 31–32. MS copy in B. L.

death of his brother. When Merlos decided to leave, the Indians surrounded his home. He told them to ask pardon for their crimes and he would go to La Plata to obtain it for them. They agreed on condition that he put his house and all his possessions under their care. Giving them the keys, he went on to the town of Ocuri, where he was surrounded by four or five hundred Indians. As a result, he could not continue on his way without treating with Nicolás Catari, but he managed to calm the natives and wrote to Nicolás explaining that the town of Macha clamored for a general pardon. The reply was so insolent that the priest hastened away and in four or five days reached La Plata.[42] Dámaso later evidently forgot his hatred for Merlos, since on the night before he was executed, he testified that the priest had taken no part in the conspiracy.[43]

The Indians soon marched to the town of Pintatora, terrifying the people along the way and enlisting all men useful for war. They showed hostility toward the Spanish people who had assembled in the church. When the assistant priest came to the door with a crucifix in his hand and urged them to keep peace, they laughed at him and threatened him with death. They went next to the town of Moromoro and committed similar outrages. There the priest closed the church door and, followed by the Spaniards of all those regions, hastened to Chuquisaca. As a result, only the governor fell into the hands of the Indians and was beheaded. The insurgents then marched to Quilaquila, near which Tomás Catari had been put to death, intending to pay their respects to him and to transfer his body from the cemetery to the church. There they beheaded the manager of the hacienda of Potolo, because he had arrested the men involved in Acuña's death, and the governor of the town, who refused to join them.

The revolutionists became bolder every day and began to throw off their masks. They killed corregidores and their dependents,

[42] Oficio de Merlos á Vertíz del 15 de Febrero de 1781, La Plata, February 15, 1781, AGN, Buenos Aires, División colonia, Sección gobierno, Tribunales, Leg. 124, exp. 3, in Lewin, *op. cit.*, 427–29.

[43] Certificación de Sebastián de Velasco, Biblioteca Nacional, Buenos Aires, Sección manuscritos, num. 2158, f. 55 and 56; also AGN, Buenos Aires, Criminales, Leg. 21, exp. 17, in Lewin, *op. cit.*, 105.

men in charge of royal revenues, and Europeans. This was the result of the first orders of Túpac Amaru.

In Chayanta another revolutionist, Simón Castillo, attracted a large number of followers. He acted with great cruelty and showed no mercy to his adversaries. The first corregidor to lose his head in that region was Manuel de Bodega from the province of Paria. He and eighteen or twenty of his servants were killed on February 15, 1781. Earlier Mateo Ibáñez Arco of Carangas and some of his dependents were attacked on January 26 and beheaded along with the governors of the town of Corque and of the doctrina of Turco. The Indians divided the fifteen thousand pesos found in the corregidor's room and also the furniture and jewels. But such violence did not satisfy them. They appointed Miguel, an Indian from the town of Andamarca, as their captain and sent him to the doctrina of Guachacalla and the town of Sabaya to behead the governors, which he did. From there the leader, accompanied by more than four hundred armed Indians from the towns of Sabaya, Rivera, Todos Santos, and Negrillos, along with a number of Spaniards and mestizos, went to Carangas on February 2. At the sanctuary of Our Lady of Purification he made them take an oath of obedience and vassalage to Túpac Amaru. They next directed their fury against the house of the accountant of the royal treasury, Juan Manuel de Gëmes y Huestes. He was imprisoned and killed by means of the stocks. The Indians then forbade anyone to care for his body, which was partly eaten by dogs the night following his execution.

The uprising spread so rapidly that it was felt simultaneously from Cuzco to La Plata, or Chuquisaca, Chichas, and Tucumán, without any one town or city being able to help any other. Fortunately, the corregidores of Tomina and Cochabamba escaped, and help came from those places. Chuquisaca, Cochabamba, and Potosí also became the refuge of many people who fled the centers of revolt.[44]

[44] Relación de los hechos mas notables acaecidos en la sublevación general . . . , 31–34, MS copy in B. L. Angelis, *Documentos*, 259–61; Oficio del oficial real de Carangas, Pablo Gregorio Castillo á la audiencia de Charcas, Carangas, February 7, 1781, in Odriozola, *Documentos*, I, 340.

Castillo now approached the town of San Pedro de Buenavista, from which his Indians cut off all food and water. For five or six days the few Spaniards remaining there resisted the invaders bravely. Then, overcome with hunger and thirst and despairing of aid from La Plata, they decided to take refuge in the church. About twelve hundred persons crowded into the building with their priest, Ysidoro Herrera, and four or five other ecclesiastics. Then, closing and barring the doors, they asked God's mercy.

The Indians hurried to the church and tried to unhinge the door with bars and sticks. A priest entreated them to spare the lives of the innocent people within, but they said they intended to kill everybody except him. Seeing that there was no hope, the Spaniards opened the doors and went out to their deaths. Although the priest took the Sacrament and tried to obtain pardon from the Indians, one of them struck him such a blow with a macana that his head was cut off. In a moment the rebels entered the sanctuary and cruelly slaughtered all the people, even the priests, and committed many indecencies. The number killed was estimated to be one thousand. There were also innumerable victims of the uprising in Oruro, Sicasica, Argues, and Hayopaya; and in the church at Caracoto the assassins were said to have waded through the blood of the Spaniards up to their ankles.[45]

Such deeds could not be continued without retribution overtaking the Indians. On February 20, the army of Dámaso and Nicolás Catari, consisting of seven thousand Indians, was defeated on the hills of Punilla, two or three leagues from the city of La Plata.[46] Dámaso fled and with some of his followers reached Oruro, where he requested a general pardon, at the same time continuing his leadership and summoning more Indians. Evidently the two Cataris hoped to take La Plata. They did their best to stir up revolt in that city, a detailed account of which will be given in the following chapter.

The inhabitants of La Plata must have felt greatly relieved when news reached them on March 30, 1781, that the Viceroy of

[45] Relación de los hechos mas notables acaecidos en la sublevación general . . . , 42–43; Odriozola, *Documentos*, I, 28–29.
[46] Odriozola, *Documentos*, I, 8–11.

Buenos Aires was sending aid. Colonel José de Reseguín was on his way with a battalion of veteran troops.[47] All along the way he met fugitives. The priest of Santa Catalina told him that proclamations had been published there in the name of Túpac Amaru, as well as in Estarca and Talina. When news came that one of the Cataris intended to invade the province, Reseguín decided to delay his march in order to check him. He went to Moraya, surrounded it, and imprisoned many people. From a fugitive it was learned that Dámaso had hidden in the mill of Oro and had sacked the mines of Vetillas, Tatasi, Portugaleta, and Chocaya, where eleven persons had been killed. When the Indian's followers learned of the troops' arrival, they deserted him; and he fled with the few men who still remained faithful. Reseguín immediately sent out a detachment to try to take Catari and recover the stolen silver and jewels. He put down uprisings in the towns of Mojo, Talina, Tarifa, and Santiaga and in the Indian communities near them which were about to follow the example of other Indian communities by joining the revolt.[48]

In revenge the Indians publicly displayed the head of Salvador Patsí on a lance. They executed Francisco Díaz de la Revilla, corregidor of Lipes, stole more than forty thousand pesos from him and the royal treasury, and killed many dependents of the corregidores. They tried to prevent aid from Buenos Aires by cutting off the roads from Jujuy to Potosí over which the mail came to La Plata.[49]

The natives of Pocoata, who had not participated in the uprising, grew tired of the turmoil and desired the general pardon offered. They therefore proposed to Francisco Javier Troncoso, their priest, that Dámaso and Nicolás be arrested and handed over to the authorities. The priest encouraged the idea and even risked his life to pacify his parishioners. When the Indians learned that

[47] Relación de los hechos mas notables acaecidos en la sublevación general . . . , 48, 51. MS copy in B. L.
[48] Carta de José de Reseguín á Juan de Vertíz, virrey de Buenos Aires. Tupiza, March 18, 1781, in Odriozola, op. cit., I, 347–48.
[49] Relación de los hechos mas notables acaecidos en la sublevación general . . . , 45. MS copy in B. L.

there was a two thousand pesos bounty on the head of each Catari, they were more eager than ever to imprison them. They soon captured Dámaso and other rebels, but Nicolás eluded them. With only six hundred Indians to guard the prisoners, they started for La Plata, remaining near Punilla for the night. On March 31, many people hastened out of La Plata to see the man who had caused so much trouble and to await the troops who were to conduct him into the city.

While this was happening, the Indians guarding Pocoata found the hiding place of Nicolás Catari. They attacked him suddenly on an estate near Clarichari and captured him with some of his famous captains. On April 1, they took him with forty-five prisoners to La Plata. There the Indian captors of the Cataris collected the two thousand pesos offered for each. Simón Castillo was still missing, but he could not escape from the Indians who were determined to sell their chiefs. He took refuge in the mine of Guanuní, twelve leagues from Oruro, where the Indians seized him and other rebels. They arrived in La Plata on April 25.

It was strange that the Indians betrayed those leaders. Likely their chief motive was to distract the Spaniards' attention from the main rebellion under Túpac Amaru, on which they placed their hope of freedom. As the roads were always open to the natives, they had news of the Inca before the royalists did. The Indians in all the kingdom of Peru and elsewhere flocked to his cause and committed revolutionary acts from the coast to the mountains. Even the barbarous Mocovies and Indians of the pampas near Jujuy and Salta received notice of the rebellion and tried to take those two cities, but were repulsed when reinforcements arrived from Buenos Aires. The Indians of Chiriguanos near the Tomina frontier also desired to recognize Túpac Amaru as their king and made costly invasions against the Spaniards.[50]

Excitement mounted when Dámaso Catari, his wife, and twenty-eight other prisoners were brought into La Plata at the beginning of April. The capture of Dámaso had been greatly desired; thus for five blocks from the Alameda to the main plaza the crowd

[50] *Ibid.*, 51–54; Odriozola, *Documentos*, I, 47–50.

was so dense that people could hardly walk and there was scarcely standing room on the balconies. The city had never before seen such a huge gathering. The chief criminal, then about thirty-five years old, looked like any ordinary Indian.

He was put in prison and his confession taken. At first he answered the charges boldly, saying that his clerk had written the letters, summoned the people, and robbed and destroyed the towns.[51] He admitted that he was the brother of Tomás and Nicolás Catari. He stated that he had never paid tribute; therefore he must have belonged to the Indian nobility. He said that he was a tailor by profession and that the Indians of Pocoata had imprisoned him in the town of Macha before bringing him to La Plata. He believed his imprisonment resulted from lies told by the people of Pocoata and from supposed documents, which neither he nor his brother Nicolás had. Questioned about the nature of these documents, he replied that they were the ones which his brother Tomás had obtained in Buenos Aires. Asked whether Tomás had been influenced by any person to go to Buenos Aires to petition the Viceroy, he said that he had no knowledge of any such influence.

He was also questioned concerning papers drawn up to advise inhabitants of the communities of Chayanta and other provinces not to pay more than half the tribute, or absolutely nothing, and of the proclamations posted in the cemeteries ordering the Indians not to pay royal dues, tenths, twentieths, and other taxes. And although his brother Nicolás had been the first person to publish the reduction of the tribute in Macha, Dámaso declared he had never heard of his brother Tomás' trying to reduce it.

The Spaniards wished to know whether Tomás had carried on correspondence with Túpac Amaru. Dámaso replied that when Ventura Cruz, an Indian alcalde of Coroma, came to Macha about the tribute, he gave his brother a letter, but he, Dámaso, was ignorant of its contents. However, he did mention an unsigned document, which had passed from hand to hand, containing information the Inca had written in letters to Potosí. Following

[51] *Revista de Archivos y Bibliotecas (Peruanas)*, V, 182–83; Relación de los hechos mas notables acaecidos en la sublevación general . . . , 52. MS copy in B. L.

receipt of this anonymous communication, a conference was held at which it was decided to send a message to Túpac Amaru offering obedience and service, but this could not be done because no one knew where he was.

Asked if there were other chiefs of the uprising, Dámaso maintained that he and his brother were the principal leaders. The Indians came to them from Paria, Porco, Carangas, and other places to relate their grievances against the caciques and certain persons who had injured them. He said that an Indian called Mateo Canaviri, living at Macha, had published the reduction of the tribute in Condo without his or his brother's orders. Furthermore, after the defeat at Punilla, Canaviri had offered to bring seven thousand Indians to Macha and put them under his orders.

Dámaso answered the question why he had gone to Punilla by saying that he had gone to Quilaquila to see Tomás' tomb. He saw the Indians of that doctrina fleeing and followed when they advised him to join them. He came to Punilla, where he tried to obtain certain papers from the possessions of the dead corregidor, Acuña, because among them were the documents given Tomás in Buenos Aires. He said that the revolt broke out because the Viceroy's decree was not put into effect. Many of the people arriving at Punilla, said Dámaso, assured him that Canaviri's seven thousand men were coming; hence he decided to enter the city on Ash Wednesday.

He declared that he had been willing to accept the pardon offered by the clergy, but his wife and many Indians did not want to do so; therefore, for fear of losing his life, he had been forced to remain in Punilla and so could not heed the warnings. He blamed Nicolás for making him write summons to be distributed throughout the kingdom.

Dámaso was tortured for an hour to find out who his accomplices were, but no information could be obtained from him except some names that he later said were false.[52] Then the Spaniards sentenced him to death. He asked pardon for his community and

[52] Confesión de Dámaso Catari, La Plata, April 1, 1781, in Odriozola, *Documentos,* I, 305–14; Decreto, La Plata, April 7, 1781, *ibid.,* I, 316–17.

showed signs of repentance. He was hanged on April 17. His body was quartered afterwards: the limbs were put up outside the walls, the torso was placed in Punilla, and the head was sent to Macha. No doubt the Spaniards followed such gruesome practices in the hope that other rebels would be deterred.[53]

When Nicolás Catari and forty-five of his followers were brought to La Plata on April 1, the excitement of the people greatly increased. Nicolás was charged with killing Villarroel, who had imprisoned his brother Tomás, and with stirring up the people of Macha, Ocuri, Ayguari, Secopoco, Paria, and part of Pocoata. The four thousand persons whom he had incited to rebel were not all Indians. Some were mestizos, particularly in Challapata, where both classes were summoned. Nicolás was not as important a chief, however, as his brother Dámaso. When asked about accomplices to his crime, he replied bravely that they were the very same persons who had taken him prisoner. Yet he did not speak evil of the people of Pocoata.[54]

The confession of Nicolás slightly contradicted that of Dámaso. Nicolás said that Tomás did not speak of the tribute until he was free because of the uprising of Pocoata, that he had obtained the title of cacique and had shown the order concerning it to many Indians in Macha. Nicolás did not know who in Macha had advised Tomás unless it was his clerk, Serrano. Asked why Dámaso went to Punilla, he said that the Indians had persuaded him to camp in that place. He also said that Dámaso wrote four letters to him from Punilla asking for men. When his brother was overthrown, he quarreled with him on account of his failure to bring aid.

The Spanish authorities wanted to know how many people were killed by order of Nicolás Catari. He replied that one night the Indians of Salguero put to death, in Challapata, one Lupercia, wife of Governor Roque Morato, since she had been administering

[53] Relación de los hechos mas notables acaecidos en la sublevación general . . . , 52; Sentencia de once reos que se ahorcaron el día 17 de Marzo de 1781, en la ciudad de La Plata, March 9, 1781, in Odriozola, *Documentos,* I, 303; Angelis, *Documentos,* 213–14.

[54] Relación de los hechos mas notables acaecidos en la sublevación general . . . , 52–53. MS copy in B. L.

the province, and her son-in-law, Martín Valeriano, who along with his mother-in-law was suspected of betraying Tomás. These two had also caused Cacique Nicolás Acho's death. By command of Nicolás Catari, the alcalde of Sicasica, Manuel Taguareja; the governor of Moromoro, Blas Aguilar; and the latter's brother were also executed.[55] This was indeed a bloody record for one man.

More criminals were brought to La Plata by many Indians who thought that thus they would gain the favor of the Spaniards. As a result, the prisons were soon filled with more than two hundred leaders of the rebellion. Commandant General Flores declared Nicolás Catari, Simón Castillo, and the other principal disturbers of the peace in Chayanta criminals of state. They were sentenced to be dragged through the plaza of the city and then hanged; their bodies were to be quartered and the heads cut off to be put up along the roads as a warning for other persons. Their names were to be called infamous, their houses burned, and all their possessions confiscated. On May 7, forty-one were executed, seven being hanged and thirty-four shot. Among the former were Nicolás Catari and Castillo, who went to their deaths chewing coca leaves.[56]

The Catari rebellion was a serious incident that showed the bravery of the Indians and their determination to get rid of abuses and inefficient administrators. It was extremely dangerous because of its influence upon regions all around Chayanta, where numerous other revolts soon sprang up. Despite efforts to put them down, new insurrections continually broke out and eventually extended for three hundred leagues from the frontiers of Cuzco to Tucumán and included twenty-four provinces. There almost at the same time the flame of revolution was kindled, and it looked as if Spain might lose a large part of her colonial possessions.

[55] Confesión de Nicolás Catari, La Plata, April 10, 1781, in Odriozola, *Documentos*, I, 320, 323, 326–29.
[56] Relación de los hechos mas notables acaecidos en la sublevación general . . . , 53–54. Sentencia expedida por Ignacio Flores, in Odriozola, *Documentos*, I, 334.

CHAPTER IV

Defense of La Plata

THE TURBULENT EVENTS in Chayanta extended to the city of La Plata.[1] As early as March of 1780 there appeared in that city a lampoon, in the form of a little verse, telling that the customhouses had been abolished in Cuzco, Arequipa, La Paz, and Cochabamba and stating that it was time to destroy the one in La Plata.[2] Then the next month, when some malcontents disturbed the city by saying that the Europeans would kill the citizens, many inhabitants wanted to go to the hills. The militia guarding the city also received an anonymous letter, supposed to have been written in Cochabamba, admonishing the people to rebel against their oppressors as the citizens of Cochabamba were going to do.[3] On September 10, the head of the unfortunate cacique, Florencio Lupa, was sent secretly to La Plata and brought to the cabildo.[4]

In the city and outside its walls a large number of Indians were ready to sack it. They had been stirred up earlier by Dámaso Catari, but, like other chiefs, he had lost time sending notes to the corrupt audiencia, thereby giving the city opportunity to prepare its defense. He had asked for the documents which his brother had brought from Buenos Aires, that Fabián Lucero be appointed pro-

---

[1] The city was founded in 1538 or 1539, at the site of the native village of Chuquisaca, by order of Francisco Pizarro, who had entrusted to his brother Gonzalo all the territory of Charcas which he had conquered. La Plata (or Chuquisaca, as the Indians preferred to call it) became the episcopal see and the seat of the royal audiencia, whose jurisdiction extended all the way to the Río de la Plata. On July 12, 1839, the name of La Plata was changed to Sucre by law, and the former was designated the archbishopric which included the departments of Oruro, Potosí, Tarija, and Chuquisaca. See Abecia, *op. cit.*, 1.

[2] Biblioteca Nacional, Buenos Aires, Sección de manuscritos, num. 2158 (cited by Lewin, *Túpac Amaru el rebelde,* 66).

[3] *Revista de Archivos y Bibliotecas (Peruanas),* Año III, Vol. V, 173–74.

[4] Odriozola, *Documentos,* I, 4.

tector of the Indians, that Juan Bautista de Ormachea be made chief justice in Chayanta, and that Father Miguel de Arzadúm be transferred to Macha. If these requests were fulfilled, the insurgents would return to their homes. If not, they would enter the city and burn it.[5] The Spaniards refused his requests, but Dámaso did not take the offensive because he knew that a revolt was being planned in La Plata. He continued, however, to send to the city officials letters full of threats, which were not answered. He said he had all his people in Punilla and there were already two thousand soldiers around the city.[6] The terrified inhabitants wanted to find means to check his insolence. On September 10 the judges of the audiencia hastily gave orders to defend the city and published a proclamation commanding all the inhabitants and even transients to come to the plaza with all their weapons.

The disturbance grew worse and fear increased, but in a short time a crowd of people appeared in the plaza. The fiscal, Pino, then asked Archbishop Francisco Ramón de Herboso to tell all priests to bring their arms, and this was done. Certain suspected persons were imprisoned and the ravines and neighboring hills examined. In the afternoon an edict was issued to summon in one hour all physically able men to enlist to form companies; the penalty for failure to obey the summons would be death and confiscation of possessions. As a crier could not be found, the audiencia regent, Gerónimo de Ruedas, cried out the proclamation while one of the judges and the president of the audiencia performed the duties of night watchman. The Archbishop ordered all church and convent bells silenced unless he ordered them to be rung since the ringing of the bells was to signal an emergency. All churches and convents were to prepare their own defenses. In the afternoon the regent had certain Indians from the town of Condo imprisoned on account of an uprising in their community. The military preparations continued for ten or twelve days, during which time even useless old men were taken into service. The chief difficulty was

[5] *Revista de Archivos de Bibliotecas (Peruanas)*, Año 1900, Vol. V, 167.
[6] AGN, Buenos Aires, Criminales, Leg. 19, exp. 21, in Lewin, *op. cit.*, 280–81.

the lack of arms; and, if the enemy had known this, they could probably have taken the city.[7]

Inhabitants of surrounding towns and villages took refuge in the capital, and the rebels easily seized those small towns and often burned them. Preparations for war went ahead in La Plata. A quantity of weapons and ammunition were collected or made, and orders sent to the towns of Laguna and Santa Cruz to obtain aid. In the meantime three or four companies of soldiers were quartered in the city, while aid was coming from neighboring towns. Viceroy Vertíz appointed Ignacio Flores, governor of Moxos and Chuquitos, commander-in-chief.[8]

The audiencia judges criticized Flores on different occasions for his irresolute conduct. They thought that if he had acted quickly, the rebellion would soon have been suppressed. Flores became angry when Tomás Catari was killed without the Viceroy's permission. He accused the audiencia of having a hand in his death because the judges believed that if the Indian was dead, the rebellion would end. Matters only became worse when Chief Justice Acuña was also killed.

The terror of the city increased when the people heard that Dámaso and Nicolás Catari were in the town of Quilaquila, only five leagues distant, with seven thousand Indians, with Sancho Acho, Simón Castillo, and other chiefs. When the Indian leaders had stirred up the neighboring towns, the cacique of Yolata sent one of their letters to the regent of the audiencia and loyally offered to serve the king with all his forces. The regent then declared him a faithful vassal and hung a medal around his neck.

The judges of the audiencia changed their minds about the effect of Tomás Catari's death when they heard that the city was surrounded. Even though he had met death in different fashion, they now tried to hide the fact that they had issued an order for his execution, but Flores had a copy of the document showing all that they had agreed in the matter. They did not know whether

[7] Odriozola, *Documentos,* I, 4–5; Carrió, *Crónicas Americanas,* 84–85; Relación de los hechos mas notables acaecidos en la sublevación general . . . , 15–18. MS copy in B. L.

[8] *Ibid.,* 29, 32.

the Indians would attack the city, but precautions were taken. Advance guards went out to observe enemy movements, trenches were dug in the streets, and companies of militia were sent to guard the outer walls. The regent took measure after measure for protection, while the lawyers formed a company to patrol the streets every night. Lacking military training, the jurists caused more confusion than security and a dispute arose concerning their assumed powers and those of the commandant.[9]

Meanwhile, from Quilaquila the two Cataris had written letters to the audiencia, asking for the release of the Indians seized at the time of Acuña's death. They said that if the president and fiscal did not grant the request, they would be killed. On account of such threats, the people decided to defend the city to the last moment. They replied to the letter by torturing two Indian messengers to death despite the presence of the enemy outside the city. While the executioner was doing his work, the crowd in the plaza witnessing it heard a loud shout and were thrown into confusion. The shout probably came from some Indians who entered the ward of San Roque to aid the victims. The people hurried to the place where they heard the noise, but, finding no enemies, returned to the plaza, where the execution was finished. When the bodies of the two Indian messengers were quartered and hung on the walls outside, the inhabitants were somewhat calmed.

This example of cruelty, however, did not check the Indians, who approaches the city on the following day, February 13, 1781. About eight o'clock that night, when they were spied on the hills of Punilla, two or three leagues distant, the church bells rang the alarm and drummers hurried through the streets to warn all the people. Nothing happened that night. Next day, from their advantageous place on the hills, the Indians began to commit hostile acts. They also hastened toward the rural districts to sack the neighboring haciendas and summoned more people from the surrounding towns to join them. As a result, Commandant Flores decided that the city must be surrounded with artillery and a company of armed men.

[9] Odriozola, *Documentos,* I, 8–9; Relación de los hechos mas notables acaecidos en sublevación general . . . , 34–35.

The priest from the doctrina of Macha, Father Merlos, was suspected of being an accomplice in the disturbances. He was arrested at his residence in La Plata, placed in the Recollect House, and afterwards taken to the public prison. The Indians continually demanded his release and threatened to take him out of prison by force if necessary.[10] The complicity of Merlos in the uprising could not be definitely proved, although Viceroy Vertíz declared him an arrogant man of bad disposition and evil conduct, who caused restlessness in all the towns where he had served. The executive thought the priest aided the insurgents in their writings because the style was too good for that of Indians, and wanted him sent back to Spain. The intimacy of Merlos with Tomás Catari and other Indians in the revolt was well known, but the judges finally pronounced him free from sedition.[11]

The people in La Plata could hardly eat or sleep or carry on business on account of the confusion, noise, and ringing of bells. To make matters worse, food became scarce and no one knew where to get more. Everyone expected an attack any moment, but conditions remained static until February 17, when many people rode out on horseback from different parts of the city to meet the enemy. As they came outside the walls without a leader to direct them, there was great disorder. The lawyers and the populace had asked Flores repeatedly to permit them to attack the enemy, but he refused to give his consent; therefore they decided to take the initiative themselves.

Alfonso González Pérez, a judge of the audiencia, and Francisco Paula Sanz, the director of the tobacco monopoly, led the royalists. Since the Indians, stationed on the hills, did not seem very near, forty Spaniards on horseback approached and soon found themselves at a disadvantage. One of the soldiers, seeing the difficulty, returned toward the city and met on the heights of

[10] Relación de los hechos mas notables acaecidos en la sublevación general . . . , 35–36; Odriozola, *Documentos*, I, 9–10.

[11] Carta de Vertíz á Gálvez sobre la conducts de Merlos y Ormachea, May 31, 1783, Correspondencia Vertíz-Gálvez, AGN, Buenos Aires, in Lewin, *op. cit.*, 429–30; Carta de Juan Josef de Vertíz á José de Gálvez, March 15, 1781, num. 485 reservada, *ibid.*, 435–37.

Zaitucancha a company of foot soldiers, who had marched out when the bells rang. Reinforced with these soldiers and with Flores in command, the Spaniards attacked a second and a third time, but could gain no advantage because of the daring tactics of the Indians. Their ammunition gone, the disappointed soldiers had to withdraw.

When night came, the people of the city remained under arms. They liked the impetuous Sanz, but complained about the circumspect conduct of Flores. Lampoons with scathing verses were put up; in them the commander was accused of cowardice and even said to favor the rebellion. Next day the inhabitants informed him that they were ready to go in search of the enemy, declaring that if he did not lead the attack, they would march out to meet the enemy without a commander.[12]

The Archbishop and the regent now decided that peace must be restored and offered the besiegers pardon in the King's name. Then the prelate walked bravely into the midst of the enemy forces to warn them to accept peace, but the Indians would agree to stop hostilities only on the conditions already proposed by their leaders. They said that they would soon have fifteen thousand soldiers to destroy the city.

The citizens of La Plata became so indignant at this answer that, on February 20, Commandant Flores ordered the troops out. Divided into three columns, the troops were to be deployed as follows: The first column, under Pedro Flores and comprised of 250 men, would attack at the right of the enemy, who were on a steep hill covered with brambles, where they waited to roll large stones down upon the Spaniards. The second, with a like number of men led by Francisco Barrientos, would advance from the opposite side. The third, which was reserved for Commandant Flores himself, with 750 men, was to attack the center. Because of various delays the army could not arrive at its destination until mid-afternoon. Most of the inhabitants wanted to see the enemy and followed the troops voluntarily. Even women were drawn up in

---

[12] Odriozola, *Documentos*, I, 10; Relación de los hechos mas notables acaecidos en la sublevación general . . . , 36–37.

battle lines with sticks and knives in their hands. The commander, deeply touched by that scene, urged them to go home, but could not make them withdraw. It was therefore necessary to place sentinels to guard the city and prevent more people from leaving.

The companies advanced in good order to the hills. When the signal was given to attack on all sides, the Spaniards began to climb the steepest of the hills because the Indians laughed at them. Stones rained upon the royalists, yet they advanced toward the summit. Some were protected by leather shields, others by the musketeers, and others by the slingers, who confused the Indians. The Indians kept their places with great tenacity, but in the end had to flee and hide among the rocks and fissures to save their lives. More than three hundred Indians were killed and still more wounded; twenty-eight prisoners were taken into the city; and the soldiers followed carrying heads. The rebel leaders and officers escaped.

This victory, which freed the city of La Plata from blockade, was celebrated with many demonstrations of joy. During a banquet at the home of Flores news came of the horrible events in the town of Oruro, which will be described later. Fortunately, the victory of Punilla had a good effect on other provinces, since many people coming to aid the Cataris returned to their homes when they heard that the brothers had fled. One division of the returning Indians entered the town of Pocopo, where they committed robberies and caused some deaths, but a detachment of Spaniards hastened there on February 24, defeated the mob, and brought seven heads and four prisoners into the city. The next day, when La Plata was threatened again, one hundred soldiers defended it and in five days returned with ten prisoners.

Eight of the captured Indians, condemned to death, were turned over to the priest of Chuquisaca, José de Rivera, for questioning. He found that, except for a few of them who had lived on distant ranches, most of them had sufficient instruction in the Roman Catholic faith. They could explain the doctrine in three languages and knew how to read and write very well. They confessed that their crimes had not resulted from lack of religion, but from desperation. Thus it seems that some Indian rebels knew more than most people thought they did.[13]

The enemy leaders finally saw the handwriting on the wall. On February 28, the regent of the audiencia received letters from Dámaso Catari asking for a general pardon for himself and the Indians. The answer was the proclamation offering two thousand pesos each for his and his brother's heads and one thousand for the head of his captain, Sancho Acho. After that conditions improved in the vicinity of La Plata, and the people could feel easy once more.[14]

Later a revolt was almost caused by a rumor that the chapetones were going to destroy the natives. An anonymous letter written in a disguised hand was sent to the militia companies defending the city. Supposed to have been written in Cochabamba, it said that "the people should not be careless, or trust in proclamations or promises, because eventually in a secret manner the Europeans wished to kill them, and that they should not wait for an attack, but strike a blow beforehand." Ignorant persons with vivid imaginations readily believed this statement, and did not stop to consider how small the number of Europeans was compared to the other groups of people.

Regent Ruedas wanted to prevent disorder. He sent a copy of the letter to the cabildo and ordered the people to meet there so that the letter could be discussed. Many men of honor, Commandant Flores, the Archbishop, and a considerable number from the lower classes assembled.

Pablo José Tarabillo stated the purpose of the meeting. He said that the discord and evil rumors must be stopped, that a city with such a glorious heritage should not be ruined by a few misinformed persons who scattered false suggestions for special purposes. He urged the residents to seek the author of those misrepresentations and punish him, whether he be native or European. He exhorted all citizens to be prompt to serve their legitimate sov-

[13] González Pavón, "Causas de la sublevación indígenes," in Loayza, *op. cit.*, Serie I, Vol. X, 79–81.

[14] Relación de los hechos mas notables acaecidos en la sublevación general . . . , 38–41; Odriozola, *Documentos*, I, 11–12.

PROVINCES OF THE VICEROYAL

BRAZIL

LA PAZ

EL BENI

• *Reyes*

Trinidad

Sorata

• *La Paz*

Cochabamba
COCHABAMBA

Oruro • *Misque*

RURO \ • *Chayanta*

SANTA CRUZ
• *Santa Cruz*

• *Sucre (Chuquisaca)*

Potosí •

POTOSÍ

Pampabamba •
CHUQUISACA

Tupiza •

• *Tarija* TARIJA

PARAGUAY

JUJUY
ARGENTINA SALTA

F PERU AFFECTED BY THE REVOLT

ereign, even at the cost of their property and lives. With shouts of, "Long live the King!" the cabildo meeting ended and the people were calmed.

The regent then issued a proclamation, on March 10, commending the people for repeated proofs of their fidelity to the King. It stated that all classes in the capital were henceforth worthy to be called faithful vassals and had set an example for other people in the dominion, while at the same time it intimated that there were subversive elements in the city.[15]

The execution of Dámaso and Nicolás Catari and many of their followers at La Plata in May calmed any seditious element still remaining there. The terrible danger which had hung over the city like a black cloud was now removed, and the surrounding regions were partly pacified. La Plata then tried to help the more distant and inland regions by collecting arms for an expedition, by gathering food, and by calling upon the people of the towns of Tomina, Misque, Vallegrande, Santa Cruz, and the provinces of Yamparaes, Cochabamba, Tucumán, and Buenos Aires for additional aid. It was difficult to obtain help from those places, however, since from the beginning of the rebellion the routes from one city or town to another had been closed.

Later, news of the disturbances experienced in Oruro, La Paz, and other distant parts of the viceroyalty reached La Plata. The Indians of the city always kept up with the progress of the uprisings and the operations of the Spaniards, but made no overt move until a new treason was discovered in Pocoata in August of 1781. An Indian governor named Pedro Caypa, who had been imprisoned during the Catari revolt and had witnessed the leaders' punishment, decided to lead a new insurrection. Taking the name of Túpa Condori, he persuaded many people to join him. But Cristóbal López, the commander in La Plata, learned of the plot and imprisoned the Indian immediately, thus keeping the revolt from materializing.

On August 11, Caypa admitted that he had been involved in

[15] Relación de los hechos mas notables acaecidos en la sublevación general . . . , 46–47.

an insurrection plot, but laid the direct blame on an Indian of Pocoata, who he said had told him that General Flores had been defeated and that this was an opportune time to attack the Spaniards. He was advised to lie in wait for the Spaniards on the heights of Morachaca. After intercepting them and putting them to death, he was to make war on Chuquisaca, Potosí, and other towns and make himself their master. He declared that he had believed the suggestion only a joke, but nevertheless had gathered together a small number of Indians. Caypa was executed on the seventeenth of August; then his head was put up in the plaza of Pocoata to terrify the people. Eight of his accomplices suffered the same fate.[16]

Quiet prevailed in La Plata until September 20, when an anonymous letter appeared on the door of the home of Regent Ruedas stating that treason was being plotted against the regent, the audiencia judges, the treasury officials, and any persons in the service of the royal treasury. These men were to be punished on account of their tyranny in the exaction of the alcabala and the collection of unbearable taxes, the letter continued. The attack was arranged for the twenty-fourth, when all Europeans would be put to death. The writer concluded by saying that he was a priest whose conscience compelled him to give information of the plot.

Ruedas was alarmed, for the plaza commandant, Cristóbal López, had only forty veteran soldiers to defend the city. And the other men mentioned in the letter were fearful because they knew Spaniards had been put to death in many places in the viceroyalty. The information was kept secret, yet on the following day a great commotion arose which made it necessary to postpone sending to Potosí one hundred bars of silver brought from Oruro. In the afternoon a curious expectation existed. Certain phrases were quoted from the letter, but no one knew how its contents were learned. Armed men were summoned from the province of Yamparaes; and within forty-eight hours its colonel, Pedro de Escobar, brought four hundred militiamen to the city. Nineteen veteran soldiers also came from Chichas. Ten cannon were loaded and cartridges distributed to the troops, who awaited an attack.

[16] *Ibid.*, 215–16.

Nothing happened until the night of September 21, when the leaders and many citizens were attending devotional services in the Chapel of Our Lady of Guadalupe. Suddenly information was received that a troop of rebel Indians had already entered the city to destroy it. When the regent ordered the large bell, used to sound alarms, to be rung, the inhabitants rushed in great disorder to the plaza. At the same time a confused shouting of "Long live King Charles III!" arose. The people swarming the plaza waited a long time for orders to attack, and when no enemies could be found, they returned to their homes.

The individuals mentioned in the letter were terrified when they saw the confusion engendered by the false report. How the whole thing had come about, no one could say, unless certain malcontents wished to rob the people and took that means to get them out of their houses. During the confusion letters were left in the judges' homes telling them to seek safety without having to be warned a third time.

Before the night of the twenty-fourth, the date set for the massacre, arrived, two communications were presented to the people of the city. In one the Archbishop threatened to excommunicate anybody who made threats against the judges and treasury officials. The other, issued by the royal council, declared all the natives of the city faithful vassals of the king and asked them to try to find the author of the letters. When the dreaded night passed without incident, the minds of the threatened men were calmed.

The audiencia urged the inhabitants of the city and its vicinity to remain peaceful, and on October 3 held an open cabildo meeting at which all the higher officials and ecclesiastics were present. A clerk read in a loud voice a proclamation of the council. Beginning with a description of conditions in the Spanish monarchy from the earliest times, it went on to relate the calamities suffered in the rebellion of the Catari brothers and in the uprising of Túpac Amaru. It concluded by extolling the city as a place of refuge for the persecuted, for its defense of religion, and for its loyalty.[17]

Even in distant Buenos Aires lampoons had appeared and ru-

[17] *Ibid.*, 187–200.

mors of dissatisfaction had been heard when news came concerning a change in the fiscal policy. The cabildo members were angered because they felt that, as representatives of the people, they should have received first notice of the new taxes. In the council meeting of October 2, 1778, Bernardo Sancho de Larrea, the attorney general, told of having been informed of the establishment of the tobacco monopoly and the imposition of new taxes, but said he was ignorant of the rules and method of their establishment and collection since the King had not yet made them known. The cabildo members then authorized him to petition the Viceroy to give them this information. The intendant general of the treasury objected on the grounds that the council had no right to ask for an explanation of the King's measures regarding any branch of the treasury. The sovereign himself sent word in March, 1779, that the cabildo had no right to have copies of royal measures and had no authority to take action in the matter, since it concerned the royal power. Further, he threatened to banish Sancho de Larrea to the Malvinas Islands. But even then the attorney general, who possessed an independent spirit, persisted in insisting on having the rules. This was the first time anybody in Buenos Aires had dared to defy royal authority.[18]

As in Peru, the alcabala had been increased from 4 to 6 per cent in Buenos Aires and was more burdensome for some articles than for others. The people paid grudgingly, protesting by posting lampoons in public places. One was attached to the house of Intendant Fernández. In it he and the accountant, Francisco Cabrera, were represented by grotesque figures going to the gallows mounted on burros. Underneath were several lines alluding to how badly they had performed their duties and making threats against them. After that incident the accountant had his house guarded.

On the following night four disguised men entered the office of Benito Gómez de la Fuente, the collector of the alcabala, threatened him, and asked him for the tax rules so that they could burn

[18] Acuerdo del extinguido cabildo, 1777–81, Serie III, Vol. VI, 289–90, 303–305, 380–87. Cited by Lewin, *op. cit.*, 68–70.

them. When they told him that he would be killed unless he obeyed, he gave them a copy of the rules and hastened off to inform the intendant and treasurer. The authorities ordered an investigation when a second lampoon was thrown at the house of Francisco Escalada, a merchant, which contained injurious remarks about certain people of the town, but the authors could not be discovered. Viceroy Vertíz took the matter seriously and fined the Escalada brothers, whom he suspected of having prepared the lampoons. They indignantly appealed to the King.[19] The Viceroy then prohibited the composition of lampoons, satires, verses, manifestos, and other seditious papers.[20]

In this account it has been noted that La Plata, threatened many times by outside insurgents, managed to defend itself successfully and put down all internal disturbances. As it was the headquarters of an audiencia, success proved to be more certain than in other places. Yet at times the powers and resources of the judges were severely strained in maintaining its defense and aiding neighboring towns and provinces. The dissatisfaction in Buenos Aires did not lead to an open revolt, perhaps because it also was the residence of higher authorities, but certain officials were badly frightened. Like La Plata, Buenos Aires did much to help quell disturbances in other areas.

[19] Lewin, *op. cit.*, 72–73.
[20] Orden de Vertíz sobre le aparición de pasquines en Buenos Aires, August 23, 1779, AGN, Buenos Aires, Criminales, Leg. 15, exp. 20 (published in Lewin, *op. cit.*, 432).

94

CHAPTER V

Revolution in Cuzco

Aᴏfᴛᴇʀ ᴛʜᴇ ᴇxᴇᴄᴜᴛɪᴏɴ of the corregidor of Tinta on November 10, 1780, the multitude vowed obedience to José Gabriel Túpac Amaru, who began to organize his forces for revolt. On the day following the execution, he took the road toward the Vilcamayo Valley and on November 12, entered the town of Quiquijana, capital of the province of Quispicanchis. There he surprised the corregidor, Fernando Cabrera, who miraculously escaped by hiding in the church and later fled to Cuzco, taking word of the uprising. The Inca obtained in his house 3,000 pesos in stamped and wrought silver and all the articles of the repartimiento. Cabrera had also left behind the royal treasury containing 25,000 pesos. This sum, with the 200,000 pesos in the treasury of Tinta, provided the first funds for the insurrection. The rich stores of the repartimientos of the two corregimientos, which the Inca generously distributed among his soldiers, encouraged men to hasten from all areas to enlist under his banner.

At first the people of Quiquijana fled, but when Túpac Amaru made his plans known to them, many returned. He told them that, if they would join his party, he would pay them salaries and regard them as his followers; if they opposed him, he would kill them all. To show that he meant what he said, he had some gallows erected in the plaza. Then he attended mass and countermarched toward Tungasuca. On the way home, he entered the workshop of Parapuquio and seized large quantities of wool, woolen cloth, tools, and other articles, which he divided among his followers. When he left, he completely destroyed the building.

In the factory at Pomacanche he obtained 38,000 yards of woolen and cotton cloth, some firearms, and two cannon. The owner estimated his loss at 230,000 pesos. In the presence of a number of neighboring caciques, José Gabriel said that he was commis-

95

sioned not only to hang corregidores, but also to destroy workshops. He then asked if the owner was a debtor to any person. Assured that he was, José Gabriel promptly paid the debt. He gave the priest 3,000 arrobas of wool, the ecclesiastic's brother a quantity of indigo, and distributed the rest of the goods to the Indians. Then he put his half brother, Juan Bautista Túpac Amaru, in charge of the workshop, although the latter said later that he took care of it only one night. Other houses and haciendas along the way were sacked. It was estimated that the total pillage amounted to 400,000 pesos. By this time Túpac Amaru had an army of six thousand men from the provinces of Tinta. Quispicanchis, Cotabambas, Calca, and Chumbivilcas, but only three hundred of them were armed with muskets; the rest had merely pikes and slings.[1]

The Inca returned to Tungasuca, where he spent much of his time sending proclamations to the neighboring provinces to raise a greater number of Indians. As the fire of revolution spread, they were distributed far and wide in all the provinces of Peru, Bolivia, northern Chile, and much of Argentina. José Gabriel himself prepared letters and edicts, which were sometimes written on pieces of fine linen and concealed in the clothing of the messengers carrying them to other places.

His orders were all very simple, like the one of November 16 to his cousin, Governor Bernardo Sacagua, which said:

> Having undertaken, by virtue of a superior order, the reform of the corregimientos, I share it with you in order that you may work in consequence of it. Consider the edict here included. Publish it in all the towns and cities and erect gallows for the rebels. Do this in the name of the King, our Lord. Assemble the inhabitants of the province, seize the corregidores and their adjutants, and place their possessions under a strong guard. This order is not against God or the King, but against the introduction of bad laws.

[1] El alzamiento de Túpac Amaru, Memorial de noticias oficiales, Lima, 1780 (copiada del original que se encuentra en el Archivo General de Indias), Colección papeles de estado, Peru, Leg. 3, in Lewin, *op. cit.*, 217; Relación de los pasages acaecidos en esta ciudad del Cuzco, Cuzco, December 3, 1780, pp. 72–74. MS copy in B. L. Valcárcel, *La rebelión de Túpac Amaru,* 47; Loayza, *Cuarenta años de cautiverio, op. cit.,* Serie I, Vol. I, 94, 97. Markham, *A History of Peru,* 198–99; Carrió, *op. cit.,* 78.

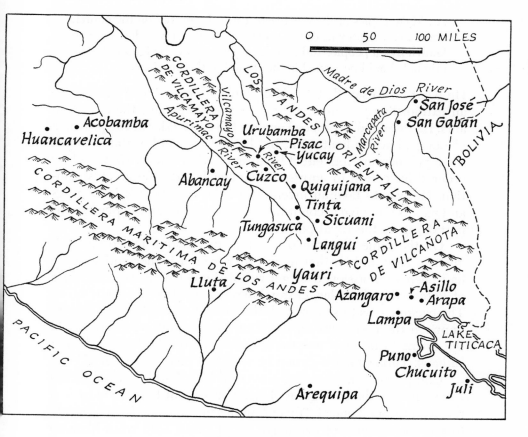

CENTRAL PERU

... Make copies of the edict that it may be posted on the church doors in all the towns of the provinces, so that my orders may be known by all people, and no one may be said to be ignorant. The original should be posted in the capital of the province.[2]

He went on to say that the King had ordered him to proceed in an extraordinary manner against corregidores and their lieutenants. He intended to proceed against the corregidor of the province of Lampa and his lieutenant, but he had not yet been able to put the royal measure into effect because of other duties. He therefore ordered his cousin to imprison the officials with the greatest caution. He was to take an inventory of the corregidor's belongings and papers and give account to Túpac Amaru of all the possessions pertaining to the royal patrimony.[3]

On the same date the Inca wrote to Cacique Diego Chuquiguanca. He told him that in an order from a higher authority he had been commissioned to get rid of the corregidores, the mitas of Potosí, the alcabalas, customhouses, and other injurious taxes. The cacique was to summon all the inhabitants of the province to imprison the corregidor in the King's name and erect gallows in the towns to be used in case of resistance by the Spaniards and Indians. Túpac Amaru signed himself his "beloved relative."[4]

Chuquiguanca, however, proved to be a faithful vassal to the King. He told the corregidor of Azángaro about the letters he had received through one of Túpac Amaru's messengers. He also wrote to the corregidores of Carabaya and Lampa, who were likewise ordered to be arrested, and asked them to take measures against the Inca.[5]

[2] Carta de José Gabriel Túpac Amaru á Bernardo Sucacagua, Tungasuca, November 15, 1780, in Odriozola, *Documentos*, I, 120; Relación de los pasages acaecidos en esta ciudad del Cuzco, December 3, 1780, p. 81. MS copy in B. L. Carrió, *op. cit.*, 80–81.

[3] Bando de José Gabriel Túpac Amaru, Tungasuca, November 15, 1789, in Odriozola, *Documentos*, I, 120–21; Angelis, *Documentos*, 12–13.

[4] Carta de José Gabriel Túpac Amaru al cacique Don Chuquiguanca, Tungasuca, November 15, 1780, in Odriozola, *Documentos*, I, 123; Angelis, *Documentos*, 15–16.

[5] Carta de Diego Chuquiguanca cacique de Azángaro al corregidor de esta provincia (unedited), in Odriozola, *Documentos*, I, 122; Angelis, *op. cit.*, 14.

Túpac Amaru also issued another proclamation on November 16 in which he summoned the Creoles and mestizos. He asked them to separate themselves from the Europeans, even if they were working for them.[6] He also sent edicts to the people of the provinces of Lampa, Carabaya, and Chinchas, assuring them that he would remove their grievances and end bad government. He told them that he had never been prejudiced against the Creoles, whom he considered brothers, and intended to destroy only Europeans; moreover, he would respect priests and members of religious orders in monasteries. He asked the people not to render obedience or give aid to judges who worked against him. He would reward the loyal, but the provinces of those who did not obey his edicts would be ruined. As a result of the edict, seven provinces soon sought his protection.[7]

At no time did Túpac Amaru say that he intended to destroy Spanish institutions. His object was to make use of them and render them more efficient rather than to get rid of them. He always showed remarkable loyalty to the church and to the crown, since, for the most part, those institutions interceded for the Indians.

No alliance was made with the Creoles, but the Inca tried to recruit as many as possible into his army because of their military knowledge. However, since the Indians hated all white men for whom special privileges had been reserved, he had to use his influence to protect Spanish Americans. Individual Creoles worked for him; for example, he had Creole secretaries, and Felipe Bermúdez of Cuzco helped him in his government. Francisco Molina, a native of Chile and a resident of Sicuani, was one of his most famous captains and urged him to besiege Cuzco. Later, when the royalists captured him, Visitador Areche banished Molina to Chile, dealing with him thus leniently because he was a relative of the Marchioness of Corpa, who resided in Lima. Mariano de la Banda, who had been Corregidor Arriaga's clerk, became a secretary of

---

[6] Valcárcel, *La rebelión de Tupac Amaru*, 48.

[7] Bando de Túpac Amaru para la provincia de Carabaya, Tungasuca, December 15, 1780, in Odriozola, *Documentos*, I, 121; Bando de Túpac Amaru, Tungasuca, November 25, 1780, *ibid.*, I, 124–25; Bando de Túpac Amaru para Chinchas, Lampa, December 23, 1780, *ibid.*, I, 42–43.

Túpac Amaru. Later Andrés Mendagure also employed Creoles who spoke very highly of him. Those Creoles tried to influence the vascillating members of their class and faithful royalists to accept the Inca cause.[8]

Túpac Amaru did not intend to exterminate the Spanish Europeans. His violent denunciations of them never included the Peninsular clergy or persons of good character. He even employed certain Europeans and gave them his complete confidence. One of them, Bernardo de la Madrid, was sent as an ambassador to Cuzco; at first he faithfully fulfilled his mission, but, when ridiculed and threatened, he committed treason against the Inca. Another European, the Galician Figueroa, used his position as armorer and artilleryman to carry on sabotage against the man who had saved his life. There were some Europeans, however, who were loyal to the Inca cause. Such was Pedro Palacios, a resident of La Plata, who was in contact with Miguel Bastidas, a cousin of José Gabriel's, when the city was attacked by the Indians.[9]

The Indians usually followed their caciques, and accepted the plans of Túpac Amaru without much urging. As soon as they heard what he intended to do, they put up lampoons criticizing the authorities and threatened to join him. Those writings were usually simple and crude in style. The Creoles helped write a number of them, displaying their discontent, but they did not definitely declare their support of the Inca. Some lampoons found in Jujuy may be considered typical. One of them said:

> Here we are waiting until these customhouses, monopolies, the new impositions of fifths and other robberies shall be removed, since it is not fitting that we shall endure such impudence. If they are not taken away, it will not be long until the heads of the thieves will be seen hanging. Long live the King of Spain, and may the thieves die! If it goes on thus, we shall defend Túpac Amaru, the Inca, as our Inca king and monarch.[10]

[8] Ballivián y Roxas, *op. cit.*, 248–49, 255–57; Loayza, *La verdad desnuda, op. cit.*, Serie I, Vol. III, 101.

[9] AGN, Buenos Aires, Criminales, Leg. 18, exp. 7 (cited by Lewin, *op. cit.*, 194–95).

[10] Pasquines puestos en Juyjuy, 1780, AGN, Peru. MS copy in B. L.

Another posted in the same town declared:

> This is to let Don José Solís, the treasury officials, governors, the receiver, and the director of monopolies know that now our supplication demands that the dues, which have been established violently in our province, must not be collected from us, or we shall place ourselves under the banner of Túpac Amaru, who has written us about the union of his crown . . . .[11]

Cuzco was greatly alarmed when news of the uprising reached there. Corregidor Inclán Váldez summoned a *Junta* of War immediately, which decided to prepare two militia regiments and establish a barracks in the former Jesuit college, which might also be used as a fort in which the royal funds could be kept. The chief sergeant, Joaquín de Valcárcel, was appointed commander of the barracks because of his military knowledge and his character. Two hundred guns, one hundred spears, and ammunition stored in the arsenal were taken to the barracks. Patrols and guards were placed on the roads to prevent the rebels from communicating with the people in the city, but the guards were ordered not to advance beyond Guarapata until more people assembled. At the same time the viceroy of Lima and the visitador-general were informed of the revolt and asked for aid.

Viceroy Jáuregui of Peru summoned his council at once and invited the visitador to be present. The executive wanted to go to Cuzco in person with the troops, but it was thought best for him to remain in Lima; therefore, Visitador Areche decided to direct the military operations and subdue the country. He notified the corregidores in all the provinces to dispatch to the capital as many soldiers as possible.

Meanwhile, the junta in Cuzco organized a company of noble Indians and caciques from its eight parishes to prevent them from joining Túpac Amaru. They were put under the command of the faithful cacique, Diego Chuquiguanca, a descendant of high Inca nobles from Azángaro, and Anselmo Bautista, for it was known that most of the Indian inhabitants favored the Inca and carried

[11] Otro pasquín puesto en el mismo pueblo de la puerta de Solís, 1780, AGN, Peru. MS copy in B. L.

on communication with him. The junta also ordered Cabrera, corregidor of Quispicanchis, to gather his militia and wait with a company in Oropesa for Tiburcio Landa, corregidor of Paucartambo. The caciques in Cuzco together with Pedro Sahuarauta of Oropesa and Ambrosio Chillitupa collected eight hundred Indians, mestizos, and a number of distinguished persons to fight in the expedition. At the same time untrained boys in Cuzco were enlisted.

Landa joined Cabrera, but was ordered to wait in Huayrapata for reinforcements. The urging of Cabrera, who was anxious to recover what he had lost, and the impatience of the soldiers, however, caused Landa to advance with the army. The royalists entered the province of Tinta and marched to the small town of Sangarara, where they arrived at sunset on November 17, 1780. The commander ordered his men to remain outside the town and fortify themselves on a hill, which he deemed a good place from which to attack the enemy. He did not know that Túpac Amaru was only twenty leagues distant and that his spies were well informed.

The Spaniards had a body of heterogeneous troops under the command of Generals Escajadilla and Landa. They consisted of 604 Spaniards and about 700 Indians under the cacique of Oropesa. They went to the main plaza to spend the night. When the watches were placed and the scouts returned saying that everything was peaceful, the soldiers undressed, resolving to fight the following day. But at midnight a multitude of Indians under Túpac Amaru surrounded the town. Their attack at four o'clock in the morning caught the Spaniards sleeping. The great confusion that followed did not allow them time even to put on their clothes.

After fighting bravely but futilely, Landa retreated to the church with his force. There the priest, his assistant, thirty Spanish women, and almost all the Indian women had taken refuge. When Túpac Amaru called for them to surrender, Landa refused. The Inca then wrote a letter to the priest, telling him to leave the building with his companions when he had consumed or disposed of the sacrament. As he did not receive a reply, Túpac Amaru ordered all the Creoles and women to come out. Many wanted to do so, but were hindered by a shower of stones. The Spaniards killed all the Indians who tried to enter the church, and the priest sent the Inca a message asking him to check the disorder. Shortly thereafter the powder in the church exploded, blew off part of the roof, and caused a part of the wall to collapse. The royalists discharged a cannon through the opening in the direction of the Inca and killed seven Indians near him.

The natives then set fire to the four corners of the church. The fire burned so fiercely that in less than an hour the edifice was reduced to ashes. Túpac Amaru later declared that he did not order the church destroyed. A number of people perished in the flames and others were killed by clubs and iron spikes when they tried to escape. Escajadilla defended himself heroically with a pistol until he died from violent blows, and a stroke from a lance killed Landa. A total of 576 other persons perished and only 28 wounded men survived, whom Túpac Amaru ordered treated and set free. All the Europeans died. After the battle, which lasted until noon, the Inca gave the priest, Domingo Sánchez, two hundred pesos to bury the dead and assured him that the sanctuary would be restored. The Inca's casualties were not so great. Some writers said that he lost only 25 men, while others believed that many Indians were killed. There was no way to count the dead Indians, whose bodies were thrown into a lake near by.

On the following day Túpac Amaru started for Tungasuca. Taking with him some cannon and the spoils of battle, he arrived at Livitaca Campino that same day, where he began to raise companies of Spaniards and mestizos. He had sent edicts to Santo Tomás, Chamaca, and Velille that the inhabitants should join him or suffer the same fate as Arriaga, and the people hastened to submit to him. The priest in whose house the Inca lodged and the tax collector escaped to Cailloma. The Indians then sacked the house, obtaining 18,000 pesos. This money and all the other articles taken were distributed among the mestizos. Túpac Amaru, it was said, kept nothing for himself.

The Inca issued additional proclamations on November 20,

and even sent one to Cuzco to be posted in a public place.[12] Next day he wrote to Bishop Moscoso and asked him to appoint intelligent priests for the doctrinas, so that the bad treatment of the Indians by priests' assistants might cease. The chief purpose of his letter, however, was to explain why he had been obliged to execute Arriaga and combat the forces sent against him. He argued that seeking relief from oppression was not opposing God and asked the prelate not to consider him evil. He reported that he had the greater part of the people of the kingdom at his command and would soon appear in Cuzco to level it to the ground if the city did not surrender to him. He also asked the Bishop to let the people know that he was not prejudiced against them and did not want to shed their blood, that his only desire was to remove the abuses against them.[13]

The prelate, who had kept quiet until after Arriaga was executed, did not do so now. He excommunicated the Inca for his attack at Sangarara, for profaning its church, for being a traitor to the King and a revolutionist, and for usurping the royal authority.[14] He sent word of the revolt to all the priests of the provinces of Tinta and Quispicanchis and asked them to try to keep the people faithful. He also reported to the Viceroy that the Inca's rebellion was the boldest since the Conquest. He advised that the repartimientos, the alcabala, the tribute, customhouses, and workshops be abolished. He said that Túpac Amaru carried on extensive correspondence with Cuzco and that it was difficult to say how many of the inhabitants belonged to his faction. The chief

[12] Relación de los hechos mas notables acaecidos en la sublevación general . . . , 19; Copia de una carta escrita por un sugeto residente en Lima con referencia á las noticias que han comunicado del Cuzco, Lima, December 23, 1780, pp. 92–94. MS copy in B. L. Funes, *op. cit.*, 237; Valcárcel, *Le rebelión de Túpac Amaru*, 50, 57ff. Markham, *A History of Peru*, 199; Relación de los pasages acaecidos en esta ciudad del Cuzco, Cuzco, December 3, 1780, pp. 74–78, 81. One account said that 595 persons perished at Sangarara and another 600, but most accounts give 576 as the number. Markham, *Travels in Peru and India*, 143; Mendiburu, *Diccionario*, VIII, 127–29; I, 324.

[13] Carta de José Gabriel Túpac Amaru al Sor. D. Juan Manuel Moscoso y Peralta, Tungasuca, November 21, 1780. MS copy in B. L.

[14] Angelis, *Documentos*, 157–71; Valcárcel, *La rebelión de Túpac Amaru*, 100–101.

objective of the rebellion, he believed, was to destroy the bridge over the Apurímac River in order to prevent supplies from and communication with Lima. Moscoso also had denunciations of the Inca posted on all the church doors in Cuzco and on some in the provinces, and exhorted the people to obey the King. He became very active now that he feared his earlier attitude toward the revolt had been made known to the higher authorities.[15]

News of Túpac Amaru's victory at Sangarara spurred many of the Indians to join him. Some hurriedly buried all their possessions that they could not carry, collected their families, and traveled over the roads of Amancai and Huamanga to join the Inca. Most of them had the misfortune to meet Lieutenant Colonel Manuel de Villalta, corregidor of the province of Abancay, who was approaching Cuzco with 450 auxiliary soldiers. The Spaniards seized the Indians' arms and forced them to go into Cuzco, allowing only the women and children to return to their homes. However, one of their most important leaders, José de Andia, escaped.[16]

At the same time the defeat of the Spaniards at Sangarara caused great consternation and confusion in Cuzco. Many people ran through the streets weeping, asking God's mercy, and seeking places to hide. Their fright increased when they heard that the Inca intended to invade the city with his army. The fear was so great that when the church cabildo met, Bishop Moscoso strongly advocated a plan to capitulate to Túpac Amaru. His proposal to send two priests to talk to the Inca made a number of persons suspicious. The Archdean resisted the plan vigorously until the Junta of War met and chose Villalta, who had been colonel in the royal navy, as commander of the defense forces of the city. The accountant of the treasury said that Moscoso influenced the Viceroy to discredit this junta because many members of it were suspicious of him. It looked as if the Inca had kept the prelate well informed or else the latter was a remarkably acute observer to know so much about the Inca's movements.

---

[15] Loayza, *Estado del Peru, op. cit.*, Serie I, Vol. V, 134–36, 146–47, 171, 198.
[16] Relación de los pasages acaecidos en esta ciudad del Cuzco, Cuzco, December 3, 1780, p. 79. MS copy in B. L.

The Junta of War took measures for defense and sent orders to neighboring corregidores to hasten to Cuzco with all their forces. Gradually the corregidores of Andahuayles, Paucartambo, Calca, and Urubamba arrived with small detachments, all except those from Paucartambo unarmed. The Junta organized an army of volunteers from among these men and made Faustino Álvarez de Fonda, the Count of Villa-Hermosa, commander. The Cabildo made powder, collected arms, and repaired the old pieces of artillery, while palisades and trenches were constructed in the main plaza and streets.[17]

These defense measures required money, and the treasury was empty; therefore funds had to be raised quickly. Certain individuals who could have contributed liberally made many excuses not to do so. Bishop Moscoso gave 12,000 pesos, the priest of San Gerónimo 40,000, and other ecclesiastics 14,000. Some 30,000 pesos were raised from other sources. Finally ten or twelve persons donated 100,000 pesos apiece.[18]

Even the clergy helped to prepare to defend the city. The Bishop made his palace into a barracks, constructed a strong parapet on the cathedral stairs, and formed a cavalry regiment under command of Manuel de Mendieta, dean of the cathedral. A secular official took charge of the military instruction of the clergy, while the Bishop walked through the public plaza carrying his banner and the King's portrait to solicit aid in providing barracks. The clergy kept guard at night in the cathedral and church towers, only four of them were exempt from this service. They did not neglect their religious devotions, however, as the city, with its eight parishes, was kept at continual prayer for more than three months.

The Bishop threatened all persons who rebelled with excommunication. He thought that the religious services, his pastorals

[17] Odriozola, *Documentos*, I, 6; Loayza, *Estado del Peru, op. cit.*, Serie I, Vol. V, 167–70; Vol. III, 203; Mendiburu, *Diccionario*, VIII, 129–30.

[18] Carta de Juan Manuel Moscoso, obispo del Cuzco, al obispo de La Paz, Dr. Gregorio Francisco del Campo, Huayallabamba, July 20, 1782, in Odriozola, *Documentos*, I, 257; Relación de los pasages acaecidos en esta ciudad del Cuzco, Cuzco, December 3, 1780, p. 80. MS copy in B. L.

directed to the doctrinas of the bishopric, and the excommunication of the Inca and his partisans after the battle of Sangarara kept many caciques faithful to the King.

This was true of Mateo Pumacagua, a descendant of the Incas and cacique of Chincheros. In the battles that ensued, with good and bad strategy, he climbed the highest hills, deceived the revolutionists with white banners, and caused great losses. Manuel Chuquinya, cacique of Copocabana, worked for the royalists and later received a reward and a pension of five hundred pesos a year for his services. Other caciques who remained faithful were Nicolás Rosas of Anata; Sucacahua of Umachiri; Huaranca of Santa Rosa; Manco, Turpos, and Diego Chuquiguanca of Azángaro; Carlos Visa of Achalla; Chuquicallota of Samán; Siñan Inca of Coporaque; Huambo Túpa of Yauri; Callu of Sicuani; Antonio of Checacupi; Cotacallapa and Huaquisto of Carabaya; Game and Carpio of Paruro; Espinosa of Cotoca; Huamanchaco of Coporque; and Pacheco Callitupa and Pedro Sahuaraura of Quispicanchis. Sahuaraura was the man who revealed Farfán's treason in the early conspiracy at Cuzco and died bravely at Sangarara; his relatives, Juan and José Rafael Sahuaraura, were also on the royalist side. On the other hand, some caciques were disloyal to the King. For example, Jacinto Inquillitupa, cacique in the parish of Hospital in Cuzco pretended to collaborate with the royalists, while he secretly assisted the rebels. Eugenio Sinanyuca, a protégé of Corregidor Arriaga, resisted the insurgents at first, but, when captured by Túpac Amaru, apparently accepted the Inca's cause and was trusted. Later, when a good opportunity arose, he escaped. Bishop Moscoso said that, with the exception of Tomasa Titu Condemayta, the woman who served as cacique of Acos, no cacique of honor followed Túpac Amaru's banner. He evidently considered all the caciques who aided the Inca dishonorable.

The prelate obliged priests to remain in their benefices and keep complete diaries of what happened to send to the Junta of War and to the Viceroy. That was the only way current news could be obtained. A number of priests remaining in the danger zones were made prisoners, lost their possessions, and some their lives. Because in places where there were no priests the revolution spread much more rapidly than where they were stationed, a La Plata citizen thought the Bishop should be called "restorer of the country."[19] Obviously he did not know about the Bishop's duplicity in regard to the revolt.

Meanwhile, people from neighboring provinces were trying to send help to Cuzco. Some thirteen thousand men, led by their corregidor, Ruiz de Castilla, went out from the province of Chilques to check Túpac Amaru's expedition to the south, but the force could not enter Cuzco because of the disaster at Sangarara. The soldiers had to return to their province to defend it from a possible similar invasion. A number of chosen men, armed with guns, swords, and daggers, were sent out from Paucartambo. The corregidor of Calca dispatched about five hundred militiamen, but they lacked arms; and Corregidor Villalta brought two hundred properly uniformed men armed with daggers and shotguns. Villalta was a great help since the members of the Junta of War lacked military experience.[20] Despite all efforts, however, by the end of November, 1780, the defenders of Cuzco numbered only three thousand.

The cabildo now took a drastic step by which it hoped to win recruits. It issued a proclamation in the King's name abolishing the repartimientos and the alcabala. It also declared that in the future Indians would not have to labor in workshops if they remained faithful. Debts owed from previous monopolies would be canceled and the natives would not be required to pay tithes or obventions to priests. This act of the cabildo did not have the desired effect, however, for most of the Indians did not hear about it until after the revolt was over.

Toward the end of November the royalists gained a little advantage over the insurgents in Guarán. In the skirmish Pumacagua so distinguished himself that he was rewarded with the title of colonel and a gold medal.

[19] Carta de Juan Manuel Moscoso, obispo del Cuzco, al obispo de La Paz, Dr. Gregorio Francisco del Campo, Huayallabamba, July 20, 1782, in Odriozola, *Documentos*, I, 254–58; Lorente, *Historia del Peru bajo los Borbones*, 189; Angelis, *Documentos*, 10; Valcárcel, *La rebelión de Túpac Amaru*, 50–53.

[20] Valcárcel, *La rebelión de Túpac Amaru*, 75–78.

While the royalist effort was being made, Túpac Amaru, on November 26, reached the town of Livitaca, where he appointed caciques and town officials, as the corregidor had fled. He had about two thousand Indians and eighty to one hundred mestizos with him. On the twenty-seventh, he went directly to the town of Coporaque. The cacique, Eugenio Sinanyuca, remained loyal to the King. He fortified himself with his people, a number from Yauri, and others from Pichiqua in a rocky ravine, which went up from Coporaque toward Cailloma. He hunted for Túpac Amaru to kill him, since he did not want to be an accomplice in his rebellion. Later the royalists honored him by giving him the title of chief justice. Some of the Spaniards and mestizos, however, were disloyal to the King. In the province of Chumbivilcas these people tried to seize the corregidor and hand him over to Túpac Amaru.

The Inca continued to recruit men for his undertaking. On November 27, he published an edict in which he explained the reason for his uprising and urged the Indians to join him.[21] Two days later he published another edict and called upon the inhabitants of the province of Chumbivilcas to enlist three hundred armed Spaniards and one thousand carefully chosen Indians. They were to march to the provinces of Carabaya, Lampa, and Azángaro, where some chapetones still oppressed the people.[22]

As the Spaniards would not negotiate with the Inca leader, at the beginning of December he marched toward the south. He crossed the Vilcañota mountain range by the pass of Santa Rosa and advanced into the Callao, or basin of Lake Titicaca, toward Pucará and Lampa. At every village he addressed the people from the church steps, saying that he came to abolish abuses and punish corregidores, that he was "the liberator of the kingdom, the restorer of their privileges, and the common father of those persons who

[21] Relación de los pasages acaecidos en esta ciudad del Cuzco, Cuzco, December 3, 1780, pp. 82–88. MS copy in B. L. Copia de una carta escrita por un sugeto redidente en Lima con referencia á las noticias que han comunicado del Cuzco, Lima, December 23, 1780, pp. 94–96. MS copy in B. L. Mendiburu, *Diccionario*, VIII, 130–31.

[22] Bando de José Gabriel Túpac Amaru, Coporaque, November 29, 1780. MS copy in B. L.

groaned under the yoke of the repartimientos." The Indians rejoiced when they heard those words and acclaimed him their "Inca redeemer."[23] He then invaded the province of Cailloma, intending to take the funds in the treasury, but discovered that the treasury officials had sent them to Arequipa. Nevertheless, he won the province over to his enterprise.

At the same time, near Ayaviri the royalists captured Simón Noguera, a nephew of Túpac Amaru. When Vicente Hore, the corregidor of Lampa, took his confession, the prisoner said that he had been sent by his uncle from Sangarara on the day of the battle with letters and edicts for various provinces. He also had taken part in destroying the workshops of Pomacanche and Paropujio. Although some people thought the evidence against Noguera was insufficient, he was put to death on December 4.

Consternation soon seized the royalists. News arrived that Túpac Amaru and his son, Hipólito, were coming from the direction of Ayaviri to attack Lampa with a large troop of Indians and mestizos and that his brother was advancing from the opposite direction. There were only twelve hundred men, with insufficient arms, in Ayaviri in the two regiments of Azángaro and Lampa. Nevertheless, the commander fortified the town for defense. On the third day a flying company from Tupacamarco was seen approaching; therefore Lieutenant Colonel Francisco Vizenteli went to Lampa to seek aid. The other officers and corregidores, who were in Lampa, held a council of war to decide whether aid should be given. As Lampa would next be exposed to the enemy, it was agreed that troops must be sent to Ayaviri and that the three regiments should withdraw to a single post, unite, and face the Indians. The royalists believed that Túpac Amaru had only two thousand men and could easily be defeated. In fact, Vizenteli declared that the Inca's army was only an Indian mob.

In the midst of preparations, on December 6, the militia of Lampa suddenly fled from the town. Some residents also left their homes and families to find a safe place for themselves, while others rallied to Túpac Amaru's banners. The officials met again in a coun-

[23] Markham, *Travels in Peru and India,* 144.

cil of war and decided to return to their own provinces during the night with their militia. The decision to abandon the defense of Ayaviri was, no doubt, influenced by the letter which Túpac Amaru had a friend write to the corregidor of Lampa stating that he intended to march with fourteen thousand men to kill the corregidor in revenge for his nephew's death.

The withdrawal from Ayaviri was a disorderly flight. Official orders were disregarded or obeyed desultorily. It seemed that most of the people and even the corregidores wanted only to hide themselves. Some officials fled as far as Arequipa, while only the young corregidor of Puno, Joaquín Orellana, was heroic enough to prepare to resist the enemy.

Túpac Amaru thus entered Ayaviri without opposition a few hours after the corregidor had ordered the soldiers to withdraw. Since many soldiers could not find mounts quickly enough, they were made prisoners and forced to travel for several days under the banner of the insurgent chief. At Pucará the Inca put to death several customs collectors and imprisoned a number of people. He then set out for Lampa, thirty leagues south of Cuzco, and entered it on the ninth. There he burned the prison and the corregidor's home and distributed among his men all the knives and flannel in the house and the irons with which prisoners were chained. The Indians sacked other houses at leisure, including that of the priest. Afterwards they went to the farms of Chingora and Guaita, which belonged to the priest, sacked them and many others, and drove off the cattle. Túpac Amaru then assumed the functions of the cacique and chief justice, Blas Pacoricona, and issued severe orders to pursue the fleeing corregidores, chapetones, and tax collectors.[24]

Here the Inca also received word from his wife about the military preparations in Cuzco; therefore he countermarched by way of Asillo and Orurillo to the Vilcamayo Valley. All along the way village priests came out to honor him with raised crosses, the

---

[24] Relación de los hechos mas notables acaecidos en la sublevación general . . . , 20–24, 201; Lorente, *Historia del Peru bajo los Borbones,* 183; Angelis, *Documentos,* 6; Valcárcel, *La rebelión de Túpac Amaru,* 65–66.

canopy, and the *Te Deum*. Some writers claim that Túpac Amaru obliged them to act thus, but in a letter written to a priest on November 12, he said that this ceremony was not necessary for him. He entered Azángaro on December 13 and completely destroyed the home of Cacique Chuquiguanca, who had refused to join him. He finally arrived at his home in Tungasuca to consolidate plans for the revolt, which had now become general,[25] and to make weapons in his foundry in Tinta.[26] The Indians of Lares constructed wooden guns and lined them with hides, but they were clumsy to use, requiring two men to fire them.[27]

By this time Túpac Amaru had invaded the provinces of Azángaro, Carabaya, Tinta, Calca, and Quispicanchis and had won over their inhabitants. The provinces of Chucuito, Pacajes, Omasuyos, Larecaja, Yungas, and part of Misque, Cochabamba, and Atacama had also decided to give their allegiance to him. In Cochabamba daily lampoons were put up opposing the Europeans and their government.[28] He could also count on many provinces to the south and east already stirred up by the Catari brothers. The revolutionary movement had also started in the large bishopric of Lima, but was quickly put down there because troops were readily available in the capital. Nevertheless, restlessness extended far—even to the provinces of Piura, bordering the Audiencia of Quito, and finally into the Quito region.[29] On December 25, 1780, in the town of Yauli, in the corregimiento of Huarochirí, a summons was posted for the inhabitants to go to Yauros, where, "according to a notification from the emperor, Túpac Amaru, arms would be provided."[30] Thus Túpac Amaru did not impulsively propose to continue a revolution for which he was unprepared.

Not many priests were found in Túpac Amaru's ranks. Because the Jesuits had participated in uprisings before their expulsion in 1767, some people believed that they actively supported the Inca.

[25] Angelis, *Documentos,* 16; Relación de los hechos mas notables acaecidos en la sublevación general . . . , 25.

[26] Valcárcel, *La rebelión de Túpac Amaru,* 81.

[27] *Ibid.,* 109.

[28] Odriozola, *Documentos,* I, 6–7.

[29] Lewin, *Túpac Amaru el rebelde,* 349, 351.

[30] Ricardo Palma, *Tradiciones peruanas,* IV, 86–87.

There may have been a few members of that order who worked for him individually from their place of exile, but never collectively. That the pretended Jesuit, Francisco José Marcano y Arismendi, played a role in the rebellion has been disproved. Arismendi was on his way to Spain when the boat on which he was a passenger fell into the power of the English, who aided him to land in America, but he could not enter Peru. Since he had mentioned uprisings in the month of October, 1780, some persons thought he had prophesied the insurrection in Tinta. Anselmo de Alivisto y Samalloa, another man said to be a Jesuit, who was the son of San Ignacio, the Paucartambino, and a friend of Túpac Catari, in 1783 confessed that he belonged to no religious order.[31] Father Juan Vizcardo y Guzmán did write a letter in which he sympathized with the Inca's uprising and mentioned the need of emancipation, but there is no evidence that the Jesuits went any further in providing aid.

Certain secular priests, like Antonio Valdés in the parish of Tinta, favored the cause. Since he was a good friend of José Gabriel Túpac Amaru, he must have had some influence on the movement.[32] Colonel Reseguín said that the priest José Vásquez de Velasco had confessed to writing some of the edicts in the name of the Inca leader.[33] José Maruri, priest of Asillo, also proved to be a partisan of the revolutionists. A copious correspondence between him and Túpac Amaru was found in his home, and he aided the Inca with men and money. Later he was arrested and brought to Cuzco, but Visitador Areche only kept him in seclusion.[34] Ildefonso Bejarano, a priest of Tungasuca who lived in the Inca's home, did not report the imprisonment of Arriaga. After the revolution, this priest and López de Sosa were banished to Spain and secluded in the Convent of St. Francis in Cádiz.[35]

In the provinces of Lampa and Azángaro the clergy sympa-

[31] Valcárcel, *La rebelión de Túpac Amaru*, 40–41.

[32] Lewin, *op. cit.*, 78, 84, 90–92.

[33] Informe de Reseguín á virrey Vertíz, April 15, 1781 (cited by Lewin, *op. cit.*, 98); Angelis, *Documentos*, V, 267–68.

[34] Loayza, *La verdad desnuda*, *op. cit.*, Serie I, Vol. III, 99.

[35] Loayza, *op. cit.*, Serie I, Vol. IX, 113n.; Serie I, Vol. III, 95–97.

thized with the rebels. From the beginning of the insurrection the priest, Isidro Escobar, marched with them and wrote letters indicating that he was devoted to Túpac Amaru. Bishop Moscoso excommunicated Friar Gregorio de Santa Cruz, who served as a chaplain, and Juan Antonio de Figueroa, chief artilleryman of the Inca. In the rebel camp Nicolás Villca, an Indian from a hacienda of Paucartambo and a member of the Ugarte family, was said to be bishop. He prayed for the Inca's success, gave blessings, and preached.[36]

The priest Bernardo de la Madrid called Túpac Amaru governor and said that he was a man of great humanity who had treated him as a son. Tomás Otazu, a parish priest in Accha Huanansayo, who spoke in favor of the Inca, was excommunicated for doing so and ordered brought to Cuzco. The priest of Pampamarca knew of the intrigues against Arriaga and did nothing. The Dominican Isidro Rodríguez was a chaplain of the rebels and said mass on a portable altar in the field.[37] José de Velasco, assistant priest of Chocalla, was active in proclaiming Túpac Amaru, scattering edicts, and persuading the people to follow the Inca. When José Gabriel was excommunicated, however, he doubtless lost the support of the greater part of the clergy, the Creoles, and many mestizos.

The majority of the clergy adhered to the Spanish cause and helped to put down the revolt. The clergy who favored the Europeans fled from their parishes when the revolt began, whereas the Creoles remained in them to work for Bishop Moscoso. Four military companies, commanded by Dean Mendieta, were formed, with money provided by the clergy. The priest of Quispicanchis, Padre Aldazabal, persuaded many Indians to desert the rebellion and aided Del Valle with provisions. Loayza, priest of Cacay, collaborated actively in the struggle by collecting armed men, giving information about the movement of Túpac Amaru's troops, and defending his town and others in the ravine. In Urcos, Pedro San-

[36] Valcárcel, *La rebelión de Túpac Amaru*, 103–105.
[37] Carta de Juan Manuel obispo del Cuzco al Señor Don Agustín de Jáuregui, Cuzco, January 5, 1780, in Loayza, *Estado del Peru, op. cit.*, Serie I, Vol. V, 198–200.

Manuel de Guiror, viceroy of Peru

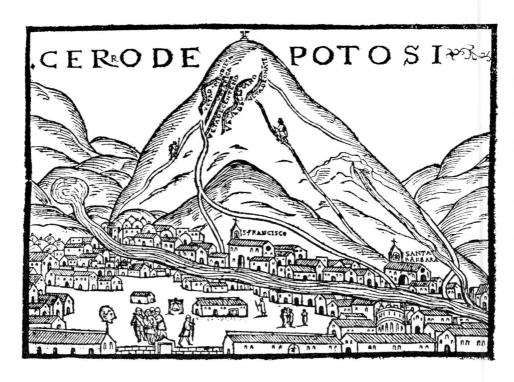

Cerro de Potosí
Pedro de Cieza de León's drawing, which appeared in the
1553 edition of his *La Crónica del Peru*.

tistebán urged the natives to be faithful to the King, assumed the town government when the corregidor fled, captured bridges, and cut off the enemy's transit. In the provinces of Calca, Urubamba, and Paucartambo priests checked the excesses of Diego Túpac Amaru's partisans, sent news to Cuzco, and collaborated in the successful resistance of Paucartambo. The priests of Aymaraes forced two of the Inca's captains to retreat toward Chumbivilcas. The priest Caviedas collected an armed force of more than six thousand men and led them himself.[38]

In the province of Cotabambas the priests were also very active. They fortified their parishes, put themselves at the head of an army of about three thousand men, and drove out Parvina, one of the Inca's captains. Later Visitador Areche thanked them in the King's name and praised them for their work. When the corregidor, José María Acuña, was restored to the province, he also spoke of the efficiency of the priests.[39] Pablo Arcos, priest of the doctrina of Paria, gathered at his own expense four hundred Indians and joined the troops of Lieutenant Colonel Reseguín.[40] The priest Gaviño, at the head of his Indians, conquered the town of Colque and pacified other towns stirred up by the agents of Tomás Catari. He captured Catari's emissaries and conducted them to Oruro to hand them over to the authorities. San Alberto, the bishop of Córdova and Tucumán, energetically condemned the uprising of Túpac Amaru.[41] Numerous other examples of the clergy's working with the royalists might be cited, but these should suffice to demonstrate their loyalty and efforts.

The question has been raised whether the Inca received help from the English. There is no indication that he did, though the authorities suspected it. When the authors of the lampoons spoke of it, all the ports on the Pacific and Atlantic coasts were closed, and a royal order was issued for a careful investigation to learn how and where the Indians obtained their firearms. Viceroy Vertíz

[38] Valcárcel, *La rebelión de Túpac Amaru,* 98–103.
[39] José Rozendo Gutiérrez, *Documentos para la historia antigua de Bolivia,* 137.
[40] Carta del cura Pablo Arcos á Vertíz, AGN, Buenos Aires, VI–XIII–10–6 (cited by Lewin, *op. cit.,* 100).
[41] Lewin, *op. cit.,* 101, 107.

said that they took some of them from the conquered Spaniards and made others. The only edited document which mentions Englishmen in Túpac Amaru's army was a diary kept in Arequipa. Under the date of July 4, 1781, it is recorded that some of the fugitives from Azángaro reported that when the Inca entered their province, he had at his side four masked men who spoke to no one.[42] Another account, signed by Túpac Catari, stated that when the Inca rode into Azángaro on a white horse, he had with him two blond men of good aspect who appeared to be English;[43] and Bernardino de Uria Illanes spoke of an Englishman as a scout of the flag. Mention has already been made of a prophecy, inscribed on the principal temple in Cuzco, which told about the restoration of the Incas with the aid of the English. While no one knew who had made the prophecy, it doubtless influenced the populace.[44] A document dated Cuzco, December 1, 1780, states that this prophecy is also found in the prologue of the *Comentarios reales de las Incas* of Garcilasco de la Vega;[45] but although there are certain vague expressions in the work of the mestizo historian which might be subject to various interpretations, there is no statement concerning English assistance in re-establishing the Inca empire. The fact that the English are mentioned in connection with the Inca empire, however, indicates that the people had at least heard about the war between Spain and Great Britain.

The only definite notice taken of an English invasion in South America is found in two royal orders of February 17 and March 20, 1781. In the former the King stated that he had learned of an English expedition of 2,000 soldiers and 15,000 arms to be sent to Buenos Aires to stir up the Indians. It was to be accompanied by the so-called former Jesuit, Arismendi. When the friar was arrested in Ostend, it was discovered that he had told the British government that all the country from the Río de la Plata to Arequipa was very much dissatisfied with the Spanish king and that the inhabi-

[42] *Ibid.*, 111, 119.
[43] Odriozola, *Documentos*, I, 119; Mendiburu, *Diccionario*, VIII, 121.
[44] AGN, Buenos Aires, Criminales, Leg. 18, exp. 7, f. 137 (cited by Lewin, *op. cit.*, 119–21); Valcárcel, *La rebelión de Túpac Amaru*, 41–42.
[45] AGN, Buenos Aires, V–32–6–25.

tants only awaited arms to rebel. He reported that an expedition would be made to Buenos Aires, that the sacking would be easy, and that the English expected to hold the city and carry on communication with the provinces of the Río de la Plata. The second decree said that the English squadron consisted of four to six ships of the line, two frigates, and 2,500 men commanded by Admiral Johnstone. The Viceroy was therefore asked to keep all forces possible in Montevideo.[46] In reply to José de Gálvez, minister of the Indies, Viceroy Vertíz suggested that the expedition would likely go to the coast of the South Sea, perhaps to Arequipa, since the town was near the province of Tinta, in rebellion under Túpac Amaru.[47] In view of the English invasion of Buenos Aires in 1806, these reports seem to have had some basis.

At first the Peruvian authorities did not seem to realize the seriousness of Túpac Amaru's insurrection. This may have been because of Bishop Moscoso's attitude. He said that the supposed conspiracy was nothing but the product of rash imagination.[48] Spanish officials no doubt thought the revolt just a repetition of the minor uprisings to which they had grown accustomed. Finally they had to pay attention to it when, on December 5, 1780, Viceroy Jáuregui of Peru received word of the Sangarara disaster. On the twelfth he issued a proclamation against the Inca, which was published on the nineteenth. He declared Túpac Amaru unworthy of the title of cacique, an apostate of the Catholic faith, and a rebel who clothed himself with an authority he did not have in order to attract the people to his cause. The Viceroy urged the people to abandon the uprising and return to their homes in order to avoid severe reprisals and offered pardon to all who would renounce their alliance to the Inca. The Viceroy also declared that he had abolished repartimientos in all the provinces of the kingdom, that the corregidores were to have fixed salaries, and that if they tried

[46] *Boletín del instituto de investigaciones históricas* (Buenos Aires), Año VIII, No. 43 (October, 1929), 459–60 (cited by Lewin, *op. cit.,* 329–30); Del Solar, *op. cit.,* 107; Lorente, *Historia del Peru bajo los Borbones,* 207.

[47] Correspondencia Vertíz–Gálvez, 1781, num. 469, AGN, Buenos Aires, in Lewin, *op. cit.,* 330.

[48] Loayza, *Estado del Peru, op. cit.,* Serie I, Vol. V, 132–33.

to distribute articles among the people, they would be severely punished.

The Viceroy had been in such a hurry to publish the proclamation abolishing the repartimientos that he had not waited for a royal decree to do so.[49] On December 22, the Audiencia of Lima notified King Charles III about the measure which had been taken without his consent, saying:

> The increase of the forces which the rebel has acquired has weakened those of Cuzco, in whose people he has infused cowardice. It is feared that the pernicious contagion will spread . . . even to the more distant provinces, where it is essential to apply extraordinary remedies. . . . It will be necessary to abolish the repartimientos of the corregidores, without waiting for the royal decision, on account of the urgent necessity in which we are . . . . And it will be necessary to assign salaries to the corregidores.

The administrative basis was thus to be changed in Peru. This shows that the revolt was feared not only by the authorities of the disturbed provinces, but also by those in Lima, who found it necessary to take quick and drastic measures.[50]

The Viceroy of Buenos Aires also recognized the seriousness of the revolt and took active measures against Túpac Amaru. On January 15, 1781, the fiscal of the Buenos Aires viceroyalty, Pacheco by name, and Viceroy Vertíz both declared him a traitor to the King and the state. They ordered war to be waged against him and his followers until they were conquered. The fiscal said:

> Already he silences the commands of the King and proceeds as the most distinguished Indian of the royal blood of the Incas to free his compatriots from the grievances, the injustice, and the servitude in which the European corregidores kept them, without

---

[49] Exorto y requirimento por Agustín Jáuregui, Ciudad de los Reyes, December 12, 1780; Copia de una carta escrita por un sugeto residente en Lima con referencia á las noticias que se han comunicado del Cuzco, Lima, December 23, 1780, p. 96; Copia de carta escrita á un Sor. ministro de Madrid por un vecino del Cuzco, Cuzco, September 1, 1782, signed "B. L. M." p. 153. Copies of all the above MSS are in B. L. Joaquín García Naranjo, *Sublevación de Túpac Amaru en el Perú*, 34–36.

[50] Informe de la real audiencia de Lima á S. M., December 22, 1780, in García Naranjo, *op. cit.*, 21–22.

attending to their complaints in the higher tribunals. . . . He only repeats the name of King Charles III to calm the minds of the natives of those provinces. . . . He intends to head the extinguished throne of the Incas.

The fiscal urged the people to imitate the loyalty of Cacique Chuquiguanca of Azángaro and his sons, who offered to sacrifice their lives for the King. He appealed to the people of Carabaya, Lampa, Chucuito, Puno, Larecaja, and other places near the viceroyalty of Buenos Aires, and also those of Cuzco, Arequipa, and other parts of the Peruvian viceroyalty, not to heed Túpac Amaru's offers. He promised that if the Indians surrendered their chief, the war against them would be suspended.[51]

The Viceroy of Buenos Aires even promised a reward for the capture of the Inca leader. He issued a proclamation in which he said that he would set aside 20,000 pesos for this purpose. He would also pardon the insurgents who repented of their errors.[52]

Even in the face of such extraordinary measures, Túpac Amaru's wife urged him to proceed with the conquest of Cuzco. She possessed a virile spirit capable of the greatest designs, so much so that it was believed in some quarters that she exceeded her husband in ardor and talents. She had advocated the execution of Arriaga and, in order to be certain that it was carried out, she had carried bullets in her mantilla to shoot him in case he was not hanged. Now both husband and wife hastened military preparations, and the Indians and mestizos were ordered to assemble in Tinta on December 19, 1780, the day the march was to begin.

On the twenty-third, the defenders of Cuzco received the alarming news of the proposed attack. They believed that the Inca hoped to sack the city and crown himself in it. The city was crowded with refugees, roads were closed to supplies, and hunger had already begun to be felt. Many inhabitants favored Túpac Amaru, but were intimidated by warnings against the rebels near

[51] Vista del fiscal del virreinato de Buenos Aires, Dr. Pacheco, Buenos Aires, January 15, 1781, in Odriozola, *Documentos,* I, 131–35; Angelis, *Documentos,* 25–29.

[52] Bando del virrey Juan José de Vertíz, Buenos Aires, January 15, 1781, in Odriozola, *Documentos,* I, 136–37; Angelis, *Documentos,* 30.

the town of Chita and elsewhere. Moreover, there was the risk of excommunication in addition to the many precautions that had been taken to prevent disorder in the city.

A number of persons were ready to hand the city over to the Inca without a fight, while others wanted it defended. These opposing views were reported to the Viceroy when aid was asked again. The extraordinary junta in Lima immediately ordered the people in Cuzco not to waste time in useless disputes, but to take every means to defend the city. A number of people fled from Cuzco and joined the enemy, some because they believed in the cause, some in the hope of saving their lives. Still others took the road to Lima in search of safety there. As a result, the corregidor issued a proclamation forbidding anyone else to go outside the city under penalty of death.[53]

Meanwhile, Túpac Amaru was approaching slowly and trying to keep order in his undisciplined and poorly armed body of forty thousand men. He brought only part of his followers, leaving one-third of them in the elevated regions with his family. He went out from Quiquijana and took most of the people with him to Urcos. Along the road he sacked all the haciendas from Quiquijana to Paylla, except that of Lucre in the district of Paucuto, where he took only horses and mules. From Urcos he marched to Andaquilas and from there to Oropesa. He then followed the direct road out of Oropesa, but returned to the heights and rested in Yanacocha, about three and one-half leagues from Cuzco. From there he sent his ambassadors, Bernardo de la Madrid, Ildefonso Bejarana, and a Franciscan friar, to the Bishop and cabildo with an ultimatum to hand over their possessions or he would overthrow the city. La Madrid had the effrontery to tell the Bishop that the Lord Governor José Gabriel Túpac Amaru had sent him a parcel of letters by his ambassador. The prelate ignored him.

At the same time Diego Túpac Amaru left Urcos and marched

---

[53] Carta de Juan Manuel Moscoso, obispo del Cuzco, al obispo de La Paz, Dr. Gregorio Francisco del Campo, Huayallabamba, July 20, 1782, in Odriozola, *Documentos*, I, 252; Relación de los hechos mas notables acaecidos en la sublevación general . . . , 201. Lorente, *Historia del Peru bajo los Borbones*, 190–91; García Naranjo, *op. cit.*, 36–37.

to the ravine to the east with six thousand men to occupy the provinces of Calca, Paucartambo, and Urubamba. He was to attack Paucartambo at the same time as José Gabriel besieged Cuzco. Before Diego arrived in the provinces he was to occupy, an agent of the Inca began to destroy the haciendas of Velasco, Astete, Camara, and Capana so energetically that they were entirely devastated, after which the Indians went down to Cacay.

The haciendas near Calca suffered the same fate. All the Spanish women in the town were killed. Some deaths occurred in Pisaca, but not so much damage was done there. On the other hand, Guayallabamba, cacique of the Chincheros, who had escaped with all his people, cruelly slaughtered the insurgents, overthrew them, and did not permit them to advance in the neighborhood of Guayacari. He then went to Cuzco and camped with his people around the ancient ruins of Sacsaguaman. Also, Rosas, the cacique of Anta, arrived with 2,500 Indians and stationed them in Picchu.[54]

Another detachment under Antonio Castelo, one of the Inca's most faithful adherents, advanced by the royal road of Cuzco. He was defeated by Valcárcel y Laysequilla in Sailla, two or three leagues from the city, and four hundred dead were left there. Only with difficulty could that vanguard unite with the bulk of the army, which José Gabriel was obliged to take over the heights.

On December 28, the Inca camped two leagues away from Cuzco on the heights of Picchu. He ordered artillery shots to be fired now and then to encourage his partisans.[55] He did not attack the city at once, but limited his activities to cutting off all outside communication and to daily excursions to near-by towns to enlist more followers. He lost valuable time sending proclamations to neighboring provinces not yet involved in the uprising, while each day's delay benefited the Junta of War in Cuzco. [56]

He also sent flags of truce and letters to the Bishop and the secular and ecclesiastical cabildos in Cuzco. In the letters he repeated that his only aim was to get rid of grievances, to work for

[54] Copia de una carta de Cuzco enviada á La Paz, January 10, 1781, in Odriozola, *Documentos,* I, 129–30; Angelis, *Documentos,* 22–23.

[55] Mendiburu, *Diccionario,* VIII, 131.

[56] García Naranjo, *op. cit.,* 28.

the general welfare of the provinces and of the city, and to uphold the glory of the church. If the city resisted, he would put all the inhabitants to the sword and burn it.[57] In a letter sent to the municipal council on January 3, 1781, he asked permission to enter the city. He said that he was forced to demand the surrender of the cabildo because it had inflicted many outrages upon his followers, who had been hanged without confession. He threatened:

> If this is not granted at once, I will not delay for an instant my entrance with fire and sword. . . . I am the only one who remains of the royal blood of the Incas, kings of this kingdom. I have decided to try all means possible that all abuses, introduced and planted by the corregidores and other persons, may cease. . . . My desire is that such officers shall be suppressed entirely; that their repartimientos shall end; and that in each province there may be an alcalde mayor of the same Indian nation and other persons of good conscience. . . . It is indispensable that in this city a royal audiencia shall be erected, where a viceroy shall reside as president in order that the Indians may have nearer access to him. I wish to leave to the King of Spain the direct rule which he has had in his possessions.[58]

He told the Bishop that he came on behalf of the whole nation to end the robberies and outrages of corregidores, to put down tyranny, and to see that the laws were obeyed. He had sent his ambassadors to the cabildo of Cuzco so that it might surrender the city to him peacefully. As his demand was refused, he would enter the city with blood and fire; but he would respect priests, all church property, women, and inoffensive unarmed persons.[59] He always kept that promise and never even urged the clergy to join his revolution.

When his messengers had not returned after twelve hours, he sent another courier with threats of a quick and destructive at-

[57] Lorente, *Historia del Peru bajo los Borbones*, 192.

[58] Oficio de José Gabriel Túpac Amaru al cabildo del Cuzco, Ocororo, January 3, 1781, in Odriozola, *Documentos*, I, 126–27; Angelis, *Documentos*, 19–20; Mendiburu, *Diccionario*, VIII, 132.

[59] Oficio de José Gabriel Túpac Amaru al obispo del Cuzco, Tungasuca, December 12, 1780, in Odriozola, *Documentos*, I, 125–26; Angelis, *Documentos*, 18–19.

tack. The royalists' reply to this message was a sally in which all classes took part. Four companies of clergy came out with the Dean of the cathedral at their head, while the Bishop walked through the streets blessing and encouraging the timid. The Indian men of the city took out their cudgels and slings, and the Indian women aided them by distributing *chicha* (the drink of the common people), by bringing stones, and by getting ashes ready to blind the invaders.[60]

The junta in Lima finally decided that the moment for combat had arrived. First it tried to obtain information indirectly from the priest of Tungasuca about Túpac Amaru's intentions, the number of men in his army, the amount of arms and ammunition he had, and how many Spaniards were helping him. The attempt was unsuccessful, but reinforcements were started toward Cuzco.[61] Earlier, on November 24, when the Viceroy had received news of the seriousness of the situation, he had dispatched toward the city two hundred militiamen under Colonel Gabriel de Avilés, a future viceroy. Then when the corregidor of Quispicanchis had arrived at Lima on December 5 with the news of the disaster at Sangarara, another force of two hundred men had marched toward Cuzco. On the eleventh another two hundred, led by Inspector General José del Valle, had left Lima. Later even Visitador General Areche started for Cuzco with a group of seven hundred men, among whom were officials, noblemen, artillerymen, and musicians armed with six cannon, three thousand guns, sabers, pistols, and other weapons. The judge of the audiencia, Benito de la Mata Linares, accompanied him as his assessor. Areche thought the rebellion would be easy to crush, but Del Valle believed a long time would be required.

When the first expedition led by Avilés arrived in Cuzco on January 1, 1781, bringing four hundred guns, five hundred swords, and twelve thousand cartridges, the defenders of the city were very much encouraged, especially because at last they had a recognized military commander. Counting the Indian auxiliaries, twelve thousand men now defended Cuzco. Without delay Avilés took charge

[60] Lorente, *Historia del Peru bajo los Borbones,* 192.
[61] García Naranjo, *op. cit.,* 37.

of directing military operations and organized an expedition under Pablo Astete and the caciques of Chincheros and Anta. On the sixth, a long skirmish occurred on a broken field; in it twenty mulattoes, who imprudently climbed the hill of Puquin, were killed.

A bloody battle, that lasted two days, began on January 8 in the suburbs of Cuzco and on the heights. Túpac Amaru found a good position on the rugged hills, used two cannon, made repeated attacks and ambushes, and employed other devices.

All the Spanish troops were put under arms. In the morning, when they occupied convenient places, the fight began. A company of merchants, consisting of 130 men under Captain Simón Gutiérrez, wanted to march at once, but were not permitted to do so until the leaders gave the order. When the command was given, they advanced up the hill in regular formation to face the enemy. A volunteer company of eighty men, led by Colonel Pedro Echave, also went to garrison the bridge of Puquin. In Belén and Guancaro a line was formed by the cavalry regiment of the city, under the command of their colonel, the Marquis of Rocafuerte. This line was reinforced by the light cavalry of Colonel Allened and by volunteers from the province of Quispicanchis under Pedro Concha. Other companies of the infantry regiment under Colonel Miguel Torrejón, the soldiers from Lima, and the other auxiliary troops remained as a rear guard.

A reinforcement of eight thousand men for the royalists arrived at Guancaro, brought by Manuel de Castilla, corregidor of Paruro, and the faithful cacique of Huraiquite, Antonio de Figueroa y Esquiluz. The new troops remained in Huancaro as a reserve body. This great assistance encouraged the army and diminished the arrogance of the enemy.

Meanwhile, the company of merchants arrived at the hilltop and made the most convenient formation possible. One-fourth of them advanced to a suitable place to discharge their guns and throw the Indians into confusion. When their grapeshot was gone, the merchants used nails instead, as they were lighter than shot, and won some advantage. It was difficult to fire the cannon since the hill did not slope enough, yet it was put to use and some Indians were killed. The Dominican friar Ramón Salazar distinguished himself as a soldier. From the protection of a large rock, he shot at the Indians and frightened them.

Many of the principal inhabitants of the city fearlessly went to the hill and joined the combatants. Important personages also served as couriers and transporters of munitions, while priests aided the wounded and dying. Even the Bishop approached the lines formed by the cavalry to administer to the soldiers, although he knew that the Indians wished to capture him. Avilés and several other generals on horseback continually inspected the posts.

The firing lasted until night, since Túpac Amaru held out a long time and encouraged the Indians to do their best. All the royalist troops remained on the hill, although they were tired and the weather foul. Needed supplies and tents were sent out to them. Colonel Villalta spent the night with more than one hundred gunners and reinforced the garrison during a heavy shower. When day dawned, a thick fog concealed the enemy. No Indians could be seen when the fog rose; only their baggage, a piece of artillery, and some munitions were visible.[62] This is the account of the battle given by the cabildo of Cuzco.

The Indians suffered even more hardships than the royalists, for they did not have tents. They fought as long as they could without sacrificing too many men, but finally had to withdraw.[63] The Bishop considered the retreat a miracle, not being able to understand why the Inca, with such a large army at his command, had not entered the city:

> A fourth part would have been sufficient to confound our small forces. . . . And the city contained many Indian and mestizo partisans of Túpac Amaru, who awaited the occasion of his entrance to declare for him.[64]

[62] Carta de Juan Manuel Moscoso, obispo del Cuzco, al obispo de La Paz, Dr. Gregorio Francisco del Campo, Huayallabamba, July 20, 1782, in Odriozola, *Documentos*, I, 255; Valcárcel, *La rebelión de Túpac Amaru*, 85–91. Garcia Naranjo, *op. cit.*, 32–33; Markham, A History of Peru, 201–202.

[63] Lorente, *Historia del Peru bajo los Borbones*, 193.

[64] Carta de Juan Manuel, obispo del Cuzco, al obispo de La Paz, Dr. Gregorio Francisco del Campo, Huayallabamba, July 20, 1782, in Odriozola, *Documentos*, I, 253.

Lack of military experience was the primary reason Túpac Amaru did not even attack Cuzco. He was quite aware that every man, woman, and child would defend the city. Moreover, he had encountered certain unexpected difficulties. When the royalists received the reinforcements commanded by Feliciano Paz, a considerable number of the Inca's men deserted him. In addition, many of his supplies were rendered useless by sabotage. To service the artillery, he had to depend upon untrustworthy Spanish prisoners. For example, prisoner Figueroa, who was faithful to the king, raised the aim so that the cannon did little damage. When he cleaned the guns, taken from Corregidor Arriaga and the defeated Spaniards, he twisted the locks and then blamed the damage on the mestizos who had stolen them. His accusation so terrified the mestizos operating the guns that they deserted, leaving the Indians unprotected.[65]

Despite the ineffectiveness of the Inca's cannon, the Spaniards suffered losses. There was desertion on their side, too. When the cholos of Cuzco heard the slings of the Indians, they fled. One writer said that the royalists lost three hundred men; however, the Bishop thought that 150 was more nearly correct.

The royalists still mistrusted Túpac Amaru, even though he had suffered defeat. It was believed that he had withdrawn toward the place where his wife was staying, to bring up the reinforcements left in Yanacocha, but when four hundred men of Paruro came after him, he was unable to return there.[66] The auxiliaries from Paruro wanted to pursue the Indians farther than Puquin, yet they were not permitted to do so because the Spaniards expected the Inca to return to Cuzco. Moreover, orders from the Viceroy prohibited really opening the campaign before the arrival of more forces from Lima.

The Inca did not consider himself conquered and apparently did intend to return to Cuzco. On January 9, 1781, he wrote another letter to the cabildo that implied that he would. He said that his

[65] Gutriérrez, *op. cit.*, 132–33, 136–37.

[66] Copia de una carta del Cuzco enviada á La Paz, January 10, 1781, in Odriozola, *Documentos*, I, 130; Vista del fiscal del virreinato de Buenos Aires, Dr. Pacheco, Buenos Aires, January 15, 1781, *ibid.*, I, 133.

Indians had urged him to let them sack the city, but he did not want to see it ruined or the inhabitants made to suffer. He asked the council again to surrender Cuzco so that this might not happen. In the town of Acomayo, where he ate in the priest's house, he stated that he would return to Cuzco later with greater forces. He attributed his retreat to his desire not to sacrifice the Indians and to the bad management of his mestizos, some of whom he punished severely.[67]

Meanwhile, Diego Túpac Amaru was also unsuccessful. His division had been detached from the main army at Checacupe, where he crossed the mountainous country and again descended into the Vilcamayo Valley. He followed the course of the river until he encountered the forces commanded by the Marquis of Rocafuerte, which consisted of the levies of Pumacagua, cacique of Chincheros, and of the caciques of Maras and Huayallabamba. A battle was fought at Huarán, on the banks of the river near Calca, where Diego met defeat and many of his Indians were drowned. On December 23, he again suffered defeat at Yucay, and was obliged to leave the valley. Crossing a mountain range, he took his stand in the town of Paucartambo on the banks of the river of the same name, while he sent his advance guards over the heights above the Vilcamayo Valley to threaten the towns of Calca, Pisac, and Taray.

The royalist José Antonio Vivar was then ordered to occupy the bridge at Urubamba and watch the enemy movement. At the same time Commandant Lorenzo Lechuga desperately defended Paucartambo and a strong fort on a rocky height on the opposite side of the river. Fortunately, Colonel Astete went to the Urubamba bridge with four hundred men and, after various encounters with the Indians, whom he defeated, arrived at the besieged town just in time, for Lechuga had used all his ammunition and was in want of other supplies. Lechuga, moreover, had suffered a wound in the mouth, which never healed.

---

[67] Oficio de José Gabriel Túpac Amaru al cabildo del Cuzco, Altos de Picchu, January 9, 1781, in Odriozola, *Documentos,* I, 128; Angelis, *Documentos,* 21; Lorente, *Historia del Peru bajo los Borbones,* 193–94.

The arrival of Astete forced Diego Túpac Amaru to retreat toward Tinta on January 18, 1781. There he aided his brother to reorganize the army. The latter made another attack on Paucar-tambo on February 11, but, after a number of unsuccessful attempts, returned to Tinta a few days later.[68]

At this time the clergy became very active once more. They took part in the warfare of the neighboring provinces, tried to prevent desertions in the towns, and guarded the bridges. They helped to protect the willow bridge at Urubamba by which traffic was carried on with the surrounding regions. They knew that if it was burned, the enemy would gain possession of the strong Vilcabamba fortress in the province of Abancay and of other places on the way to Lima; then Cuzco would lack supplies and cattle. The priests of Cotabambas cut off the contagion of revolution in that province and from Chumbivilcas.[69]

Members of the clergy were also working for peace. The Dean of the cathedral in La Paz, Antonio González Pavón, made wise suggestions to the King for halting the revolt. He and other reformers agreed that the office of corregidor and the repartimientos must be abolished. In addition, the Dean believed that justices must prevent the selling of *aguardiente* and other liquors, made from certain fruits, to the Indians, since it was bad enough that they got drunk on their chicha. The Dean advised, moreover, that cattle and farm implements be given to the Indians as a means to promote peace. He and other officials maintained that the office of cacique should not be hereditary, but should be held for only three years by any one man, and that great care should be taken to select competent men for the position.[70]

Hostilities nevertheless continued in the province with alternate reverses and success. The brave and loyal Tomás Pavina obtained decisive advantages in Chumbivilcas, but could not check

[68] Markham, *Travels in Peru and India*, 146–47.
[69] Carta de Juan Manuel Moscoso, obispo del Cuzco, al obispo de La Paz, Dr. Gregorio Francisco del Campo, Huayallabamba, July 20, 1782, in Odriozola, *Documentos*, I, 259.
[70] González Pavón, "Causas de la sublevación indígena (Documento inédito del año 1788)," in Loayza, *op. cit.*, Serie I, Vol. X, 78–79.

the Indian army in Cotabambas which was led by disloyal priests. In the province of Paruro the enemy were driven back from the capital; but they pillaged the town of Pilpinto, which the women had heroically defended, and committed outrages in many other near-by places and on the haciendas. In the province of Calca the fury of the Indians reached such an extent that they divided the heart of a Spanish gentleman and drank his blood, saying that it had a very good flavor. The following day the terrible Pumacagua, an ally of the Spaniards, fell upon the insurgents and showed no mercy.[71]

Túpac Amaru was working hard to recover from his losses. He fortified Tinta and placed sixty thousand men around it, but they were undisciplined and lacked arms. He therefore decided to make more weapons. By this time all but sixteen of the caciques supported him, for most of the Indians wanted his revolt to succeed. The Inca also visited the distant provinces of Chuquibamba and Cotabambas, while Isidro Mamani, an Indian of ferocious character and a native of Pomata, Pedro Vargas, and Andrés Ingaricona controlled the country in the basin of Lake Titicaca. Indeed, the insurrection had spread through all parts of the south, center, and west of Peru.[72]

Cuzco had to remain always in a state of defense. A short time after the Inca's retreat the city learned of an Indian uprising in a near-by province. A party of seventy-five armed men marched out under Isidro and Pedro Gutiérrez to put it down. As they did not have much military experience, they were surprised by an ambush. Both leaders and some of their soldiers lost their lives, but fortunately a cacique arrived with his men just in time to save the others. Then the royalists attacked the Indians fiercely and killed more than five hundred of them.[73]

Areche and Del Valle finally arrived in Cuzco with their forces on February 23, 1781. There they found some fifteen thousand men,

[71] Lorente, *Historia del Peru bajo los Borbones,* 194.
[72] Markham, *Travels in Peru and India,* 148; Mendiburu, *Diccionario,* VIII, 136–37.
[73] Relación de los hechos mas notables acaecidos en la sublevación general . . . , 202. MS copy in B. L.

consisting of the followers of the loyal caciques, Negroes, mulattoes from the east, and Spaniards. Areche and other officials reviewed the city's armed forces, asked the Viceroy for more soldiers, made plans, and enlisted militias.[74] The visitador published a proclamation on March 5 putting a price on the heads of Túpac Amaru and all men exempted from the general pardon. He hoped that this move would cause the Indians to desert the Inca's cause.[75] At the same time Del Valle was preparing to begin the campaign early in March.

Before the army left Cuzco, Areche received a long letter from Túpac Amaru declaring that he had gone down to Cuzco to put the King's orders into effect and to make terms with the members of the cabildo. He said:

> My intention was not to maltreat or disturb the inhabitants of Cuzco, but the interested corregidores imagined that I was going to demolish the city, which act would have been directly against the royal crown of Spain and the King, my lord. When they resisted me with great instruments of war, I was compelled to respond. I do not have a heart as cruel or depraved as the tyrannous corregidores and their allies, for I am a good Catholic Christian.

He added that he had great pity for the suffering of the city and was postponing further action until he received a reply from Areche. Furthermore, two years earlier the King had issued a royal decree abolishing the repartimientos and the office of corregidor, which, however, still existed in opposition to the sovereign's will. "These evil names must be blotted out from our imagination," he said, "and in their place alcaldes mayores should be established in each province . . . in order to administer justice to us."

The Inca leader went on to say that he felt relieved that the visitador had arrived, and he eagerly summed up the grievances of the natives for him. He suggested that Areche examine the reports of Gregorio Francisco Campos, bishop of La Paz, of Manuel

---

[74] Lorente, *Historia del Peru bajo los Borbones,* 195.

[75] El mariscal de campo D. José del Valle escribió y firmó en el Cuzco en 30 de Sete. de 1781 un manifesto que no sé si se imprimió y que acredita el desacuerdo y enemistad en que se hallaba con el visitador Areche, AGN, Peru. MS copy in B. L.

Gerónimo Romani, of Agustín Garrochátegui, bishop of Cuzco, of Ignacio Castro, and of other clergymen in the latter bishopric in order to realize the Indians' suffering because the sovereign did not seem to know about them.

Túpac Amaru also spoke very highly of the King and his just laws, which supported the natives. He was certain that the corregidores paid no attention to laws, for they killed the Indians like dogs and without allowing the necessary sacraments. He believed that the Indians had rendered the King a great service when they executed the wicked corregidores, and should be rewarded. He blamed the latter officials and the reluctance of administrators to enforce royal measures for the revolt. He also refuted the report that the Indians wished to abandon the faith and refuse obedience to the King, and denied that he wished to crown himself and return to idolatry, by declaring his loyalty and that of the Indians to the monarch. He said: "We have lived and live now under the royal sovereignty and power. We have nowhere to flee, but must sacrifice our lives before these sovereign altars, in order that, with the red tint of our blood, his royal heart may remain calm." He avowed that he always put royal orders into effect and had even endangered his life to do so. If he had made a mistake by sending ambassadors with dispatches, if he had violated any prerogatives of the King, he alone was guilty, and he alone should be punished.

The Inca asked the visitador to send good men to help his people. He wanted one or two lawyers who had taken oaths of fidelity to the King to be the Indians' protectors and direct their affairs according to the sovereign's will. He also asked that two virtuous and learned priests be sent to show him the way of truth.[76] His ably written letter is a notable document which reveals the Inca's character and views.[77]

The visitador's brutal reply of March 12, 1781, left no alternative for Túpac Amaru except to resist to the end. Areche refused

[76] Carta escrita por D. José Gabriel Túpac Amaru al visitador, D. José Antonio de Areche, Tinta, March 5, 1781, in Odriozola, *Documentos*, I, 145–52.

[77] Sir Clements Markham believed that the Spanish authorities never intended this letter to be preserved, and it was only "through a curious accident" that it was (*A History of Peru*, 203).

all negotiations, threatened the most horrible vengeance, and proceeded to point out to the Inca his errors. His letter sounded
sincere, yet he deduced from it that the Indians were badly governed and that the Inca had little understanding of the extent of
his crimes. Even if the evils of the corregidores were certain, Túpac
Amaru should not have usurped the authority of the King, who
would have remedied the evil. The Inca was blamed for not coming
to Areche's tribunal to seek a remedy for the injustice until the last
moment, although the visitador had served in and worked for the
Americas for seventeen years. Perhaps the Inca imagined that he
had bona fide orders to kill corregidores and Europeans, but, according to the law, it was not just to hang a man without a trial,
as he did in the case of Arriaga. In doing that, he harmed the courts
and the King. Indeed, José Gabriel was guilty of treason even if he
pretended to be a Christian.

The visitador pointed out that it was cowardly to injure the
government or kill anyone appointed in the monarch's name. The
abuses of the repartimientos were about to be abolished by the
sovereign; therefore it was unnecessary to put the corregidor to
death. Orders had also been issued to extinguish the mitas and to
pay just wages to the laborers in workshops. If the Inca had consulted Areche before acting so violently, he would have seen how
complete was the King's plan for Peru. He asked Túpac Amaru
to consider the deplorable desolation of the invaded territory.

> Count with the imagination the many thousands of deaths
> which you have caused. Meditate about the end which these mis-
> erable souls, seduced with so many errors, have had. It would have
> been better to suffer the old evils a little longer, to intercede with
> God for their removal, and to inform the higher chiefs of the nation
> about them.

Areche castigated the Inca for mentioning laws without intelligent knowledge of them and for being ignorant of their spirit. The
laws forbade anyone to usurp their authority, yet the Inca and his
followers were doing just this by taking vengeance into their
own hands.

It is not a good means to break one law to try to fulfill another, since both are injured, as it happens with you. You have filled the provinces with deaths, burnings, insults, robberies, sacrifices, and immunities. Without authority you pretend that you are trying to free the Indians from the evils they say they suffer, but now their sufferings are doubled.

Areche went on to enumerate the severe measures he intended to take against the Inca. He had prepared a large army to fight him; all men deserting his cause would be pardoned; and a substantial reward was offered to bring him, his family, and his principal captains alive to Cuzco to be imprisoned. If he surrendered at once, the manner of his execution would be less cruel. The ruthless Areche said:

Let me persuade you of the humanity and the desire which I have that, while you may be lost to the world, you will be saved for Heaven with your followers, who are in a similar condition. You will say that the answer is terrible, but I reply that the danger in which you are is more terrible. Eternal salvation is the first essential.

He informed Túpac Amaru that the Bishop and other clerics to whom he had written felt the same way about him. He therefore hoped that the Inca would surrender so that many lives might be spared.[78]

General del Valle protested the brutality of this reply, for it made surrender and peace impossible. He said that if he had given such an answer, Areche would have denounced him, declared that his hard spirit had exasperated the Inca and had closed the door to reconciliation, and that he only engaged in the war so that his soldiers might carry everything at the point of the lance. "But as he was the visitador, I kept quiet; and on my part, to make me hated, he said I was ungovernable. If he had heard Túpac Amaru in terms of humility, misfortunes like those of La Paz and others and their results would have been avoided."[79]

[78] Contestación de José Antonio de Areche á José Gabriel Túpac Amaru. Cuzco, March 12, 1781, AGN, Peru. MS copy in B. L.

[79] El marischal de campo D. José del Valle escribió y firmó en el Cuzco en 30 de Sete. de 1781 un manifesto . . . , AGN, Peru. MS copy in B. L.

Thus Túpac Amaru was brought to the realization that there was no middle ground, no chance for negotiation or compromise with the visitador. The brutal, inflexible attitude of the man made it only too clear that the Inca must carry on or die.

It is significant that Túpac Amaru in his edicts, proclamations, letters, and other writings always stressed his loyalty to the King and neither mentioned nor implied that he was fighting for independence—with a single exception. That exception is an undated, unsigned document entitled "Proclamation of His Coronation," found on April 6, 1781, among his papers. Most authorities consider it a forgery by a Spaniard who wanted to provide evidence of treason and thus make Areche's sentence seem less harsh. The document, which is inconsistent with all the Inca's other written statements, reads:

Don José I by the grace of God, Inca king of Peru, Santa Fe, Quito, Chile, Buenos Aires, and the continents of the seas of the south, highest duke and lord of the Césars and Amazonians, with dominion in the Gran Paititi, commissary and distributor of divine piety . . . decided in my council . . . on repeated and secret occasions, already made public, that the kings of Castile usurped the throne and dominion of my people three centuries ago, making them vassals with unbearable services, tributes, money, duties paid to the Spanish government . . . customs dues, alcabalas, monopolies . . . tenths, and fifths. The viceroys, audiencias, corregidores, and other ministers [are] all equally tyrannous, selling justice at auction; and to him who bids most, most is given. Ecclesiastical and secular officials enter into [administering justice] without fear of God, trample upon the natives of this kingdom as beasts, and take away the lives of all those who do not wish to rob. . . . In the name of God, all powerful, we order and command that none of the said pensions shall be paid to the intrusive European ministers of bad faith or shall they be obeyed in anything. Respect shall only be held for the priesthood. We shall pay the tenth and first fruits [*primicia*], which are given to God and the tribute and the fifth [*quinto*] for the King as the natural Lord; and this with the moderation which shall be made known with the other laws to be observed and kept. . . . I command . . . an oath to be taken to my

134

royal crown in all the cities, towns, and places of my dominions; and [I wish] to be informed briefly of the ready and faithful vassals, for rewards, and of those who rebel, for imposing fitting penalties.[80]

The Inca's wife said that an Indian from Marcapata took this document from the pocket of the alcalde of Marcapata, who had been killed.[81] An identical document was published in Silos, New Granada, on May 2, 1781, during the revolution of the *comuneros*. How it came there no one knows. Also among the papers given by Francisco Miranda to William Pitt, is one in which the Inca leader is addressed in the same manner as in the above-quoted excerpt. Because of those two documents, Boleslao Lewin believes that the proclamation of April 6 is authentic. He says that since no one denied the idea of independence in the precursory movements, it must be included in Túpac Amaru's uprising.[82] The fact remains, however, that such an idea is at variance with all the other writings of the Inca, who always spoke respectfully of the Spanish king and showed no desire to abolish the institutions established by the conquerors.

A portrait of Túpac Amaru was found which showed him crowned. At his feet, as trophies, were the dead in the first battles of the rebellion. This, too, was without doubt the product of imagination rather than a delineation of actual fact.[83]

Spanish authorities likely exaggerated when they suggested that José Gabriel had for five years been preparing for a great revolution to re-establish the Inca empire. Their purpose was to diminish the blame placed on corregidores and make the people believe that abuse of their monopolies was not the chief cause of the disturbances. There is no proof that Túpac Amaru sent agents to other places to prepare the people for an Inca monarchy. It was only

[80] Bando sobre la coronación de José Gabriel Túpac Amaru que se encontró entre sus papeles, in Odriozola, *Documentos,* I, 206.

[81] Confesión de Micaela Bastidas, Cuzco, April 22, 1781, in Loayza, *op. cit.,* Serie I, Vol. IX, 116.

[82] Carlos A. Villanueva, *Napoleón y la independencia de América,* 39; Archivos de Lord Chatham, South America, Ley 345, Diario de Mr. Edmond Bott (cited by Lewin, *op. cit.,* 202–203).

[83] Odriozola, *Documentos,* I, 206.

after the uprising began that he issued circulars urging them to support him. Most of these were obtained by the Spaniards. The majority of them concerned reforms to eliminate abuses; nowhere was the re-establishment of the ancient empire mentioned. Caciques and noble Indians helped put down the rebellion, and if there had been any serious attempt to restore the old empire, they surely would not have aided the Spaniards. Túpac Amaru's writings, moreover, were not always dictated by him, but sometimes by his mestizo friends. It is possible, therefore, that the proclamation of April 6 may have been composed to flatter him and compare him to a king. Moreover, the mestizos would have been a great obstacle to restoring the ancient monarchy, the castes would have opposed it, and even Indians hostile to José Gabriel would have tried to prevent it.[84]

The lampoons were a different matter. In some of them Túpac Amaru was called "king," but he did not compose them and often he could not restrain his enthusiastic followers. For example, on December 25, 1780, three Indians of Tungasuca posted a lampoon on the church door at Yauli, in the province of Huarochirí, and were hanged immediately. It said:

> Know, all you who are aggrieved by the alcabalas and new impositions, that Emperor Túpac Amaru has notified us and all his friends in this province of Huarochirí, and that we already have arms at Chicoxira, four leagues from the town of Yauros.[85]

A lampoon in Oruro declared that the people in Cuzco wanted to throw off the yoke of the foreign king and crown one of their countrymen. Another attached to the door of the Audiencia of La Plata began, "The Inca general lives; we already swear to him as king because he is very just . . . ."[86] One of the most efficient revolutionary leaders of High Peru, Pedro de la Cruz Condori, in a letter of March 19, 1781, speaks of himself as governor of the provinces in the name of Túpac Amaru, Inca king of the vast viceroyalty of

[84] Mendiburu, *Diccionario*, I, 335–37.
[85] José M. Valega, *El virreinato del Peru; historia crítica de la época colonial, en todo sus aspectos*, 105; Palma, *op. cit.*, IV, 88.
[86] Lewin, *op. cit.*, 205–206.

Peru.[87] The comuneros of New Granada called Túpac Amaru "king of the Indies";[88] and after his death, Diego, his nephews, and his generals spoke of restoring the Inca empire. It is certain that they, and not José Gabriel Túpac Amaru himself, spread the idea of a new Inca empire.

Túpac Amaru was also accused of telling his people that all persons who died for his cause would be resurrected. It was reported that some women whose husbands had been killed in the war came to him asking when they would see them alive, and he replied that this would happen three days after his coronation in Cuzco.[89] Such a statement is inconsistent with his other actions, although he may have made such a reply to satisfy his superstitious followers. It is more likely, however, that his ignorant partisans spread the idea of the resurrection of the dead. After his brother's death, Diego Túpac Amaru was wise enough not to promote such an idea.

José Gabriel established a kind of government for the conquered territory under his control. At the head of it he placed a junta composed of five members, one of whom was the Creole from Cuzco, Felipe Bermúdez. The Inca's army was led by brave men with considerable ability in military and administrative matters. Among them was Diego Túpac Amaru; and in the provinces, bordering the viceroyalty of Buenos Aires, Andrés Ingaricona, Nicolás Sanca, and Ramón Ponce were active. Antonio Bastidas and Pedro Mendagure occupied the greater part of the province of Quispicanchis. Bastidas believed in great precaution, took care of the military operations, and watched the conduct of all officials appointed by the Inca; Mendagure wanted more action. Other notable military officers were Bermúdez, Tomás Parvina, Juan de Díos Valencia, Carlos Niña Catari, and Alejandro Callisaya. The last two controlled the provinces of Larecaja and Omasuyos.[90] The unnamed authors of certain reports admired the promptness with

[87] Angelis, *Documentos*, 46–48.   [88] Manuel Briceño, *Los comuneros*, 46–47.

[89] Carta de Juan Manuel Moscoso, obispo del Cuzco, al obispo de La Paz, Dr. Gregorio Francisco del Campo, Huayallabamba, July 20, 1782, in Odriozola, *Documentos*, I, 257.

[90] Valcárcel, *La rebelión de Túpac Amaru*, 92–97, 158.

which the people obeyed their leader and were amazed at the rapidity of the conquests, which encompassed great distances.[91] Those conquered areas had to be administered very well indeed to prevent chaos.

The Inca or, in his absence, his wife issued passes for using the roads in the revolting provinces. And his military assistants did the same in distant places. So effectively were the roads closed to the royalists that Commandant Flores complained to José de Gálvez that not a single Spaniard remained in the region from Oruro to Cuzco. The commandant tried to discover the condition of the natives, but he never obtained the least information on account of the vigilance they exercised. Neither could Field Marshal del Valle, when he was in Azángaro, obtain information about La Paz, the charcas, and the hill provinces because all the passes were closed, communication was cut off, and messengers were seized if they tried to slip through the blockade.[92]

Túpac Amaru could not always restrain his followers, who sometimes did their work too thoroughly. They had no respect for haciendas because property rights did not seem sacred to them when they had been despoiled of their lands and wages. Neither did they honor the laws on account of the scandalous corruption among persons entrusted with their enforcement. Túpac Amaru did not approve of widespread destruction of property or of excessive bloodshed. When one of his generals, named Cicenaro, put to death four inhabitants of different castes in the town of Ayaviri, he was severely reprimanded by the Inca. The General answered, "If all people of Spanish blood are not exterminated, some class will dominate the Indians." Túpac Amaru replied: "It is not time. We are thinking now only of obtaining possession of the vast and extensive regions. Soon a method will be sought to destroy all embarrassments and obstacles which are presented to us."[93]

[91] *Revista de Archivos y Bibliotecas (Peruanas)*, Año 1900, Vol. V, 185.

[92] El alzamiento de Túpac Amaru, Memorial de noticias oficiales, Lima, 1780 (copiada del original que se encuentra en el Archivo General de Indias), Colección papeles de estado, Peru, Leg. 3 (cited by Lewin, *op. cit.*, 211); Odriozola, *Documentos*, I, 68.

[93] Odriozola, *Documentos*, I, 51.

It has been noted that the Inca protected his Creole friends, declared himself the liberator of all oppressed races, and was even willing to employ Europeans who could be useful to him. His principal targets were grasping and dishonest corregidores and tax collectors. His only aims were to abolish unjust taxes, to give satisfaction to the offended, to place chief justices who were men of honor and sons of the country at the heads of provinces, to create an audiencia for Cuzco, and then to retire to private life. With it all, he desired to uphold religion and give just praise to priests. Unfortunately, his moderate policy could not be enforced on account of the hatred felt by his partisans. Some of his captains believed that in order to keep from falling again under the yoke of oppression, it was necessary to exterminate all people who were not Indians. Others extended the proscription to as many as wore the Spanish jacket. As a result, as the revolution spread, many acts of cruelty were committed which were never sanctioned by the Inca. If he had had eight or ten experienced generals of first rank, he might have freed Peru. Unfortunately, this was not the case.

CHAPTER VI

Sedition in Oruro

THE TOWN OF ORURO, south of La Paz, was another center of disturbance, which, while not actually a part of the Inca rebellion, nevertheless was superficially linked with it.

The tragic events in the provinces of Chayanta and Tinta were made known to the Creoles in Oruro through an edict of Túpac Amaru, in which he stated his intentions. When those purposes and the Indian ravages in the provinces of Lampa and Carabaya were brought to the attention of Corregidor Ramón de Urrutia, he prepared to check any such movement in his province. He feared that the Creoles and other inhabitants of Oruro would join the Inca uprising, since their hatred for the European Spaniards was well known. He organized companies of whites to train the rest of the inhabitants in the use of arms and designated different places for instruction twice a week. Many men eagerly took advantage of this instruction, but the followers of Túpac Amaru went only to criticize.

At the same time they insolently put up lampoons which opposed the King and censured the administration of the corregidor and other magistrates. On December 25, 1780, a lampoon appeared which announced the assassination of Europeans and censured the conduct of Fernando Garruchagua, the *alcalde ordinario*. Members of the cabildo were warned not to choose European alcaldes, who would become the victims of the Creoles' anger and would not last eight days, but to appoint Juan de Dios Rodríguez and Jacinto Rodríguez, two wealthy Creoles of the town. The former was the proprietor of a famous and very productive silver mine near Oruro.

The corregidor was not frightened by these bold threats, however, and tried diligently but vainly to discover the persons responsible for the lampoon. When election day for the year 1781 arrived, he favored José Miguel Llano y Valdés, Joaquín Rubín de Celis, and Manuel de Mugrusa, all Europeans and efficient men. Differences arose over the election, but Urrutia's candidates won.

The Rodríguez clan could not hide their hatred when they saw the power they had held for eighteen years taken away from them. Juan de Dios left town quickly, leaving word that none of his clients were to attend the bullfights to celebrate the election of the new alcaldes. Even the priest sided with the Rodríguez faction. When the cabildo members went to the church to hear mass, as was the custom after elections, the sacristan met them at the door and told them that there would be no mass because none of them had given alms.

Matters had reached this critical stage when news was received of the death of Tomás Catari. Earlier the corregidor of Paria, Manuel Bodega, had asked Urrutia to help him remove Catari. He believed that it would be easy to subjugate the province of Chayanta and collect the tribute and repartimiento dues. When Urrutia refused, Bodega collected fifty men at his own expense and marched to the town of Challapata, where he and most of his followers lost their lives.

The Indians of Challapata, Condo, Popó, and other near-by towns, convinced that Urrutia had supported Bodega, threatened to kill the corregidor and all the inhabitants of Oruro. Then the Rodríguez family chaplain, Bernardino Gallegos, a Franciscan friar, told Urrutia that he had heard that the Indians of Challapata were ready to invade Oruro. When the official ignored his warning, the clergyman became so resentful that he spread the word that the Indians were surrounding the town.

The terrified Spaniards held council meetings in which nothing was decided on account of lack of money. They discovered that Jacinto Rodríguez years ago had appropriated all the funds in the local treasury. Nor could the corregidor obtain money from the royal treasury, the treasury officials declaring that they had no power to remove money from the strong chest without an express order from a higher authority. Urrutia then proposed that the inhabitants should make contributions, but they were too poor to do so. Finally the treasurer, Salvador Parrilla, gave two thousand pesos of his own funds for barracks and munitions, and three hundred men were armed by means of his money. Information concerning the critical condition was also sent to the audiencia. When the troops were formed, however, many dissensions arose because of military insubordination.[1]

The corregidor had a large house erected near his own to be used for barracks and required the soldiers to stay there. At first all seemed harmonious among the Europeans and Creoles. Dissatisfaction arose later when it was noticed that the Creoles received three reales a day, while the other men served without pay. The rumor that the Europeans intended to kill the natives was spread on February 9, 1781. How the rumor started no one knew, but the natives believed they would be put to death that night before aid could be obtained.[2] The Creoles had some reason to suspect the Europeans from certain rash statements made by three of them, Francisco Santelices, José Caballero, and José Bullain. Santelices had proposed that a *fandango* be held and the Creoles killed at that time.[3]

Certain soldiers of the company of Manuel Serrano became panic stricken. They ran out of the barracks at ten o'clock in the evening, shouting for aid from the others. When inquiry was made as to the cause of the commotion, Sebastián Pagador answered in a loud voice that the chapetones were trying treason against them and that they must have nothing to do with the Europeans. Pagador was a troublemaker and caused resentment to spread all over the town. He had served in the Rodríguez mines for a number of years, and that afternoon he went to the mines near the town and got drunk, making all kinds of absurd statements. He said that the corregidor wanted to hang him, his brothers, Manuel de Herrera, and other inhabitants. Since Nicolás de Herrera, lieutenant of the troops

---

[1] Odriozola, *Documentos*, I, 12–15; Edmond Temple, *Travels in Various Parts of Peru, including a Year's Residence in Potosí*, II, 29–30; Lewin, *op. cit.*, 287–88.

[2] Relación de los hechos mas notables acaecidos en la sublevación general . . . , 55–56. MS copy in B. L.

[3] Confesión de Juan Gualberto Mexía, AGN, Buenos Aires, Revolución de Oruro, Vol. VI–8–5–5, Leg. 1 (cited by Lewin, *op. cit.*, 288–89).

and a man who had been tried many times as a public thief, desired plunder, he saw to it that Pagador's irresponsible remarks were spread. The ignorant soldiers believed that the Europeans and the corregidor had conspired against them.

Next day the soldiers refused to remain in the barracks. Some went to their homes, and others, accompanied by Pagador, visited Jacinto Rodríguez. They told the latter that they were ready to follow him, and he laid out a course of action.[4] When Corregidor Urrutia tried to make them enter the barracks again, they insulted him and said he wanted to shut them up in order to kill them. He and other officers tried to reason with them and calm them, but were unsuccessful. The Creoles answered that Rodríguez had ordered them not to go into the barracks.[5]

For some days before this Rodríguez had been preparing for insubordination. He had sent the priest Gallegos to Challapata to summon the Indians for February 10 and had distributed his Negro servants on the farms and in neighboring towns to increase his forces. Now he rode to the mines, where he united all the Indians, mulattoes, and mestizos working there, and told them to come down from the hill of Conchopata to the town as soon as it grew dark. Then José Azurduy, an officer of the company of Menacho, was sent through the streets and plazas of Oruro to proclaim the treason of the corregidor and the Europeans. He said that Urrutia, accompanied by thirty or forty Europeans, could kill more than five thousand people. A fragment of a letter was also found in which Gallegos advised his brother, Friar Feliciano, that on the night of the tenth the town would be invaded by the Indians of Challapata. He told him not to be afraid since their purpose was to kill the corregidor and the treasury officials. As a matter of fact, the Indians of Challapata had no thought of coming that night, but the false rumor was spread to increase the fear in the town.

Another cause for the disturbance was the serious condition of the mines. Because of financial losses in the past ten years, mine-

---

[4] Odriozola, *Documentos*, I, 15–16; Ordóñez López and Crespo, *op. cit.*, 114–15.
[5] Relación de los hechos mas notables acaecidos en la sublevación general . . . , 56; Oficio del corregidor de Oruro, Ramón de Urrutia y las Casas al virrey de Buenos Aires, La Plata, March 15, 1781, in Odriozola, *Documentos*, I, 342–43.

owners, except the Rodríguez family, could not pay the workers or obtain sufficient labor. Only the Europeans had cash, and they refused to invest in the mines. They did not realize the danger of withholding financial aid from people who despaired of paying their debts and were eager to rebel.

At four o'clock in the afternoon of February 10, the corregidor summoned the militia. The soldiers still did not want to go into the barracks, and clustered in groups at the corners of the plaza. Pagador, who was among them, discussed the acts of José Gabriel Túpac Amaru, the vexations suffered on account of the corrupt government of the king's ministers, and the heavy burdens imposed upon the people. The corregidor tried to persuade the soldiers to enter the barracks, first with kindness and then by threats, but they only wanted to remain in the plaza and wait for the Indians. Urrutia offered to sleep with them, told them that when a conspiracy was proved, they might take his life first, and begged them not to listen to such falsehoods. They only became more insolent and began to manipulate their slings.

Finally the militia entered the barracks to collect their pay. While they were inside, boys could be heard shouting in the streets and plazas. The youths shot stones with their slings, causing dismay in the town, while church bells rang out. No one took the time to investigate the ringing of the bells or the boys' pranks.[6] Night had scarcely fallen when horns, *polulos* (warlike musical instruments), and stringed instruments were heard on the hill of Conchopata, making the people think that the Indians were entering the town.[7] When a European went out to inspect the suburbs, he found out that the noise was made by the natives. He told them to stop and come down from the hill, but when they threw stones at him, he returned to the plaza, where many people had assembled. Later it was discovered that the trumpets were blown by the Negroes of Rodríguez, Nicolás de Herrera, and Isidro Quevado to induce the Europeans to assemble, so that it would be easier to attack them.

6 Odriozola, *Documentos*, I, 16–18.
7 Confesión de José Azurduy y Lazarte, AGN, Buenos Aires, Revolución de Oruro, VI–8–5–5, Leg. 1 (cited by Lewin, *op. cit.*, 290).

Learning that the town was not under siege, many Europeans went to the home of José de Endeiza, a citizen of Buenos Aires and a merchant, to dine. He had arrived from Cochabamba twenty days before with more than 60,000 pesos. To this amount were added some gold ingots that his dependent, Francisco Gutiérrez Palazuelos, a resident of Salta, had transported from the province of Larecaja, making a total of 140,000 pesos in all. Other merchants also brought their funds to his home for protection, so that more than 350,000 pesos were in the house.

As the first course of the dinner was being served, José Cayetano de Casas entered the dining room covered with blood. He had been stabbed by the Creoles because he had opposed their entrance at the church corner, which was guarded by his company. He assured the diners that the Creole conspiracy against them was certain. Soon the crowd in the plaza began to throw stones at the house and balconies, and continued to do so all night. The Europeans were determined to defend themselves to the last, but Endeiza was a man of peace. When he saw that death was inevitable, he assured his companions that their only crime was that they were Europeans and had collected their wealth in his house in view of the Creoles. He told them to discharge their guns into the air to frighten the rebels without wounding anybody. More than two hundred shots were fired thus. Then José Larrar was killed when he slipped down from the balcony as he tried to flee, and Casas died from his wound.

Some four thousand Indian insurgents had assembled, but the corregidor knew they were not causing the disturbance. He hastened to the house of Manuel de Herrera, the alcalde, and asked him to calm the crowd. Herrera answered that it was not yet time and went on playing cards with the priest of Sorasora, Isidro Velasco, and other persons. When the corregidor realized that he could accomplish nothing there and that he would be killed if he remained, he rode to Cochabamba, where he found refuge.[8]

Meanwhile, the rebels decided to set fire to Endeiza's house

[8] Odriozola, *Documentos,* I, 18–19; Relación de los hechos mas notables acaecidos en la sublevación general . . . , 56–57 (MS copy in B. L.); Carrió, *op. cit.,* 88.

on all sides and quickly burned the balconies and principal shops. Thus the Europeans were forced to come out by way of the roofs, and when all retreat was cut off for them, they were killed in the cruelest manner. They were left nude and cut to pieces. The rabble then rushed into the house, sacked it like wolves, and destroyed it, along with a shop belonging to a Creole named Panteleón Martínez, on the pretext that he was an accomplice of the chapetones and had sold powder to them. He was entirely ruined. It was said that the mob obtained about 700,000 pesos from the Europeans.

At half-past five in the morning the friars tried to calm the mob by bringing the sacrament out of the Convent of Mercy, but the people paid no attention and continued their brutal acts. Eleven dead Europeans were lying in the plaza, twelve Negroes had been killed, and many persons were wounded. The bodies of the dead were taken to the prison threshold and left unburied for two days. Next the rabble freed all the prisoners. Then, shouting "Long live our chief justice, Jacinto Rodríguez!" and joyfully blowing trumpets, they went to Jacinto's house. When the priest asked what they wanted, they said that they wanted the corregidor and other chapetones to be banished from their sight.[9]

Deciding that something must be done to pacify the mob, the priest told Rodríguez that it was his duty to go out and calm the people. The two men walked to the main plaza and soon appeared on a balcony overlooking the square. The priest addressed the people, advising them to recognize some superior, and asked whether they would accept Rodríguez as such. They responded that they would obey him in everything, but that they must kill the corregidor and the Europeans. The priest urged them to lay aside their ill feeling and pardon the Europeans who still remained alive since they had avenged themselves sufficiently.

The rebels were calmed, but laid down conditions under which the chapetones must surrender their arms. The pardon would not include Xavier de Santelices, they said, who must die if they found

---

[9] Relación de los hechos mas notables acaecidos en la sublevación general . . . , 58–59 (MS copy in B. L.); Odriozola, Documentos, I, 20–21; Carrió, op. cit., 88–89.

146

End walls of the Temple of the Sun, Cuzco

Door of the Jesuit Church, Cuzco

him, whereupon the priest admonished them to hand him over to the chief justice instead.

The peace was short lived. The mob had acquired a taste for plunder and sacked the establishment of Manuel de Santander, a European merchant from Lima, leaving only an empty trunk. They even killed his dogs. They did the same to the homes of other Europeans, so that the disorder continued until midafternoon.

Meanwhile, around noon, the parties of Indians summoned by Rodríguez began to arrive in Oruro. They came blowing trumpets and armed with slings and cudgels. Jacinto Rodríguez and the Creoles had gone out into the country to meet them. The Indians willingly promised obedience to Rodríguez, and when he took them to the plaza to show them the unfortunate dead, they tore them to pieces. Afterwards they got drunk and paid no heed to a devout procession that came out of the church.[10] Then they went to the homes of Manuel de Herrera, Captain Menacho, and Antonio Quirós, whom they honored. They spent the rest of the afternoon searching houses for hidden wealth, while other Indians continued to come in troops with their white banners.

The Creoles hardly knew what to do when they could not control their guests. They finally urged them to enter the church to seek fugitive Europeans and make them surrender their arms. The Indians did this willingly. When the priest handed some weapons over to them they were not content and asked for more. As the priest could not check them, he went up to the pulpit, began to preach and give them advice. They laughed insolently and hurled stones with their slings, making him come down quickly. By this time the prior of the Augustinian Order had come out in procession with the communities of Franciscans and the Order of Mercy; they carried the image of the holy Christ of Burgos. Only old women followed the procession. The Indians shouted that the image was nothing more than a piece of maguey wood and paste and that the painters had deceived them.[11]

[10] *Relación de los hechos mas notables acaecidos en la sublevación general* . . . , 59–60 (MS copy in B. L.); *Revista de Archivos y Bibliotecas (Peruanas)*, Año III, Vol. V, 189.

[11] Odriozola, *Documentos*, I, 21.

All that night the Indians and Creoles kept breaking into shops and houses of Europeans. By the next morning (the twelfth) they were more dangerous because they had become thoroughly drunk. In the afternoon more processions came out of the churches, but had no effect upon the rebels. By night many other Indians had arrived and helped to plunder the town. The dead bodies were left unburied until the priest finally ordered them taken to the cemetery, where a pit was dug and they were thrown into it one upon another.[12]

The Creoles grew dismayed at the destruction. Twenty-five went out of the town to try to prevent any more Indians from entering, telling them that since victory had been attained, they were not needed. The Indians, however, paid them no heed, for they had received word of the sacking. Europeans hurried to take refuge in the churches and implored the mercy of God, while Creoles tried to stop the robberies. But nothing checked the mob, which shouted, "Death to the alcalde!" And that officer quickly fled to save himself.

Conditions were getting beyond anybody's control. Rodríguez therefore ordered that the cabildo be opened on February 13 and steps taken to receive the chief justice. He tried to keep the people from entering the building, but twelve of their leaders did so, thinking the corregidor was hiding there. The priest, who accompanied Rodríguez, assured them that the official was not there, but he rashly added that four Europeans already confessed were. Then the mob rushed to the parish church to look for them and even opened vaults when they did not find them (the unfortunate refugees had committed suicide). The Indians cut open the casket of Francisco Molliendo, who had died a few days earlier, because they believed the corregidor was in it. When they did not find him, they took their vengeance upon the corpse, stabbing it many times. They searched the church again and found Miguel Estrada, whom they killed. They took Miguel Bustamante alive to Jacinto Rodríguez and asked whether they should put him to death. When

12 Relación de los hechos mas notables acaecidos en la sublevación general . . . , 60. MS copy in B. L.

the officer arranged to imprison him, they became angry and killed Bustamante anyway, by beating and stabbing him.[13]

The Indians continued their outrages all that day and the next, while more kept coming. Reinforcements from Sorasora, Jayaquiza, Bombo, and Antequera were led by the royal ensign bearer, Diego Antonio Flores, one of the principal chiefs of the rebellion, who was dressed like a native, wearing the uncu.[14] From the unpublished material it is certain that Flores, Jacinto Rodríguez, and Manuel de Herrera were in contact with Túpac Amaru's organization, although the exact nature of the connection is unknown.

When the mob entered the Convent of Mercy secretly by the roof, they found José Bullain and killed him. They returned again and found José Ibaraquen, who was dressed as a woman, dragged him out of the arms of his wife, and cut him to pieces even though his wife asked Rodríguez to pardon him.

They also sacked and robbed the Convent of St. Augustine. Then outside in the streets they saw Agustín Arregui, whom they wished to kill as a European. He said, "I am not a chapetón, but a Creole. Enter the convent where there are five chapetones with arms." They took him along to make sure that he was telling the truth, and when they did not find the Europeans, they killed him. Later they discovered three Spaniards and a Frenchman, dressed in habits of the religious order, and murdered them.

They searched the Convent of St. Dominic diligently four times and obtained buried jewels, money, and wrought silver. They found the treasury official, Parrilla, hiding in the building, and dragged him out to the plaza. Fortunately, someone recognized that he was a Creole. He was saved, but the Indians left him without clothing. José Caballero, an unfortunate European, had escaped in the garb of an Indian and hid among them until midnight of February 14; then someone saw through his disguise and took him to Rodríguez, who pretended not to know him. Caballero

[13] Odriozola, *Documentos*, I, 21–23.
[14] AGN, Buenos Aires, VI-8-5-6, Leg. 2; *Revista de Archivos y Bibliotecas (Peruanas)*, Año III, Vol. V, 191.

claimed to be from Arequipa, but the rebels killed him just the same.[15]

Matters had reached a climax. The robberies now amounted to 2,000,000 pesos; even Europeans of near-by towns had been killed and their heads brought to Rodríguez. Finally, the five or six thousand guests in Oruro, who expected to be feasted, became burdensome. When there were no more houses of Europeans to rob, they demanded money from the native inhabitants and threatened to sack their homes. The town leaders hastened to consult about how to expel the Indians. Since there was no money to buy them off, they decided to get it from the royal treasury. They proposed to Rodríguez that the Indians should be given one peso each to keep them from attacking the treasury. At last the treasury officials, who had been in hiding, were found and handed over the keys to the chief justice. He and the priest took 25,000 pesos out of the treasury, although they were authorized to use only 10,000.

They then went to the camp where the Indians waited. The priest thanked them in the name of the people for defending the town, and told them that if they would return to their homes, each would receive a peso and that the other funds would be kept in the treasury for King Túpac Amaru. When the Indians asked whether they would get the Spaniards' lands, Rodríguez answered, "Yes, and in the future you need not pay the tribute, the diezmos, or first fruits of the church."

The distribution of the money caused great confusion. No record was kept of how much was spent or to whom it had been given. After the Indians were paid, there was a surplus of 2,500 pesos in a bag, but it is not known whether anybody returned it to the treasury. When the Indians entered the town again under the pretext of getting their belongings, they and the inhabitants publicly proclaimed allegiance to Túpac Amaru as their king. At that time an Indian arrived from Tinta saying that he had been sent by Túpac Amaru. He told Jacinto Rodríguez that the Inca ordered

15 Odriozola, *Documentos*, I, 23–24; Relación de los hechos mas notables acaecidos en la sublevación general . . . , 61–62 (MS copy in B. L.); Carrió, *op. cit.*, 89–90.

him to have more respect for temples and priests and not to harm the Creoles; chapetones only were to be persecuted.

Rodríguez decided that all the Spaniards should wear Indian costume and soon appeared dressed in black velvet ornamented with gold. He declared that everybody would be victims of the Indians unless they followed his example, for they would be considered Europeans. Then a great transformation occurred in the town, when the men adopted the uncu of the natives and the ladies took off their elegant short skirts and donned the long ones of Indian women.

The change in costume did not induce the Indians to stop their plundering. They continued drinking and that night visited the house of Joaquín Rubín de Celis, a wealthy European who had been spared the sacking because he was a friend of Rodríguez and had put up a white banner over his door. Since the banner had been removed in proclaiming the name of Túpac Amaru, his house was now robbed.[16]

The same disorders lasted during February 15 and increased when news came that the Indians of Challapata were approaching. The people went out into the country to receive them as usual, but only forty of their leaders arrived. At the head of them came Juan de Dios Rodríguez, accompanied by Mariano Lope Chungara, cacique of Challapata, and other chiefs from Paria. As soon as they entered the plaza, Rodríguez ordered the bells to be rung and afterwards took the visitors to his home, where they were feasted. The guests said that they had come to aid the town and had forty thousand Indians for its defense. When they passed the post office, they took down the arms of King Charles III from above the door.

Next day, when the commotion increased, the inhabitants were thoroughly disgusted. They decided to expel the Indians by force if they would not leave voluntarily. The natives wanted to remain, and spent their time asking owners of haciendas for land and

---

[16] Odriozola, *Documentos*, I, 23–25; Relación de los hechos mas notables acaecidos en la sublevación general . . . , 61–64 (MS copy in B. L.); *Revista de Archivos y Bibliotecas (Peruanas)*, Año III, V, 193–95; Carrió, *op. cit.*, 90–91.

remuneration. Fearing to lose their lives, the owners gave them money and signed over their property to them. Thus the Indians became the possessors of the town and grew bold. Juan de Dios Rodríguez spoke kindly to them and advised them to go home, but this insulted them. One threatened him and was immediately put to death, after which they withdrew temporarily.

That night many returned and sacked the shop of Francisco Polo, a Creole. He hurried off to find Jacinto Rodríguez and asked redress for such an outrage. Then the Rodríguez brothers, with the help of the cacique of Challapata, who ordered all the Indians resisting to be killed, finally settled the disturbance. Treaties of alliance and mutual defense were signed between the townsmen and the people of Challapata. Juan de Dios thus helped to establish peace in Oruro, although he had caused the uprising in Challapata, the death of Corregidor Manuel Bodega, and many other acts of violence there.[17]

Jacinto Rodríguez ordered the Indians to return all articles stolen from the chapetones. Part of the people, led by a man named Torreadorcito, opposed his order, but he was soon arrested. The Indians then attacked the prison and even the home of the Rodríguez family; they were repulsed and Torreadorcito was put to death.[18] On the seventeenth, the chief justice sent men outside the walls to see if the Indians had left the booty, and they found a considerable portion of it. Then the division of the spoils prompted a serious dispute and almost caused another uprising.

The Rodríguez faction still tried to dominate affairs and spread false reports to keep the Creoles under control. It was alleged that in La Paz and Potosí the Creoles and Indians had united and killed all the Europeans, and therefore there was no more work for them to do. The clergy also aided in restoring peace and, carrying sacred images, marched through the streets. The priest then went up to the cabildo gallery and urged the people to repent and ask pardon for their crimes. He finally absolved them on condition that they

---

[17] Odriozola, *Documentos*, I, 25–26; Relación de los hechos mas notables acaecidos en la sublevación general . . . , 64–65. MS copy in B. L.

[18] Lewin, *op. cit.*, 295.

would not continue their excesses. After that day peace was restored again.[19]

About this time Tiburcio Ríos, a representative from Chayanta, came to Oruro and asked for orders from Túpac Amaru in connection with the war against the Spaniards. He wanted to know when the Inca would be in Oruro. Rodríguez told him "in the month of May," and gave him some documents signed by his clerk, Josef Contreras. Later Ríos was arrested, and two documents were found among his possessions, but only one was signed by Jacinto Rodríguez and witnessed by Contreras. It mentioned Catari's name and said that he had ordered the people not to pay the tribute. "All the places notified—this town and the others of the province, Antequera, Popó, the others near by, and Chayanta—must comply with this command. This advice is given until the return of our monarch." Evidently Túpac Amaru was the person alluded to as monarch.[20]

Even the expulsion of the Indians from Oruro did not bring a rupture with the movement of Túpac Amaru. Their resentment at being driven out of Oruro no doubt was the reason for the killing of the Inca's ambassador. They also put to death Pagador, the cholo, who first harangued them in the name of Túpac Amaru, because he had killed an Indian during the distribution of the money from the royal treasury. Jacinto Rodríguez did not intervene to save him. Later, in his confession, Juan de Dios said that the chief justice had told him that he governed for Túpac Amaru. At least his brother had been confirmed in office by the rebel multitude in the name of the Inca.[21]

The situation changed when, on March 9, 1781, the first invasion of the Indians of Sillota, Paria, and the neighboring estates occurred. They had killed the cacique, Lope Chungara. Then they turned against Jacinto Rodríguez, who had trusted them,

[19] Relación de los hechos mas notables acaecidos en la sublevación general . . . , 65–66 (MS copy in B. L.); Odriozola, *Documentos,* I, 26–27.

[20] AGN, Buenos Aires, Criminales, Leg. 18, exp. 3, in Lewin, *op. cit.,* 296–97.

[21] Confesión de José Manuel Montesinos, AGN, Buenos Aires, Revolución de Oruro, VI–8–5–6, Leg. 2; Confesión de Juan de Dios Rodríguez, *loc. cit.* VI–8–5–5, Leg. 1 (cited by Lewin, *op. cit.,* 297).

struck at his door, and shouted that they had come for his head. It was therefore necessary to summon the militia to drive them back, and sixty were killed. The natives changed their tone toward Rodríguez when they withdrew, and declared that they would come to his aid if he summoned them. The Indians next began to collect from the neighboring provinces and brought the silver stolen from Oruro; they occupied the roads and cut off supplies for the town. In one of the expeditions, sent out to open the roads, the cacique of Oruro and his purveyor were cruelly killed. This angered the people of the town so much that they hurried out and burned Paria.

Rumors spread that the Indians intended to destroy Oruro. On March 18 at dawn, Indians from the province of Oruro, the greater part of those from Paria, and some from Carangas and Pacajes surrounded the town, until six or seven thousand natives were seen on the hills of San Felipe and Tetilla. The greatest anxiety reigned in the town. Skirmishes were fought, which drove the Indians back temporarily, but they always obtained reinforcements and returned to the hills. This time when the people of Oruro saw the multitude of Indians, they decided to forgive the Europeans, who were still in hiding, and asked them to come to their assistance. Nineteen men appeared, who were embraced and welcomed, but about half of them proved to be useless for war because of age or infirmities. Finally after the Europeans and townspeople killed fourteen Indians and put the head of one of their captains on the point of a lance, the natives respected them.[22]

The enemy were carefully watched until dawn of the nineteenth. No action was taken until the greater part of the Indians crowded onto the hill of San Pedro near the town. The Orureños wanted to attack, but the priest persuaded them to wait and see what would happen. The commander and three or four persons then cut off a party of one hundred Indians, who had come to join the others, and killed fifteen. The event inspired such terror among

---

[22] Odriozola, *Documentos*, I, 27–28; Relación de los hechos mas notables acaecidos en la sublevación general . . . , 66–69 (MS copy in B. L.); *Revista de Archivos y Bibliotecas (Peruanas)*, Año III, Vol. V, 198; Angelis, *Documentos*, 29.

the enemy that in the night they abandoned the hill. On the following day not an Indian was seen, but they soon came out to attack any stray persons they could reach.

The freed Europeans aided in defending Oruro; six thousand cartridges were made, weapons collected, and militia organized. Almost every day soldiers marched out into the country to search for enemy forces. Even the priest, Patricio Gabriel Menéndez, formed a detachment of churchmen and led them to the combat. The Indians of Challaocollo, Popó, Sorasora, and Antequera asked pardon, after 120 of them were killed; but those of Paria and Sillotas remained obstinate.

Another conspiracy against the Europeans was planned by Domingo de Ramos. It did not materialize, however, for the troops under José de Ayarza, who had gone out of Cochabamba a month before and defeated the Indians of Colcha, had received notice that Oruro suffered on account of the Indians and lacked supplies. Ayarza decided to aid the town and fortunately appeared on the very day that the new conspiracy was to break out. The chief justice tried to prevent his entrance, but the commander quartered his troops near the town. Then Rodríguez had to welcome him. With the arrival of Ayarza the loyal vassals of the King had the satisfaction of seeing the royal arms and the sovereign's portrait put up again on the balcony of the Rodríguez house. Ayarza remained for three days and then returned to Cochabamba, leaving provisions. As soon as he was out of sight, the King's arms were taken down a second time by the disloyal faction.[23]

Later, after the death of the Inca, Andrés Túpac Amaru sent edicts and letters to Oruro. In a letter of September 5, 1781, he said that he was well satisfied with the way the wishes of José Gabriel and Diego Túpac Amaru, Tomás and Julián Túpac Catari, and himself had been carried out there. He acknowledged Jacinto Rodríguez, Manuel de Herrera, Diego Flores, and Fulano Rocha as followers of the Inca and as wise men. He sent the rector, Fran-

---

[23] *Relación de los hechos mas notables acaecidos en la sublevación general . . . ,* 69–71. MS copy in L. L. Odriozola, *Documentos,* I, 28, 31; see also the AGN, Buenos Aires, Legajos sobre la Revolución de Oruro.

cisco de Miranda y Montoya, an edict which he and the four persons mentioned in it were to transmit to the inhabitants of Oruro. It concerned punishing and removing corregidores and their followers, abolishing customs dues and the frauds of quicksilver distribution in Potosí, and ruining the chapetones.[24]

The people of Oruro, who had committed such great misdemeanors, were all, except the instigators, later included in the general pardon. On January 20, 1784, Colonel Sebastián de Segurola marched there with a detachment of soldiers to arrest certain individuals. The most notable among them were Jacinto and Juan de Dios Rodríguez, Diego Flores, Manuel de Herrera, Fulano Rocha, and Clemente Machado, all persons of wealth and importance in the town. Segurola took them, well guarded, to Potosí, where they were kept for some time in the public prison. Early in March they were sent to Buenos Aires by order of the viceroy, the Marquis of Loreto, who was quite lenient with them, only Herrera being executed.[25] Juan de Dios Rodríguez was kept in confinement for twenty years, and died soon after he was set free.[26]

Potosí might have suffered the same fate as Oruro if it had not been for the active measures of its governor, Jorge Escogedo. He summoned and disciplined the militia, organized cavalry and artillery forces, collected supplies and armaments, carefully patrolled the region, and ordered the approaches to the town to be cut off by trenches. In this manner he saved the rich mining city.[27]

Various opinions have been expressed about sedition in Oruro and how it began. Some people attributed it to the treason of the Europeans and others to the wickedness of the Orureños. The latter alleged that the corregidor was their enemy, that he gave their firearms to the chapetones to destroy them, and that there was a cellar in the barracks filled with powder to blow them up. In truth, the cellar was nothing more than an ancient drain. The corregidor

[24] Carta de Andrés Túpac Amaru al rector Don Francisco de Miranda y Montoya, La Paz, September 5, 1781, AGN, Buenos Aires, División colonia, Sección gobierno, VI–VIII–5–6 (published by Lewin, *op. cit.*, 475–76).

[25] Relación de los hechos mas notables acaecidos en la sublevación general . . . , 229. MS copy in B. L.

[26] Temple, *op. cit.*, 31.

[27] Valcárcel, *La rebelión de Túpac Amaru*, 132.

had collected firearms in order to distribute them at the proper time. And the soldiers did not lack weapons, for they already had knives and lances, which they used later in killing the Europeans. As there were thousands of Orureños and only forty-five Europeans, the argument that the latter were trying to surprise them in the barracks was also weak. It is certain that Jacinto Rodríguez and other Creole leaders of the town had a hand in the rebellion. It is also known that copies of Túpac Amaru's edicts were scattered among the people. To save themselves if the revolt should be successful, it seemed advisable for the leaders to cast their lot with the Inca. They therefore showed all the hatred they could for the Europeans, exaggerated the stories of their wealth, received the Indians as friends and allies, and condescended to dress like them and even chew coca leaves.

It is obvious that the Creoles used the Indians as pawns to gain their ends and claimed allegiance to Túpac Amaru to win the support of the natives. The Oruro uprising was thus not really a part of the big Inca rebellion, but primarily a Creole revolt. The Indians thought, however, that the revolt was connected with the larger movement, and the Inca leader counted the Orureños among his followers.

CHAPTER VII

Resistance in Cochabamba

Tʜᴇ ᴘʀᴏᴠɪɴᴄᴇ ᴏꜰ Cᴏᴄʜᴀʙᴀᴍʙᴀ, a food-growing area for the mining industry, was also influenced by the disturbances in Chayanta, Oruro, and elsewhere. The malice of the Indians became so great that they not only destroyed the isolated towns of those provinces, but also stirred up the neighboring regions. Thus Cochabamba could not escape, since the influence of Túpac Amaru spread to the most remote parts of Peru and to many areas in the viceroyalty of La Plata.

As in other districts, the first disturbances in Cochabamba, on April 6, 1780, began with lampoons. Written satires against officials were posted at night on public buildings. Three of these, with identical contents, began thus:

> Long live the King and destruction to bad government! My beloved countrymen, how long shall we endure the violence which we suffer? How long shall we sleep in this confused abyss of oppressions, robberies, and thieves?

Although the anonymous author pretended that the movement was spontaneous and mentioned events in Arequipa, Cuzco, and La Paz as influencing him, the truth was quite different.

Cochabamba had a revolutionary organization months before the lampoons appeared. Armed persons who spoke of casting off the tyranny that oppressed them held nightly meetings. Andrés de los Ríos, a priest, reported that one night, before the posters appeared, many people passed through the streets and he heard them say that they expected to resist the government and throw off its oppressive yoke. Friar José Bustillos said that more than seven penitents had confessed to him that the plotters had assembled the night of Holy Thursday to strike the first blow at the royal treasuries and take the funds. Various women also reported the plot to Friar Bustillos. Many citizens heard the tramping of people on foot and the clatter of horses' hooves in the streets. There must have been constant activity on the part of the conspirators for some weeks before the open cabildo met on April 7 and temporarily closed the customhouse. The people must have been on the verge of rebelling or the town council never would have taken this drastic measure.[1]

People came to Cochabamba from the neighboring regions that were in revolt. When Phelipe Ayaviri, cacique of the town of Sacaca, heard of the revolution in Chayanta, he hastened to Cochabamba with his family; and crowds of Indians pursued him as far as Arque and Colcha. Then the corregidor of Cochabamba, Felipe José de Villalobos, decided to check such disturbances by sending out a party of six hundred soldiers under José de Ayarza to investigate the ravages in the province. That commander marched through the ravine of Arque in search of the enemy, who waited for him near the town of Colcha. A battle ensued in which the Indians resisted boldly, but were finally put to flight.

The Indians of Cochabamba refused to pay the royal tribute in December, declaring, however, that by Ash Wednesday every real of it would be collected, if it had to be paid. Evidently they expected the revolts in the other provinces to spread to their own. The corregidor, who did not wish to use pressure, was lenient with them. He was willing, however, to help check the disturbances in neighboring provinces when, on January 21, 1781, he received a letter from Commandant Ignacio Flores in La Plata declaring that intervention was needed in Chayanta to stop the excesses of the Indians, which grew worse every day. Flores said that he would aid the province by recruiting troops in Sacaca, the cost of which could be met by the royal treasury. Although the treasury officials did not want to furnish the money, the corregidor urged them to do so and began to make military preparations. Iron lances and leather shields were made and measures taken to defend the capital, which had only eighteen unserviceable guns. Since only Ignacio

[1] AGN, Buenos Aires, Criminales, Leg. 17, exp. 24 (cited by Lewin, *op. cit.*, 64–66); *Revista de Archivos y Bibliotecas (Peruanas)*, Año III, Vol. V, 204.

Muñoz had had any military experience, he was appointed commander. Then the people waited patiently for Flores, who did not come.

At that time Francisco Paula Sanz, director of the tobacco monopoly, was in Cochabamba. To obtain more revenue from the monopoly, he fixed the price of twenty-four cigars at one real. This caused great dissatisfaction among the common people, who published at night satires against the tobacco employees. They accused them of disobeying the King, burdening the poor with unjust contributions, and preferring the friendship of the rich. Such actions aroused great anxiety in Corregidor Villalobos, the cabildo, and the inhabitants generally because of what had happened in Oruro. An open cabildo meeting was therefore held to find means to calm the lower classes, at which it was decided to increase the number of cigars to forty for a half-real and to sell tobacco at the former price. This brought a temporary peace.

Soon Corregidor Urrutia and other officials of Oruro came fleeing to Cochabamba and caused great excitement. Then on February 15 authorities in neighboring regions asked the corregidor of Cochabamba for aid again, but it could not be granted on account of turbulent conditions in his own capital.[2]

Meanwhile, many Indians hoisted their banners on the heights of Quirquiavi and proclaimed Túpac Amaru their leader. They sent ambassadors to arm all the Indians of that region and then approached the parish of Colcha on February 21. They took vengeance upon all persons who failed to join them. They killed the assistant priest of the parishes adjoining Quirquiavi and Tocopaya and many other inhabitants, whom they dragged out of the sanctuary where they had sought refuge. They next went down to the town of Colcha, where they killed the priest's two servants and broke his head open with the blow of a stone. They continued their outrages until they reached Arque, where they also did much damage.

Juan Fernando Pacheco, the corregidor's lieutenant, attempted

[2] Relación de los hechos mas notables acaecidos en la sublevación general . . . , 72–75. MS copy in B. L. Odriozola, *Documentos*, I, 31.

to defend the territory with the faithful inhabitants, but, unfortunately, the leaders appointed to put down the disturbances proved to be unfaithful. They committed robberies, profaned churches, and killed all persons who resisted them. They deposed priests, chose others for their positions, and appointed Pedro Salamanca chief justice. Their outrageous acts continued for ten days, and then, after having completely corrupted the Indians, they withdrew to Colcha. With the natives corrupted, many other places in the province and at the mine of Choquecamata suffered the same calamities.

Quick and effective measures had to be taken in the town of Cochabamba to calm the populace. The free use of tobacco was therefore permitted on February 24, in the King's name. In the afternoon clamorous noise accompanied by the ringing of the cabildo bell gave the alarm that invaders were entering the town. The confused shouting was unbearable. Shortly more than five thousand men congregated in the main plaza, while in the fields outside the town a large number of people on horseback were assembled, and among them the women and children suddenly appeared to be armed. But when a detachment of soldiers went outside the walls to search for the enemy and find out which road they had taken, they could not be found.

Corregidor Villalobos was on the alert. The day before the commotion, he had ordered 450 men under José de Ayarza to march without delay to the towns of Caraza, Ytapaya, and Charamoco to punish traitors. Ayarza killed in skirmishes more than 160 of them and hanged others. When he entered Capinota, he found the Indians apparently quite peaceful; therefore he camped on the hacienda of Vinto near the town of Arque. There he again had encounters with the Indians from Colcha, who had united with many others from the provinces of Paria, Sacaca, Acasio, and other towns in the province of Chayanta.

At the same time he received word of the general uprising in all the towns of the province and of the killings and robberies in them. Friar Santos de la Rea, assistant priest, and other persons told him that many Indians had gathered on the heights of the

161

town of Tapacarí, intending to enter it, and that a few days before this Francisco de Mendoza, the corregidor's lieutenant, the alcalde mayor, most of the Spanish inhabitants, and even the caciques had fled. The Indians entered the town on February 25 while the priest was celebrating mass. Showing no respect for him, they dashed through the church and cruelly killed more than four hundred people inside and outside the building. Discovering a man hidden behind the high altar with his wife and children, they killed the whole family. They planned to bury Spanish women alive, and dug a ditch in the plaza for that purpose.

Similar outrages were committed in Palca. At the foot of the altar the Indians killed the priest, José de Arnao, with the sacrament in his hands. And four hundred other persons perished in the church. An Indian woman ran through the streets with the consecrated Host in her hands, crying that the priest had made it from flour she had brought from the valley and then pretended it was a sacrament. Such blasphemies were common during the revolt. At Calliri, at other less protected places along the roads, and on the haciendas the revolutionists robbed and put to death many unfortunate persons.[3]

The Indians took possession of the beautiful Clisa Valley, noted for its fertility, abundance of grain, mild climate, and healthful waters. The valley included the parishes of Tarata and Punata, with 860 Indians in the first and 700 in the second. These people, who were strong, robust farmers, were scattered over the Spaniards' haciendas, some as day laborers and a few as yanaconas, but most as muleteers. The same rebellious spirit was infused into these peaceful people as into the others, and they decided to put to death their masters, patrons, and any persons they disliked.

In the center of the valley on the hacienda of Clisa, which belonged to the monastery of Santa Clara, unlawful meetings were held. There the Indian captains, Marcos Churata and Manuel Colque, decided to kill the overseer, Canchero, and other officers

[3] Relación de los hechos mas notables acaecidos en la sublevación general . . . , 75–77 (MS copy in B. L.); Odriozola, *Documentos*, I, 29–30; Lorente, *Historia del Peru bajo los Borbones*, 185–86; Carrió, *op. cit.*, 92–93.

on the estate. Fortunately, Antonio Luján, provincial alcalde, Manuel de Villarroel, alcalde of the Santa Hermandad (or brotherhood, which summarily tried and executed criminals), the corregidor's lieutenant, Miguel Sainz, and certain other officials appeared unexpectedly. They quickly overthrew the natives. No part of the valley was free from fighting, but only one Spaniard perished. The ministers of justice then had to use their influence to keep the Spaniards from exterminating the Indians.[4] In the towns of Punata and Arandi many of the Indian leaders were hanged, while in skirmishes out in the country many other natives lost their lives. Just as everything seemed to be quiet, trouble broke out in Paredón, a sub-parish of Tarata, where the Indians killed the Spaniards.

The valley of Quillacolla, including the four towns of Quillacolla, Sipesipe, Paso, and Tiguipaya, suffered minor calamities. When the cacique of Paso publicly declared that he recognized Túpac Amaru as king, the loyal inhabitants killed him instantly. The corregidor's lieutenant then raised some militias in that region, to which were added three cavalry companies under Pedro Gari. The soldiers surrounded the rebels in Sipesipe and took them prisoner; but, after they were convicted by their governor, Ventura Mamani, the Spaniards took pity on them and decided merely to disarm them. As a result, only nine were put to death, while others were whipped or punished in various other ways. Both Spanish commanders resolved to overthrow the enemy near the rugged mountain of Targuani. They went down to the town of Calliri with 700 soldiers and volunteers, hoping to rescue many women from captivity in that town. They arrived at Calliri too late, finding it strewn with corpses. Only forty rebels were put to death.

When the troops hastened their march, the Indians attacked them on the rugged edges of the ravine in Milloma. There the Indians were checked and more than 150 of them killed. The rest of the terrified rebels united with 300 others who waited for the Spanish troops in Cambuyo, four leagues above the ravine on the road to Tapacarí. It was difficult terrain for a battle, as it was narrow and steep, with numerous crevices. In the bloody struggle

[4] *Relación de los hechos mas notables acaecidos en la sublevación general* . . . , 83–85. MS copy in B. L.

that ensued more than 500 Indians perished. The fact that the Spaniards were victorious, although the insurgents had the advantageous position, plainly demonstrated the inequality of the arms of the two contending forces.

Finally overcoming the difficulties of the transit, the Spaniards reached the town of Tapacarí. The Indians opposed their entrance, but the royalists forced their way into the town, killed three hundred insurgents, and set free a number of persons condemned to be buried alive that very day (March 3). On the outer wall of the cemetery the Spaniards found a paper, signed by Carlos Silvestre Manco Túpac, which read in part:

> My beloved countrymen and compatriots . . . I advise you that our monarch, Don José Gabriel Túpac Amaru . . . does not wish to harm the Catholic religion, but desires to suppress disorder . . . after having taken those means considered fit for the preservation and tranquility of the Spanish Creoles, mestizos, Zambos, and Indians.

It went on to exhort the people not to obey the judges of the province.

From February 24 to March 8, the Indians swarmed like locusts through the towns and doctrinas of Machaca and near-by places, robbing and killing the people. Even then their anger was not appeased, and they executed a priest and robbed his church.[5]

At the beginning of the uprising Carlos de Valencia, lieutenant of the district, had come to the provincial capital and asked for men and arms for its defense because the inhabitants had fled in terror. Corregidor Villalobos aided him promptly by sending out a detachment under Ambrosio Yañez de Montenegro, which soon joined the Lieutenant and some of his fugitive people. Another group commanded by Ignacio Muñoz marched out armed with hurriedly made lances. As these arms were insufficient, the soldiers used *chicotes,* Indian weapons made of ropes twisted together like a cable and used like clubs. When the first expedition arrived in Machaca, it found the Indians celebrating their triumph.

[5] *Ibid.,* 77–80.

A bloody encounter soon took place in which eighty insurgents were killed. Expecting the bulk of the enemy to attack any moment, Montenegro withdrew to the town of Chinchiri and sent word to the second detachment to hurry. The two military forces united on March 12 in Santa Rosa, where the Indians chose to make their stand because of the ruggedness of the mountain ridge. The royalists had to ascend the ridge from the side of the Santa Rosa River, but fortunately managed to do so without detection. The Spaniards won the battle that ensued in a few hours. They killed more than three hundred Indians and then advanced five leagues, leaving the corpses of fleeing enemies all along the way until they arrived at Palca. The sight that met their eyes there was awful. The church contained the dead bodies of four hundred men, women, and children, stacked one above the other, even on the altars; the priest, clad in his sacred vestments, had been torn in pieces.

All the provinces now burned with civil war. The military forces were not prepared for defense, although lances were made as rapidly as possible. The corregidor raised companies of infantry and cavalry and appointed as officers Pedro Ramón de Arauo for the valley of Punata, Juan Ventura Ferrufino for Tarata, and Pedro de la Via y Maldonado for the capital; he gave the last named the title of governor-at-arms. At the same time the cabildo of Cochabamba chose four suitable persons as alcaldes of the Santa Hermandad. Trenches were dug in strategic places in the capital, patrols and sentinels distributed, soldiers enlisted, and a company of noblemen organized to remain under arms and come to the cabildo at the first signal of danger.

Lack of money was a great hindrance to military preparations. The 11,000 pesos in the treasury and 4,000 given by the alcalde mayor of Tapacarí were used as a beginning. As the sum was insufficient, a council meeting had to be held, at which it was decided to ask the national government for guns. So much enthusiasm was shown in the council that one man offered to conquer the rebellious towns of Tiguipaya and Paso and put the Indians to the knife with only fifty armed men. This was rash boasting, as the towns had been surrounded by Indians for a long time and the caciques and leaders co-operated with the besiegers. Furthermore, three hundred natives of the Sacava Valley communicated with those towns by the same mountain ridge and helped to increase the number of rebels. The two chiefs in the valley were Esteban and Pedro Gutiérrez, father and son, capable men who had some education, and some wealth. They began their revolt by putting up a lampoon in the town of Sacava to summon the insurgents, but the priest, Domingo Sempertegui, used his influence and kept the insurrection from becoming serious.[6]

Meanwhile, the brave soldiers, victorious at Tapacarí and Ayopaya, marched toward the capital. Some were barefooted and others in Indian dress. Fifty men got separated from the detachment of Tapacarí and took another road through the heights, where a considerable number of Indians attacked them. They fought desperately for a whole day without food, but finally saved themselves with the loss of only twelve men and left fifty dead Indians along the way. They had scarcely reached Cochabamba when news came that the Indians were holding a junta on the heights of Tapacarí to unite all the forces possible to repeat their attacks on the towns near the provinces of Sicasica, Paria, Carangas, and Chayanta. Reports also came from Ayopaya that the Indians were doing the same in the town of Cavari and other places in the province of Chulumani. Two more expeditions were therefore sent against the rebels. When the first, under Commander Gari, reached Tapacarí, it found in that town and its deep ravines an Indian army protected by moats and trenches. The courageous natives had improvised armor by covering their bodies above the waist with rawhide, and were provided with shields and lances which they managed with dexterity. The battle lasted most of the day, but finally the insurgents were decisively defeated. Fleeing, they were forced to leave four hundred dead and some captives. The Spaniards lost forty men killed, and many others were dangerously wounded.

The second expedition, led by Marzelo Pérez, which marched

6 *Ibid.*, 80–83.

166

to the province of Chulumani, was not so successful, likely because of dissension among the officers. The brave soldiers, however, managed to save the army, defeat the Indians at the cost of many wounded, and set free three captive priests.

After the withdrawal of both detachments, the Indians of Macha sent the corregidor word of their repentance and professed obedience. He gladly answered the letter and exhorted them to be peaceful.[7]

While these exploits were underway in the province, the judges in the capital were employed in punishing rebels. Every day guilty persons were executed. The Indians went to their death calmly, as if going to a banquet; one of them even ate at the foot of the gallows. This fortitude seemed to stem from the common belief that the dead would be resurrected when Túpac Amaru established his kingdom. In the town of Sipesipe, Captain Antonio Lizarazu was also busy putting conspirators to death. There was hardly a post, plain, or road where parts of bodies were not hanging to show that justice had been carried out.

The capital was stirred when Father Martínez de Tineo, the wounded priest of Colcha, appeared. The rebels had broken open his head because he said that he would give fifty lashes to any Indian who did not want to learn the Christian doctrine. He had placed a medal of the Virgin of Copacabana in the wound and now walked through the streets of Cochabamba, shouting, "Where are the loyalty and religion of the Cochabambinos, who do not prevent such injuries and sacrifices? Look how ministers of the sanctuary are treated! Do not believe the vain offers of the traitor, Túpac Amaru! You shall all be victims of his tyrannous ambition, because his purpose is to shed all Spanish blood." The priest thus moved the minds of the vascillating about to join the rebels.

Shortly a desire for revenge caused commotion in the streets and plazas. As a result, the detachment of 400 men under Captain Ayarza was increased to 1,100 infantrymen and cavalrymen. They marched out of Cochabamba to inflict retaliation on the Indians of Colcha. This expedition was one of the most important because

[7] *Ibid.*, 85–87.

in a two months' campaign the Spanish Army was victorious, killing about 1,500 Indians while losing only 12 royalists. So many chiefs and sacrilegious women, who had co-operated in putting priests to death, were shot and hanged in the towns of Colcha, Quirquiavi, Tocopaya, Sacaca, and others that the inhabitants came humbly in numerous groups, knelt down, and asked pardon. Finally commerce and communication were opened again with the town of Oruro.

At this time Thadeo de Arze, a hacendado in Veuchi, informed the corregidor of another danger spot. He said that between Caraza and Capinota on the mountains near Tapacarí and Arque the rebels had met and appointed a captain. An expedition soon overthrew them, killed about seventy Indians, and set fire to all their supplies.

The province of Cochabamba was one of the objectives of Túpac Amaru, who made many attempts to take it. Consequently, always some part of it was in turmoil, and people in areas thought to be pacified rebelled again. Notice soon came to the capital concerning the disastrous events in the provinces of Yungas and Chulumani, where all the people, the corregidor, José de Albizuri, and ten priests had been captured. Then Corregidor Villalobos ordered Commandant Juan de Ormachea to take his volunteer troop of four hundred men without delay to investigate the situation; at the same time another small detachment was being prepared in the capital under Yañez de Montenegro, but it was not used because in a few days a letter came from Corregidor Albizuri, saying that he was marching to Cochabamba with more than five thousand inhabitants of his province.[8]

Then it was reported that the Indians of the heights of Tapacarí, Challa, Tallija, Legue, and other towns, who had been punished with the lash and in other ways, had reinforced their party and formed a treasury with the funds stolen in Oruro and other places. The corregidor therefore, on April 27, sent out a detachment under Pedro de Zerro, which was to be incorporated in the

[8] *Ibid.*, 87–90; Odriozola, *Documentos*, I, 29; Lorente, *Historia del Peru bajo los Borbones*, 186–87.

Quillacolla Valley with fourteen infantry and cavalry companies. They were to join with three or four companies of Indians from the three other towns in the valley, so that the force would total more than one thousand men. This battalion went out of Quillacolla on the thirtieth, and on May 3 arrived at Tapacarí. Although the Indians attacked it in different areas, they were defeated and about three hundred of them killed.

The expedition then marched to the town of Mohoza in the province of Sicasica, where a number of faithful Indians, many priests, and Spaniards had asked aid. With the entrance of the troops many evils were remedied. Montenegro was appointed commandant and judge, peace was supposedly restored, and the expedition returned to Cochabamba. Meanwhile Esteban Barbeito, priest of the doctrina of Ynguisivi in the province of that same name, sent reports to the capital of Cochabamba of the outrages committed upon his Spanish and Indian parishioners. The expedition of one thousand men, under Lieutenant Carlos de Valencia, went out again on May 17, 1781, without waiting for preparations or pay, to check the boldness of the rebels. It came to the aid of Commandant Montenegro, who had been defeated in the town of Cavari, set free some priests and captives, and put the rebels to flight.

Another letter imploring aid reached Cochabamba. It reported that the enemy were attacking in different places, with Túpac Catari as leader. A letter from Commandant Ormachea, dated June 16, also told of the large number of enemy fighting near Palca. He related that when the soldiers reconnoitered the interior, they saw a man wearing a large crown of strange design who was accompanied by many Indians. Behind him walked many Spaniards, dressed in the same costume, who seemed to be captives. The chief fought furiously, obtained all the cattle and grain brought by the royalists, and killed some of the men, among them the faithful cacique Pasqual Calli. Thus it was necessary for the royalists to retreat to Chinchiri to seek aid. The Indian chief struck another blow at the towns of Cavari and Mohoza, desolated them, and killed the Spaniards who had remained. When eighty or ninety men came out from Calchani, the doctrina of Gharapaya, and other places to try to check him, most of them were killed.

Upon receipt of such bad news, a detachment of five hundred men was quickly raised in Tapacarí and the surrounding country. Gerónimo Mohedano, an experienced soldier, was appointed commander, and on May 20 went out to meet the enemy. At the same time Lieutenant Marcos Mercado of Quillacolla hastened to the Apopaya Valley with four infantry and cavalry companies and the two detachments. Later, when the Indians attacked the rich mine of Choquecamata, thirty leagues from the capital, Lieutenant Juan Postigo and Captain José de Pereyra raised one hundred soldiers for its relief, captured the leaders, and brought them to Cochabamba.[9]

Despite their many difficult problems in dealing with the Indian revolt, the people of Cochabamba were always willing to help other provinces. The corregidor appointed Ayarza for a third time to lead an expedition to be incorporated with Gavino Quevado's force in the middle of May. It consisted of one thousand infantrymen and cavalrymen of Cochabamba, volunteers from the Clisa Valley, Caraza, and other towns, and all the retinue possible. This poorly equipped body joined another group leaving Tarata on May 17, but the latter was not any better prepared. Quevado arrived at Oruro two days later, and without waiting for Ayarza, as had been ordered, left for La Paz on the twenty-first with all his people. He reached Sicasica at daybreak of the twenty-third and entered into combat with the Indians, who resisted a long time, although they did not have sufficient firearms and only three cannon. He then entered the plaza and repulsed the enemy, but the soldiers could not be restrained from plundering. Meanwhile, the insurgents regained their strength, renewed the battle, pursued the soldiers to Panduro, and let only thirty of them return to Oruro. Over three hundred royalists perished, including the best officers; and the enemy captured two fieldpieces, many guns, and ammunition.

9 Relación de los hechos mas notables acaecidos en la sublevacion general . . . , 90–94. MS copy in B. L.

Túpac Catari then boldly wrote to Ayarza, threatening to destroy him and his forces. He bragged that he had eleven thousand soldiers, and servants in addition, with which to defend himself. He said that since the Europeans of Peru wanted to be absolute rulers, he would punish them as traitors, since he was lord of the land and sea.

Ignorant of the disaster, Ayarza advanced toward the town of Sicasica. He was terrified at the sight he saw, for the field outside was strewn with corpses. It was necessary to withdraw to Oruro to obtain reinforcements before the army could go farther because Túpac Catari had cut off communications. At the beginning of June, Ayarza reached Cochabamba and raised five hundred recruits there and in the valleys of Clisa and Sacava; then he started out again to join Commandant General Flores, who was coming with troops from Buenos Aires.[10]

It can be seen thus that the province of Cochabamba was threatened in all directions by the uprising of Túpac Amaru and that the flame of revolution spread rapidly. At first it looked as if the province would go the way of others, but by desperate efforts Corregidor Villalobos managed to check the flame and preserve the loyalty of most of the inhabitants. He was even able to furnish troops to aid the neighboring province of La Paz, which was in a critical situation. The Cochabamba soldiers were brave, although hard to discipline because they loved plunder. They nevertheless played an important part in protecting their strategic province— which Túpac Amaru wanted on his side—and thereby shortened the revolution.

[10] *Ibid.*, 98–102.

CHAPTER VIII

Auxiliary Expedition from Buenos Aires

THE WHOLE NORTHWESTERN PART of the viceroyalty of La Plata was stirred up by the rebellion of Túpac Amaru. It was necessary, therefore, to dispatch troops from Buenos Aires, La Plata, and elsewhere to pacify the area. Never before had there been such a large insurrection in South America or one that covered so much territory.

No armed movement broke out on the east coast, yet great uneasiness prevailed there also. In a letter of April 30, 1781, to José de Gálvez, Viceroy Vertíz said that if the British should come to Buenos Aires, he had no way to defend it except with a body of dissatisfied militia, vascillating in obedience and ready to imitate the Peruvians. He knew that the inhabitants of Córdoba were discontented and had protested the increased price of tobacco, but they did not follow the example of Peru. On the other hand, the Andean region from Jujuy to Mendoza, which had been influenced by Inca civilization before the Conquest, was deeply affected by the disturbances in Tinta. The Viceroy said that there the people "follow the bad example of the day, look with indifference upon the many horrors committed, and some with satisfaction."[1]

The harassed towns and provinces were glad to hear that forces with competent commanders were coming from the capital of the viceroyalty of La Plata. The first detachment ready to march consisted of two hundred veteran soldiers under Sebastián Sánchez, captain of infantry; and in a few days another, with the same number, started out. The commander in chief of the expedition, José Reseguín, left Montevideo with the greatest speed. Then, as soon as he obtained his instructions from the Viceroy, he departed from Buenos Aires, on February 19, 1781, hoping to overtake the

---

[1] Correspondencia Vertíz-Gálvez, 1781, Oficio 464 escrito en Montevideo, AGN, Buenos Aires (cited by Lewin, *op. cit.*, 303–304).

first detachment, which had left two months earlier. He caught up with it on March 13 at Los Colorados. Fugitives along the road assured him that the provinces of Chichas, Cinti, Lipés, and Porcó, between the city of La Plata and Potosí, were all involved in the uprising. This news was confirmed by the corregidor of Chayanta, Joaquín Alós, who had fled disguised as a Franciscan friar.

Fifty men deserted from the expedition when it crossed the province of Tucumán. That loss was made up by a company of militia from Salta, although the men had little military training. With these small detachments and little ammunition, Reseguín marched as rapidly as he could. On February 16, he arrived opportunely near the town of Moxos in the province of Chinchas. Antonio José de Iribarren, priest of Talina, came to meet him and told him of the ferment in the neighboring provinces and the difficulty of keeping his parishioners faithful.[2] He described the terror of the Spanish inhabitants when they saw the outrages committed by the Indians, mestizos, and cholos, who had united. He also reported that on March 6 the rebels had killed Francisco de Prado, the corregidor of the province of Chichas, and some of his dependents in the town of Tupiza.[3]

The author of that crime was Luis Lazo de la Vega, a very bold cholo, more Spanish than Indian, who was serving as sergeant of the militias. Prado had favored him, but he had exhibited the greatest ingratitude toward his benefactor by plotting to usurp command of the provinces of Chichas, Lipés, Cinti, and Porcó. He took advantage of the ferment stirred up by Túpac Amaru's edicts, the efforts to collect ammunition for the corregidor, and the plan to raise cholo and mestizo militias in Tupiza.

Lazo de la Vega persuaded his soldiers to obey his orders rather than those of the corregidor, and the Indians of the surrounding towns followed their example. When Prado learned what had happened, he could do nothing except seek refuge in his home with some of his followers. After Lazo de la Vega and his partisans

---

[2] Odriozola, *Documentos*, I, 32–33.
[3] Relación de los hechos mas notables acaecidos en la sublevación general . . . , 45. MS copy in B. L.

barricaded him there, the corregidor tried to break out on horse-back, but seeing that this was impossible, decided to defend him-self to the last. He began to shoot at the crowd from the doors and windows. The shooting continued until midnight, when some of his dependents had been killed and others were too fatigued to continue the defense. The rebels set fire to the house, causing the powder stored inside to explode and part of the wall to collapse. The Indian Nicolás Martínez then entered the corral, where he found the corregidor sitting stupefied in a corner. He beheaded him forthwith and drank a quantity of his blood. Prado might have saved himself if he had tried to flee sooner, but he did not want to abandon his possessions.

When the other insurgents learned that the corregidor was dead, they entered the house, sacked it, and committed many out-rages during the night. The Indians on the hacienda of Salo fol-lowed the example of those in Tupiza and attacked the owner, Salvador Paxsi, cutting off his head and taking his abundant pos-sessions.

Lazo de la Vega could control the Indians only by letting them commit such crimes. He now called himself governor and captain general of the province for Túpac Amaru, and sent out summons through his secretary, Fermín Aguirre, ordering the people to unite with him, contribute to the common defense, and do away with corrupt government and all forms of oppression.

The parish priest, José Dávalos, tried to calm the rebels by hum-ble supplications and prayers. But he obtained nothing more than the right to bury the corpses, which he did with great solemnity.[4] The following day the insurgents dug up Prado's body and took it out of the church with the intention of sending the head to La Plata. Agustín Solís, the faithful Indian governor of the town of Santiago de Cotagaita, however, obtained it and buried it in the church.[5]

When Reseguín heard of Prado's death, he wanted to hasten

[4] Odriozola, *Documentos*, I, 37–39; Angelis, *Documentos*, 270–71; *Revista de Archivos y Bibliotecas (Peruanas)*, Año 1900, Vol. V, 173.
[5] Carta de José de Reseguín á Juan José de Vertíz, virrey de Buenos Aires, Tupiza, March 18, 1781, in Odriozola, *Documentos*, I, 39, 347.

his march, even though the roads were steep and wound through many narrow passes where Indians obstructed them. He hesitated at first, for if his soldiers perished, the ruin of La Plata, Potosí, and other towns was certain because all communication between them and Tucumán and Buenos Aires had been cut off. Delay, on the other hand, was also dangerous since it encouraged seditious-minded persons. Moreover, Reseguín did not know the fate of La Plata and Potosí. Spanish fugitives, who had witnessed the outrages committed by the Indians, began arriving from all directions and reported that no one was safe; therefore Reseguín decided to conquer or die.

He allowed his troops to rest for some hours, while he conferred with the priest Iribarren concerning the best means to surprise Tupiza and capture Lazo de la Vega. When the parish of Mozo furnished two hundred mules, on March 16, 1781, Reseguín advanced toward the town of Moraya, three leagues distant on the royal road of Potosí. He decided not to change his orders to march to join General Flores and help save the city of La Plata. He sent men ahead to observe the movements of the enemy. Reaching Moraya safely, he ostensibly made preparations to spend the night there. Then, designating one officer and twenty soldiers to remain in camp under orders to keep the fires hidden, raise the camp at dawn, and follow him with the baggage and equipment, he crept out silently with the remainder of his forces and took the road to Tupiza.

In their orderly march the Spaniards eluded the vigilance of the enemies, so that on the following day the Indians could not imagine what had become of them. The road to Tupiza was very rough. Half of it traversed hills and precipices, and the other half a deep ravine, through which a river, which had to be forded many times, descended. Two leagues from Tupiza there was a pass, extending for a quarter of a league, bordered by high crags, forming a winding, narrow lane through which not more than two men could go abreast. The Indians knew the advantage of this type of terrain for an attack and always chose such positions.

The troops arrived safely at that natural fortress, but soon heard the noise of slings and saw stones falling from the heights. The commander, perceiving that the danger was inescapable, resolved to make a run for it. He ordered the soldiers to follow him quickly and negotiated the narrow lane without hindrance, emerging into a more spacious ravine. There Reseguín made his formation, extending the front part as far as the width of the road allowed. He divided his two hundred men into five divisions, putting four under command of veteran officers and the fifth, the largest, under himself, and instructed all to be silent until they arrived at Tupiza.[6] They reached there at four o'clock on the morning of the next day, March 17.

Reseguín intended first to capture the chief, Lazo de la Vega. Without waking the inhabitants of the town, he went to the chief's home and called his name, but was answered coldly because the man did not want to be disturbed. Finally Lazo de la Vega came to the door half-dressed, with a blunderbuss in his hand. He stood immovable, like a statue, when he saw the Spaniards, and could not even pull the trigger. They imprisoned him and also his secretary, Fermín Aguirre, a Spanish subject of rather high birth, who had been appointed viceroy of the province by the seditious party. Many other men were also taken. Then the soldiers examined the outskirts of the town for two leagues to find accomplices. By afternoon 160 of the principal members of the conspiracy were in prison. Reseguín took the greatest precaution to guard against a surprise attack to free the chiefs, placed double guards, sent out patrols, and summoned the militias of the towns of Suipacha and Tarija, which remained loyal because of the imprisonment of their chiefs and the terror infused in them by the royal arms.

Every day widows, orphans, and refugees arrived in Tupiza to tell the commander about their suffering. Some had lost fathers, husbands, and all their belongings. They reported that the insurgents had destroyed all the machinery in the mines of Tomabe, Ubina, Tatasi, Portugaleta, and Gran Chocalla. Moreover, they had abused priests, profaned churches, and murdered citizens. Rese-

[6] Odriozola, *Documentos,* I, 33–36.

guín heard the unfortunate individuals kindly and promised to restore their possessions if it took the last drop of his blood to do so.[7]

On March 18, he received packets of letters from General Flores telling about the fortunate outcome of the attack at Punilla, near La Plata, where the forces of the Catari brothers had been defeated. That same afternoon Domingo de Reguera, a fugitive from Oruro who came dressed as a priest, informed him that Pedro de la Cruz Condori, who was the Indian chief of Challapata in the province of Chayanta, governor of the town of Cerrillos, and a faithful adherent of Túpac Amaru, was there with more than four thousand rebels. Reguera said that Condori had distributed many edicts among the people and planned to attack Tupiza and free the prisoners. There were also three brothers, one with the name of Túpac Amaru and the other two with that of Catari, who had such a large following that they were able to overcome the few loyal inhabitants in the town and commit many atrocities there.

The commandant decided to put a stop to those evils before the chiefs became bolder. He sent out three detachments of veteran soldiers and the militia to go by different roads to Condori's camp and try to capture him. When they arrived, the Spaniards saw that the Indian did not have many men. Condori approached with a few of his followers to speak to the commander of the dragoons, Lieutenant José Vila, and warned the royalist to join him or become the victim of his people's fury. While they talked, the Lieutenant showed not the least fear, although one of the Indians accompanying the chief got his sling ready to discharge at the Spaniards. Luckily, Alonso Mesias, a leader of one of the militias, noticed this and killed the Indian with a pistol shot before he could carry out his intention. This terrified the followers of Condori so much that they fled and joined other forces a little distance away. The latter also fled, leaving their venerated chief in the hands of the Spaniards, who took him with them well guarded to Chocalla to search for the three brothers, who were also captured.

[7] *Ibid.*, I, 36–37; Carta de José de Reseguín al virrey de Buenos Aires, Juan José de Vertíz, Cayza, April 15, 1781, *ibid.*, I, 345–46; Carrió *op. cit.*, 94.

The royalists arrested the assistant priest of Chocalla, José de Velasco, because he had helped Condori acclaim Túpac Amaru in his doctrina. He had made demonstrations in favor of the Inca's troops and had agreed to follow their leader even in the planned attack on Tupiza, and had also aided in scattering edicts and seditious letters and in influencing the people.

Twenty-three of the principal criminals were put to death and the rest condemned to the presidio or whipped. Active measures were next taken to recover the stolen possessions of the Spaniards who had died or fled; more than 2,500 pesos were found and returned to their owners. Parties of veteran soldiers went through the province, instilling so much respect in the inhabitants that Indian governors came to Tupiza to ask pardon.[8] The soldiers saved the priest of Chocaya, killed more than five hundred Indians in skirmishes, and captured an Indian chief called Tomava, said to be a relative of Túpac Amaru. They remained in the province until the road was opened and peace restored in neighboring areas.[9]

At Tupiza on March 20, 1781, Reseguín issued an edict to be published in all the churches. He informed the people that part of the soldiers sent by the Viceroy of Buenos Aires had already arrived to establish peace, that the citizens would be maintained in their homes, and that their work was to continue as before the uprising. Anyone who tried to seduce the people, robbed haciendas, or committed other crimes would be severely punished. Priests were to tell their parishioners that the King's troops came to punish the guilty, establish good order, and administer justice everywhere. They were also to urge the people to remain loyal vassals of the sovereign. The proclamation had the desired results, for many Indians came to assure Reseguín of their loyalty. Mines were worked again, the roads opened, the mail detained at Moxos sent to its destination, and peace restored.[10]

The inland regions still had to be dealt with. Pedro Corbalan informed Reseguín that the Indians of the interior provinces had

---

[8] Odriozola, *Documentos*, I, 39-44.

[9] Relación de los hechos mas notables acaecidos en la sublevación general . . . , 45. MS copy in B. L.

[10] Odriozola, *Documentos*, I, 44-45.

collected an abundance of arrows and arms and were marching to the aid of the Inca king.[11] Reseguín then started out for the town of Santiago de Cotagaita on April 5, sending Captain Joaquín Salgado ahead with fifty men to calm the area and encourage the people to remain loyal. The commandant spent only two days on the road, imprisoning more than eighty criminals; among them were the chiefs of the conspiracy in the province of Lipés and accomplices in the death of Corregidor Francisco la Revilla. Eleven were condemned to death and the rest to the presidio.[12] In Santiago de Cotagaita nine persons were sentenced to death for conspiring and publishing an edict of Túpac Amaru. Condori had ordered them to do so to make Túpac Amaru's wishes known. He said that the Inca had promised to relieve all Spaniards, Creoles, mestizos, and other persons born in the country of oppression, and at the same time expected them to be his vassals. If they disregarded his peaceful invitation, they would experience severe penalties.

Reseguín thanked the loyal inhabitants for their fidelity to the King and urged them to continue to be faithful. Then he sent detachments of soldiers to all parts of the province of Chichas, pacified it, and persuaded the people to return to their homes and farms.[13] He decided to march boldly forward, although the transit was flooded with enemies. As the people of Tupiza did not want him to leave their province, they tried to frighten him. They said that the King would lose one million pesos annually from the tribute, the fifths on precious metals, the alcabala, and other revenues if Reseguín abandoned the province, and that communication would be cut off again between Peru and Buenos Aires. In reply, Reseguín promised to leave Lieutenant Joaquín de Soria with twenty-five veteran soldiers to guard them, since he was anxious to send an expedition into the province of Lipés. There he hoped to free the dead corregidor's wife, who was a prisoner. He marched as rapidly as he could and overcame great obstacles. With the

---

[11] Carta de Pedro Corbalan al teniente Manuel Padilla, Hacienda del Remate, March 28, 1781, in Odriozola, *Documentos*, I, 358.

[12] *Ibid.*, I, 45–46.

[13] Carta de Pedro de la Cruz Condori á los habitantes de la doctrina de Santiago de Cotagaita, Chocalla, March 19, 1781, in Odriozola, *Documentos*, I, 41.

approach of the army peace was restored in Yura, Tomabe, and other towns in the province of Porcó. And so the people of Potosí, frequently threatened by insurgents from those places, drew a breath of relief. By this time Reseguín had established such a good reputation that the towns all along the way tried to give him substantial proof of their fidelity. He now decided to heed the many requests of General Flores and go to La Plata.

Repeated information from Cristóbal López concerning sedition in the mountain provinces made Flores hasten his march. When he was near Salta, Colonel Andrés Mestre, governor of Tucumán, sent word for him to hurry because three hundred men assigned to serve in Peru had deserted and returned to their homes, and the Tobas Indians were going to take advantage of the desertion to attack the city of Jujuy.[14] He feared that they would ally themselves with the people of Jujuy to attack Tucumán.[15]

As the commercial route of high Peru passed through Jujuy and Salta, those strategic towns were naturally influenced by Túpac Amaru's revolution. José Quiroga, a Christian mestizo and an interpreter in the reduction of San Ignacio, led the movement in the Jujuy region and made an alliance with the Tobas Indians and the Matacos Indians of Chaco not in the mission towns. He maintained that the poor wanted to defend themselves against Spanish tyranny and that the Indians should be governed only by their Inca king.[16] In that region the uprising was not so much the work of the Indians as of native Spanish adherents to the cause of Túpac Amaru. It was they who entered the reductions of the Tobas and the Matacos and made a profound impression on the people by promising to free them from Spain and put them under the Inca king. As a result, the inhabitants of Jujuy, Islas, and Carril were ready to join the revolutionists as soon as they approached. The

[14] Odriozola, *Documentos*, I, 47–50; *Revista de Archivos y Biblioteca (Peruanas)*, Año 1900, Vol. V, 185.

[15] Vista fiscal del 15 de Junio de 1781, respectiva al informe de Mestre de 26 de Mayo de 1781, AGN, Buenos Aires, Tribunales, Leg. 127, exp. 13, in Lewin, *op. cit.*, 442.

[16] Angelis, *Documentos*, 275–77 .

Tobas delayed the attack on Jujuy because of high water in the Río Negro.[17]

A priest by the name of Albarracín informed the authorities of Jujuy of the uprising, saying that the people of Perico, Islas, and Carril and the Tobas Indians were in the woods of Pongo waiting for three other barbarous tribes with whom they had made alliance. The city officials did all they could for protection, but had accomplished little by March 28, 1781. The military commander, Gregorio Zegada, summoned the militia to aid the Río Negro fort, which was attacked on that date, and found that the people had gone to the mountains in groups of forty to fifty to hide until they received word of the revolutionary activities. When Zegada learned that the enemy were preparing to launch an attack on the city, he struck first, on March 31, and took twenty-seven prisoners. The rest of the insurgents fled to the hills and warned their allies, who were determined to take Jujuy.

Commander Zegada appealed to Governor Mestre for help, which could not be sent at once because the Indians of Cuzco and Chaco, allied with Salta, were rising. Zegada then sent in vain to Flores for aid. During April, 1781, the uprising spread over the whole province of Tucumán, so that reinforcements finally had to go to Salta. It commonly happened that before companies of militia reached their destination, they were needed elsewhere, for it was difficult to catch up with the fast-moving Indians.[18]

The attorney general of Salta summed up the reasons for the uprising. He said that the exactions of customhouses, the oppression of corregidores, the burdens imposed by the repartimientos, the high parish dues and the cost for the rites of the church, and the high price of tobacco had brought it about. He proposed therefore that all the new dues should be discontinued and the old ones paid, that the office of corregidor be abolished and in its place ministers or judges be designated because the natives hated the word "corregidor." The new officials should be paid from the treasury and

---

[17] Odriozola, *Documentos*, I, 105–106.
[18] Angelis, *Documentos*, 273–75, 284.

not allowed to impose repartimientos or carry on business, since trade should be free in all the towns and cities except for the alcabala. If priests of the doctrinas should receive a stipend provided by law, people would not need to pay for church services. Finally, two hundred men should be quartered in the cities of La Plata, Cochabamba, La Paz, Cuzco, and Arequipa to forestall the vexations caused by the Indian rebels, and a general pardon should be proclaimed.[19] Members of the Cabildo of Córdoba, where there was also dissatisfaction, cited the same causes of the insurrection, declaring that when Túpac Amaru offered relief, the people were eager to follow him.[20]

The disturbances continued in April. Five hundred men assembled in the plaza at La Rioja, overthrew the monopolies, took the money, and ordered tobacco to be sold at a much reduced price. When certain priests tried to stop them, they paid no attention to their entreaties. There was another uprising at Belén, in the province of Salta, caused by a company of militia.[21] People also expressed sympathy for Túpac Amaru in a number of other places; and in the province of Tucumán a military insubordination might have led to open rebellion, but did not because the insurgents of Jujuy failed to create a common center from which the movement could spread.

Governor Mestre was quite active in the midst of danger. He brought a force from Tucumán to provide timely aid for a party of veteran soldiers under López when the people of Jujuy were defeated by the Tobas. Some of the criminals were soon left hanging from the trees. The relief party had scarcely left Jujuy, however, when a force led by the Tobas besieged it again.[22]

On his way to La Plata, Reseguín helped to save Jujuy a second time. He traveled fifty leagues in two days, passed Salta safely,

[19] Informe del procurador general de Salta sobre los motivos de la sublevación, Salta, June 9, 1781, AGN, Montevideo (published in Lewin, *op. cit.*, 477–79).

[20] El cabildo de Córdoba dictamina sobre los motivos de la sublevación, Córdoba, June 8, 1781, *ibid.*, 479–81.

[21] AGN, Buenos Aires, Tribunales, Leg. 127, exp. 13 (cited by Lewin, *op. cit.*, 310).

[22] Odriozola, *Documentos*, I, 105–106; Carta de Andrés Mestre á Juan de Vertíz, virrey de Buenos Aires, Jujuy, April 24, 1781, *ibid.*, I, 355–57.

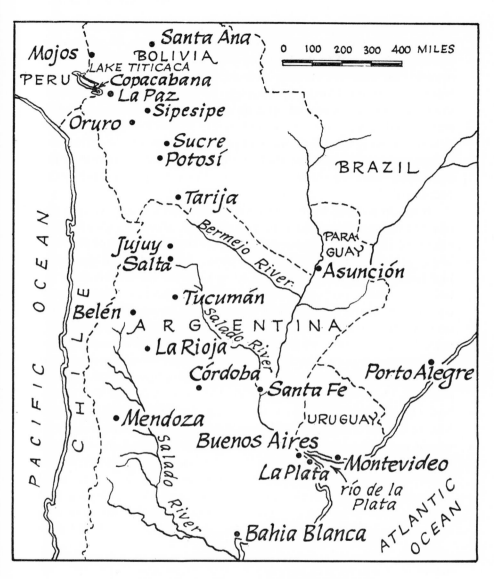

THE AREA OF REVOLT IN ARGENTINE TERRITORY
(Modern boundaries shown)

and arrived at Jujuy just in time to aid in repulsing the Tobas. They were forced to surrender their principal chiefs, Santiago and José, who were put to death along with five others. Peace was thus established, and the Viceroy sent an infantry company to occupy Jujuy. As a result, Córdoba, Santiago del Estero, where a threatening lampoon had been put on a grocery door, San Miguel del Tucumán, Salta, and Jujuy were not active in the extensive revolt.[23] When the King heard of the campaign, he was pleased that the Tobas were subdued and that the city of Jujuy remained calm. He hoped that all the campaigns in the province would be as successful.[24]

It might be well to digress here to mention the agitation in the city of Mendoza toward the end of the year. Mendoza also felt the effects of the Túpac Amaru rebellion. At the beginning of November, 1781, it was reported that a group of people had paid two hundred pesos for a portrait of King Charles III which they intended to burn, perhaps publicly, and then declare allegiance to the Inca of Peru. The Viceroy of Buenos Aires ordered a careful investigation to be made. A number of witnesses, whose testimony varied, gave ample evidence that the dissatisfied element knew about Túpac Amaru. José Carrera testified that certain persons had burned a piece of braid, or, rather, a royal effigy, not the King's portrait. Quinoñes, a European doctor, reported that the rebels had said they would have a new king. Another witness, Manuel Rodríguez, had heard that Túpac Amaru would be crowned and would enter the city to overthrow the Europeans. Reference was also made to the *comuneros* of New Granada, in Martín Cevallo's report that he had heard three men on the street say, "Why shall we not rise as the people have risen in Santa Fe de Bogotá and other places? They have obtained what we want." Another witness, Captain Pedro Encinas y Salas, declared that he had heard

23 Odriozola, *Documentos*, I, 49–50; Pasquín fijado en Santiago del Estero, Acuerdo de cabildo del 31 de Mayo de 1782, AGN, Buenos Aires, Sección gobierono, VI–VII–7–5 (published in Lewin, *op. cit.*, 451).

24 Real orden de 12 de Enero de 1782, El Prado, January 12, 1782, Biblioteca Nacional, Buenos Aires, Sección manuscritos, Revolución del Peru, num. 2158 (published in Lewin, *op. cit.*, 447–48).

Francisco Aguilar (alias Chachingo) speak for Túpac Amaru and his revolt. When the cabildo let the results of the secret investigation become public, there was quite a stir in the city. All the inhabitants and even the clergy hastened to swear their loyalty to the Spanish monarch, and nothing definite could be proved against them.[25]

To return to Commandant Reseguín and earlier events, the commandant arrived with his 200 veteran soldiers at La Plata on April 19, 1781, where the people gave him a joyful reception. He learned that just the day before, the first detachment of 500 men had gone out of that city to aid other regions still ravaged by revolt. It was followed immediately by another, consisting of 200 men under Gavino Quevado, who went first to the town of San Pedro de Buenavista, which had suffered so much in the revolt. On May 10, Lieutenant Colonel Diego de Velasco led 330 soldiers out of La Plata, and on the fourteenth another 150 men followed. Finally, on the sixteenth two companies of veteran soldiers left, taking six additional fieldpieces and 50,000 cartridges, two engines for throwing stones at the Indians, and the necessary baggage and supplies. All were under the commandant general of the expedition, Flores, who followed his men on the eighteenth, accompanied by Sebastián Velasco, the auditor of war, his assessor general, and a body of dragoons from Buenos Aires for his rear guard. Only one company, under Captain Sebastián Sánchez, was left in the city. In the town of Macha on May 22, 1781, Flores joined forces with most of the troops of his command.

On May 29, Reseguín left La Plata with the last men from Buenos Aires to join Flores. He met the Commandant General on June 7 at Oruro and found him very sad because of a defeat suffered by the detachment under Quevado at Sicasica on May 23. The defeat also caused great grief in La Plata.[26]

The Commandant General was very anxious to leave Oruro as

[25] AGN, Buenos Aires, División colonia. Sección gobierno, Mendoza, 1759–1782, VI–III–I–I, in Lewin, *op. cit.*, 315–24.

[26] Relación de los hechos mas notables acaecidos en la sublevación general . . . , 97–103. MS copy in B. L.

quickly as possible, for he had received news of the trouble in the city of La Paz. Two companies of militia from Oruro, 200 Indians from the town of Toledo, and 250 men who lived near Paria offered their services for the expedition. Even the sad remnant of the troops of Quevada and Ayarza enlisted. Everything was ready by June 15, when an army of 700 men, most of them without firearms or military instruction but desirous of freeing the inhabitants of La Paz, left Oruro.

The royalists soon received information that 20,000 Indians were waiting at Sicasica to destroy them as they had destroyed the detachment under Quevado. Flores tried to send word to Corregidor Segurola of La Paz that he was coming, but could not do so. At Caracollo, Ayarza joined the expedition with 500 Cochabambinos, two pieces of artillery, and other military supplies. When the volunteers from Oruro arrived, the army had a total of 1,300 soldiers. The expedition then started for Sicasica, meeting on the way parties of Indians who were spies of the Indian viceroy, Túpac Catari.

When the Commandant General, disregarding warnings, approached Sicasica on June 19, some two thousand shouting Indians rushed out of the town to the open field, using their slings to hinder the royalists. Royalist forces were quickly drawn up in battle formation. The infantry comprised three divisions, with the cavalry on the flanks and the troop of Cochabambinos as a rear guard. The army was ordered to march forward in this formation until it arrived within firing distance of the enemy. Before opening fire, Flores gave the Indians a chance to ask pardon, urging them to disregard the commands of Túpac Catari and put themselves under the King's banners. They replied with a volley of shots and innumerable stones; then the Indians on horseback began to attack. A party of veteran dragoons and volunteers, followed by the cavalry, came immediately to defend the Commandant General and forced the enemy to flee to the near-by hills after twenty-five were killed and many wounded.[27]

The Indians then took possession of two hills and an elevated

[27] *Ibid.*, 103–105.

slope. On the right they were defended by four to six hundred men; on the left by nine hundred to one thousand; the rest were on the slope between the two hills. The battle was desperate. The Indians fought bravely, but finally they were defeated and many lost their lives. Since more than eighty royalists had been wounded and it was growing late, they withdrew. Great precaution was taken during the night. Flores decided to issue a warning to the enemy and then set fire to Sicasica. Therefore, next day the royalist army marched to a near-by town, where the assistant priest talked with the Indians, urging peace, which they haughtily refused.

The enemy army kept increasing all the time and carefully observed the Spanish forces. The Spaniards had scarcely begun their march when the rebels started to move also, keeping time with their musical instruments. The Indians approached and distributed four thousand men over the brow of the hill, while another party of five hundred came to join them. The royalists discharged their cannon against them, but they dared to go down the hill, and a party of three hundred tried to seize the baggage of their adversaries. The Indians were overthrown, however, and did not cause more trouble that day. When pardon was offered again on the same terms, they answered that they would accept peace only when Túpac Catari surrendered.

The Spaniards fell back to seek pasture and water and camped on the slope of Vicario. While they were there, two hundred men sent by the priest of Tarata, Angel Moscoso, and five hundred additional Cochabambinos arrived. Both detachments were under the command of Ayarza, who was received with great joy.

General Flores now realized that he had accomplished very little. His forces were small, many of his men wounded, his supplies scarce, and a multitude of Indians awaited him near La Paz. In this critical situation he called a council of war. All the participants favored an effort to save La Paz with the exception of Captain Francisco Xaviar de Cañas of La Plata, who was opposed because of the small size of the army.[28] After celebrating mass on St. John's Day (June 24, 1781) and leaving two hundred Cochabam-

---

[28] *Ibid.*, 105–107.

binos behind to hide the supplies which had arrived from Oruro the day before, they raised camp.

The troops formed in two columns and marched along the road to La Paz. They had safely passed Sicasica and had almost reached Calacoto when about six thousand Indians came out determined to fight. Eight hundred of them were on the slope and the rest on a hill in front, which Túpac Catari had fortified with three bronze cannon, which fired frequently upon the Spaniards. Flores had a cannon placed on the slope to check their shooting and stationed the Chuquisaca companies there to keep the enemy from coming down for water.

When the Cochabambinos approached near the insurgents' artillery, they were attacked repeatedly with stones and spears. A company under Mariano Ybáñez went to their aid and routed the Indians. Then the Cochabambinos took the rebels' cannon, two of which had been obtained from La Paz and the other from Quevado at Sicasica. The soldiers pursued the Indians so fiercely that even the highest hill no longer served as a refuge. The rebels ran more than half a league and lost 150 of their men. That night the royalist camp was made very near the insurgents.

At dawn next day the Indians covered the hills, but were silent. They traveled over the heights, followed the march of the Spanish army, and made no demonstrations. That night the royalists placed their camp on the burned plantations of Patacamania, where they found some Spanish women hidden with two servants. On June 26, the army arrived at Ayoayo without opposition, but found no food there. Some women reported that Túpac Catari had just passed by with his forces to unite with other Indians in Calamarca for the purpose of cutting off the march.

Next afternoon the army arrived in Calamarca. Before camping, the soldiers saw some Indians near the town; and above on the slope there was one Indian wearing a bright red riding coat, whom Flores judged to be the chief. When the Spanish commandant drew near the enemy, the Indian leader acted as though he wanted to treat with him, but he was drunk and had to be carried away. A number of gunners and cavalrymen approached the Indians and

188

skirmished with them, but Flores, fearing an ambush, ordered a retreat. He still insisted upon offering pardon to the Indians and urged them to desert Túpac Catari. He sent a written dispatch, delivered by means of a prisoner, to this effect, but Túpac Catari answered that he was not interested in peace since he had twenty thousand soldiers above the city.

The Spaniards did not want to fight with the insurgents immediately because they had not won great advantages in past encounters. When they did not engage the enemy at once, the Indians became careless, and on June 28 began to entertain themselves, dancing, shouting, and blowing trumpets. More than six thousand of them taunted their opponents as they marched, threw stones, and even left the hills that protected them. The royalists then attacked on all sides, killed fifteen hundred, and pursued Túpac Catari, but he escaped by throwing himself off his horse into a narrow ravine. Afterwards the royalists spent a peaceful night at Capilla.

The Commandant General hoped to reach Ventilla the next day, but could not quite get there. Some flying companies going out to search for cattle had several encounters with the Indians, killing many of them,[29] yet the insurgents resisted the auxiliary forces almost to the last moment. When the royalists moved their camp on the thirtieth and passed Ventilla, they began to see Indians in the narrow Achocalla Valley. These rebels remained at the rear guard of the column, but shortly a multitude of them appeared at the vanguard. When the Spaniards feared they would be surrounded, they formed a large square, mounted six cannon, and advanced in that formation. The Indians marched in two divisions in good order, and placed an ambush of three hundred men to the right. But the Spaniards discovered it and put the enemy to flight. Then they came to a place a quarter of a league from the rebels' encampment and caused two thousand Indians there to scatter.[30]

Aid was thus temporarily brought to La Paz by regular troops

29 *Ibid.*, 107–10.
30 *Ibid.*, 111–12.

from Buenos Aires, Tucumán, and Cochabamba after a long, hard march and many difficult encounters with the insurgents. The besiegers withdrew farther from the city, but the unruly Cochabambinos deserted in such large numbers that Flores had to withdraw to Urcos with the remnant of his army to seek reinforcement. When he left La Paz on August 4, 1781, the Indians returned and continued the siege.[31]

Flores finally reached Oruro on August 14, and immediately sent Reseguín to Cochabamba to obtain four thousand to six thousand soldiers and to collect as many provisions as he could. Flores himself went to Potosí and asked the treasury officials to give him 100,000 pesos and to buy a quantity of hung beef for him. Returning to La Plata on the twenty-ninth, he was well received. He then ordered Lieutenant Joaquín de Soria to proceed to Potosí with twenty soldiers to get the 100,000 pesos and the provisions left there for Oruro. He next prepared the militias of La Plata which were to unite with those of Oruro. On September 7, he started for Cochabamba, gathering soldiers all along the way; he arrived there on the twentieth and arranged for the troops to go on campaign two days later. They were divided into three divisions; one under Pedro Ramón de Arauco, the second under Joseph Ignacio Severicha, and the third under Pedro Gari. Many volunteers followed them, so that when the Cochabambinos united with the forces waiting at Oruro, the number of men rose to nine thousand. They consisted of poorly armed militias of Cochabamba and Charcas and companies from Salta, Jujuy, and Tucumán. The command of that force was given to the brave, hard-working Reseguín since Flores preferred to remain in Cochabamba to direct the movement of the army.

The second auxiliary expedition left to go to the aid of La Paz on October 1, 1781. The Indians intended to attack this force, and with this in view, Túpac Catari's two generals, Juan de Dios Mullapuraca and Diego Quipe, united their troops near the town of Yaco. Reseguín divined their plans and decided to upset them.

[31] *Ibid.*, 113–15; Ballivián y Roxas, *op. cit.*, 81–86; Odriozola, *Documentos*, I, 108.

Therefore, at the head of a detachment of two thousand men, he marched to Yaco during the night. He ordered his men not to light campfires, but it was very cold and some disobeyed. The Indians saw the fires and attacked. At the first firing, however, they fled, more than three hundred of them being killed. Reseguín burned the town and returned to his encampment. This victory removed all obstacles, making it possible for him to reach the heights of La Paz and enter the city on October 17.[32]

The efficiency of Viceroy Vertíz and of the troops from Buenos Aires prevented the Inca revolt from spreading to the eastern and southern part of the viceroyalty of La Plata. The Spaniards were also able to put down the revolts in Tucumán, Salta, Jujuy, and other smaller towns in the northwest. Then they aided other regions to the north and even reached La Paz, the recovery of which was highly important for the pacification of the two viceroyalties of Peru and La Plata. Without the assistance of the auxiliary forces from Buenos Aires, La Plata, Cochabamba, and elsewhere, this tactic could hardly have succeeded.

[32] Relación de los hechos mas notables acaecidos en la sublevación general . . . , 216–27 (MS copy in B. L.); Odriozola, *Documentos,* I, 111. The siege of La Paz is treated in Chapter XIII.

CHAPTER IX

The Distaff Side

WOMEN PLAYED AN IMPORTANT PART in the last Inca revolt. Chief among them was Micaela Bastidas, wife of José Gabriel Túpac Amaru, an unusual woman who was very active in his behalf. During the Inca's absence, she took over matters at home, issued passports, provided for collection of supplies, spread information about his cause, and even rode over the countryside recruiting. Other women, like María Esquivel, wife of the Spaniard Francisco Cisneros, who served in the Inca's secretariat, and Francisca Herrera and Catalina de Zalas y Pachachutti, worked with Micaela. Tomasa Titu Condemayta from Acos corresponded with the Inca, aided his directly, and was considered one of the principal instigators of the revolt. Cecilia Túpac Amaru, half sister of José Gabriel, also took part, though inconspicuously.

The Inca's wife was involved from the beginning of the revolt, and by November 27, 1780, was already issuing passports. She ordered all Spanish guards, Indians, and spies who served under her husband to give free passage to the cargoes of Agustín Herrera, and allowed him to travel through the towns where it was necessary for him to go to sell his products.[1] Later (January 25, 1781) Micaela ordered alcaldes and caciques in the towns of Corma and Sanca not to molest Francisco Torres, a sincere partisan of the revolt, since this was her husband's wish.[2] The priest Antonio José Centeno asked her for a safe-conduct when it became necessary for him to go down to the city of Cuzco for eight days.[3]

[1] Pasaporte dado por Doña Micaela Bastidas, Tungasuca, November 27, 1780, in Loayza, *Martires y heroinas (Documentos inéditos del año de 1780 á 1782)*, *op. cit.*, Serie I, Vol. IX, 9.

[2] Salvoconducto dado por Doña Micaela Bastidas, Tinta, January 25, 1781, *ibid.*, 15.

[3] Carta de Dr. Antonio José Centeño á Micaela Bastides, San Pedro de Cacha, December 8, 1781, *ibid.*, 93–94.

Micaela helped to control roads and bridges. When José Gabriel was ready to go to Lampa, he sent word to her to see that the roads through the ravine were guarded.[4] On January 28, she notified Tomás Parvina, one of her husband's generals, that the roads to Cuzco must be cut off and that if this had not been done already, he should do it.[5] She was no doubt glad to receive a letter from Ramón Ponce promising to take the bridge of Curbamba, thereby preventing supplies from reaching Cuzco.[6] Micaela had written her husband to dispatch men to destroy the bridge at Pachachaca, saying that if he could not do so, she would destroy it herself.[7] She asked Governors Agustín and Lucás Núñez de la Torre and Matías Canal to send an Indian secretly to burn the bridge on the Apurímac, so that the chapetones could not flee to Lima.[8] On the other hand, she issued a command to guard the rope bridge at Yanaoca for the sake of transporting supplies.[9]

The collection and distribution of supplies were highly important, and in this connection Micaela proved to be very helpful. She gave orders for the cloth seized in Guaraypata to be sent to Quiquijana, but unfortunately the caciques transporting it were overcome by hostiles from Cuzco.[10] She reported to Juan de Zubizarreta, chief justice of Livitaca, that there was no one in Quibis to deliver the copper, and asked him to go in person to give it to the muleteers, for which service she would pay him.[11]

Pedro Venero, chief of the Commissary Department at Tinta who was married to Bartola Escobedo, José Gabriel's sister, sent the Inca's wife two pounds of powder. He reported that he and

[4] Carta de José Gabriel Túpac Amaru á su esposa, n.p., n.d., *ibid.*, 61.

[5] Carta de Doña Micaela Bastidas á Tomás Parvina, Tinta, January 28, 1781, *ibid.*, 16.

[6] Carta de Ramón Ponce á Micaela Bastidas, Velille, January 28, 1781, *ibid.*, 35.

[7] Carta de Micaela Bastidas á José Gabriel Túpac Amaru, November 24, 1781, *ibid.*, 43-44.

[8] Carta de Micaela Bastidas á los gobernantes Don Agustín y Don Lucás Núñez de la Torre y Don Matías Canal, Tungasuca, December 7, 1780, *ibid.*, 11-12.

[9] Carta de Micaela Bastidas á José Gabriel Túpac Amaru, Tinta, March 23, 1781, *ibid.*, 57.

[10] Carta de Micaela Bastidas á José Gabriel Túpac Amaru, Tungasuca, November 26, 1780, *ibid.*, 45.

[11] Carta de Micaela Bastidas á Juan de Zubizarretta, Tungasuca, December 2, 1780, *ibid.*, 10.

his men had seized the cattle and other items from Juan de Dios Ingarroca in the parish of San Sebastián and that the latter was coming to see her. Venero advised her to examine him carefully, since he was reported to be the cacique of that place.[12] Micaela ordered Venero to collect two and one-half fanegas of flour. He obeyed her, dispatched it with other articles toward Sicuani, and told her that she would also receive fifteen boxes of hardtack, which her cousin had provided.[13] Diego Bisa Apasa wrote Micaela that he was sending two hundred baskets of coca by way of Lauramarca.[14] Julián de Escalante informed her on January 28, 1781, that he had collected 130 pieces of coarse cloth badly needed by the Indians, but was unable to find sacks in which to bring the wheat from Antabamba.[15]

The Inca's wife wanted the alcaldes of Sanca to do their part in furnishing supplies. She ordered them to assist Bernardo Carrasco in bringing to the cabildo at Tinta the potatoes, peaches, and other food taken from the Spaniards' haciendas, but the cattle seized were to be kept for her husband.[16]

Micaela and her brother, Antonio Bastidas, one of the Inca's trusted officers, corresponded frequently. On February 13, Antonio asked his sister to send a servant to attend to his sick wife.[17] Two days later he wrote again, asking her to send him coca and aguardiente for the use of the army, and to include jerked beef or wheat, powder and shot, and silver for expenses.[18] A little later Micaela sent him six molds of cheese, along with rice, sugar, and yerba maté, for which he was very grateful.[19]

[12] Carta de Pedro Venero á Micaela Bastidas, Tinta, November 30, 1780, ibid., 20.

[13] Carta de Pedro Venero á Micaela Bastidas, Tinta, December 9, 1780; also his carta of December 10, 1781, ibid., 20–21.

[14] Carta de Diego Bisa Apasa á Micaela Bastidas, Capana, December 13, 1780, ibid., 28.

[15] Julián de Escalante a Micaela Bastidas, Acos, January 28, 1781, ibid., 37.

[16] Orden de Micaela Bastidas, Tinta, February 18, 1781, ibid., 16–17.

[17] Carta de Antonio Bastides á Micaela Bastidas, Pucacasa, February 13, 1781, ibid., 39.

[18] Carta de Antonio Bastidas á Micaela Bastidas, Pucacasa, February 15, 1781, ibid., 40.

[19] Carta de Antonio Bastidas á Micaela Bastidas, Quiquijana, March 29, 1781, ibid., 42.

Rodríguez de Ávila, the priest of Yanaoca, wrote Micaela asking her to send him a two-arroba loaf, fifty pounds, of sugar, since he had heard that she had some.[20] It is not known whether she complied. Another priest, Gregorio de Yépez, informed her that he was collecting supplies for her husband. She was to tell José Gabriel that he had a bay horse, which he was fattening, and that two other men had thirteen mules for him.[21]

Micaela continually provided her husband with things he needed. On November 23, 1780, she wrote that she had sent him six hundred pesos, in addition to fifty-six which her brother Juan was bringing. She also included a goatskin bag of aguardiente and the letters she had just received. (She signed her letters to José Gabriel "Mica" or "Micaco" and addressed him as "Chepe," terms of endearment.[22]) On November 26, José Gabriel wrote to her to send him 2,000 pesos, saying that he was on the heights of Livitaca where he would remain for five or six days. He also asked her to be very careful about the letters going back and forth from Cuzco. He signed this letter "your Chepe."[23] On November 28, he asked Micaela to send the large cannon brought from Quipococha, with shot and powder, and to tell Figueroa to come along to operate it.[24] In another two days José Gabriel dispatched porters to his wife with bales of goods, which she was to keep until they could be disposed of properly.[25]

At another time she sent a porter to her husband with 526 cartridges for guns and ammunition for the cannon. She thoughtfully included six pesos and two baskets of coca. Again, on March

[20] Carta del Dr. Rodríguez de Ávila á Micaela Bastidas, Yanaoca, December 26, 1780, *ibid.*, 74–75.
[21] Carta de Gregorio de Yépez á Micaela Bastidas, Pomacanche, March 4, 1781, *ibid.*, 82–83.
[22] Carta de Micaela Bastides á José Gabriel Túpac Amaru, Tungasuca, November 23, 1780, *ibid.*, 43.
[23] Carta de José Gabriel Túpac Amaru á su esposa Micaela, Altos de Livitoca, November 26, 1780, *ibid.*, 59.
[24] Carta de José Gabriel á su esposa, Coporaque, November 28, 1780, *ibid.*, 61–62.
[25] Carta de José Gabriel Túpac Amaru á Micaela su esposa, Coporque, November 30, 1780, *ibid.*, 63. Carta de José Gabriel Túpac Amaru á Micaela su esposa, Yauri, December 1, 1780, *ibid.*, 64.

195

23, 1781, she said that she had sent more ammunition.[26] She had even aided Diego Túpac Amaru with a troop and arms when he was in Lauramarca and insisted that he was going against Paucartambo at the end of January, 1781.[27]

Spreading propaganda in favor of the revolt was another of Micaela's duties. She wrote to the governors Agustín and Lucás Núñez de la Torre and Matías Canal to inform them what her husband was doing and asked them to relay the information to the Indians and caciques in the towns under their jurisdiction. She had no doubt that the governors would help him and told them that if they had people enough to take the corregidores and Europeans, they should do so. She greatly exaggerated her husband's forces, likely for propaganda purposes, saying that he had more than 86,000 Indians under him and, in addition, the principal inhabitants and Spaniards of eight parishes in Cuzco. She assured the governors that they would be protected and freed from taxes. In a short time the Inca would go to Cuzco with his garrison, and they were to hasten there also as soon as they received the news of his arrival. If they refused, she threatened to exterminate them. Micaela was indeed a brave and determined woman.[28]

She wrote José Torres that her husband was trying to free the kingdom from the evil practices of corregidores. She asked him to take all his people to Cuzco immediately to help put a stop to the injuries caused by such thieving officials. The revolt, she declared, had the support of the provinces of Urubamba, Paucartambo, the eight parishes of Cuzco, of Quispicanchis, Paruro, Tinta, Lampa, Azángaro, Paucarcolla, Carabaya, the city of Chucuito, and of other towns.[29] She wrote practically the same thing to the governors Baltasar Cárdenas, Tomás Enríquez, and Mariano

26 Carta de Micaela Bastidas á José Gabriel Túpac Amaru, Tinta, March 7, 1781, and *carta* of March 23, 1781, *ibid.*, 57.

27 Carta de Micaela Bastidas á José Gabriel Túpac Amaru, Tinta, January 24, 1781, *ibid.*, 54; Valcárcel, *Le rebelión de Túpac Amaru*, 93.

28 Carta de Micaela Bastidas á los gobernadores Don Agustín y Don Lucás Núñez de la Torre y Don Matías Canal, Tungasuca, December 7, 1780, in Loayza, *op. cit.*, Serie I, Vol. IX, 10–12.

29 Carta de Miguel Bastidas á gobernador Don José Torres, Tungasuca, December 15, 1780, *ibid.*, 13.

Flores, and asked them to bring their people to Tungasuca to assist the Inca.[30] In fact, her commands were respected as much as her husband's were.

Micaela received correspondence from many of his generals. Her brother-in-law, Pedro Mendagure, married to Cecilia Túpac Amaru, wrote that he had marched to Checacupe and Pitamarca with his people, where he learned that Rafael Rada and Felipe Castro had gone out to Quiquijana with the forces they commanded to find out whether the enemy soldiers were there. From a priest in Checacupe, Mendagure heard that Simón Noguera was shut up in Lampa.[31] The alcaldes of Yauri informed the Inca's wife that all their caciques and people had left to accompany José Gabriel and that they intended to send him all the other inhabitants in the district.[32] From the alcaldes Andrés Cotates and Marcos Chasares of Pichigua, she received word that the caciques and their people had not yet arrived. They had perhaps tarried in the town to celebrate the day of Santa Lucía. The alcaldes promised, nevertheless, to go where they were ordered.[33]

Fernando Gurpide and Agustín Aucagualpa wrote that they had learned from an Indian of Paruro that the people of that town were leaving on December 12 or 13, 1780. They had been awaiting the results from Cuzco, but they would now march by way of Acchas and place guards along the route.[34]

Melchor Castelo had followed Micaela's orders and had made them known to the people of Maranganí. They had responded, and some were already with José Gabriel Túpac Amaru. Castelo assured Micaela that the rest of the Indians would soon go to join

---

[30] Carta de Doña Micaela Bastidas á los gobernadores Don Baltasar Cárdenas y Don Tomás Enríquez y Don Mariano Flores, Tungasuca, December 15, 1780, *ibid.*, 13–14.

[31] Carta de Pedro Mendagure á Micaela Bastidas, Checacupe, November 30, 1780, *ibid.*, 19.

[32] Carta de Alfonso Guissa y Diego Chilo á Micaela Bastidas, Yauri, December 12, 1780, *ibid.*, 21.

[33] Carta de Andrés Cotates y Marcos Chasares á Micaela Bastides, Pichigua, December 12, 1780, *ibid.*, 22–23.

[34] Carta de Fernando Gurpide y Agustín Aucagualpa á Micaela Bastidas, Pirque, December 12, 1780, *ibid.*, 24.

him.[35] Diego Bisa Apasa wrote that he had received her letter, that his people had gone to Capana, Catca, and other places, as she had ordered, and that they would send her letter on to Marca-marca.[36]

Marcos de la Torre, one of José Gabriel's captains, sent word that he also had carried out her orders. He had gone with all his people to Guatua, the sentinels had not been removed, and various persons from Cuzco said every day that neither the people from that city nor those from Pilpinto, Accha, or Paruro would go out to fight.[37] In another letter La Torre reported that the people from Paruro, Accha, Pilpinto, and other places were going to Acos, Acomayo, and other towns to attack the revolutionists. He hoped that Micaela would check them from the rear with forces from Livitaca so that the river could be crossed, and asked her to fix a day when his force should advance to the other bank. He asked for one hundred soldiers with guns and ammunition and an officer of high rank to govern the disorderly town of Acomayo.[38]

Tomás Guaca reported to Micaela that he had very few soldiers and no food. He knew the enemy awaited them in Pilpinto and that in Acomayo the alcaldes and caciques had given the people sufficient food, as a result of which they sided with the royalists. He hoped that she could send him relief soon.[39] Fernando Gurpide and Agustín Aucagualpa were hard pressed by the enemy and awaited her orders. They wrote that the royalists were expecting them to come to Acos and that many soldiers from Cuzco had joined those of Paruro to defeat the revolutionists.[40]

Julián de Escalante sent information that soldiers from Cuzco

[35] Carta de Melchor Castelo á Micaela Bastidas, Sicuani, December 13, 1780, ibid., 25–26.
[36] Carta de Diego Bisa Apaca á Micaela Bastidas, Capana, December 13, 1780, ibid., 28.
[37] Carta de Marcos de la Torre á Micaela Bastidas, Acomayo, December 13, 1780, ibid., 28.
[38] Carta de Marcos de la Torre á Micaela Bastidas, Acomayo, December 15, 1780, ibid., 31.
[39] Tomás Guaca á Micaela Bastidas, Pomacanche, December 15, 1780, ibid., 31–32.
[40] Carta de Fernando Gurpide y Agustín Aucagualpa á Micaela Bastidas, Pirque, December 16, 1780, ibid., 32–33.

were in Guaro. He said that on January 29, 1781, his people must go to Yanacocha, but he did not know how this could be done since his force was threatened by the inhabitants of Pilpinto, who had taken away from them thirty loads of reeds for making boats. With sufficient boats the people of Paruro could get away; therefore many soldiers were needed to guard the transit.[41] Micaela's brother, Antonio Bastidas, wrote her that his forces had entered Urcos, where they had destroyed all the houses. Now the people of the neighboring towns threatened his men, and Antonio asked his sister to send commissioners to those towns to drive out the rebels.[42]

Like her husband, Micaela respected priests and the church. She ordered the people who joined the revolt not to harm them and, like good Christians, they were to wear crosses on their caps and hats.[43] She ordered the alcaldes in the town of Marcapata to hasten to Juan Salazar, the assistant priest, with the accustomed fees, and said that if she noticed the slightest omission, those officials would be punished.[44]

When Micaela believed that priests could assist her, she did not hesitate to call for their services. She told Antonio de Chávez y Mendoza to administer the sacrament in Sicuani and to take charge of the possessions of that church, for Pedro de Landa, who had served it, had been sent to Pampamarca to conduct religious services.[45] On March 24, 1781, she asked Pedro Santisteban and other priests to come to Tinta immediately to remedy certain wrongs which the Indians did to the people.[46] She ordered Justo Gallegos, her chaplain, to celebrate mass in the church at Langui. Diego Túpac Amaru was present and, after the service, started

[41] Carta de Julián de Escalante á Micaela Bastidas, Acos, January 28, 1781, *ibid.*, 38.

[42] Carta de Antonio Bastidas á Micaela Bastidas, Pucacasa, February 15, 1781, *ibid.*, 39–40.

[43] Edicto de Micaela Bastidas, Tungasuca, December 13, 1780, *ibid.*, 106.

[44] Orden de Doña Micaela Bastidas, Tinta, January 23, 1781, *ibid.*, 15.

[45] Bando de Micaela Bastidas, Tinta, February 6, 1781; Carta de Antonio Chávez Mendoza, Sicuani, February 8, 1781, *ibid.*, 107–108.

[46] Carta de Micaela Bastidas á Pedro Santisteban, Tinta, March 24, 1781, *ibid.*, 17.

with his followers for another province.[47] Later Micaela had another chaplain, Chávez y Mendoza, who conducted church services and also gave her advice. He wrote her that the people were perishing from hunger and that it would be cruel to ask obventions from them. He said that he had buried certain valuable possessions of the church and every Sunday told the caciques and Spaniards to protect the Inca, Túpac Amaru.[48]

Micaela noticed that many people respected the church. She wrote to her husband on November 27, 1780, that the people in Tungasuca were dissatisfied because the church was closed and wanted to desert his cause. Two days later José Gabriel wisely ordered the assistant priest to open the church and administer the sacraments to the Indians.[49]

A number of priests corresponded with Micaela during the revolt about various matters. Pedro Juan de Luna, a chaplain, asked her to give him satisfaction for certain calumnies spread against him by Juan de Dios Valencia, who had been commissioned by her husband. The chaplain claimed that he had been detained in Livitaca on February 3, 1781, where more than two thousand Indians had insulted him. He had been falsely accused of summoning soldiers.[50] The chaplain was later punished for writing to a woman who had been excommunicated.[51]

The priest Domingo de Escalante appealed to Micaela in behalf of his brother, Julián, whom the Indians of Pomacanche were conspiring to kill, declaring that his brother had not harmed anyone.[52] At the beginning of the revolt Domingo de Escalante was assistant priest in Marcaconga, a town near the doctrina of San-

[47] Carta de Justo Gallegos á Micaela Bastidas, Layo, December 9, 1780, *ibid.*, 23.

[48] Carta de Antonio Chávez Mendoza á Micaela Bastidas, Sicuani, March 25, 1781, *ibid.*, 41.

[49] Carta de Micaela Bastidas á José Gabriel Túpac Amaru, Tangasuca, November 27, 1780, *ibid.*, 45.

[50] Carta de Pedro Juan de Luna á Micaela Bastidas, Livitaca, February 10, 1781, *ibid.*, 67–68.

[51] Acusación del promotor fiscal, Dr. Iturrizarra á Pedro de Luna, June 22, 1782, *ibid.*, 69.

[52] Carta de Domingo de Escalante á Micaela Bastidas, Acos, February 12, 1781, *ibid.*, 70.

garara. Later the royalists tried him for writing this letter to Micaela, but he was not convicted since he was not aware that Micaela had been excommunicated when he wrote.[53]

Other priests who corresponded with Micaela were Rodríguez de Ávila, Gregorio de Yépez, Martín Castilla, and Antonio José Centeno. The first was later declared guilty of treason, but since he was so well liked where he lived, nothing could be done to him. When questioned, he claimed that he had been forced to write to Micaela because he was surrounded by rebels; moreover, he wanted to keep the Spaniards in his parish from being killed.[54] Yépez had sent his brother to Cuzco and thereby lost the Inca's favor. In the letter to Micaela, Yépez claimed that the Bishop wanted his brother there, and that he, too, had gone to Cuzco because of a report that José Gabriel had ordered all Spaniards in Pomacanche to be killed. The priest said that neither he nor his brother found fault with the acts of Túpac Amaru. Micaela sent him a loaf of sugar, telling him to say mass for her husband. He answered that every time he drank maté he commended the Inca to God.[55] Yépez was also later condemned for having correspondence with an excommunicated woman.[56]

One Castilla, an assistant priest, wrote to Micaela asking a favor. One night Gregorio Chávez, a boy of his parish who lived in the priest's house, had robbed him. Castilla had put the boy in prison by order of the alcalde, and now, when Chávez wanted to be freed, Castilla feared him and was appealing to Micaela for protection.[57] No positive charges could be made against Castilla later because he claimed that he had written the letter before

[53] Informe de Dr. Matías de Isunza, abogado de la real audiencia de los reyes y juez comisionada de Domingo de Escalante, Cuzco, May 17, 1782; Acusación del promotor fiscal, Dr. Matías de Isunza, contra Domingo de Escalante, May 22, 1782, *ibid.*, 71–74.

[54] Decisión del Dr. Iturrizarra á Dr. Carlos Rodriguez de Ávila, Cuzco, October 22, 1782; Confesión de Carlos de Rodríguez de Ávila, Cuzco, June 18, 1782, *ibid.*, 77–82.

[55] Carta de Yépez á Micaela Bastidas, Pomacanche, March 4, 1781, *ibid.*, 83–85.

[56] Opinión del promotor fiscal, Dr. Iturrizarra, Cuzco, October 3, 1781, *ibid.*, 87–88.

[57] Carta de Martin Castilla á Micaela Bastidas, n.p., n.d., *ibid.*, 91–92.

Micaela was under excommunication.[58] The priest Centeno had merely asked for a safe conduct; hence the Bishop cleared him from all suspicion.[59]

The Inca's wife took charge of prisoners sent to her and tried to prevent crimes. On December 10, 1780, she commissioned Diego Berdejo to go to Quiquijana and, with the aid of the alcalde, seize Francisco Sucacahua for contradicting her husband's orders. The culprit was then to be brought to Tungasuca to prevent him from asking aid of the enemy caciques in Combapata and Checacupe.[60] On another occasion Micaela ordered the alcaldes and caciques of Yanaoca to bring the alcalde of Machacayo to her in order that he might explain a certain demand he had made."[61]

Marcos Reynoso Yáñez and Juan de Dios de la Borda wrote to Micaela that they were sending Luis Rodríguez and two Indian companions to her as prisoners. They had burned a mill on the hacienda of Quellouno, belonging to Lucás Puma Inga of Quiquijana, and had sacked and destroyed other ranches. Two Indians of the same town—Santos Oquendo and José Mayna—who had been caught stealing seventy-six sheep from General Gabriel Ugarte on the estate of Hayune, also were sent under guard to Micaela. When cows and sheep on the haciendas of Ayuni, Camara, and elsewhere had been stolen or killed, it was necessary for her to punish the culprits, as well as other persons who did not obey her orders.[62]

Agustín Mercado sent her word that the jailor of Sicuani was bringing a captured Indian who had been in Cuzco and, perhaps, was carrying letters.[63] Antonio Bastidas informed his sister that Marcelo Vargas was persecuting the people of Sangarara, both Spaniards and Indians, that he injured their cattle and their homes, and did great damage on the hacienda of Buenavista, where he

[58] Carta de Dr. Iturrizarra al obispo Cuzco, October 2, 1781, *ibid.*, 92–93.

[59] Decisión de Juan Manuel obispo del Cuzco, August 12, 1781, *ibid.*, 93–94.

[60] Comisión dada por Doña Micaela Bastidas á Don Diego Berdejo, Tungasuca, December 10, 1780, *ibid.*, 12.

[61] Orden de Micaela Bastidas, Tinta, January 28, 1781; Orden de Ramón Moscoso, Yanaoca, January 29, 1781, *ibid.*, 107.

[62] Carta de Marcos Reynoso Yáñez y Juan de Dios de la Borda á Micaela Bastidas, Quiquijana, December 13 and 14, 1780, *ibid.*, 26–27, 30.

[63] Carta de Agustín Mercado á Micaela Bastidas, n.p., n.d., *ibid.*, 34.

killed the cattle and sheep. Antonio therefore asked Micaela to remove Vargas from his position as commander.[64]

Micaela had heard that Andrés Castelo had used extortion to make the people rebel. She disapproved of this action and asked her husband to send him to her. In this case she seemed to have been mistaken, for Castelo later died a hero.[65]

The Inca did not comply with her request in the case of Castelo, but several days before he had sent Eugenio Sinanyuca, cacique of Coporaque, to her as a prisoner. He told Micaela to let him and his wife live together, and not to put him in prison because he was sick.[66] Later when José Gabriel had been defeated and Micaela was about to flee from Tinta, he told her to guard the prisoners well with fetters. He also hinted that if it were possible to give them some poison, it might be well to do so, for they could cause no more trouble.[67]

Micaela issued edicts and appointed officials when necessary. She had an edict drawn up on December 13, 1780, which was to be proclaimed by the crier to inform the people that they were to have José Mamani as colonel and Simón Ayuni Túpa as captain. They must obey their measures; disobedient persons and deserters would be punished.[68] Another edict of March 22, 1781, ordered Bernardino Zegarra in Quiquijana to check abuses against Spaniards and their possessions in that town, and stated that if the people disobeyed, they would be hanged and their property confiscated.[69]

Micaela appointed Santos Corma Condori chief justice of Tinta on April 1, 1781, because of the illness of Juan Chunca Tuna, who had held the position. She informed the new official that she expected him to perform his duties well.[70]

[64] Carta de Antonio Bastidas á Micaela Bastidas, Sangarara, February 7, 1781, *ibid.*, 38–39.

[65] Carta de Micaela Bastidas á José Gabriel Túpac Amaru, Tungasuca. December 2 and 3, 1780, *ibid.*, 47.

[66] Carta de José Gabriel Túpac Amaru á Micaela su esposa, Coporaque, November 30, 1780, *ibid.*, 63.

[67] Carta de José Gabriel Túpac Amaru á su esposa, n.p., n.d., *ibid.*, 66.

[68] Edicto de Micaela Bastidas, Tungasuca, December 13, 1780, *ibid.*, 105–106.

[69] Bando de Micaela Bastidas, Tinta, March 22, 1781, *ibid.*, 107.

[70] Carta de Micaela Bastidas á Santos Corma Condori, Tinta, April 1, 1781, *ibid.*, 17.

Francisco Molina, a Spaniard, later testified that Micaela's orders given to various persons were more vigorous than those of her husband. As she could not write, the edicts were written by scribes, Felipe Bermúdez, Mariano de la Banda, Diego Ortigosa, Estebán Escarcena, and Dios Berdejo, who worked for José Gabriel. Molina said that many people in the provinces who refused to join her cause were terrorized, imprisoned, and killed.[71] This statement, coming from a Spaniard, must be discounted to a certain extent.

Micaela went out with the expedition to Caylloma. When news came that her husband was in Velille and had asked for aid, she quickly hastened there on foot. She declared, "I will die where my husband dies." It was also said that she commanded troops in Pilpinto, Pomacanche, Caylloma, and Velille; she thus personally had charge of the Inca's guerrillas and managed them well.[72]

At the same time she showed that she was a sympathetic woman. When she asked Eugenio Canatupa Sinanyuca to send her a priest's habit, she asked him also to see that the Negro women were not neglected and to give them beds.[73] She wrote to Francisco Molina, "As soon as you receive my letter take the road for this town [Tinta], in order to save your life."[74] She was always glad to hear that her husband had arrived safely at his destination and repeatedly cautioned him to be careful. As she had heard that the people in Cuzco had great foresight in coming out of the city, she warned him, "When you go down there, you have the same foresight."[75]

Micaela had to face great difficulties despite her apparent success. On November 23, 1780, she wrote to her husband, "It is necessary that you take the proper remedy . . . since the Indians say they

[71] Declaración de Don Francisco Molina, Cuzco, April 21, 1781, *ibid.*, 97.

[72] Loayza, *ibid.*, 102–103n.

[73] Doña Micaela Bastidas á gobernador Don Eugenio Canatupa Sinanyuca, Sangarara, December 29, 1780, *ibid.*, 14.

[74] Carta de Micaela Bastidas á Don Francisco Molina, Tinta, January 22, 1780, *ibid.*, 15.

[75] Carta de Micaela Bastidas á José Gabriel Túpac Amaru, Tungasuca, November 26, 1780, *ibid.*, 45.

are divided."[76] Two days later she informed him that soldiers were coming from Lampa and Arequipa in considerable numbers intending to pillage the revolutionists, that the priest had fled, and that the imprisonment of Noguera caused her great anxiety, but that she had sent letters to check the hostile Indians coming from Marangani, Langui, and Layo. She told her husband that his absence had caused trouble and that it was necessary for Diego Túpac Amaru to assist her.[77] She reported that the priests of Pampamarca and Yanaoca had written to authorities in Cuzco, to the Bishop, and to other persons about what happened in Tungasuca and about the number of soldiers the revolutionists had. She had also heard that those priests, Fathers Bejarano and Ramón Mostoso, were conspiring to hand her and her son over to the enemy. All these things worried her very much.[78]

Micaela was also troubled because José Gabriel advanced so slowly. When he had delayed in Yauri for two days, she wrote that she did not have patience to endure all this. She threatened, no doubt as a means to make him hurry, to hand herself over to the enemy or take her own life. She was worried about the danger to her sons and his other followers. She asked her husband not to tarry in towns where there was nothing to do, because delay would make it possible for the enemy forces from Lampa, Arequipa, and other provinces to unite. She advised him to go to Cuzco at once before they could unite with the soldiers from Lima, but he believed in more thorough preparation. She seemed to have a clearer vision of the operations than her husband. She knew the people of Cuzco were in a panic because of their defeat at Sangarara and believed a surprise attack during the confusion in Cuzco would offset the superiority of Spanish arms. As has already been pointed out, Bishop Moscoso shared her opinion.

Micaela was grieved and scolded the Inca in the manner of a provoked wife:

[76] Carta de Micaela Bastidas á José Gabriel Túpac Amaru, Tungasuca, November 25, 1780, *ibid.*, 44.

[77] Carta de Micaela Bastidas á José Gabriel Túpac Amaru, Tungasuca, November 27, 1780, *ibid.*, 44–45.

[78] Carta de Micaela Bastidas á José Gabriel Túpac Amaru, Tungasuca, November 26, 1780, *ibid.*, 46–47.

If you wish our ruin, you may go to sleep. You are so careless that not only do you pass through the streets of Yauri, but also you go up to the church tower. . . . Such actions do not add to your honor; they detract from your fame.

She perhaps did not know that he had entered the towns to learn whether he could depend upon the people and climbed the towers to see if they would make good fortresses. Micaela told him that she no longer believed him. She was ready to travel with her people and would leave Fernando at a designated place, since the Indians were incapable of hurrying in a time of great danger. She threatened, "I am going to travel even though I may lose my life."[79] She told José Gabriel that she had summoned Indians from all the towns for the purpose of surrounding Cuzco, where the people were badly frightened and many had fled to the hills. "I have not been careless in writing to the caciques of Maras and Paucartambo," she said, "But you are inactive and give the enemy time to arm and destroy us." She relayed the latest intelligence from Cuzco, that more than one thousand soldiers were drilling on the highway, there was a barracks in San Borja, and the corregidores of Abancay, Paruro, Calca, Cotabambas, and Chumbivilcas had offered their services and their soldiers.[80]

Three days later she informed José Gabriel that people had marched out from Cuzco in three divisions. One division had gone to Catca and destroyed the town. She said that Sacacahua had committed treason and that she had very few people. "You have taken little notice of my letters telling you that I will give myself over to the horns of a bull. You do not permit me to take my life, yet your absence has been the cause of all this." She added that next day the enemy would enter Quiquijana, Acos, and neighboring towns and thus cut off the passes.[81] On December 16, 1780, she was in Pomacanche gathering more recruits and awaiting her

[79] Carta de Micaela Bastidas á José Gabriel Túpac Amaru, Tungasuca, December 6, 1780, *ibid.*, 48–51; Valcárcel, *La rebelión de Túpac Amaru*, 108–109.
[80] Carta de Micaela Bastidas á José Gabriel Túpac Amaru, Tungasuca, December 7, 1780, in Loayza, *op. cit.*, Serie I, Vol. IX, 52.
[81] Carta de Micaela Bastidas á José Gabriel Túpac Amaru, Tungasuca, December 10, 1780, *ibid.*, 52–53.

husband's advance because the first troops from Cuzco were already in Urcos.[82]

When José Gabriel finally advanced toward Cuzco, his wife marched to Sangarara and then to Yanacocha. After he had to withdraw from Cuzco to save his men, Micaela was his chief collaborator. She detained two priests from Cuzco to obtain news. They told her that when the Inca's force left the heights of Picchu, all the common people wanted to go over to him, but the sermons of different clergymen prevented their doing so. The Bishop himself was ready to go out and speak to José Gabriel, but the enemy checked him by saying that a shot could kill him. They made the prelate believe many falsehoods about the Inca, including the allegation that he would destroy Cuzco entirely. Micaela learned that the Bishop had changed his mind about the Inca when he discovered that José Gabriel respected religion. She gave José Gabriel all this information and added that she would detain the captured priests until he decided what to do with them.[83]

The Inca seemed to have great respect for his wife, entrusted her with important measures, and was anxious for her safety. On November 26, 1780, he wrote her to take care of the people at home and to see that Figueroa was not careless in keeping the arms ready.[84] Next day he told her to order the people to station themselves on the hill of Chullocani until he returned to Velille. Figueroa was to take all the cannon to that hill, but he must go with Francisco Molina and Basilio Morales, so that there would be no treason. José Gabriel evidently did not trust Figueroa entirely and thought that if he was in the company of other Spaniards, he would not have so much of a chance to turn traitor.[85] The Inca said he was safe at present, but precautions had to be taken. He

[82] Carta de Micaela Bastidas á José Gabriel Túpac Amaru, Pomacanche, December 16, 1780, *ibid.*, 53.

[83] Carta de Micaela Bastidas á José Gabriel Túpac Amaru, Tinta, January 24, 1781, *ibid.*, 54–55; Valcárcel, *La rebelión de Túpac Amaru*, 73–74.

[84] Carta de José Gabriel Túpac Amaru á su esposa Micaela, Altos de Livitaca, November 26, 1780, in Loayza, *op. cit.*, Serie I, Vol. IX, 59.

[85] Carta de José Gabriel Túpac Amaru á su esposa, Velille, November 27, 1780, *ibid.*, 60–61.

advised his wife to guard herself with soldiers and spies.[86] He understood her anxiety, and he, too, was anxious, but, if it was God's will that they should die, His will must be fulfilled.[87]

When five corregidores were in Lampa waiting to catch José Gabriel, he told Micaela that there was nothing to worry about. She and the people were to remain in their town and post sentinels. If she had to flee, she was to go with the family to Vilcañota by way of Layo. She was to keep the prisoners fettered and well guarded and leave the servants, in whom she had the greatest confidence, at home to take care of them.[88]

The Inca became still more anxious about her when he heard that the corregidor of Chumbivilcas had ordered soldiers to go to Tungasuca. He greatly feared this corregidor, who had given commands that Indians belonging to the revolutionary party were to be hanged. José Gabriel wrote Micaela to ask Molina to issue orders to the people of Pomacanche, Pueblo Nuevo, Pitamarca, Checacupe, Combapata, Tinta, and especially of Sicuani to unite and go to the height of Pongoña to await him. She herself should summon the Indians of Yanaoca, Pampamarca, Tungasuca, and Surimana. The Indians were then to march under Molina, Morales, Rafael de Rada, Melchor Castelo, Agustín Richarte, and other Spaniards who had remained in the towns mentioned. Furthermore, Figueroa was to bring a cannon and sufficient ammunition.[89]

José Gabriel made elaborate preparations for the safety of his wife and family later, when Micaela informed him that soldiers were coming from Cuzco toward Tinta. He told her to hasten with all the soldiers guarding her house toward Langui, where she could stay with her sons, Mariano and Fernando. She could do this under the pretext of sending out soldiers, and then she must remain with the forces in Langui and Layo so that she would be safe. She was

[86] Carta de José Gabriel Túpac Amaru á su esposa, Corporaque, November 29, 1780, *ibid.*, 62.

[87] Carta de José Gabriel Túpac Amaru á su esposa, Coporaque, November 30, 1780, *ibid.*, 63.

[88] Carta de José Gabriel Túpac Amaru á su esposa, Yauri, December 1, 1780, *ibid.*, 63–64.

[89] Carta de José Gabriel Túpac Amaru á su esposa, n.p., n.d., *ibid.*, 64–65.

not to neglect to send Pedro Mendagure and José Unda to advise the caciques of Marcaconga, Sangarara, Aumayo, Acos, Pirque, Pacres, and Rontocán to come to the heights of Chacamayo, where the revolutionists were stationed. The people from Checacupe and Pitamarca should take care of the sally from Quiquijana, and Tomás Rada and Felipe Castro should go with all the people. The Inca added that he would be on the boundary of Vilcañota on Sunday and that his wife should bring as much silver as possible, and he cautioned her not to forget the cannon.[90]

A number of women worked with Micaela, but only a few of their names are known. María Esquivel collaborated in the revolt; therefore Micaela protected her.[91] María did not live long, the priest Chávez y Mendoza reporting to Micaela on March 25, 1781, that he had buried her.[92] Francisca Herrera from Combapata was another woman who put herself under the orders of the Inca's wife.[93] Angela Pacuri also showed great respect for Micaela's authority in the revolt and applauded the Inca's success.[94]

Catalina de Zalas y Pachacutti helped Micaela collect supplies for Túpac Amaru. On one occasion Catalina wrote that the porters had been detained because there was no money to pay them and that even the priest had no funds, but she sent Micaela some provisions anyhow.[95] Catalina said that she was praying for the Inca's success.[96]

The most important woman revolutionist other than Micaela was Tomasa Titu Condemayta, who governed Acos. She was very brave and bold and from the beginning of the revolt worked directly with José Gabriel. She furnished him silver and supplies,

[90] Carta de José Gabriel Túpac Amaru á su esposa, n.p., n.d., *ibid.*, 65–66.

[91] Carta de Melchor Castelo á Micaela Bastidas, Sicuani, November 14, 1780, *ibid.*, 18 & n.

[92] Chávez Mendoza á Micaela Bastidas, Sicuani, March 25, 1781, *ibid.*, 41.

[93] Carta de Francesca Herrera á Micaela Bastidas, n.p., n.d., December 13, 1780, *ibid.*, 25.

[94] Carta de Angela Pacuri á Micaela Bastidas, Coporaque, December 12, 1780, *ibid.*, 22.

[95] Carta de Catalina de Zalas y Pachacutti á Micaela Bastidas, Yanaoca, December 16, 1780, *ibid.*, 32.

[96] Carta de Catalina de Zalas y Pachacutti á Micaela Bastidas, Yanaoca, n.d., *ibid.*, 34.

gave him information, corresponded with him, and took orders from him.[97] She did not wait for Micaela to write to her, but sent a letter to the Inca without knowing his exact whereabouts. She said that she had her people ready to help him, since she heard it was necessary to advance to the heights of Yanacocha because many soldiers from Cuzco were surrounding the revolutionists. She was therefore determined to take out her people, and she prayed for his health.[98]

She also corresponded later with the Inca's wife. On December 4, 1780, she lamented that she had waited for Micaela's arrival and the return of her own brother, José, about whom she was greatly worried because she had not heard from him. She said that she had nobody to put in his place, and could not rely upon the people of Acomayo and Corma, since they had fled. She had protected the inhabitants of Acos, but for two years they had suffered hunger and the food situation was getting worse. She therefore asked Micaela to send grain from Veleta. She felt certain of help, for the Inca's wife had twice assisted Acomayo.[99]

Five days later Tomasa informed Micaela that inhabitants of Cuzco and Chumbivilcas were determined to come out against the revolutionists. Juan Zubizarreta, whom Micaela had appointed chief justice in Livitaca, had fled with all his people toward Cuzco, but was arrested in Paruro. As the people from Quiquijana and all the ravine knew that the Inca was far away, they were going to ambush the inhabitants of Acos.[100] Another time Tomasa wrote that it was very difficult for a woman to defend herself. She had prepared as many people as possible, but her forces could not leave from Acos or Acomayo, as they were in a critical situation. She advised the Inca's wife to appoint a new chief, similar to Julián Escalante, who was young and more intelligent than Marcos de

[97] Carta de Tomasa Titu Condemayta á José Gabriel Túpac Amaru, Acos, November 21, 1780, *ibid.*, 157–58.

[98] Carta de Tomasa Titu Condemayta á José Gabriel Túpac Amaru, Acos, November 30, 1780, *ibid.*, 159–60.

[99] Carta de Tomasa Titu Condemayta á Micaela Bastidas, Acos, December 4, 1780, *ibid.*, 160.

[100] Carta de Tomasa Titu Condemayta á Micaela Bastidas, Acos, December 9, 1780, *ibid.*, 161.

la Torre. She hoped that Micaela would not let her people be ruined.[101]

The part that the Inca's half sister, Cecilia Túpac Amaru, played in the revolt is rather hazy. No letters written by her have been found. The reports of her enemies comprise the only known source of information about her, and they were no doubt greatly exaggerated. Some individuals maintained that she gave orders in the Inca's house, declared it necessary to kill Spaniards, and had gone on the expedition to Picchu. It was reported that she declared the mestizos traitors, that she had stirred up the Indians to kill Spaniards, telling them to begin with her husband, Pedro Mendagure, because he had at first refused to aid the Inca, and that she gave silver and coca to natives who put Spaniards to death.[102] Andrea Esquivel said that Cecelia was worse than Micaela, that she wanted her brother to succeed in the rebellion, and that she bragged about having the pelts on which corregidores had slept.[103] Francisco Molina said that Cecilia had influenced Micaela to kill and mistreat Spaniards as traitors and rogues. He also testified that when Cecilia came to the hill of Picchu and did not find powder, she blamed Francisco Cisneros, maltreated him, and tried to put his eyes out with a broomstraw.[104]

It can be thus concluded that women of eighteenth-century Peru were no weaklings, despite conservative Spanish conventions, and took an active part in the most significant event of the era. José Gabriel Túpac Amaru's wife naturally assumed the leading role in carrying out her husband's orders and in governing the people during his absence. She was helpful in collecting supplies, spreading propaganda, giving orders, and at the same time making appointments and administering justice. Tomasa Titu Condemayta and Cecilia Túpac Amaru were also important to the cause, as were other, nameless, women who participated in the revolt.

[101] Carta de Tomasa Titu Condemayta á Micaela Bastidas, Acos, n.d., *ibid.*, 161–62.

[102] Declaración de Manuel Galleguillos, Cuzco, April 26, 1781; Declaración de Diego Ortigosa, Cuzco, May 4, 1781; Declaración de Francisco Noguera, n.p., n.d., *ibid.*, 190–91.

[103] Declaración de Andrea Esquivel, Cuzco, May 5, 1781, *ibid.*, 191.

[104] Declaración de Francisco Molina, Cuzco, June 1, 1781, *ibid.*, 192.

CHAPTER X

Defeat and Death for the Inca

IN CUZCO many preparations were made to press the campaign against the Inca. The army consisted now of the forces from Lima, militia from Huamanga, forces of Cuzco, and the faithful Indians. According to Odriozola, the number of men under arms expanded to 15,210, while other sources give 17,116, at least 14,000 of them loyal Indians. These soldiers were divided into six columns, a body of reserves, and two detachments. The six columns and the reserves were all to advance over different routes towards Tinta. The two detachments of 1,846 men were assigned to take the posts of Urubamba, Calca, and Lares for the purpose of cutting off the enemy's retreat in that direction.[1]

At first Visitador Areche hoped to win over some of the rebels by offering a pardon. On March 8, 1781, therefore, he offered pardon to those who would lay down their arms and return to their homes. Not included in this general amnesty, however, were caciques who had allied with the Inca or the leaders of the rebellion. Areche also declared that he would liberally reward anyone who delivered to him the insurgents not included in the pardon. Among them were José Gabriel, Hipólito, Mariano, Fernando, and Diego Túpac Amaru; Francisco Túpac Amaru, the Inca's uncle; his nephew, Andrés Mendagure; his cousins, Patricio and Francisco Noguera and Diego Berdejo; his brother-in-law, Pedro Mendagure; his wife and her brother, Antonio Bastidas; and many of the Inca's secretaries and officers. Areche promised to reward their captors with a pension of eighty pesos a month, a captain's salary, for the rest of their lives. He would even pardon the chiefs in the

---

[1] Odriozola, *Documentos*, I, 55–56. Lorente said the number of men was 17,116 (*Historia del Peru bajo los Borbones*, 195). The men of Del Valle's army gave the number as 17,116 (Diario de los soldados que vienen del Cuzco con José del Valle, Cuzco, March 19, 1781, in Odriozola, *Documentos*, I, 137; Angelis, *Documentos*, 34–37).

rebellion if they would capture José Gabriel, his sons, brother, wife, and relatives.[2]

Leaving a garrison of one thousand soldiers in Cuzco, Inspector General del Valle took the army with its six cannons out of the city next day. He advanced slowly over the mountains toward the east of the Vilcamayo Valley. On the march he suffered greatly from snowstorms and lack of food and fuel—the latter because the visitador had not attended to the provisions and the enemy had cut off communication with loyal neighboring provinces. When the army was without meat and biscuits for three days, Del Valle gave his own supplies to the troops. Colonel Gabriel Avilés, chief of the reserves, had to take cattle by force and pay for them with his own funds, for the rebels had seized the meat for the rest of the campaign. By March 12, only seven head of cattle had been collected for 2,760 men.

Nor did the authorities assist Del Valle with money. In fourteen months of the campaign he received only one full salary; and on one occasion the enemy came close to getting 20,000 pesos of the loyalists' funds. In the column from Cochabamba only fifteen tents and 6,000 pesos were furnished for approximately three thousand men, the army was clothed in flannel of inferior quality, and no muleteers had been provided to transport supplies.

Medical supplies were also short. A box sent from an apothecary shop in Lima was broken to pieces on the road. When the corregidor of Paruro, Manuel Castilla, was wounded, he had to seek a little brandy from a distance to alleviate the pain. There were only two surgeons in all the columns. Men were treated with red oxide of iron, and many suffered from dysentery.

The expedition was composed of a heterogeneous group of Spaniards, mestizos, and Indians. With the exception of about fifty men from Callao, they were ignorant of military matters, and all but ten or twelve officers were untrained. Del Valle said that they were rustics incapable of discipline, and there was no time to train them properly. These men had abandoned their crops to

[2] Bando de José Antonio de Areche, Cuzco, March 8, 1781, in Loayza, *op. cit.*, Serie I, Vol. IX, 147–50 n.

serve, with their mules, for the meager pay of fifty to one hundred pesos, believing that they would have to fight for only twenty days. When they learned that the time of service was indefinite, many deserted.[3]

In the province of Cotabambas the fifth division fought during a snowstorm with Indians under the command of Tomás Parvina and Felipe Bermúdez. This battle brought many hardships to the Spaniards, but more than one thousand Indians were killed. Among them were both of Túpac Amaru's brave chiefs, who, with five thousand to six thousand men under them, died fighting on foot in a canyon. The loss of these two capable officers was a great blow to the Inca.[4]

Near Pucacasa the Spaniards suffered from another severe storm and had to take shelter in their tents, while the Indians watched their movements from the hills. Túpac Amaru sent the royalists a message on March 18, in which he repeated the proposition he had made to Visitador Areche to end the evils suffered. He added that if they did not give protection to all his family and his proposal was not accepted, he would continue to fight.

The Spaniards remained under arms all night, yet no attack was made. At dawn they noticed that the Inca's army had gone. Túpac Amaru's purpose in withdrawing was to prepare a surprise attack for March 21, hiding in an unfrequented ravine with ten thousand men. His plan would have succeeded if a traitor Zumiaña Castro by name, had not given Del Valle information about his movements. The Spaniards quickly broke camp and changed their position, while the Inca passed the night looking for them.[5]

The soldiers from Lima and the coastal regions suffered so

[3] El mariscal del campo D. José del Valle escribió y firmó en el Cuzco en 30 de Sete. de 1781 un manifesto . . . . MS copy in B. L.

[4] Decada 4ª· de la rebelión de José Gabriel Túpac Amaru, Cuzco, May 22, 1781. MS copy in B. L. Diario de los soldados que vienen del Cuzco con mariscal del campo, José del Valle, Cuzco, March 19, 1781, in Odriozola, *Documentos*, I, 138; Lorente, *Historia del Peru bajo los Borbones*, 195.

[5] Markham, *Travels in Peru and India*, 150–51. Decada 4ª· de la escena en la rebelión de José Gabriel Túpac Amaru, Cuzco, May 22, 1781. MS copy in B. L. Copia de carta escrita á un Sor. ministro de Madrid por un vecino del Cuzco, September 1, 1782, signed "B. L. M.," copied from the Archivo General del Peru. Copy in B. L.

214

much from the high altitude that they could scarcely manage their arms during the cold nights. As General del Valle was over seventy years of age and could not himself endure the excessive cold of the mountains, he took the troops down from Pucacasa to the town of Andahuaylas in order that they might recover from their illness. From there he continued his march through the temperate regions to the town of Quiquijana.[6]

The inhabitants of Quiquijana had been very obstinate in supporting the insurrection. General del Valle therefore thought it would take many days to reduce them to obedience without shedding excessive blood. He decided to camp in the vicinity, and was soon saluted by the fire of enemy artillery and guns, which had no effect because they were too far away. At dawn of the following day the priest of the town informed the General that the rebels had abandoned their advantageous position for the purpose of uniting with the army of Túpac Amaru, who was in Tinta, and that they had destroyed the bridge to delay the advance of the Spanish troops. The royalist army then entered Quiquijana, where they found only old men and women. All had sought refuge in the church and, with many tears, showed signs of repentance and asked pardon. This was granted, but Luis Poma, a cousin of Túpac Amaru, and Bernardo Zegarra, his confidant, were hanged.

After stationing guards about Quiquijana, the army continued its march without delay. At the next camp the enemy were seen occupying the mountain heights, where they had a cannon and large stones which they intended to hurl on the Spaniards when they entered a narrow pass near a river that had to be forded. To avoid this danger, gunners of the light troops and Indian auxiliaries from Anta and Chincheros dislodged the enemy from three very advantageous posts on the mountain crest.[7] Then it was reported that Túpac Amaru camped on a hill between Tinta and Sangarara with seven thousand Indians.

According to plan, the reserve army under Colonel Avilés

[6] Lorente, *Historia del Peru bajo los Borbones,* 197; Mendiburu, *Diccionario,* VIII, 141.

[7] Odriozola, *Documentos,* I, 57–58; Diario de los soldados que vienen del Cuzco con el mariscal del campo, José del Valle, Cuzco, March 18, 1781, *ibid.,* I, 138.

arrived, on March 23, two leagues from Sangarara. When Avilés reconnoitered the enemy's location, he saw that it was advantageous on account of the nature of the land and the entrenchment they had constructed. He sent word to Lieutenant Colonel Villalta, commander of the third column, to hasten there, which he did with the greatest precaution, arriving on the twenty-fifth. The two forces camped there until April 4, when all the other columns reached their assigned destination.

General del Valle made a new reconnaissance (April 4) and summoned a council of war, which decided that the enemy camp was too strong to attack, for the Inca had at least fourteen thousand men in that region, and that the Spaniards should form a blockade. Indian deserters brought news that Túpac Amaru had collected few supplies and would have to go down to the plain to seek hay for the mounts of his four thousand cavalrymen, at which times he would be vulnerable to attack. The royalists surrounded the area, but the enemy kept quiet in their camp until April 5. Then fifty Spaniards advanced boldly under constant fire near to the enemy entrenchment and made a careful reconnaissance. When a large number of Indians came out, the royalists fought bravely for a quarter of an hour, after which the number of Indians increased so greatly that the soldiers retreated, in good order and losing only two men. From two Indian prisoners it was learned that Túpac Amaru had supplies in camp for scarcely two days.

That night royalist sentinels were doubled. They were ordered to observe the enemy closely and to discharge their guns if they noticed any movement. It was feared that the Inca might attempt to surprise them, since lack of provisions was making him desperate. On the night of April 5, Túpac Amaru tried to do just that. He believed the royalists had not withdrawn farther than to the open road and decided to surprise Villalta's column and the body of reserves. Therefore, shortly after midnight he came out of his camp very silently with all his people and beheaded four of the Spanish sentinels. Another guard, who was fifty paces distant from the others, heard a noise and fired his gun. The Spaniards were half-asleep in their tents, but they seized their arms without delay and in five minutes were drawn up in battle formation. The musketeers attacked the enemy flanks with a lively fire, while the reserves struck their rear guard. Although the Indians fired six cannons as well as guns, they could not withstand such an assault. When the Inca saw that his cannons and munitions were taken, he fled, leaving a large number of dead on the field and all the baggage and war equipment. It was now four o'clock in the morning.

Túpac Amaru realized that he was completely defeated. He rode horseback up the hill of Sangarara and then descended on the opposite side. Forgetting the ford in the river which he had to cross to reach Tinta, he swam across and almost drowned. Eighteen mulattoes of the Lima infantry followed him because they wanted the 20,000 pesos' reward offered for him, but two of them drowned and the rest had to turn back.[8] Before the Inca arrived at Tinta, he wrote to his wife pathetically, "Many and brave soldiers are coming against us. There is no other remedy for us but to die." His wife and some members of his family then hurried away toward the province of Carabaya to seek refuge among the Indians of the more elevated towns.

The Spanish army decided to follow even to Tinta. They could not do so quickly, however, because the river was high. When night approached, it became necessary to camp near the town of Combapata, one league distant from Tinta. In the morning the enemy fired on the royalists, but caused no damage.

At two o'clock on the following morning 150 gunners of the light troop were ordered to surprise the insurgents. They went out with the Indian auxiliaries of Anta and Chincheros to occupy a mountain overlooking a tract of level land over which the army would pass to go to Combapata. The Indians had surrounded that town with an adobe wall covered with thorns to obstruct the march. The General then ordered a battery of five cannons placed in a post

[8] *Relación de los hechos mas notables acaecidos en la sublevación general . . . ,* 207–10. MS copy in B. L. Diario de los soldados que vienen del Cuzco con el mariscal del campo, José del Valle, Cuzco, March 19, 1781, in Odriozola, *Documentos,* I, 137–38; Diario de los soldados que vienen del Cuzco con mariscal del campo, José del Valle, Cuzco, March 19, 1781, *ibid.,* I, 138–39. Noticias recibidas del campo Tungasuca con proprio que salió del Cuzco en 8 de Abril, y llegó a Lima el 16 del mismo mes, in Lewin, *op. cit.,* 239–41.

dominating the enemy position. As the firing was well directed, it was not long before thirty inhabitants of Tinta presented themselves for pardon. They said that Túpac Amaru's family had left the town, taking with them the stamped and wrought silver, jewels, and other things of value obtained at the beginning of the revolt. Juan Bautista Túpac Amaru, the Inca's half brother, had been put in charge of the transportation of arms, money, and cattle.

Inspector General del Valle ordered the army to go to Tinta and sent detachments in all directions to try to capture the fugitives. He caused the pass of the Andes through the province of Carabaya to be closed to prevent the Inca and his family from seeking refuge in those mountains among the barbarous Indians.[9] Túpac Amaru's wife, two sons, and five other members of the family fled by the road of Livitaca, hoping to reach La Paz with their twelve loads of stamped silver, but were arrested by the column under command of Francisco Laesquilla and Domingo Marnara.[10]

José Gabriel took the road to Langui, a town six leagues distant on the shore of a wild mountain lake. The desire to save part of his funds to continue the war caused him to lose time loading his mules in Tinta, and so he did not get started until six o'clock in the evening and had to travel slowly. At Langui he intended to rally his scattered forces, no doubt to pass into the jurisdiction of Buenos Aires and offer resistance in the Callao region. He entered the town confident of the fidelity of Colonel Ventura Landaeta, whom he told about his ill success and his plans for continuing the revolution. The Colonel persuaded him to remain there until recruits could be collected. The Inca agreed, and waited while breakfast was prepared for him. Meanwhile, the Colonel went to seek confederates to help him carry out a traitorous plan. Upon his return, Túpac Amaru detected his cunning and tried to get away, but two women seized him by the shoulder and detained him. They were indignant and overcome by grief on account of the war. One had lost a husband and the other two sons in the revolution. The latter,

[9] Odriozola, Documentos, I, 58–59; Markham, A History of Peru, 204; Carrió, op. cit., 97; Valcárcel, La rebelión de Túpac Amaru, 119.
[10] Museo de Mitre, Armario E. Cajón 10, in Lewin, op. cit., 241.

Juana Portilla, wife of Tomás Rodríguez and probably a Spaniard, remained in Langui to become the victim of the Indians a few days later for her part in their leader's apprehension.

The people of Langui, aided by the assistant priest, Antonio Martínez, guarded Túpac Amaru. Soon Colonel Landaeta obtained fifty dragoons from Sicuani to escort him, the greater part of his family, thirty-two of his captains, and certain of his followers to the camp of General del Valle. Some members of the Inca's family were not captured. His brother Diego, his son Mariano, his nephew Andrés Mendagure, and Miguel Bastidas, a nephew of his wife, escaped by taking different roads. They established residence in Azángaro and continued to support the revolt.

Meanwhile, Del Valle entered Tinta with his troops. He found an effigy of Túpac Amaru on horseback and trophies of the battle of Sangarara hanging on the gallows. As the people received him willingly and tearfully, he was kind to most of them, but he put sixty-seven Indians to death and placed their heads on posts along the road. He also immediately utilized the Inca's foundry in Tinta.

News of the Inca's capture soon reached Cuzco, where there was great rejoicing. When Visitador Areche heard that many valuables were hidden in Tinta, he asked the church to issue a general censure against any person who usurped or concealed Túpac Amaru's possessions. This was done without delay.

Leaving most of the army in the camps at Quiquijana, Tinta, and Langui, Del Valle conducted the retinue of prisoners to Cuzco. The entrance on April 14, 1781, was one of the most solemn events ever seen in that city. Even the visitador went out to the town of Urcos, eight leagues distant, to meet the captives, triumphantly entered Cuzco with them, and received public acclamation. The militia was drawn up to form two passageways from the little plaza of Limapanpa, near the church of Santo Domingo, to the prison, which was the old Jesuit College. All the city turned out to see Túpac Amaru, his wife and sons, and allies who came with uncovered heads. The first objects that the unfortunate captives saw were the gallows. After passing through the aisles bounded by militiamen, they dismounted from their mules at the prison doors, where

Areche separated them. There Túpac Amaru took leave of his wife and sons with the promise that he would see them in eternity. They were soon placed in different prisons, and the visitador commissioned Judge Benito de la Mata Linares to preside at their trial.[11]

At six o'clock in the morning of the same day Francisco Túpac Amaru, the Inca's uncle, and a cacique, called Marcos Torres, had been conducted into the city. Both were famous captains. The first wore the royal vestments of the Incas.

Two trunks full of papers were also brought into Cuzco, and several persons were kept busy all night examining the contents. Two other trunks containing wrought silver and many of the Inca's jewels were likewise found.[12]

Visitador Areche immediately informed the Viceroy of Buenos Aires of the capture of the long-sought prisoners.[13] It was not until June 23, however, that the inhabitants of Buenos Aires heard about the Inca's imprisonment. At that time Bishop Sebastián Malvar y Pino issued a pastoral letter summoning them to the cathedral on the morning of the twenty-eighth to give thanks to God for his mercies and to sing the *Te Deum*. He exhorted all the people to remain obedient to the King and the Viceroy.[14]

Meanwhile, the Inca wrote to the Bishop of Cuzco asking that his life be spared and stating once more the things for which he had been working:

> I am considered a rebel or infidel to our monarch, Charles III. Time will tell that I am a faithful and loyal vassal and that I have not retracted a bit from my due esteem for the holy church and his Majesty. . . . I will refrain from asking divine mercy and general

11 Decada 4ª. de la escena en la rebelión de José Gabriel Túpac Amaru, Cuzco, May 22, 1781. MS copy in B. L. Copia de carta escrita á un Sor. ministro de Madrid por un vecino del Cuzco, Cuzco, September 1, 1782, signed "B. L. M." MS copy in B. L. Lorente, *Historia del Peru bajo los Borbones*, 197–98; Odriozola, *Documentos*, I, 59–60. One account said that Juana Portilla took hold of the reins of the Inca's horse and he could not free himself (Loayza, *op. cit.*, Serie I, Vol. III, 174n.)

12 Diario de los soldados que vienen del Cuzco con mariscal del campo, José del Valle, Cuzco, March 19, 1781, in Odriozola, *Documentos*, I, 139.

13 Oficio del visitador general D. José Antonio de Areche al virrey de Buenos Aires, Cuzco, April 12, 1781, *ibid.*, I, 139–43; Angelis, *Documentos*, 38–39.

14 Pastoral del obispo de Buenos Aires, Fray Sebastián, Buenos Aires, June 24, 1781, in Odriozola, *Documentos*, I, 164–66; Angelis, *Documentos*, 57–59.

pardon for myself. I realize that I did not show the proper vassalage that I desired, but I tried only to abolish all customhouses.

He asked to have all his documents sent to Cuzco and carefully
examined.[15]

Areche kept Túpac Amaru in prison without a trial for more
than a month while he was taking measures for the conquest of
the provinces still in rebellion. Since the Inca refused to confess
during the trial when it finally took place, he was tortured by
means of the *garrucha,* or pulley, until an arm was dislocated.
Afterwards the visitador, pretending to be humane, served him
food, and ate at the same table with him.[16]

Reports that José Gabriel had tried to escape hastened his trial.
According to one account, the Inca, using his own blood as ink,
wrote instructions for his people on a piece of lining from his
clothes, then endeavored to bribe the sentinel to smuggle the message out of the prison. The man proved to be a faithful subject of
the King and reported the incident to Visitador Areche.[17] Inspector
General del Valle also reported that the Inca had asked Cayetano
Vilches, a soldier stationed at the prison door, to bring him a file
so that he could free himself and also asked him to carry some
papers for him. He had offered the man an immense amount of
money, which he said was buried in a certain location. Vilches,
however, reported to his chief, José de León, commander of the
troops of the Cuzco garrison, who informed the visitador. The
latter was assured of the truth of the accusation because he had
eavesdropped on the soldier's conversation with León.[18] Areche
declared that Túpac Amaru had tried to flee from the prison on
two occasions.[19] Moreover, by May 2 the Inca's health was break-

[15] Carta escrita del Inca Túpac Amaru al Illmo. obispo del Cuzco [n.d.]. Copy
of the original sent by the Bishop to the Viceroy. MS copy in B. L.

[16] Decada 4ª· de la escena en la rebelión de José Gabriel Túpac Amaru, Cuzco,
May 22, 1781, MS copy in B. L. Gutiérrez, *op. cit.,* 149.

[17] Copia de carta escrita á un Sor. ministro de Madrid por un vecino del Cuzco,
Cuzco, September 1, 1782, signed "B. L. M." MS copy in B. L.

[18] Mariscal del campo D. José del Valle escribió y firmó en el Cuaco en 30 de
Sete. de 1781 un manifesto. MS copy in B.L.

[19] Sentencia dada por el Sor. visitador D. José Antonio Areche al rebelde José
Gabriel Túpac Amaru en la ciudad del Cuzco, Cuzco, May 15, 1781. MS copy in B. L.

ing; and so the trial was hurried for fear that death would deprive the executioner of a victim.[20]

At the trial the accusations against the Inca included almost every possible crime. Túpac Amaru was charged, first of all, with plotting the rebellion in almost all the territory of two viceroyalties for more than five years before it broke out in order to have himself crowned lord of the country, although he pretended to be the liberator of the people. Hanging Corregidor Arriaga was his first crime. He displayed an implacable hatred of Europeans and all other white people. He committed innumerable outrages, insults, and robberies. He caused death, ravishment, and unspeakable acts of violence. He had profaned churches and their ministers and ridiculed excommunication. He had made himself a legislator, thereby usurping the King's authority. Without legal authority, he had put priests in the Indian villages, let them receive him under the canopy, appointed justices in the provinces, abolished repartimientos, extinguished customhouses and dues called unjust, abolished the mita, burned workshops, and had taken funds from the royal treasuries. He had imposed the death penalty upon all persons who did not obey him and had hanged many in every town. He had compelled many persons to pay tribute to him and had induced them to disobey their legitimate king. He had let the wicked rumor spread through his troops that after he was crowned, the men who had died in his behalf would come to life again. He had persuaded the Indians to believe that his cause was just, had had cannon made to oppose the King's authority, had fixed the place for his palace, had taken royal titles, had used the royal insignia of early Inca kings, and from the beginning had commanded like a monarch. Many of the charges, of course, were never proved.

On May 15, 1781, the visitador pronounced his terrible sentence. In the public plaza in Cuzco the Inca was to witness the execution of his wife, son, other relatives, and captains. After they had been put to death, his tongue was to be cut out by the executioner. Then his limbs were to be tied by strong ropes to the

[20] Valcárcel, *La rebelión de Túpac Amaru*, 121.

girths of four horses, which were to be driven in four different directions, so that his body would be dismembered. His remains were then to be taken to the hill of Picchu, where he had had the boldness to ask the city to surrender, and the trunk burned in a bonfire, the ashes to be cast into the air. A flat stone was to be erected on which his crimes were to be enumerated. His head was to be sent to Tinta and kept on the gallows for three days and then put up on a post at the entrance of the town. The same thing was to be done with one of his arms in Tungasuca, and the other arm would be exhibited in the capital of the province of Carabaya. One leg was to be sent to Livitaca in the province of Chumbivilcas, and the other to Santa Rosa in the province of Lampa. His houses were to be demolished completely and the sites publicly salted. All his possessions would be confiscated, and the members of his family would have no inheritance whatever. The proclamations concerning his descent were to be collected and publicly burned by the executioner to blot out the memory of them. Any future claims of descent from the ancient Inca kings were not to be handled by any court, but were to be sent directly to the Spanish sovereign.

The office of cacique was no longer to be hereditary, but corregidores henceforth were to appoint men of good character to the position. The Indians were forbidden to wear the costumes of the Inca nobility because they only reminded them of the Inca kings and generated hatred for the Spaniards. Indians were not to dress in black as a sign of mourning for their dead monarchs. This proclamation was to be published in every province of South America, so that the people could hand over to their corregidores whatever clothes of that nature which they had. Spanish dress must be worn by all Indians. All pictures and portraits of the Incas were to be collected so that they could not be used for adornment or decoration.

Areche went so far as to forbid the production of comedies and other ancient dramas. Use of conch-shell horns was prohibited. The Indians were not to be called Incas henceforth. All persons who had genealogies were to send them, free of charge through the post office, to the secretaries of the two viceroyalties. The use

223

of the Quechua language and the reading of the *History of the Incas* by Garcilaso de la Vega were forbidden. Finally, no cannon of any kind could be made under penalty of ten years in a presidio in Africa for a nobleman and two hundred lashes for a plebeian.

Areche wanted this sentence to be published immediately in all the kingdom of Peru because the Indians thought that the death penalty could not be imposed upon a person of such high Inca rank as Túpac Amaru held. Further, a day was to be set aside by the authorities on which each year the inhabitants of the towns were to be told about his fate.[21] As it turned out, however, later viceroys, in order to prevent the Indians from learning what they considered harmful things, prohibited the reading of the part of the sentence treating the Inca's past.[22]

The questioning of the Inca's wife at her trial was so rigorous that she confessed her guilt, while cleverly refusing to reveal what she did not want known. The charges against her were made by prejudiced Spaniards and other enemies. Francisco Molina declared that Micaela had imprisoned Spaniards, called corregidores and their followers public thieves, and said that the high courts condoned their acts. He also testified that she had said that Spaniards were traitors, that she wanted to destroy the whole race, and that her partisans had been responsible for many deaths.[23] Francisco Cisneros, a scribe of Corregidor Arriaga and an inhabitant of Sicuani, said that her orders were more vigorous than her husband's. They were written by his secretaries, but when she did not like them, she blotted them out and had other papers drawn up.[24]

Manuel de San Roque avowed that she had guided her husband's conspiracy, excited the Indians, armed them, and encour-

21 Sentencia dada por el Sor. Visitador D. José Antonio Areche al rebelde José Gabriel Túpac Amaru en la ciudad del Cuzco, Cuzco, May 15, 1781. MS copy in B. L. Angelis, *Documentos*, 44–52; Markham, *A History of Peru*, 205.

22 Lewin, *op. cit.*, 16.

23 Declaración de Don Francisco Molina, Cuzco, April 21, 1781, in Loayza, *op. cit.*, Serie I, Vol. IX, 98–99. Although Molina had been one of the most bloodthirsty of the rebels at the battle of Sangarara, he was merely banished after the revolution.

24 Declaración de Francisco Cisneros, n.p., n.d., in Loayza, *op. cit.*, Serie I, Vol. IX, 99–100.

aged them with silver, coca, and food. Although Spaniards and mestizos made many complaints about the outrages committed by certain Indians, she did not check them. She had let him understand, contended the witness, that her husband intended to reign, and, in order to do so, would imprison the Europeans in the Jesuit College, where they would be killed.[25] Manuel Galleguillos, one of the secretaries, declared that she led the expedition to Pilpinto personally as far as the workshop of Pomacanche, from there returning home with her people. He said her orders were stronger than the Inca's and that she wanted to kill all Spaniards in cold blood. He heard her say to José Gabriel that if any Spaniards remained alive, he was to make them work hard. She rejoiced greatly when she learned that the King's soldiers had died and gave anyone bringing such news silver and clothes. She was reported to have said that when she and her husband were victorious, they would thrust Spanish men, women, and priests into a house and burn them.[26] Most of these accusations were lies.

Micaela confessed (April 22, 1781) before Judge Mata Linares. She said that she had been born in Pampamarca and was twenty-five years old. Earlier, on April 2, however, she had admitted that she was thirty-five, and this age seems more accurate, since she had married José Gabriel on May 25, 1760. She declared that she was imprisoned because her husband had killed Corregidor Arriaga. When asked what motive the Inca had for executing the corregidor, she replied that Arriaga had wanted to put José Gabriel and Pedro Mendagure to death. The judge asked when her husband first told her that he intended to kill Arriaga. She replied that he did not communicate anything to her until after he had imprisoned the official; then he told her and Diego Túpac Amaru that he had a decree from the King to seize corregidores. The judge asked whether she had tried to dissuade him and why she had not fled. She stated that she had tried to make José Gabriel change his mind, but he would not listen to her, and that she could not get away, although she wanted to go to her relatives in Cuzco.

---

[25] Declaración de Manuel José de San Roque, n.p., n.d., *ibid.*, 100–101.
[26] Declaración de Manuel Galleguillos, n.p., n.d., *ibid.*, 102–104.

She admitted that her husband had ordered Corregidor Arriaga to be executed and that a Zambo called Antonio had volunteered to hang him. She gave the names of the priests who administered to the corregidor before his death because everybody knew them already. They were the priest of Pampamarca, Antonio López de Sosa, Ildefonso Bejarano, Jacinto Castañeda, and Clemente Vergara. Asked whether José Gabriel was friendly with and consulted other priests, she said he did not ask their advice. She made this answer to save the priests. Questioned whether priests did not remonstrate with her husband about what he intended to do, she replied that the priest from Pampamarca asked why he acted as he did and if he had a wife and children, but the other priests did not say a word. She said that José Gabriel answered that he knew what he was doing.

Asked if she gave orders and collected people during her husband's absence, she replied that she did so at his command. She answered the question of whether José Gabriel influenced caciques and natives by claiming to be of royal blood by saying merely that the Indians called him "Inca." She declared that she did not know who had advised him, or with whom he had communicated; only his agent, Mariano Barrera, wrote to him from Lima about his lawsuit.

The judge was curious about the caciques to whom the Inca wrote after Arriaga's death about seizing other corregidores. Micaela cleverly said that she knew of only two—Chillitupa and Sahuaraura—both traitors to Túpac Amaru. She was asked whether her husband corresponded with members of the Ugarte family in Cuzco, but pretended not to know. In fact, there were many proofs that this family had worked secretly for the revolt, and when it was over, in 1787, Antonio and Gabriel Ugarte were taken as prisoners to Spain and banished from Peru. The judge hoped that Micaela would give the names of the Inca's assistants, but she said, "Everybody was his friend." She did not hesitate to tell who his secretaries were, since they had already testified against her, perhaps to save themselves. Micaela refused to list any of the captains, saying that the Inca himself was the principal leader of the expeditions.

She denied that she had tried to take up arms against the King because she believed her husband would be victorious. The judge refuted her statement by saying that it looked as if she were interested in the Inca's victories when she gave out his orders. She retorted that Mariano de la Banda wrote the orders, that she did not examine them since she did not know how to read or write. When asked why she did not abandon her spouse after he was excommunicated, she said he had assured her that the penalty of the church did not include them since God knew his intentions; therefore, she had no fear.

The Spaniards were particularly interested in knowing whether Micaela had hidden gold, silver, jewels, or documents. She declared that she had given everything to Inspector del Valle. When the judge asked whether her husband had a hidden mine, she answered, "No." He next wanted to know if the Indians had brought him gold or silver as tribute. She said, "Yes, but not as tribute." The judge made her enumerate all her personal jewelry at the time of her imprisonment. All this, she said, the people of Langui took and gave to the inspector, except for a chest of silver, which she let the priest of Yara have. She pretended not to know anything that had happened in Cuzco. The judge showed her José Gabriel's portrait painted on a piece of linen and asked who had painted it. She said that Antonio Oblitas had made the picture at her husband's request, so that if he was killed, some memory of him would survive.[27]

The judge questioned Micaela again on May 1, 1781. He was most persistent, repeating some of his questions in an attempt to break down her resistance. He asked her whether her husband had decided upon the uprising because he had lost his lawsuit in the Audiencia of Lima and on account of the dispute between the priest of Coporaque and others. She acknowledged that the charge had been made, but declared that José Gabriel did not know about

[27] Confesión de Micaela Bastidas, Cuzco, April 22, 1781, *ibid.*, 108–18.

it until he came from Lima.[28] The judge wanted to know if it was true that her husband had considered the uprising seven years before it broke out and that he had consulted Barrera and Lucás Aparicio about it when they were in Potosí, if the latter had advised him to go ahead with the rebellion, and whether, while he was in Lima, the Inca had conferred with people of high rank who had urged him to go ahead. Micaela answered that the charge was true concerning Barrera and Aparicio and that he had corresponded with Miguel Montiel, but the rest she denied.[29] Her answer contradicted the testimony of several witnesses who had made statements earlier. For example, Bernardo de la Madrid had declared that Micaela had said that three years earlier her husband had considered the revolt and on his way back from Lima had spoken of it to the caciques of Huarochirí as he passed through that province. La Madrid testified that he heard the rebel say to his wife or another person in his house that a storekeeper in Lima had aided him with eight thousand or more pesos and that the Inca had invited him to come to Tinta.[30]

Romauldo Ordóñez, a Spaniard and teacher of Túpac Amaru's sons in Tungasuca, related that he had heard Micaela say that her husband had seven lawyers in Lima, but she did not reveal their names.[31] Figueroa had testified that on April 28, 1781, in the camp at Sicuani, he had heard her say that when her husband came from Lima, certain people awaited him in Cuzco with supplies, and that it was then that revolt had been decided upon, but no leader had been appointed. Figueroa added that a number of Indians from Huarochirí were in Lima concerning a lawsuit at the same time as José Gabriel, but the fiscal dismissed them saying that he was very busy with matters of their King Túpac Amaru. Because of the incident, José Gabriel believed that the fiscal was friendly and sent him a gift through a Dr. Isunza, a resident of Cuzco,

28 Testimonio de Micaela Bastidas, signed by José Esteban Escarcena del Villanueva and Manuel Espinarete López, Cuzco, May 1, 1781, *ibid.*, 118–19.
29 Testimonio de Micaela Bastidas, signed by Francisco de Cisneros and Manuel Espinarete López, Cuzco, May 1, 1781, *ibid.*, 121.
30 Testimonio de Bernardo de la Madrid, signed by the scribe, Pedro de Alarcón y Moscoso, Sicuani, April 26, 1781, *ibid.*, 123–25.
31 Testimonio de Romauldo Ordóñez, Cuzco, n.d., *ibid.*, 126.

whom he asked to tell the official not to believe those lies concerning his (José Gabriel's) inciting a revolution. The fiscal replied to the doctor that he "would not be surprised if one day the kingdom should be handed over to Túpac Amaru." In 1777, Figueroa had also heard Micaela say that when her husband came from Lima, he would start the uprising. Figueroa reported that she had said often, "This is the hour when Lima is to be ruined." He maintained that she corresponded with both Lima and Potosí, but he did not know with whom. He said that she was not ignorant of her husband's ideas, despite her statement that the Inca had forced her to do what she did. He told that she had rejoiced that Dr. Astete in Cuzco had offered coca for the undertaking.[32] Andrea Esquivel also said that Dr. Astete offered coca for the uprising,[33] but Micaela declared that he did not offer anything.[34] The answers to the many charges against her show that Micaela was not ignorant, and that she must have been a very clever woman.

Pablo Figueroa, a lawyer of the Audiencia of Lima who served as fiscal in the case, proposed the death penalty for Micaela. All of her possessions were to be confiscated and her house in Tungasuca demolished. No one might perpetuate her memory, and all children of her relatives to the fourth degree should be killed.[35]

Micaela's lawyer and defender, Gregorio Murillo, asked that she be banished to one of the overseas presidios. He contended that she was forced to carry out her husband's orders. Moreover, although she had given orders, taken severe measures when they were disobeyed, and advised her husband to exterminate Spaniards, allowance should be made for her sex. After all, she was not in the army, and, not knowing how to write, had had to depend upon other people. The lawyer pointed out her difficult situation since the Inca had refused to excuse the smallest mistake. The defender argued further that her family should not be exterminated, for it was unreasonable to put the innocent to death; moreover, no evil could be found in her youngest son, who was

[32] Testimonio de Juan Figueroa, April 28, 1781, *ibid.*, 126–29.
[33] Testimonio de Andrea Esquivel, *ibid.*, 130.
[34] Testimonio de Micaela Bastidas, *ibid.*, 131.
[35] Recomendación de Pablo Figueroa, Cuzco, May 3, 1781, *ibid.*, 132–34.

only a child.[36] On the other hand, Figueroa did not favor leniency if the crime were completely proved according to law.[37]

Francisco Loayza believed that Micaela's defender did not try to save her, only wanting to smear her husband. José Gabriel was in a predicament. If he denied the charges, he would save his dignity but would not help his wife's cause. And if he ignored the false accusation, his honor would suffer. He finally decided upon the latter course and thereby baffled the judge.[38]

Murillo also insisted upon questioning the Inca about his wife and did so ruthlessly. He asked him why he had sometimes overlooked her conduct and at other times beat her. The Inca said that he had whipped her occasionally prior to the revolt, but not afterwards. Murillo wanted to know whether it was true that, when he proposed to hang Corregidor Arriaga, Micaela had begged him on bended knees and with tears not to do it because his whole family would suffer. The Inca answered that he was uncertain whether he had consulted his wife. Murillo persisted, asking whether four priests—Antonio López, Ildefonso Bejarano, Clemente Vergara, and Jacinto Castañeda—were present when Micaela was on her knees and whether the Inca said he would hang her first and then turned his back on her and the priests. Túpac Amaru again replied that he was not certain. To the question whether his wife was afraid of him, he answered that she obeyed his orders, and he did not know whether or not she was afraid. Asked if Micaela was uninformed of the uprising and if he had kept his purpose secret, he now replied that after he came home from Lima, he had told her only of his intention. The judge said he had heard that Arriaga had been imprisoned on Saturday and that on the following Thursday, Túpac Amaru had informed his brother, in Micaela's presence, that the corregidor had threatened to hang him and that it was necessary to take action. The Inca replied that this threat had been made one month before he had seized Arriaga and that he had told

---

[36] Argumento del abogado defensor, Gregorio Murillo, Cuzco, n.d., *ibid.*, 135–38.
[37] Argumento de Pablo Figueroa, Cuzco, May 7, 1781, *ibid.*, 139.
[38] *Ibid.*, Serie I, Vol. IX, 140 n.

Micaela about it then.[39] Túpac Amaru did not sign this declaration, however, because of his injured right arm.

Visitador Areche found Micaela guilty of complicity in the rebellion. He declared that she had summoned people to send to her husband in order to invade and subject the provinces. Moreover, she had condemned individuals to death who did not obey his orders and had rejoiced publicly over his victories. She had aided and encouraged the Indians, appointed officials, spoken evil of the Spaniards, and caused the natives to hate them. She had told the Indians to pay only the tribute. She had assured them that they would enjoy perfect liberty as in the time of their idolatry. She had despised the penalty of the church, had taken the ban of excommunication off the doors, and had posted her own edicts there. She had appointed men to take charge of administering the sacraments, ordered the churches closed, published decrees, given commissions, and issued passes.

Areche therefore condemned her to death. She was to be taken out of prison, dragged along the ground with a rope around her neck and her hands and feet tied. The crier was to make known her crimes, as she was taken to the place of execution, and the corregidores were to publish her sentence by proclamation.[40]

Micaela confessed to Mata Linares. She stated that before coming to Picchu, she had kept in her house the furniture, church ornaments, and wrought silver belonging to the priest of Pampamarca, not because he sent them but because she respected him. She said that the articles were not stolen, and carefully enumerated them. She told the judge that she had some remnants of woolen and silk cloth, which were an inheritance from Ollapata, that she owed Mariana Fuentes twenty marks of broken silver pieces for remelting, and that an unfurnished house belonging to the Fuentes family had been taken.[41]

---

[39] Interrogación de Gregorio Murillo, Cuzco, n.d.; Declaración de José Gabriel Túpac Amaru, Cuzco, n.d., *ibid.*, 141–45.

[40] Sentencia dada por José Antonio de Areche, Cuzco, May 15, 1781, *ibid.*, 145–48.

[41] Declaración de Micaela Bastidas, Cuzco, May 16, 1781, Rúbrica de Mata Linares, *ibid.*, 148–51.

Witnesses also testified to the revolutionary activities of Tomasa Titu Condemayta. Manuel Galleguillos said that at the beginning of the revolution he had heard her say that she had sent people to the Inca. He also stated that she had fled from Acos because the Indians threatened to kill her and because her son-in-law was a chapetón.[42] José Aresmendi declared that Tomasa wrote to the Inca's wife, telling her that Indians had gone out of Acos to find Túpac Amaru, and that she sent word for the caciques to bring all their people and come with her to the workshop of Pomacanche, where José Gabriel was at that time. The accuser also said that he was informed that her soldiers left Acos regularly and that the Inca had admitted that she aided him.[43]

The confession of Tomasa did not furnish the judge with much information. Asked whether she had aided Túpac Amaru with soldiers and had advised him, she said she had not. She cleverly declared that when Andrés Castelo, a royalist, came to Acos with an edict from the King, the Indians left the town voluntarily. When Judge Mata Linares showed her letters which she had written to Micaela, she admitted that she wrote them because she wanted to please the Inca's wife. Other letters, which told how she tried to subject the people in her town and indicated that she was a follower of Túpac Amaru, she did not remember. She contended that she had gained nothing from the Inca, since he had burned her houses and destroyed her property. When the judge wanted to know what property she had, she answered that she had none, although the fact was that she had enough to be considered rich. To the question, "Who aided, wrote to, or encouraged the rebel in his undertakings?" She replied only that she had heard from Patricio Noguera that the priest of Pampamarca was to blame for everything.[44] When Túpac Amaru and other prisoners testified that she had sent help to them, she said that she had been forced to do so.[45]

Again Fiscal Figueroa advised the death penalty for a woman

[42] Declaración de Manuel Galleguillos, Cuzco, April 25, 1781, *ibid.*, 164.
[43] Declaración de José de Aresmendi, Cuzco, n.d., *ibid.*, 166.
[44] Confesión de la cacica de Acos, Cuzco, April 26, 1781, *ibid.*, 167–68.
[45] Declaración de José Gabriel Túpac Amaru and Mariano de la Banda, Cuzco, n.d., *ibid.*, 169.

because of her complicity in the revolt.[46] On the other hand, Murillo recommended banishment in the absence of clear proof that she belonged to the Inca's party.[47]

Murillo also questioned the Inca about Tomasa. Asked whether he had told her about the hanging of the corregidor, he said he had not. To the question whether he had ordered people killed for refusing to obey him, he declared that he was uncertain. He refuted the belief that he had had Andrés Noguera killed by saying that the Indians had put him to death in Yanaoca. He said that they had also burned Tomasa's house in the belief that she was harboring Spaniards. When asked whether he took everything she had, he pretended not to understand the question. Yet he proffered the information that she had sent ten loads of flour to him with her people. When the judge asked why the Inca had imprisoned Tomasa, he replied that he had merely taken her with him to protect her from the Indians when he withdrew from the hill of Picchu. Asked whether he had persecuted her because she refused to obey his orders, he said that she always carried out orders promptly and sent recruits to him.[48]

The judge even questioned Micaela about the valiant woman. The Inca's wife declared that she was uncertain about everything. She admitted, however, that Tomasa kept Indian soldiers to follow Túpac Amaru and was anxious for him to enter Cuzco because the King's forces were threatening to kill her.[49] The priest Melchor Huamán testified concerning the property of Tomasa and her husband. He said that he himself had sold the latter 520 sheep and that they had much farming land.[50]

Tomasa was condemned to death for aiding Túpac Amaru. She was to be taken out of prison and, with a hemp rope around her neck and her hands and feet tied, mounted on a beast of burden. As the crier made known her crimes, she was to ride to the place

[46] Recomendación de Pablo Figueroa, Cuzco, May 3, 1781, *ibid.*, 170.
[47] Recomendación de Gregorio Murillo, Cuzco, May 7, 1781, *ibid.*, 170–72.
[48] Declaración de José Gabriel Túpac Amaru, Cuzco, n.d., *ibid.*, 175–77.
[49] Declaración de Micaela Bastidas, Rúbrica de Mata Linares, *ibid.*, 178–80.
[50] Inventario de las posesiones de Tomasa Titu Condemayta, Acos, May 11, 1781, *ibid.*, 181–82.

of execution and be put to death by the garrote. Afterwards her body would be hanged on the gallows and exposed to the public. Her head was then to be cut off and sent to Acos and, after her crime was published, placed there on a gibbet in the most conspicuous place. All her possessions were to be confiscated for the treasury.[51]

Cecilia Túpac Amaru showed great bravery and cleverness when she was questioned. At first she denied her name, saying that it was Cecilia Escalera. She declared that she was over twenty-five years old, a native of Surimana, married to Pedro Mendagure, and had no employment. She presumed that she had been imprisoned because she was in Túpac Amaru's house. Asked whether she had shown great hatred for Spaniards and had tried to influence Micaela to believe that they were traitors, she pretended not to understand the question. She said that she did not reside in Tinta; when she went there, Micaela had treated her badly, called her a fraud, taken away her cattle, and ordered her killed. This exaggerated statement was no doubt made for the benefit of the judge. She did not understand the question asked about whether she had served in the rebel's house. When the judge repeated it, she said that she was there only on three occasions and on each one merely for a day.[52]

She confessed that she had gone to Picchu, although she desired to remain at home. Her brother had told her that everybody must go to Cuzco. She denied that she wanted him to succeed. The judge inquired whether she had maltreated Francisco Cisneros when she found no powder at Picchu and whether she had written to the Inca and advised him of a junta, which a number of hostile Spaniards had held, and had told him to kill them. Again she did not understand the question. Asked if she knew who had aided Túpac Amaru, who wrote to him, and who were his captains, she declared that she did not, since she was always in Surimana. She also pretended not to understand the question whether she encour-

<hr/>

[51] Sentencia dada por José Antonio de Areche, Cuzco, n.d. *ibid.*, 183–84.
[52] Declaración de José de Tapia y Sarmiento, notario de su majestad, Cuzco, May 18, 1781, *ibid.*, 185.

aged the Indians to kill Spaniards. She was no coward, for she ended by saying, "What I confessed, I confessed; and what I denied, I denied."[53]

The fiscal again recommended the death penalty. He maintained that there was no reason to doubt that Cecilia was involved in the revolt, since she was the wife of one of Túpac Amaru's noted captains.[54] Manuel de Dios Pereyra, a lawyer from the Audiencia of Lima, defended her. He asked to have her excused from capital punishment since the crimes attributed to her were merely desires. He also tried to excuse her actions on the ground of poverty, but this was a false basis, because she had cattle and her husband owned land. Her defender declared that she could not have aided Micaela on account of her frail constitution; her small stature, however, did not mean that she was weak. The judge also believed that she was incapable of influencing or advising the Inca because of her ignorance of military matters. He said that she could not have influenced Micaela for Micaela had a much keener mind than hers, and that, since no one was able to know Cecilia's intentions clearly, she should not be put to death.[55]

Visitador Areche ordered that she be given two hundred lashes as she rode through the streets of Cuzco and then banished for ten years to a convent in Mexico. Every year the Peruvian government was to be informed of her conduct.[56]

The convicted rebels were soon prepared for death. First they were absolved from the ban of excommunication, on May 16; and the penitentiary canon, José de Pérez, and several other learned ecclesiastics aided them. Even the Bishop visited them in their separate prisons on the eve of execution. He urged them to repent and not to leave this world without naming all the accomplices in the rebellion, for, if it continued, God would hold them responsible. He paid particular attention to José Gabriel Túpac Amaru and later

[53] Confesión de Cecilia Túpac Amaru, Cuzco, June 7, 1781, *ibid.*, 183–96. Other documents give her age as less than thirty-five years. She did not sign her confession because she could not write.

[54] Condemnación de Cecilia Túpac Amaru, Cuzco, June 11, 1781, Rúbrica de Mata Linares, *ibid.*, 197–98.

[55] Defensa por Cecilia Túpac Amaru, Cuzco, n.d., *ibid.*, 198–200.

[56] Sentencia dada por José Antonio de Areche, Cuzco, n.d., *ibid.*, 202.

235

said that the Inca shed many tears and that all the condemned persons told him that they had disregarded their consciences.[57]

The cruel sentences were to be carried out on May 18, after the prisoners confessed, heard mass, and took the last communion. When the day came, the city militiamen, armed with daggers and side arms, surrounded the large plaza; and the four sides of the gallows were circled by a body of mulattoes and soldiers from Huamanga, all having guns and fixed bayonets. Nine persons were to be put to death on that day: José Berdejo, a Spaniard and son-in-law of Francisco Noguera, the Inca's commander; Andrés Castelo, a captain; Antonio Oblitas, the Zambo who had hanged Corregidor Arriaga in Tinta; Antonio Bastidas, a brother-in-law of Túpac Amaru; Francisco Túpac Amaru, an uncle; Hipólito Túpac Amaru, the twenty-year-old son of the Inca; Tomasa Titu Condemayta; Micaela Bastidas, the Inca's wife; and José Gabriel Túpac Amaru himself.

All the prisoners wore handcuffs and fetters and came out at one time, one behind the other. They were put in sacks and dragged along the ground tied to the tails of horses. All were heavily guarded and accompanied by priests, who comforted them as they approached the foot of the gallows, where two executioners awaited them. Berdejo, Castelo, Oblitas, and Bastidas were simply hanged. Francisco Túpac Amaru, a man almost eighty years old, and Hipólito had their tongues cut out before being hanged. The Indian woman Tomasa was garroted, or strangled with an iron collar or screw, mounted on a little platform with an iron wheel on it, never seen before in Cuzco. The Inca and his wife had to witness all these executions, and finally that of their oldest son. Then the Inca's wife, Micaela, dressed in the habit of the Order of Mercy, mounted the little platform. Her tongue was to be cut out, but she refused to let the executioner do it; and so it was taken out after her death. She was also subjected to the garrote, but because she had a very small neck, the screw caused intense suffering without strangling her. The executioner then put a lasso around her neck

[57] Decada 4ª· de la escena en la rebelión de José Gabriel Túpac Amaru, Cuzco, May 22, 1781. MS copy in B. L. Gutiérrez, *op. cit.*, 149.

236

and pulled it one way and another, all the while repeatedly striking her, until she died.

José Gabriel was then brought out to the center of the plaza. There the executioner cut out his tongue and threw him on the ground face down. He tied his hands and feet with four cords, fastened these to the girths of four horses, which four mestizos then drove in four different directions. Either the horses were weak or the Inca unusually strong, for he was not immediately torn to pieces, but remained suspended in mid-air, spider-like, for some time while the horses strained to pull him apart. The hard-hearted visitador, who witnessed the execution from the Jesuit College, finally ordered the Inca's head cut off. At the same time he arrested the corregidor of Cuzco and another official for not providing suitable horses. The Inca's body was dismembered, as were the bodies of his wife, son, and uncle. Only the heads were removed from the bodies of the remaining victims.

Many people were there that day to witness the execution, for such a spectacle had never before been seen in Cuzco. Not a single spectator shouted or raised a voice. No Indians were seen, at least not in native dress. At twelve o'clock, when the horses were pulling the Inca, a strong gust of wind arose, followed by hard rain, which made the spectators and even the guards withdraw hurriedly. The Indians said that even Heaven and the elements mourned for the Inca on account of the inhuman death that the Spaniards inflicted upon him.

The trunks of the mutilated bodies of the Inca and his wife were taken to the height of Picchu. There they were thrown into a bonfire and reduced to ashes, which were scattered into the air and cast into the Huatanay River. The rest of the gruesome sentence was carried out to the letter. Hipólito's head was sent to Tungasuca, and his limbs were scattered in different places. Francisco's head was taken to Pilpinto, one leg to Carabaya, the other to Puno, and an arm to Paruro.

Visitador Areche's conscience must have hurt him, for it was said that he attended confession after his terrible sentence had been carried out. He also provided many masses to be said for them.

237

The Inca's youngest son, Fernando, a nine-year-old child, was exempted from capital punishment. With a chain on his foot and guarded by four soldiers, he was taken to the foot of the gallows and forced to witness the cruel deaths of his parents. His heart-rending shrieks resounded for a long time in the ears of the people who heard them. Afterwards, the boy was passed under the scaffold, sentenced to a presidio in Africa for life, and left Callao with Areche toward the end of 1781.

Later, on different days, many of the other rebels were tortured and executed. Among them was Puma Inca, cacique of Quiquijana and Túpac Amaru's chief justice, who was broken to pieces by swords.[58]

José Baquijano, a professor in the University of San Marcos, condemned the bloody work of Areche. He believed that the visitador thought it weakness to yield to pity, yet nothing was gained by destroying a man, and seeking peace was always better than fighting. He concluded, "It seemed to be the destiny of all savage and barbarous peoples to be extinguished by communication with the civilized."[59]

The Creoles also did not like the bloody work of Areche and seemed more inclined than ever to take action. They said in a lampoon found in Cuzco in 1781:

> Oh, King Don Carlos III, by the grace of God, if you knew the great danger your kingdom of Peru is in, because of the tyranny of the corregidores, the visitador, and other tyrants, you would come from Spain and take measures against the persons who are the cause of this hell that we suffer. Know especially that your most distinguished Creole people are not very contented because the [tyrants] wish to monopolize salt, and discontent fills the breasts of these your loyal vassals. Although Túpac Amaru is

---

[58] Relación de los hechos mas notables acaecidos en la sublevación general . . . , 211–13; Odriozola, *Documentos*, I, 161–64; Decada 4ª. de la escena en la rebelión de José Gabriel Túpac Amaru, Cuzco, May 22, 1781; Lorente. *Historia del Peru bajo los Borbones*, 198–99; Menduburu, *Diccionario*, VIII, 143–44; IV, 343; Angelis, *Documentos*, 53–54. Declaración de José de Palacios, excribano real y público, Cuzco, May 18, 1781, in Loayza, *op. cit.*, Serie I, Vol. IX, 152–53.

[59] Barreda Laos, *Vida intelecual del virreinato del Peru*, 321–22, 329, 332.

dead, others are not lacking to get rid of tyranny by killing the cruel visitador.[60]

The King grew indignant when he heard of the awful sentence imposed upon Túpac Amaru. He was horrified that the Inca had had to witness the death of his wife, son, and relatives, and by the manner of his death. To his confessor, he said: "I fear to speak of it. . . . What is this, Padre . . . to kill successors of the kings of Peru? There comes to my imagination the conquest of Peru by blood and deceit, killing kings without cause and even despising their friendship." The sensitive monarch even questioned the legitimacy of his title to the Indies, declaring he did not want to possess what did not belong to him.[61]

Cecilia Túpac Amaru was punished as Areche had ordered. Naked to the waist, she was mounted on a burro and whipped through the streets by the hangman until two hundred lashes had been given. She was detained in Callao awaiting passage for Mexico, but the general pardon of 1781 freed her from the penalty of banishment. She died in Peru some months before July, 1783.[62]

Juan Bautista Túpac Amaru was surprised on the heights of Surimana and captured through the treachery of certain women. His captors entered his house, took all his possessions, and fettered him. They found one hundred pesos on him and tortured him to make him tell where he had more money hidden. They placed his little fingers inside the lock of a gun and pressed it down until they were certain that he had nothing further to confess. Then they took him well guarded to Cuzco, shut him up in a dark prison among assassins and robbers, and would permit no outside communication, even with his wife and mother, who were in separate prisons. They kept him there for a year and half-starved him. On the day

[60] AGN, Buenos Aires, VI–XIII–10–6, in Lewin, *op. cit.*, 193.

[61] Copia de un capitulo de carta escrita por el confesor del rey Carlos III de España en 6 de Enero de 1782, al P. Fray Pedro de Parros, franciscano, rector del colegio de Monserrat de Córdova, in Lewin, *op. cit.*, 245–56.

[62] Loayza, *op. cit.*, Serie I, Vol. IX, 205n. See also Vol I, 123–24; Valcárcel, *La rebelión de Túpac Amaru*, 124; Valcárcel, *Rebeliónes indígenes*, 132; Loayza, *Cuarenta año, de cautiverio*, *op. cit.*, Serie I, Vol. I, 26–27.

they executed Pedro Mendagure, he was put on a donkey and whipped through the streets until he had received two hundred lashes. He was given such a blow on the head that he bore the scar for the remainder of his life. Areche then sentenced him to ten years of banishment to the Fortress of San Juan de Ulloa in Mexico. The visitador did not send Juan Bautista, Mariano, or Fernando Túpac Amaru to presidios in Africa, as was the custom, because he feared they might be able to flee with the help of a foreign power.[63]

The revolt did not end with the Inca's death since many Indians still remained under arms. The 1,200 soldiers left in Langui were insufficient to pacify the Indians because 6,000 natives waited on the other bank of the Pisac River. A Spanish troop of some 3,000 men, commanded by Miguel Velasco, was sent against them, but had to withdraw to the town of Urcos. The saddest event occurred when the irritated natives killed all the Spaniards in the town of Quiquijana. The bloody acts in Cuzco had only infused new fury into the rebels, so that the war now was to become a war of extermination. During the following years at least 80,000 people became victims. As the whole basin of Lake Titicaca was in a state of insurrection, the Spaniards had to flee for their lives to La Paz, Puno, and Arequipa.[64]

Diego Túpac Amaru now became the leader of the revolt, which spread with remarkable rapidity. He was aided by Mariano, the second son of the Inca, who had reached sixteen years of age when his father died, by a nephew, Andrés Mendagure, by Miguel Bastidas, a nephew of the Inca's wife, and by some of his faithful generals.

José Gabriel Túpac Amaru was a remarkable man whose service to his nation is unforgettable. A wealthy and influential cacique of considerable culture, he performed his duties conscientiously and intelligently. When he assumed the role of defender of the oppressed, he was zealous and able in promoting their cause. He

[63] Loayza, *Cuarenta años de cautiverio, op. cit.*, Serie I, Vol. I, 25–28, 103, 138.
[64] Decada 4ª. de la escana en la rebelión de José Gabriel Túpac Amaru, Cuzco, May 22, 1781, MS copy in B. L. Markham, *A History of Peru*, 208.

used every peaceful means at his command to obtain redress for the grievances suffered by his people at the hands of the Spaniards. Forced to take up arms when persuasion failed, he put forth every effort to achieve victory. His edicts were sensible and humane. He phrased the aims of the rebellion in the language of administrative reforms and did not promise his followers an independent Indian state, although others did so in his name after his death. Even after the revolt began, he preferred to obtain his objective by negotiation rather than by war. When the Spaniards of Cuzco refused to make terms with him, he continued fighting, willing to lose everything, even his life, for his cause. Fate was against him, however, and he was defeated and captured, yet he met disaster with stoic courage. He did not deserve the horrible penalty exacted, but he met it like a hero without flinching and won the admiration even of his enemies.

That José Gabriel failed to achieve his immediate goals— whether because of Spanish superiority of arms and knowledge of military strategy or his own inability to make effective use of other revolts or his uncertain ambitions, or a combination of all of these factors—is unimportant in the long span of history. What is important is that his efforts paved the way for the later successful revolution against Spain. In effect, his rebellion marked the beginning of the end of Spanish colonial Peru.

CHAPTER XI

Túpac Amaru's Generals Take Over

THE REVOLT TURNED INTO A HOLOCAUST after the Inca's death. When Diego Túpac Amaru, a talented and rather cultured Indian, and the Inca's generals took charge, they showed little mercy toward Spaniards or Spanish sympathizers. They were burning with the desire to avenge José Gabriel's cruel death; as a result, the bloodiest period of the conflict followed.

Diego did not forget to refer to the royal edicts that his brother was supposed to have had. He evidently was not as bloodthirsty as the other chiefs and on one occasion at least he seemed quite just. He advised Miguel Bastidas to investigate carefully the case of Lucás Baco Tupa, who had been charged with treason, before passing judgment on him. All of Tupa's pleas were to be heard, and if convincing evidence of his guilt was not forthcoming, he should not be punished. Diego said, "It is never my will to punish the innocent, but real traitors who are sufficiently guilty." He asked Bastidas to heed the ideas of Juan de Dios Mullapuraca, a good Christian, since the man always spoke as his feelings dictated.

> Hear the reasons and exceptions of both sides and, if there is any doubt about the punishment, or whether not to punish, communicate with me, or you may send Chuquiguanca or Baco Tupa (himself) to me with the reasons or motives which you shall explain, so that I, in view of all, may take just measures.[1]

No better advice could have been given today.

The edicts of the Inca's generals had a different tone, yet these men claimed to be working for the same just cause as José Gabriel. Their edicts were still issued in the name of the King; continuing connection with Spain seemed to be desired; and the generals still

---

[1] Carta de Diego Cristóbal Túpac Amaru á Miguel Bastidas, Azángaro, November 7, 1781, in Odriozola, *Documentos* I, 233; Angelis, *Documentos*, 134–36.

pretended to be punishing corregidores under the claimed royal order. Andrés Mendagure, the dead Inca's nephew, a gallant and handsome youth of eighteen who called himself José Gabriel's son and took the name of Túpac Amaru, also made use of the supposed royal decrees, saying:

> In the name of King Charles III, Andrés Túpac Amaru, Marquis of Alcalises, Inca descendant of the royal blood and principal throne of the monarchs, who governed these kingdoms of Peru, makes known to all the natives of the provinces of Pacajes, Sicasica, and other places . . . that the King, our Lord, being informed of the great excesses, disorders, and abuses which were caused by the corregidores, customs collectors, and usurper chapetones, sent his commission from Spain, directed to my father, José Gabriel Túpac Amaru, Marquis of Alcalises, Inca descendant of the royal blood and principal throne of the monarchs, who governed these kingdoms of Peru, and told him that the corregidores, custom officials, and chapetones should be removed and punished; and that at the same time the mita of Potosí should be abolished. The corregidores pretended that a just opposition should be made, as they did it, bringing together many inhabitants, soldiers, and Creoles; on account of this many of them were punished and the same corregidores, who fled, were overthrown; and by virtue of the royal order these were acts of justice.

Andrés made many extravagant statements in his proclamation; for instance, that his "father," José Gabriel Túpac Amaru, because of having discharged his commission so well, was already viceroy of Lima.

An edict issued by Diego Túpac Amaru makes practically the same statement. He declared that, as the Inca's descendant, he, along with Julián Túpac Catari, was ordered to get rid of the corrupt government under the corregidores. He said that he intended to carry out the order and to see that José Gabriel's son was crowned and placed in the viceroyalty of Lima.

Immediately the new leaders began to organize the Inca's scattered forces and collect more troops. They summoned for the war young boys and men of sixty, threatened the disobedient with severe punishment, and appointed captains. Andrés promised that all men who obeyed would receive the title of marquis and other honors, that they would possess the land and haciendas of the enemy in La Paz, and would be forever free from repartimientos, mitas, customhouse dues, and other burdens because King Charles III wished to abolish them.[2]

Diego Túpac Amaru was also able to obtain priests to assist his cause. Manuel Castro, assistant priest of San Pedro de Acora; Atanacio Loza, priest of Asunta de Yungio; the priest of San Pedro, Ventura Ibero; the priest of Zepita, Esteban Mogrovejo; the priest of Puno, Zuñiga; the priest of Azángaro; the priest of Carabaya, who formerly served as assistant priest in Chupa; Antonio Palacios, assistant priest of Crucero; Fulano Baldez, vicar of the province; and Josef Ochoa, priest, and Josef Bustamante, assistant priest, of Vsicaios—all worked for the movement. Each one of these priests advised the Indians in their parishes to aid the new Inca leader. Josef Manuel, priest of Asillo, gave Diego powder and lead and told him to make guns.[3]

The revolutionists now committed numerous outrages. They horribly mutilated all persons caught with messages for their enemies. They came down from their posts on the summits of the Vilcañota Range and spread desolation and terror. In high Peru they also fought furiously. Among the chiefs, perhaps the most outstanding was Pedro Vilca Apasa, a native of Tapatapa about eighteen miles east of Azángaro, who was devoted to Andrés Túpac Amaru. Others were Alejandro Calisaya and Julián Apasa, who had first taken the name of Niña Catari.

It is difficult to characterize Apasa, perhaps the natural son of the sexton in Ayoayo, because all accounts of him were written by his enemies. He had been a sacristan and later a peon in a sugar mill before becoming the most terrible of the revolutionists. He was a man of extraordinary boldness.[4] He was of medium stature and

[2] Bando de Andrés Túpac Amaru, Quincocera, July 13, 1781, Odriozola, *Documentos*, I, 207–208; Bando de Diego Cristóval Amaru, Azángaro, August 20, 1781, *ibid.*, I, 209–10; Angelis, *Documentos*, 106–10.

[3] AGN, Buenos Aires, Criminales, Leg. 21 (cited by Lewin, *op. cit.*, 98–99).

[4] Lorente, *Historia del Peru bajo los Borbones*, 200–201.

had an ugly face, but his eyes, although small and sunken, showed great vivacity and determination. He was rather white for an Indian.[5] Aided by another Indian, Marcelo Calle, in a few days' time he acquired great authority and devotion in his province of Sicasica, in Carangas, Yungas, Pacajes, Omasuyos, Larecaja, Chucuito, and others.

In the early stages of the revolt he had accidentally intercepted Túpac Amaru's correspondence with Tomás Catari of Chayanta. Not knowing how to read or write, he took the documents to a cholo of La Paz, named Bonifacio Chuquimamani, to learn the contents. After that he pretended to be related to the Inca and took the name of Viceroy Inca Túpac Catari, thus combining the names of two leaders of the revolt. When he raised the standard of rebellion, the Indians rendered almost divine homage to him, although he was more autocratic than Túpac Amaru and believed in forceful methods. He intended to overthrow foreign domination, kill all the Spaniards if necessary, and separate from Roman Catholicism. As a beginning he ordered the people not to bare their heads before the sacrament of communion, not to eat bread from the church or drink water from baptismal founts, and not to say their prayers. He then proceeded to slaughter Europeans, Creoles, and mestizos and in some places did not even spare priests.[6]

Túpac Catari was very ambitious. Although he lacked the education of José Gabriel Túpac Amaru, he tried to maintain a viceregal court on the heights of La Paz. In that court he exercised the right of life and death over everyone, yet he wanted a priest to officiate for him in a kind of chapel.

Friar Matías Borda, a royalist sympathizer, was one of the men to serve there. On March 19, 1781, an Indian named Tomás Calisaya, who called himself a messenger of the fiscal king, arrived in the Tiguina Pass, where Borda was serving as assistant priest. Calisaya had a rope around his neck and a cord with a knot in his hand. He said he had orders to hang with that rope all persons who

[5] Cánovas del Castillo, *op. cit.*, V, 460.

[6] *Relación de los hechos mas notables acaecidos en la sublevación general . . . .* , 121–22. MS copy in B. L. Odriozola, *Documentos*, I, 62; Ballivián y Roxas, *op. cit.*, I, 10–11; Temple, *op. cit.*, II, 109–10.

did not tell the truth, that when the knot was untied it signified a kind of proclamation, and that he alone had the power to open it.

After he had walked around Tiguina three times and all the Indians of the community had assembled, he made his message known. After telling that Túpac Catari, the Inca king, was already fighting on the heights of La Paz with many soldiers, he read in a loud voice:

> The sovereign Inca king orders me to put to the knife all corregidores, their ministers, caciques, collectors, and other dependents; likewise all chapetones, Creoles, women, and children without regard for sex or age, and every person who may be or seem to be Spanish, or at least is dressed in imitation of such Spaniards. And if this kind of people is favored in any place or places of refuge and, if any priest or other person hinders the beheading of them, he also shall be trampled under foot by all. The priests shall be put to the knife and the churches burned. Mass shall not be said, or confession made, or the least adoration given to the most holy sacrament.

Instantly the natives became submissive.

The friar was giving the *viaticum*, or sacrament for the sick, to Nicolás Carreño, Francisco Salinas, and other Spaniards who had found refuge in the church. The Indians did not show the least reverence, keeping their caps on. When Borda reprimanded them for lack of respect toward the sacrament, they answered that they would do what the Inca king and Calisaya had commanded. When the indomitable friar told the rebels that God would punish them for daring to profane the temple, they paused to consult. Then each refugee picked up a crucifix or some other sacred symbol of Christianity and went out of the church expecting to die as a martyr. New cries soon arose from the Indians, who entered the sanctuary again and put to death the Spaniards found there. Julián Ticuna, who was appointed captain by the so-called fiscal king, wanted to lock the priest in the church with the refugees and set fire to the building.

Most of the Spaniards of the town went to the cabildo building. There Indian men seized the Spanish men and Indian women took

246

the Spanish women and executed all of them, causing a veritable lake of blood. About one hundred people who did not want to join the rebels were put to death. The friar proposed that a tomb should be opened and he would bury the bodies, but the Indians refused to allow this, saying that it was the order of the Inca king to throw the bodies out in the fields like those of excommunicated persons.

The Indians left Borda alone for three days, but he could not escape. He went to see his prelate in the Convent of Copacabana, where on March 24, 1781, another slaughter of Spaniards occurred. The prelate and all the members of the order made public penitence and were ready to die to quiet the Indians, but it was impossible to do so. Those men who directed the uprising threatened that the friars and monks would be beheaded, the temple destroyed, and the miraculous image of Our Lady of Copacabana taken to another place if they did not find the corregidor of the province of Omasuyos. The Indian fiscal king, the captain, and others of their rear guard entered the sanctuary and searched every corner without the least respect. Two Indians, who were still devoted to the Virgin, witnessed this act; and, after a conference, the insurgents beheaded them. The Indians were now like ferocious beasts, hunting the miserable refugees in caves, on the hills, and on farms. They brought all they found to the church, where they beat them to death and committed other atrocities.

From the heights of La Paz, Túpac Catari sent a message to the prelate, Gregorio de Suero, asking for a priest to be brought to him within four days. If this was not done, all the priests would be killed and the church and convent destroyed. After a consultation, Borda decided to sacrifice his life to save the friars and the sanctuary, and so he set off like a criminal with sixty Indians. In the town of Guarina he learned that Friar Antonio Barriaga of the Franciscan Order had been beheaded on the heights of La Paz. Then Borda wanted to return to Copacabana, but the Indians threatened him with death if he tried to escape. He went on with them, expecting to be killed.[7]

[7] Relación de Friar Matías de la Borda, La Paz, May 30, 1781, in Relación de los hechos mas notables acaecidos en la sublevación general . . . , 173ff. MS copy in B. L.

Arriving on the height (April 15), Borda was taken into the presence of Túpac Catari in the third cabildo, one of the twenty-four which the chief had. The friar saw an Indian thirty years of age who cut a ridiculous figure in a uniform with an undershirt of black velvet. He was surrounded by his staff and many other persons, whom Borda addressed in Spanish, for which Túpac Catari severely reprimanded him, ordering him to speak only the Aymará language under penalty of death. Then the friar was taken to a large shed or tent, called the palace. There he met Túpac Catari's wife, Bartolina Sisa, a half-blood twenty-six years old, four judges, many ambassadors, and two priests, Isidro Escobar, adjutant of the town of Palca, and Julián Bustillo, adjutant of Pucarani, who were chaplains.

Borda also saw the chief's secretary. He was an Indian who for many years had been a resident of La Paz and a clerk in the church cabildo and who had changed his name, Bonifacio Chuquimamani, to Manuel Clavijo. He sent out summons and other measures of the Indian leader under the title of "I Túpac Catari." Túpac Catari no longer used cords, knots, and other devices, but did what his secretary told him to do; the judges also listened to Clavijo.

Borda witnessed the beheading of many Spanish prisoners, and thought that he was also marked for death. For the first thirty days of captivity he and the other priests were often disturbed suddenly and threatened with execution. Then they would cast themselves at Túpac Catari's feet and try to make him believe that they were glad to be in his company. As a result, their lives were spared. The priest Gisvero, of the town of Songo, was put to death by one of the twenty-four cabildos; and Túpac Catari himself ordered Father Sebastián Limachi of Guaqui beheaded because he did not want to absolve him. Borda wrote a letter in behalf of the two priests, but it almost cost his own life and the lives of four other priests.

According to Borda, Túpac Catari remained sober for only two hours a day. He and his assistant chiefs went out to patrol the vast population during the day and night and searched carefully for all the women capable of satisfying their carnal desires. Túpac Catari whipped his captains and other officials and even beheaded those who showed carelessness in battle.

His patrol ended near the priests' tent, when he would make the priests come outside, where he lined them up in a row according to their alleged faults or merits. Sometimes he taunted them all, at other times only two or three, and meted out punishment. Borda tried to appease the Indian's wrath by throwing himself at his feet and asking him to do quickly whatever he intended to do with him. The chief only turned his back upon him and went into the palace to his queen, whom the priest thought more bloodthirsty than Túpac Catari. When her husband was in a pious mood, however, she found it expedient to pretend to support his ideas and also to soothe his rage by endearments.

Borda believed that all the priests would die and prepared them for death. He seized every favorable moment to implore mercy for them and succeeded in getting many cruel sentences revoked by Túpac Catari, who would then say to his wife, "For you, my queen, I make this pardon." Immediately she would go with Borda to the prison and angrily ask the priests to send her husband powder and shot under penalty of death. The priests were saved and ordered to say mass daily, yet they always lived in terror because of Túpac Catari's erratic disposition.

Borda noticed that not everything was satisfactory in the enemy camp. Although the chief's subjects generally obeyed him blindly, there was dissatisfaction among some, who despised his acts. Others wanted to usurp his position. Among them were Marcelo Calle, Phelipe Apaza, and the chief's uncle, the one-eyed Pedro Obaya, who pretended to be a nephew of Túpac Amaru. They contended that an Indian of such low rank had no right to rule, even though he had married the so-called queen and had crowned himself. They asked why they could not be leaders, since they were chiefs, respectable, and of legitimate birth. Túpac Catari was so powerful, however, that they did not dare move against him. To secure unquestioning obedience, the twenty-four cabildos had erected twenty-four gallows, which were never idle. The secretary, Bonifacio, also worked with Túpac Catari and professed great hatred even for the word "Spaniard." He wrote letters full of flattery to the Indians in La Paz, telling them that the Spanish king had usurped the kingdom and that it was time they obtained what belonged to them by right.

The people in the camp, elated with repeated victories, revered Túpac Catari as if he were a god and showed constant attention when he was present at mass, at the table, and about his daily business. He was surrounded with great elegance, and sometimes ordered the priests to wait on him at table. His wife was always at his side, and used much wrought silver, all stolen from the Spaniards who had died in the towns.

After beheading prisoners, the chief would attend mass in a chapel. It was formed by poles with blankets stretched over them and adorned with an organ and the images taken from the churches of La Paz. There all the priests in the camp officiated in their surplices and stoles. Túpac Catari had a canopy put up for himself. At one side of him was his wife and at the other his assistants, judges, ambassadors, and other followers according to their rank. A mirror was placed in front of the canopy, and the chief continually looked in it during the mass and made faces that seemed to interest him more than the service, yet he did not refrain from maltreating individuals or giving blows in the chapel to anyone who did not confess.[8]

This was the man who, with an army of thirty or forty thousand Indians, besieged La Paz for months. He must have been very energetic and not as bad as the royalists described him or he could not have kept the loyalty of so many natives. He was not an imposter, as some people thought. At least three times he had gone to Tungasuca to confer with Túpac Amaru; therefore the Inca must have approved of his name and generalship.[9] He was probably not

[8] *Ibid.*, 176–82; Advertencia del Dr. Gregorio Funes, deán de la catedral de Córdova, publicó en Buenos Aires, en 1817, in Odriozola, *Documentos,* I, 102; Temple, *op. cit.,* 119–32; Ballivián y Roxas, *op. cit.,* I, 209–28.

[9] Documento fechado en Oruro el 30 Octubre de 1781, AGN, Montevideo, Coleción de documentos para la historia del Uruguay, copiados del Archivo General de Indias en Sevilla, in Lewin, *op. cit.,* 266.

of such low station as commonly represented, since the name Apasa was peculiar to the Incas of Chucuito and belonged to many chiefs. The mestizo Bonifacio Chuquimamani would hardly have worked for an Indian of low rank. Túpac Catari traveled over the country engaging in commerce in coca and blankets, and no doubt at the same time he organized revolutionary centers among the natives. Diego and Andrés Túpac Amaru both mentioned that José Gabriel had commissioned Apasa to help direct the rebellion.[10] The Inca's family also must have regarded Túpac Catari favorably because after his death Túpac Amaru's stepmother cared for his son, Julián, until the Spaniards found and imprisoned the ten-year-old boy.[11]

The fact that Túpac Catari had been a sacristan likely had something to do with his desire to worship God. If the form of worship seemed fantastic, it was at least according to his interpretation. It is true that, despite his display of devoutness, he had killed two men, Antonio Barriaga and Sebastián Limachi, alleged to be priests, although Victor Santa Cruz believes that they were probably sacristans dressed in church vestments to save themselves rather than real priests.[12] A number of Spaniards donned clerical garments to escape the fury of the Indians.

To return to military matters, when José Gabriel Túpac Amaru had been captured, the royalist troops from Lima wanted to go home to harvest their crops, and some deserted. The Indians of Anta and Chincheros and the greater part of the militia troops, which had formed the bulk of the Spanish army, scattered, as did members of the other columns. After the division at Langui had been attacked by Diego Túpac Amaru on the nights of April 18 and 20 in two bloody skirmishes, in which many Spaniards were wounded, the royalists spent eleven days getting new recruits. Then the army marched to the town of Sicuani to aid all the columns entering into the Lake Titicaca basin and also to win the

[10] Testimonio de las confesiones del reo Julián Apasa, alias Túpac Catari, AGN, Buenos Aires, Revolución de Oruro, Leg. 1 (cited by Lewin, *op. cit.*, 266–67); Ballivián y Roxas, *op. cit.*, I, 246–48; Angelis, *Documentos,* 160 ff.

[11] La prisión del hijo de Túpac-Catari, La Paz, April 8, 1783, Biblioteca Nacional, Buenos Aires, Sección manuscritos, num. 6139 (in Lewin, *op. cit.*, 476).

[12] Santa Cruz, *op. cit.*, 111–12.

people back to the King. The column under Manuel de Castilla, corregidor of Paruro, followed the road from the town of Macari. The division of Cotabamba, commanded by its corregidor, José María Acuña, proceeded to Checa, Quequi, Yauri, and Choraque to reduce those towns for the King; and the mestizos and Indians of the province of Quispicanchis joined them. Another column of one thousand men under Colonel Avilés approached the town of Muñoa to obtain information in that region and to punish the rebels. With the rest of the army Inspector General del Valle crossed the boundary dividing the viceroyalty of Peru from that of Buenos Aires. There the rebellion still continued with the greatest fury because Diego Túpac Amaru suspected the whites and mestizos of those areas of treason on account of the rewards offered for his capture. He therefore ordered all persons who were not of his race to be executed immediately, not even respecting the sacred calling of priest, as his brother had.

All along the way Del Valle suffered for want of provisions since the towns were deserted and the crops and cattle had been destroyed. When he approached the plain of Quesque, where he passed the night, more than one thousand rebels boldly fired at the vanguard with only three muskets. They accompanied the firing with shouting that they were not cowards like the people in the province of Tinta, and that soon the Spaniards would experience the bravery and strength of the Indians from the Collao. When they discovered the size of the royalist army, they went up to the summit of a very high mountain covered with snow, taking all their cattle with them. Antonio Ternero, second major of the Cuzco regiment, was sent up the mountain with eighty men to punish the natives for their boldness. He killed twelve and took some horses and many cattle.[13]

Shortly afterwards four prisoners reported that the inhabitants of Santa Rosa were the most important followers of Túpac Amaru. Deciding to punish them, the commandant entered the town without resistance and put twenty people to death. The army went next to Orurillo, where only some old men and a few women were

[13] Odriozola, *Documentos*, I, 61–62.

found. Asked why the inhabitants had abandoned their homes, the priest answered that he could not persuade them to remain there and calmly await the arrival of the King's troops because they had obstinately denied obedience and followed the banners of the rebellion. Two Indians were captured and treated well; then the Spaniards told the inhabitants that they would be punished with all the rigors of war if they did not obey the King. These mild measures caused the few people there to go in search of their relatives and friends and persuade them to come back. All promised to be faithful vassals upon their return.

Colonel Avilés was already camping with his division in the vicinity of Orurillo on his way to Muñoz. He ordered a detachment of ninety men to attack the Indians on the heights. Although there were not more than 400 of them, they made an obstinate resistance, but were, nevertheless, overthrown and about 150 killed. On May 6, 1781, Avilés commanded an attack to be made upon more than 100 rebels on a hill called Ceasirí. After a lively fire, the Spaniards espied 500 mounted enemy troops, with good lances, charging them. The Indians waged battle in three different areas with dogged determination; however, they were overthrown, and over 100 of their dead were left on the battlefield.[14]

When Avilés' column had united with the rest of the army, the royalists advanced to the town of Asillo, which was also deserted. Only the priest, accompanied by four servants, came out to receive them. He said that when the people saw the vanguard of the troops, they all left—even those who wanted to ask pardon. Afterwards, when it was learned that the priest had persuaded his parishioners to enlist under the banners of the rebels and had aided them with funds, Del Valle seized all his papers, which revealed that he had carried on friendly correspondence with José Gabriel and Diego Túpac Amaru. Then the royalists imprisoned the priest and sent him, shackled, to Cuzco. That same night Avilés marched out of the town at the head of a strong detachment. He surrounded the enemy and killed more than one hundred next day without losing a man; as a result, the rest of the Indians fled.

14 *Ibid.*, 62–64.

The following day, May 7, the Spaniards came to a place where they could see the famous Condorcuyo Mountain. There in 1741 the Indians of Azángaro had made an obstinate defense against their corregidor, Alfonso Santa, because of abuses of the repartimiento. It was obvious that the people of that region were still determined to stand up for their rights, for the mountain was covered with them. They made such a loud noise with their musical instruments and their insulting cries that it seemed as if there were 100,000 of them. The Spanish attackers did not obey orders to unite; therefore the Indians killed fifteen of the Lima troops.

The entire Spanish army soon approached the insurgents on the slopes of the mountain, where Pedro Vilca Apasa, one of Diego Túpac Amaru's best commanders, had charge of the encampment. Diego was there also with all the Indians from the provinces of Azángaro and Carabaya. The loyal Indians of Anta and Chincheros shouted to the enemy to come down and pledge obedience to the King so that they could be pardoned and return peacefully to their homes. But the rebels were stubborn and answered boldly and defiantly that they intended to go to Cuzco to set their idolized Túpac Amaru free.[15]

The Spaniards soon realized that it would be impossible to win these rebels by kindness, and an attack was planned for the following day. The commandant ordered his army divided into four columns to be situated so that the mountain could be besieged on all sides. He assigned one division to pursue any fugitives and ordered the other three not to move from their posts until the signal was given for battle. When two cannon shots were fired, the royalists began to climb up the mountain and the rebels to climb down. As the combat spread, the Indians made an obstinate resistance, being well defended by the fortified corrals of 1741. Lieutenant Colonel Manuel Campero, at the head of a column of 1,500 men, attacked the rebels on the left, yet they stood their ground in the face of heavy fire in order to defend a very necessary pass.

[15] *Ibid.*, 64–65.

The royalists, with the help of the Indians of Anta and Chincheros, finally overcame the insurgents. Even in the face of overwhelming odds, the rebels displayed remarkable bravery. One Indian pulled a lance out of his breast with his own hands and pursued the Spaniards with it until he fell dead. Another, whose eye had been put out by a lance, followed his attacker and would have killed him if another soldier had not come to the rescue. The heavy fighting lasted for two hours, and more than six hundred Indians were killed.

After the battle, the Spaniards advanced to the deserted town of Azángaro, where they found only the assistant priest left. Avilés pitched camp half a league distant in order to include in the center the columns from Paruro and Cotabamba, which had arrived a few days before. When a prisoner reported that Diego Túpac Amaru was in that region on his way from Puno and had passed very near the column from Paruro, the General ordered that the Marquis of Rocafuerte, colonel of the regiment, be informed. Shortly the Marquis departed the camp accompanied by his second in command, Isidro Guisasola, who knew that Diego slept that night at the hacienda of one of his followers only one and one-half leagues distant from the Spanish camp. At half-past eleven, Colonel Avilés also started out with a detachment of two hundred men, but they could not find Diego. They blamed Guisasola for not taking active measures for his capture.[16]

At dawn of May 9, the General himself marched toward Putina to try to overtake the rebel chief, but he went in the wrong direction. Although the march was varied the next day, the Spaniards considered it useless to follow Diego Túpac Amaru, who withdrew hurriedly to the province of Carabaya. Some residents along the way told them that the Indians of the provinces of Chucuito, Omasuyos, and Pacajes continued to besiege the town of Puno, which was now in a critical position. Therefore, a detachment of one thousand cavalrymen and two thousand Indian auxiliaries from Anta, under Major General Francisco Cuellar, hastened to the province of Carabaya, intending to pursue the rebels before

[16] *Ibid.,* 65–67.

they reached the Andes. As the provinces of Paruro and Chumbivilcas were still active in the uprising, Manuel Castilla, corregidor of the first, and Francisco Laesquilla, chief justice of the second, were sent there at once with their forces, while Del Valle took the rest of the troops to relieve Puno. He also wanted to obtain news of La Paz, Charcas, and other provinces in the mountains, whose fate was not known because the Indians had closed all the passes and intercepted communications.

That night (May 10) the royalists camped at Ocalla, near which Friar José Acuña of the Dominican Order was found killed. Next day, half an hour after the march resumed, the soldiers saw from an extensive plain the high mountain of Puquiona Cancari. The mountain was solid stone and so steep that it could be ascended only by a narrow pass. When the vanguard approached, a soldier noticed two or three Indians in a glen ahead but ignored them. About a quarter of a league farther on, eighty inhabitants came out to receive the troops, fell on their knees in front of the General, and with many tears asked pardon for their crimes. He granted their request, and ordered them to bring provisions for the army, offering to pay just prices for them.

When José María Acuña, commander of the Cotabamba column, arrived, he informed the General that as his men passed the mountain, the Indians had hurled huge stones at them. The march was accordingly delayed while a detachment of eighty gunners went out to punish the Indians. At the same time Del Valle himself fell back with the Cuzco regiment to surround the mountain and prevent any of the seditious Indians from escaping. The Indians, however, refused to be intimidated and were obstinately determined to defend the post they occupied, or die. When an officer of the Cotabamba troops offered them pardon, they answered with fury that they would rather die than be pardoned. Then the royalists attacked fiercely. To prevent capture or surrender, some Indians threw themselves over a cliff more than two hundred yards high. Others hid in crevices between large rocks, paying no heed to another offer of pardon, and defended themselves until all died.

256

After the battle the army went directly to Puno, which had been under siege for a long time.[17]

José Gabriel Túpac Amaru's capture and horrible death thus became the signal for the most terrible and cruelest Indian revolt South America had ever witnessed. Blood flowed freely on both sides, and little mercy was shown noncombatants. The untamed savage spirit in the natives was unleashed, and the uprising now became a war of vengeance, with extermination of the whites its goal. It caused untold misery and destruction of property and severely taxed the strength and resources of Spain to put it down.

[17] *Ibid.*, 67–69.

CHAPTER XII

The Siege of Puno

ALMOST FROM THE BEGINNING of the revolution Puno, the capital of the province of the same name, was among the towns which suffered most. Situated on the northwestern end of Lake Titicaca and elevated 12,874 feet above the sea, its main street sloped by a gradual descent toward the reed-bordered lake. Near the town on the south were the famous silver-bearing mountains of Cancharani and Layacayata to which Puno owed its existence. Since the town lay in the midst of enemy territory, it was like a little island of loyalty in a sea of rebellion. Even though it was beset by many dangers on all sides, expeditions of loyal citizens marched out of it against the Indians.[1]

The corregidor of Puno, Joaquín Antonio de Orellana, was the first official to return to his province at the beginning of January, 1781, after being driven out of it in the early stages of the revolt. He had offered his services at the outset of the revolution (November, 1780) when the corregidor of Lima, Vicente Hore, called for help against José Gabriel Túpac Amaru. The forces of the corregidores from Azángaro, Carabaya, Puno, Chucuito, Arequipa, and La Paz were ordered to be united in Lampa; and Francisco Dávila, a marine officer, was appointed commandant. The colonel of the Azángaro militia and the colonels of Lampa, however, did not obey the order.

Orellana then received orders to go to the important town of Ayaviri with his people to reinforce it, but after a two days' march, he was told to withdraw. In the retreat many men and the greater part of the ammunition fell into the hands of the enemy. Orellana finally returned to Lampa. The same command to retreat came to the colonel of the Lampa militia, who wanted to remain in Ayaviri, but he put the order into effect with the loss of many men, who

[1] Markham, *Travels in Peru and India*, 88, 94–95, 134.

were either seized by the insurgents or joined them voluntarily because of their attractive promises.

A council of war was called to consider the situation. It was decided to withdraw the forces to the town of Cabanilla, which was done, but some of the militias did not want to reunite and feared to obey. Orellana and the corregidores of Lampa, Azángaro, and Carabaya then returned to their own provinces to defend them, while the other officials marched to Arequipa to seek the aid already asked. The corregidor of Chucuito became suspicious of the movement of his provincials, who were very much agitated, and he, too, went to Arequipa. These men all knew that after they withdrew from Lampa, Túpac Amaru would enter the town.

Orellana asked for help from La Paz and Chucuito, which could not be granted. He was also vexed by the clamors of the inhabitants of Puno, who wanted to flee the town, but finally he allowed them to seek refuge twelve leagues distant, to wait for the expected aid. He urged them to remain faithful to the King and not to listen to the deceitful promises of Túpac Amaru. He had a force of 1,031 soldiers. Leaving the few arms he had under guard to prevent the enemy from getting them, on December 11, 1780, he marched quickly to the mountains. There he heard of the outrages committed by the rebels in the province of Lampa and of the secret order sent to his people for his arrest. Then he withdrew with his troops toward Lima, hoping to obtain aid. When it did not come, he determined to go personally to Arequipa to ask again.

A messenger told the corregidor that Visitador Areche did not intend to continue his journey to Arequipa, but was going directly to Cuzco, and would not provide the desired assistance. This report filled Orellana and his people with dismay, but he returned to Puno with them. Deciding to defend the town, he took extraordinary measures to keep the people loyal in the face of Túpac Amaru's seductive offers. He disciplined the militias, instructed them in the use of arms, and paid them daily wages from the tribute money, hoping to hold out until he could incorporate his soldiers into the forces expected from La Paz. When he heard that José Gabriel Túpac Amaru was marching through the province of

Lampa, it became necessary to assemble as many troops as possible to be prepared for an attack. He sent again to the commandant of La Paz for aid, but the commandant replied that the order to help him had not yet arrived, and that if he could not obtain aid from the neighboring provinces or his forces were not sufficient to maintain the honor of the King's arms, he could withdraw.[2]

Orellana was worried. He learned that the neighboring provinces of Lampa, Azángaro, and Carabaya were in the greatest confusion because of robberies and deaths instigated by the Inca's captains, who were collecting supplies and enlisting men. They had tried to attack Puno and to reduce the neighboring city of Chucuito in order to obtain its three hundred quintales of quicksilver. Orellana raised a force of 824 men, including priests, to defend Puno.

Then he decided to go in search of the Inca, setting out on February 7, 1781, in a rainstorm. The river was high, but he crossed it on the eighth and entered the towns of Paucarcolla and Caracoto, where he received information that the Indians commissioned by the Inca traveled in parties and that the first division was in the vicinity of the towns of Samán, Taraco, and Pusi. They were reported to be burning prisons, killing Spaniards, and forcibly enlisting recruits to Túpac Amaru's cause. Orellana decided to surprise them. Accordingly, he marched to the Juliaca River, ordered the cavalry to ford it and attack suddenly. However, when he received word from the priest of Taraco that the Indians had already crossed the Samán River and were only six leagues away, he cancelled the order. He sent twenty-four gunners and sixty-two cavalrymen to the three towns, but the Indians had been warned and left hurriedly.

Then he ordered his soldiers to cross the river without delay. This they did at two o'clock in the morning. At six o'clock they fought a skirmish with a division of fifty-two Indians. Orellana

---

[2] Odriozola, *Documentos,* I, 71–74; Relación del cacique de Puno, Joaquín Antonio de Orellana de sus expediciones, Cuzco, July 17, 1781, *ibid.,* 167–70; Angelis, *Documentos,* 60–64; Markham, *Travels in Peru and India,* 158.

called for the surrender of cruel Nicolás Sanca, an Indian who had been chanter in a church and had become one of Túpac Amaru's colonels. The Indians answered angrily, called the Spaniards revolutionists, and attacked them furiously with their cudgels, but the royalists repulsed them, killing twenty-five. Among documents found were some original edicts of Túpac Amaru regarding the enlistment of recruits and the punishment of priests who opposed his orders. One document was addressed to the chief justice of Azángaro, urging him to join Andrés Ingaricona on the farm of Chingora, two leagues from Juliaca, and to enlist men in the towns of Achaya, Nicasio, and Calapuja so that they could attack Orellana's troops as they crossed the Juliaca River.

This information caused Orellano to search immediately for the rest of his troops, who he found had already crossed the river. Then, in order to prevent the union of Ingaricona and Sanca, he started toward Lampa. When an Indian woman told of the violence she had suffered in Calapuja from a party of three hundred Indians under Ingaricona, the corregidor hastened to Calapuja. But he could not find the enemy, although he had brought with him a prisoner, Cacique Pacaricona, as a guide. The commander was obliged to spend the night on the plains of Surpo. A spy in camp, after being whipped, revealed that the Indians were on top of Mount Catacora. The army hastened to the heights, but when the Indians saw the Spaniards, they abandoned their post and went up higher into the mountains.

Orellana sought a pass to go up the mountain, but was impeded by a storm which lasted a long time. His men were eager, to attack, however, so he divided them into two groups, which marched in different directions, seeking protection among the large rocks from the stones shot by the enemy slings. The royalists fought bravely and obtained some advantage. They killed thirty Indians and wounded many others. When night came, the General ordered a retreat, as he believed it impossible to hunt the Indians in the dark; moreover, he himself had received a blow on the leg and a wound in the breast. It was then that he learned that the rebel chief, Colonel Sanca, had burned Lampa and was camped on some hills one and one-half leagues from the Spanish quarters.[3]

Under such conditions Orellana considered it useless to go on with the undertaking. He therefore decided to withdraw to the lakes of Juliaca to forestall the assaults on his province and to keep the Indians of Puno, Caracoto, Cabana, and other towns loyal. During the march the prisoner Pacaricona showed signs of unfaithfulness, so he declared him a traitor.

At Chingora, on February 13, 1781, Indians were seen drawn up in two divisions on the mountain summit. A division marched toward the lakes of Juliaca to cut off a royalist retreat. To prevent their doing so, the Spaniards raised their camp and advanced two leagues toward the town of Coata. From there part of the troops marched to meet the Indians at the lake, but the rebels immediately returned to the heights. The chief of the Indians asked why the Spaniards had taken Cacique Pacaricona prisoner and wanted Orellana to surrender him, but this was not done.

Next day the loyal cacique of Caracoto showed the commander an order from Colonel Sanca to enlist people of the town in the name of the Inca king of Peru and cut off the lakes of Juliaca and Suches. Orellana inferred that the Indians intended to attack the towns of Puno and Chucuito; therefore he advanced to Coata and camped on the riverbank. He ordered twenty-five boats brought from Capachica, rested the troops for a day, inspected arms, and on February 16 sent out a detachment to investigate the enemy's intentions. An Indian informed the Spaniards that the rebels were preparing to attack. Shortly afterward they appeared on the hills and then swarmed down to besiege the Spanish camp, which fortunately was in an advantageous location. On the left it was protected by the deep Coata River, on the right by a lake, and at the back on the peninsula by a narrow pass. Twenty-five men on horseback were stationed as a rearguard at this pass.

[3] Odriozola, *Documentos,* I, 74–76; Relación de . . . Orellana de sus expediciones, Cuzco, July 17, 1781, *ibid.,* 170–74; Angelis, *Documentos,* 64–68; Mendiburu, *Diccionario,* VIII, 144–45.

A dispute arose between the rebel leaders, Ingaricona and Sanca, about whether they should begin battle in this location. Ingaricona wanted to attack, believing the number of royalists small, but Sanca was opposed. When the cacique of Carabaya became involved in the dispute and supported Ingaricona, the latter decided to go ahead with the attack. The contention had lasted until three o'clock. Meantime, the royalist infantrymen were sitting on the ground with their baggage carts, bundles of clothing, and beds placed as a rear-guard wall behind them. The Indians, who did not see the men, wanted to seize the arms for Túpac Amaru. When they approached, a number of priests tried to persuade them to surrender, accept pardon, and obey the King. They retorted that they did not need pardon, that they recognized only Túpac Amaru as their king, and that they would come in the night with all their army.

The Spaniards kept perfectly quiet until the Indians had formed a semicircle around the camp. Sanca directed the left flank, Ingaricona the right, and the cacique of Carabaya the center. Then the twenty-five royalists on horseback, who guarded the pass which covered the rear guard and the cattle, began the battle. When the enemy tried to take the cattle, another twenty-five men arrived to reinforce the first group. Next the main body of the Spanish army drew up in battle array. Half of the soldiers, with lances, sabers, and cudgels, were placed on each wing and reinforced by the cavalry. The right wing dealt with Ingaricona and the left with Sanca. Colonel Sanca and his men, reluctant from the start, suffered very little because after a few Indians were killed, they fled in great disorder to the near-by mountain. On the right and in the center the enemy fought stubbornly, but when many were killed and the remainder terrified by the continuous firing, they finally fled and were pursued to the hills.

The battle lasted until half-past six. It was called Mananchili because it was near that place that more than 370 natives died, including many women who had come to aid their husbands and relatives by bringing stones. About 5,000 rebels were engaged in the struggle, not counting the women. That no royalists were killed was attributed to the protection of the images of the Virgin placed on the principal banner and over the soldiers' hearts.

Not an Indian was seen on February 17. Orellana crossed the river, hoping to cut off the rebels who went by way of Juliaca, but found none. As the people of the town of Guaca and its vicinity came to ask pardon, which was granted on the nineteenth, the corregidor returned to Puno, after having been on the campaign twelve days.[4]

The Indians were still seditious, lost no opportunity to attack Puno, and made invasions into the provinces of Chucuito, Pacajes, and Sicasica. Orellana realized that he could not resist them on a campaign; therefore he decided to prepare defenses at Puno and wait for them there. He had trenches dug, collected ammunition, made cannon, stored up provisions, and combined his forces with those of Ramón de Moya y Villarroel, governor of Chucuito, who had returned to his province. Even then Orellana's force was inadequate. He gave account of his successful expedition to the commandant and Board of Finance in La Paz and asked for aid. The commandant, thankful for what he had done, sent him 10,000 pesos, but no soldiers arrived because the Indians had defeated them on the march from Omasuyos to Larecaja.

Word arrived that a native army had already reached the town of Juliaca, only nine leagues from Puno. It consisted of 18,000 men under Diego Túpac Amaru, not counting other parties from Atuncolla, Vilque, and Totorani. The main army was led by Lieutenant General Ramón Ponce, a mestizo, and two colonels, Pedro Vargas and Ingaricona, who had already shed much Spanish blood. On the other hand, the Spaniards had only 1,400 men. On the morning of March 10, the shouting enemies appeared on the heights near Puno and fired. They surrounded the town for more than three leagues, except for the hill of Azogue, which 120 faithful Indians of Puno, under Cacique Anselmo Bustinza, held. The

[4] Odriozola, *Documentos*, I, 76–79; Relación de . . . Orellana de sus expediciones, Cuzco, July 17, 1781, *ibid.*, 174–78; Markham, *Travels in Peru and India*, 159; Angelis, *Documentos*, 68–72.

latter were attacked so fiercely that it was necessary to send help to them. The enemy was repulsed, however, and thirty killed. They did not make another attack that day or the following night, but the Spaniards doubled their guards and cavalry pickets.

The royalists soon abandoned the hill of Azogue as being too difficult to defend. The enemy occupied it immediately and fired on near-by ranches, the garrison, and the main plaza. Six gunners were placed in the church towers, while other pickets marched to Orcopata with a cavalry company from Chucuito. They finally drove back the Indians and kept the road to Chucuito open.

The Indians then advanced with all their forces to the foot of Mount Queroni, leaving the town free only on the side facing the lake. On the higher part of the hill of Azogue they burned some ranches not far from the church of St. John, took the suburb of Guansapata, repulsed the loyal Mañazos Indians who defended it, and put up a banner on a large rock near the town. The Spanish attack accomplished very little, but they did drive the insurgents from the town. The fighting lasted until six o'clock in the evening. Orellana suffered a foot dislocation when his horse fell, but he remained in action. As the enemies hid their dead and withdrew in good order, it was not known how many of them were killed.

Using priests as intermediaries, the Indians on March 12, 1781, asked the people to surrender the corregidor of Puno and publish a proclamation of Túpac Amaru's. Orellana in reply sent a detachment under Captain Nicolás de Mendiolaza more than a league and a half from town, but told him not to risk unnecessary danger. When the royalists were attacked from a mountain along the royal road of Cuzco, the first gunners opened fire. They drove the rebels up to the highest part of the mountain where their companions were stationed. When the battle was renewed, both sides fought fiercely, but the loyalists finally had to retreat to Puno.[5]

Although the rebels were repulsed at Puno, they caused much

[5] Odriozola, *Documentos,* I, 79–83; Relación de . . . Orellana de sus expediciones, Cuzco, July 17, 1781, in Odriozola, *Documentos,* I, 178–83; Angelis, *Documentos,* 73–78.

damage elsewhere. In Coata and Capachica they massacred a number of Spaniards and mestizos. They persuaded the towns of Yanguyo, Desaguadero, and Zepita in the province of Chucuito to join them and united with the people of the province of Pacajes southwest of La Paz. They hindered the delivery of a dispatch from Orellana to the commandant of La Paz, in which Orellana had asked that a capable officer be sent to maintain the defense of Puno, since he was confined to bed on account of his injured foot. When the messenger returned without delivering the message, Orellana made the greatest effort to direct the defense.

When the governor of Chucuito asked for help, the junta of war proposed that soldiers be sent to check the movement in his province. Orellana opposed this move since the forces were small; moreover, he thought such a measure would stir up the whole province. But when the cacique of Pomata, José Toribio Castilla, took out twenty-five men and they were all killed, Orellana quickly dispatched all the militias under Captain Santiago Vial. When they arrived at Juli, they found the plaza and streets filled with corpses and no one to explain what had happened until several priests came out of hiding. As the rebels were on the near-by mountains, Captain Vial fell back to Ilabe to give account of the event in a council of war. It was decided to retreat, but Vial did not withdraw until the hostile Indians of Acora forced him to do so; then he had to call for help. Shortly after Orellana reached Vial, he received word that the Indians had arrived at Puno. He broke camp hurriedly and marched at twelve o'clock at night. As soon as he left Juli and Ilabe, the Indians entered and sacked the towns.

The Spaniards had more success in the region of Azángaro when on March 23 a small detachment under Andrés Calisaya, cacique of the town of Tiguillaca, was sent there. The loyalist soldiers aided the town of Capachica, defended Pusi, Samán, Taraco, and Caminaca, punished the enemy, and took away their cattle. Orellana sent another detachment over the royal road to Arequipa which defeated a party of thieves led by the Indian Juan Mamani, who was captured after an obstinate resistance and put to death with many of his followers. Twenty imprisoned Spanish women were freed.

Meanwhile, Captain Vial returned to his capital of Chucuito and consulted the junta of war at Puno. He asked whether he should withdraw or defend his city in case of an attack. The council promised that men and munitions would be furnished him as soon as information concerning the number of enemies was received. The garrison of Chucuito then decided to attack a party of Indians which was approaching. The soldiers went out half a league, but obtained no advantage; next day they advanced again and fought a long time without effect. In the afternoon the enemy attacked suddenly, took the Spaniards' fieldpiece, killed many loyalists, and followed the troops to the city, yet did not dare enter. When the fleeing Spaniards reached Puno, Orellana had to take measures to keep his troops from abandoning the town.

On the following morning he sent three cavalry companies toward Chucuito to aid in the withdrawal of the white people remaining there. The royalists entered the city without trouble and escorted the people out of it, but the Indians came down to occupy a narrow pass, making it necessary for them to retreat quickly. As the commandant was obliged to break through the pass, some of his soldiers were killed. Among them was the priest of the church of Santa Cruz in Juli. When the first refugees to arrive at Puno told of the conflict, Orellana started out quickly with all the musketeers to aid his cavalry. Refugees along the way said that the greater part of the people had freed themselves and that those in the pass were without doubt already dead; therefore the march was halted. That night, when certain persons were missed, boats were sent to the shores of Chucuito to rescue those who hid among the rushes.

As soon as the Spanish soldiers had left Chucuito, the Indians entered the town and cruelly killed everybody except two priests and a few other individuals. Then they burned the town, 250 quintales of quicksilver, and some important papers that had been transferred to Chucuito by a treasury official the day before. Orellana was grieved at what he saw, but since there was nothing to be done about it, he had to start for Puno. The Indians tried to cut off his march in the same pass, but he repulsed them and killed four of the boldest.[6] At the same time the Indians of Azángaro and Lampa attacked the town of Capachica again, where at the beginning of the revolt the faithful Indians and mestizos had repulsed the insurgents, who had killed many Spaniards.

Orellana now heard that the Indians of Desaguadero, Omasuyos, and Pacajes, in co-operation with those who occupied the provinces of Lampa and Azángaro, planned to attack Puno. Therefore he quickly asked the aid of a detachment of five hundred men, sent out by the Viceroy under Captain Ramón de Arias and Colonel José Moscoso, which had come from Arequipa and was now only nine leagues distant. The officers answered merely that they did not have orders to help him; nor did they send the supplies and ammunition requested. The corregidor thus remained alone in the midst of his enemies.

After the royalists left Chucuito on April 10, the rebels again appeared on the mountains around Puno. But Orellana had prepared for them, and the defense was stronger than at their first attack. He had built a small fortress at the advantageous site of Guansapata, had new trenches dug, three more cannon made, and powder provided. When the Indians tried to drive off the cattle, the corregidor sent out a cavalry contingent, telling them, however, not to begin the battle. The soldiers did not obey. As soon as they were near enough, they attacked the Indians, killing one hundred of them and dislodging them from their position.

On their return the companies were stationed outside Puno toward the road to Chucuito. There they fought skirmishes with the rebels until two o'clock in the afternoon. Soldiers also fired continuously upon the Indians from the tower of Guansapata and the plaza, forcing them to withdraw to the hill of Orcopata.

On the opposite side of Puno, at the hill of Azogue, the enemy had been attacking since morning. A company of cavalry, aided by

6 Odriozola, *Documentos*, I, 83–87; Relación de . . . Orellana de sus expediciones, Cuzco, July 17, 1781, in Odriozola, *Documentos*, I, 184–88; Mendiburu, *Diccionario*, VIII, 145; Angelis, *Documentos*, 79–84.

loyal Indians from Paucarcolla, Guaca, and the estate of Moro, was sent out to keep them from uniting with their companions. Two pickets of gunners also went out to reinforce them, but since it was late and the ascent steep and dangerous, the rebels could not be forced to surrender. The gunners withdrew to the plaza, while the faithful Indians remained in their posts all night; but the slowness of Cacique Bustinza, who withdrew from his assigned post, permitted the enemy to escape after the second invasion of Puno. Although the number of besiegers was not as great as in the first siege, they were as confident of taking the town.

When the garrison went to defend the Indians of Icho, all the Indian women were found to have been beheaded because their husbands were faithful to the royalists. Pascual Alarapita, an Indian of low station from the province of Paria, directed the natives with Isidro Mamani as his subordinate. The former had been cast out of his province as a delinquent and now undertook the conquest of the provinces of Sicasica, Pacajes, and Chucuito, which were terrified by his bloody acts. The Indians of Acora finally imprisoned Mamani and surrendered him with two of his captains to Orellana, who treated him kindly since he was of inferior rank.

The people of Azángaro, Lampa, and Carabaya soon attacked the heights of Puno again. In a skirmish with the faithful Indians and three companies of gunners, they tried to take the cattle and reduce the inhabitants to the greatest want. Although their number was much larger than that of the Spanish forces, Orellana marched against them next morning with the greater part of his people. The enemies' chief purpose was to unite with the inhabitants of Chucuito, but as soon as they learned of Mamani's imprisonment, they withdrew, drove off the cattle, and set fire to the town of Paucarcolla. The cavalry company marching ahead fought with them near the hill of Yupa, where they awaited the corregidor. The Indians then took refuge on the mountain summit, where stone walls protected them. In the late afternoon the people of Cabana and Cabanilla, who were on their way to Puno, arrived, for it was feared that Diego Túpac Amaru intended to attack Puno. This new force with the troops of Vilque and Mañazo was sufficient to surround the insurgents that night despite their advantageous location.

The Indians, fatigued from the afternoon sun and constant shouting, could not quench their thirst because the Spaniards controlled all the brooks. Their condition was critical. Therefore, they made one last effort to break through the military lines around them. This they did, and the greater part of them, including Ingaricona, escaped. Those who could not follow were brutally slain by the loyal Indians whose wives and children had been put to death. Many rebel colonels and captains also perished.[7]

Orellana now received a letter from an Indian of Acora telling that the enemy troops were coming there again to take vengeance on the faithful Indians. The rebels had withdrawn to Ilabe and Juli, where they had been reinforced with people from Pacajes. The corregidor arranged to send aid to Acora, but had to keep his soldiers in Puno when he heard that the revolters were preparing to attack again. The roads were cut off; no word could be sent to Lima; and the visitador seemed to ignore the critical situation in Puno. Orellana therefore repaired the fortifications again, barricaded the corners of the plaza and the streets, and took the greatest precautions.

The enemy forces approached Chucuito, where they stopped for some days to await the orders of Diego Túpac Amaru. Meanwhile, Orellana wrote Pascual Alarapita to ask pardon and thus save the province of Chucuito. Alarapita did not answer, and, in a note which he sent to the prisoner Mamani, he said that he had burned the letter without reading it. He also made many threats against Orellana and the men defending Puno. As a result, the corregidor sent a last request to Arequipa for men, munitions, and supplies to ward off the third siege of his town.

On May 7, Diego Túpac Amaru appeared on the heights of Puno with all his troops. He took no action, however, until the

[7] Odriozola, *Documentos*, I, 87–91; Relación de . . . Orellana de sus expediciones, Cuzco, July 17, 1781, in Odriozola, *Documentos*, I, 188–92; Angelis, *Documentos*, 84–89.

afternoon of the eighth, when he attacked the loyal Indians on the hill of Azogue. Since he dislodged and pursued them to the fortress of Santa Barbara, it was necessary to send the cavalry and gunners to halt the Indians near the church of St. John, which they tried to occupy. The enemy were finally repulsed with a loss, withdrew to the heights, and did not attack on the following day.

The royalists now noticed that the men who had come from Chucuito had camped very near the town on the royal road. They helped Diego Túpac Amaru surround Puno on all sides, and soon attacked boldly. Their numerous cavalry fought along the lake so that it was impossible for shepherds to bring their sheep into the town. The rebels withstood the artillery fire from the fortresses of Guansapata, Santiago, and Santa Barbara, and that of the gunners in the trenches. Full of pride and confidence on account of the easy conquest of the provinces of Sicasica, Pacajes, and Chucuito and encouraged by the presence of their generals, they took the exterior and interior breastworks and tried to seize the trenches near the inn of Santa Rosa, but failed. They finally had to fall back because of the firing from the nearby fortress of Santiago. In the upper part of the town, despite shooting of cannon from Guansapata, they penetrated the street where Licenciado Mongrovejo's house was located. Orellana then gave orders to concentrate on driving them away, and they lost what had been gained on that side of town.

At the rear of the parish of St. John the insurgents forced a detachment of lancers to seek refuge in the inside streets. Shortly the cavalry, pursued by Indians, fled in disorder, leaving the gunners separated from the rear guard. Orellana went out to meet the cavalrymen, reproached them for their dishonor, and stopped the retreat. The royalists then turned around and charged the enemy, who had already crossed the first streets, and drove them out of town, killing many of them in the process.

The fortress of Santiago was attacked many times and had to get aid, since the Indians swarmed around all parts of the town. They tried to take the trenches a second time, but were repulsed.

As the Spaniards repaired the trenches immediately, the invaders did not obtain any advantage except the burning of several ranches and houses a short distance away.

Orellana was forced to withdraw the garrison of Santiago to the plaza because of lack of men to operate the cannon. The officers and men remained armed in the trenches all night; the loyal Indians were placed all around the town; and patrols were kept on duty until dawn. On the following day (May 11), the rebels made a similar attack, concentrating on the area back of the church of St. John in the belief that it had not been repaired. They were driven back.

At two o'clock in the morning the Spaniards noticed that the Indians had come down to the slopes. Confident of success, at half-past six they divided into many parties and began the fourth attack. The royalists were tired, yet each man took his assigned place. The enemy now directed their greatest efforts at the trenches under the command of Francisco Barreda, Juan de Monasterio, and Juan de Cáceres, for they knew that the fortress of Santiago had been abandoned. They did not gain the trenches, and fell back. At the rear of the church of St. John they again attacked boldly, but were repulsed by Martín Zea and his picket of gunners and cavalry. They made another attempt on the trench under Cáceres, hoping to open a way by which to enter the town, but this effort, too, failed. The insurgents then destroyed the walls with small bars, penetrated to the back of the inn of Santa Rosa, and set fire to the houses on that side of the town, but even from here they were dislodged.

The artillery commandant, Francisco Vizenteli, was extremely watchful. When he saw any place in great danger, he directed a lively fire toward it from the plaza. Antonio Urbina also kept up a continuous fire from the fortress of Guansapata and contributed greatly to repelling the natives, who tried to seize the more exposed trenches held by Barreda and Monasterio. From the trench of Santa Barbara, Martín Esquiros directed the shooting upon the enemy cavalry; and from each of the four corners of Anselmo Bustinza's house cannon fire was aimed toward the country. This kept the Indians from entering and burning in that ward. Gradually the Indians were forced to the edge of the town and up to the heights. Diego Túpac Amaru's men went to their barracks first, but the men from Chucuito fought stubbornly for half an hour longer.

At dawn next day the royalists discovered that Diego Túpac Amaru had departed so hurriedly that he had left behind his rich parasols and many provisions. But the rebels from Chucuito, who were believed to be commanded by Túpac Catari, remained and fought skirmishes with the cavalry until May 22, when they also left because troops were approaching from Lima. Inspector General del Valle, after overthrowing the Indians in Combapata, marched toward Puno to relieve the hard-pressed defenders.[8]

Orellana had received a letter from Del Valle, dated May 19, stating that help was on the way. His message caused great joy in Puno, but precautions still had to be taken. When six leagues distant, Del Valle received word from the corregidor that Puno was still besieged by twelve thousand Indians under Túpac Catari. Del Valle hastened his march, and soon the arrival of the royal troops in Puno was announced by the ringing of bells, salutes of artillery, and illuminations. The rebel Indians made similar demonstrations. They boldly shouted to the people in the town that the King's army had arrived, commanded by the Visitador himself, who came to punish them for the many dead Indians, and that it would soon be proved that José Gabriel Túpac Amaru had acted by authority of a royal order.

Del Valle had intended to spend the night two leagues from Puno, but when he learned that the enemy intended to attack again before assistance came, he hurried to the town, arriving there the afternoon of May 24. The enemy forces withdrew to a high mountain, and the Spanish army camped at its base.

Orellana brought out the garrison to attack on the following morning. Accompanied by many officers, he went to the enemy

<hr />

[8] Odriozola, *Documentos*, I, 91–97; Relación de . . . Orellana de sus expediciones, Cuzco, July 17, 1781, in Odriozola, *Documentos*, I, 192–200; Mendiburu, *Diccionario*, VIII, 145–46; Markham, *Travels in Peru and India*, 160–61; Angelis, *Documentos*, 89–97.

camp, and was pleased to find that the Indians had abandoned their position. They had divided into many parties, each going in a different direction. At last silence reigned on the mountains which had been occupied for more than fifteen days. The captured priest, Casimiro Ríos of Puno, had escaped during the retreat and made his way to the town. He reported that Andrés Guara, one of Túpac Catari's generals, who commanded the rebel army, had convinced his followers that he had raised the camp because he was very ill.[9]

The corregidor wanted to search for the enemy. He proposed to Del Valle to pursue the rebels to the province of Chucuito, where supplies were abundant and pasture lands good. He also wanted to find out whether the people would surrender Túpac Catari or any other commander. But one great obstacle stood in the way of his proposal—desertion among the royalist troops. The forces had left Cuzco 15,000 strong, but now were reduced to only 1,100 soldiers and 450 Indians. In six days 1,950 men had deserted. The Indian allies had become disgusted with the rigorous discipline, their small wage, and the poor food, and many had gone to assist Diego Túpac Amaru in harassing the Spaniards and cutting off supplies. A council of war was therefore held, in which it was determined to withdraw immediately to Cuzco lest the remaining men be lost. When the troops learned of this decision, they celebrated, and that night 30 more militiamen and 150 Indian allies deserted.

The fate of Puno hung in the balance. When Del Valle asked Orellana if he considered one hundred men sufficient to continue its defense, he replied that he did not have confidence in his soldiers and had no food for them. It was then planned to evacuate the town so that the inhabitants would not be exposed to the atrocities committed in Chucuito and elsewhere. This decision caused great dismay among the inhabitants of Puno, especially since they were given only three days to get ready to leave, and the confusion increased when Del Valle shortened the time to two days.

The sad exiles had to abandon their town on the twenty-sixth,

[9] Odriozola, *Documentos*, I, 69–71; Angelis, *Documentos*, 98–99.

Inca battle scene, showing *macanas* (swordlike clubs) and the "star-headed mace." After Felipe Guaman Poma de Ayala in *Nueva crónica y buen gobierno.*

From *Handbook of South American Indians*
(ed. by Julian H. Steward), II: *The Andean
Civilizations* (Washington, 1947)

The great Inca city of Machu Picchu

leaving behind practically all their possessions, including their cattle. Even the women and children had to travel on foot. About five thousand people evacuated Puno after the cannon had been thrown into deep wells to keep the Indians from obtaining them. It was difficult to maintain order on the march, for each man had his family. Only one or two leagues could be traveled in a day. A few people decided to go to Arequipa, thinking they could live better there, but most did not want to leave Orellana and marched toward Cuzco with the remnant of the army. Fortunately, the corregidor had obtained some food from Arequipa for the garrison, which he now distributed among the people, but a heavy snowstorm made it almost impossible to cook the scant provisions.

The Indians caused no problems until the refugees reached Lampa. They then attacked the flanks and rear guard and killed all persons who got separated from the main group. Near the town of Pucará some of the travelers took the road to Ayaviri. Noticing that they were separated and defenseless, the enemy charged them, cruelly killed many of them, took possession of the greater part of the baggage, and pursued the retreat to the Vilcañota Mountains. There they attacked again unexpectedly and seized the cattle and beasts of burden, but since there were only one thousand Indians, they were easily repulsed.

Orellana soon realized that it had been a mistake to leave Puno. He sent word from Yanarico on May 29 to the Inspector General that it was necessary for the viceroyalties to hold Puno. Del Valle's reply, received in Quiquijana, described the sad conditions in the viceroyalty of La Plata and the results of the depopulation of Puno. He ordered Orellana to suspend his march in the town of Sicuani so that all the refugee families might return to their homes. Both the Viceroy of Peru and Visitador Areche also wanted to hold Puno; they regarded its evacuation as an abuse of authority on the part of the Inspector General and feared that La Paz would be in great danger as a result of it. Since he was so near Cuzco, Orellana decided to go there at once with his people, arriving on June 5, after forty days of great hardships and leaving many dead along the way. There he found an order for him to take the people back to Puno.

The visitador promised him help, but Orellana said that he would need four thousand men, eight hundred guns, and ten cannon to undertake such a journey.[10]

Del Valle had not marched all the way to Cuzco with Orellana. He found Major General Francisco Cuellar still in Sicuani, where the General had detached a body of eight hundred soldiers and two thousand friendly Indians to pursue Diego Túpac Amaru in the province of Carabaya and, if possible, take him with his nephews and followers. As the rebels had cut off communications so thoroughly that Cuellar had received only one letter in all the time he had been in Sicuani, he knew nothing about the situation of the army and could not send help. This was not strange since the Indians treated messengers cruelly. For instance, in the town of Santiago de Pupuja a messenger on his way to Sicuani had his ears and nose and hands cut off. This barbarity horrified the inhabitants so much that none of them would consent to carry letters even when offered large sums of money.

After a short delay in Sicuani, Del Valle's army passed the frontier dividing the two viceroyalties. There desertion from the militia and among the Indian auxiliaries was so great that Del Valle feared they would all abandon him entirely. He finally arrived in Cuzco with the remnants of his force two days ahead of Orellana.[11]

He reported to the Cuzco officials concerning the desperate condition of his army. He declared that it was impossible to correct in four days what the insurgents had done in four years and that criticism of the retreat was unjust.[12] He did not have enough troops to engage in battle with Diego Túpac Amaru; furthermore, a number of the men were ill, there were many desertions, the tents had been destroyed, and many mules had died for lack of pasturage. Del Valle said that he and the council of war both realized that

[10] Odriozola, *Documentos*, I, 97–100, 102, 201–206; Carta de Dn. Agustín de Jáuregui á Dn. Ramón de Arias, Lima, December 11, 1781. MS copy in B. L. Angelis, *Documentos*, 99–103. Markham says in *Travels in Peru and India*, 161, that General del Valle had 1,443 men left after the desertions. According to Valcárcel, in *La rebelión de Túpac Amaru*, 153, some 8,000 persons accompanied Orellana in the retreat from Puno.

[11] Odriozola, *Documentos*, I, 100, 102.

[12] Del Solar, *op. cit.*, 106.

Cuzco also was exposed to the insurgents and had only two hundred soldiers to defend it. He had decided to assist the town because the Indians from Calca, Paucartambo, and part of Tinta surrounded it.

When the Viceroy ordered an army to be gathered to retake Puno, the Inspector General asked the various corregidores for recruits. Although the order was repeated, they all excused themselves by saying that it was impossible on account of lack of money, hunger, illness, and the fact that the natives' mules had not been paid for.[13]

The refugees in Cuzco could see that armed Indians surrounded the city. The rebels were especially bold on the heights above Urubamba and Calca and at Lauramarca and Ocungate. Those near Calca fortified themselves in a place called Chuña-casa, but they were defeated with great loss by a force of four hundred men under José de Barala, while Joaquín Valcárcel kept the insurgents who threatened Paucartambo in check.

Meanwhile, Diego Túpac Amaru had established his headquarters in the elevated town of Azángaro, which for a short time became the Inca capital. He lived in the home of Cacique Chuquiguanca, a circular building with a remarkable Inca roof and called the *Sondorhuasi*. In it there was a long room in which Diego held receptions. Wrapped in a long cloak, he went from his dwelling to the fine old church every night. It was reported that fifteen muleloads of treasure, consisting of spoils from the provinces of Omasuyos and Larecaja, were brought into Azángaro and buried near Diego's house, but the riches have never been found.[14]

The revolt was now directed from Azángaro. From there Andrés Túpac Amaru, who paid more attention to the formalities of war than other leaders, and Miguel Bastidas, accompanied by Vilca Apasa, overran the provinces on the western shores of Lake Titicaca and established communication with the insurgents in Upper Peru. The priest Pacheco, a captain in the army of Colonel Arias,

[13] Mariscal del campo D. José del Valle escribió y firmó en el Cuzco el 30 de Sete. de 1781 un manifesto. MS copy in B. L.

[14] Carta de Diego Chuquicallata á Agustín Jáuregui, Cuzco, February 18, 1781. MS copy in B. L.

called Andrés a fine boy. He cited his bravery in daring to pass the royalist camp alone, although Diego Túpac Amaru refused to do so because he feared an ambush. Andrés knew how to win the sympathy of the Creoles, among whom he found Gerónimo Gutiérrez a capable assistant. He evidently had larger plans than merely avenging the death of his relatives. The siege of the town of Sorata firmly established his reputation.

The Spaniards of neighboring districts had taken refuge at Sorata with their families and their wealth. The faithful Diego Chuquicallata was among the refugees. He had been serving with the troops of the corregidores of Lampa, Azángaro, and Carabaya, with those under Cipriano Cabrera in the province of Larecaja, and with those under José Pinedo in La Paz. He had unselfishly refused to accept pay for serving the King, but because of the pursuit of his enemies it was necessary for him to seek refuge in Sorata.[15]

Sorata was surrounded for fourteen days by the three Indian generals, Andrés Túpac Amaru, Bastidas, and Vilca Apasa, with four or five thousand men. In Sorata, Manuel Asturizaga assumed the leadership of the royalists and formed an army of eight hundred to one thousand men, who killed more than three hundred Indians. The enemy then raised the seige and left the town in peace for twenty days. During that time Asturizaga took all measures possible for its defense. The people heard that General Cuellar, corregidor of Cangaio, was bringing relief, but he had to withdraw. It was this retreat that really caused the ruin of Sorata, for shortly thereafter eighteen thousand to twenty thousand Indians, led by Andrés Túpac Amaru, besieged the town.

The firing was continuous, day and night, for ninety days. As a result, the people of the town lived entrenched in the center of the plaza. Including the refugees who came there from Lampa, Azángaro, Carabaya, and elsewhere, the fighting men in Sorata now numbered two thousand. They were commanded by Anastasio Suárez de Verela, an inhabitant. During the siege the Spaniards had received three messages concerning surrender from Andrés

[15] Markham, *Travels in Peru and India*, 162, 209–10; Lewin, *op. cit.*, 257, 262–63.

278

Túpac Amaru and had paid no attention to them. Now they were almost starved and had been eating mules, dogs, cats, and rats. Prices were so exorbitant that a mule's leg cost fifty pesos. Under such conditions the people were willing to treat with the besiegers. For two days after the firing ceased, the royalists made use of the truce to collect supplies until the day came to treat for peace.

When the Spaniards went to the place appointed for making the treaty, the Indians dealt treacherously with them.[16] It seems, however, that they brought this kind of treatment on themselves. According to an unedited document, José Pinedo had earlier pretended great friendshop for Andrés Túpac Amaru, all the while planning to kill him. He went to the Inca's lodging near the town for that purpose, but before he could get out his hidden pistols, one fell to the ground. When the Indian leader cried, "Treason!" the warriors caught Pinedo before he could mount his horse and killed him and Gregorio Santalla, who had accompanied him.[17]

The third message from the rebels was delivered by Tomás Segovia, priest of Challanta. In it the people were asked to surrender and put themselves under his banners, but they refused. Then Andrés Túpac Amaru took an extraordinary measure to reduce the town—a strategy which would have done credit to any general. He had the water coming from the snow-covered Ancoma Mountain collected behind a dam, and on August 4, 1781, directed the water toward the earthworks defending the town. The torrent of rushing water broke through the trenches and obliged the guards to flee. The enemy immediately entered the plaza and killed more than ten thousand persons, all the inhabitants except the clergy. Their barbarity exceeded that employed in the death of José Gabriel Túpac Amaru. Finally they burned the town and Andrés Túpac Amaru took Eustaquio Caravedo along with him as his chaplain.

The Indians ordered Chuquicallata sent to the gallows. He saved his life by pretending to be a priest, but was taken to the

---

[16] Ballivián y Roxas, *op. cit.*, 249–55.
[17] Informe fechado en Arequipa el 22 de Agosto de 1781, AGN, Buenos Aires, VI–XVI–9–12, in Lewin, *op. cit.*, 256.

stopping place of Andrés three quarters of a league from Sorata. There he saw the 40,000 pesos taken from the town and surrounding area. Andrés sent to Azángaro for his uncle, Diego Túpac Amaru, to dispose of the booty. Diego and his colonel, Vilca Apasa, went away with forty mules loaded with trunks full of gold and stamped silver, which they sent to the province of Carabaya and the doctrina of Sandia. On the same occasion Chuquicallata saw Colonel Diego Quispe, from the town of Patambuco, load six mules with gold and silver from the same source, while Andrés took large amounts with him to La Paz. The prisoner was conducted to Azángaro, presented to Diego Túpac Amaru, and remained there from October 7, 1781, to January 21, 1782, when he traveled with the Inca to Sicuani.[18]

Andrés returned to Azángaro, where he made frequent visits to the home of Vilca Apasa's sister, in which the beautiful Angelina Sevilla lived. The friendship of the young people ripened into love, but since large reinforcements were being gathered in the two viceroyalties, evil days were coming for the lovers.[19]

In this account it has been noted that Puno was important because of its strategic location in the valley of Lake Titicaca. If the town could have obtained substantial assistance after heroically withstanding three sieges by the Indians, it might have aided the surrounding territories and perhaps prevented the siege of La Paz from being so severe. With his limited forces and resources its corregidor, Orellana, accomplished wonders in defending the town and helping the near-by villages. He was very sad when the long-expected reinforcements arrived under Inspector General del Valle and were unable to lend effective assistance. From this distance in time, it appears that Del Valle could have made a greater effort to hold Puno. After the town was abandoned, the enemy took possession of the whole Lake Titicaca region, concentrated all their forces in besieging La Paz, and thereby prolonged the revolt.

[18] Ballivián y Roxas, *op. cit.*, 249–55; Miller, *op. cit.*, I, 71. Miller said that twenty thousand people were put to death in Sorata. Odriozola, *Documentos*, I, 109–10; Carta de Diego Chuquicallata á Agustín de Jáuregui, Cuzco, February 18, 1782. MS copy in B. L.
[19] Markham, *A History of Peru,* 211.

CHAPTER XIII

The Siege of La Paz

Lᴀ Pᴀᴢ, ᴀ ᴄɪᴛʏ ᴏғ 20,000 ɪɴʜᴀʙɪᴛᴀɴᴛs, suffered two severe sieges, the first lasting 109 days and the second 75. The Indians of the area had been dissatisfied and restless since 1777, when the customhouse was established, and were also angered by the high taxes. On February 2, 1780, a lampoon appeared on the customhouse door containing insulting remarks and a drawing of the corregidor and treasury officials hanging from gallows. Another lampoon threatened that if Bernardo Gallo were not removed from the customhouse, the Indians would drink out of his skull. These threats indicate that the natives had begun to rebel against the royal tax measure of July 26, 1776, when their petitions to have it rescinded had gone unheeded. The merchants had demanded from the natives a 6 per cent tax on yerba maté, coca, salted mutton, flannel, and other coarse cloth. Now officials began to take fright as the lampoons continued. A lampoon posted on March 4, 1780, was particularly forceful. It read:

> May the law of God and the purity of Mary live and may the King of Spain die ... if he does not know the insolence of his ministers, their public robbery, and the crimes they commit against the people! Let the King live, and let all those public thieves die![1]

The next overt act occurred on the night of March 12, when groups of masked men forced the sextons to ring the church bells to summon the insurgents. When the sextons objected, they threatened to burn the parish church of Santa Barbara. After two thousand people assembled, Fermín de Gil y Alipassaga, the corregidor, the treasury officials, and other authorities went into hiding. Next day an Indian arriving from Puno reported that there were many

---

[1] Lewin, *op. cit.*, 54–57; Cánovas del Castillo, *op. cit.*, V, 449–80; Loayza, *op. cit.*, Serie I, Vol. XIII, 112.

people on the heights above the city. When he asked them why they were there, they said that they came from the provinces of Pacajes and Sicasica to destroy the customhouse. Moreover, they wanted to emulate the thirteen English colonies in North America by joining the general uprising to be led by Joseph Chino and Eugenio Quispe.

When the corregidor himself received a lampoon threatening him with death if he kept the customhouse, he summoned the cabildo to meet on March 15 to consider the critical situation. On the morning of that day the councilors were assailed by more lampoons. Realizing the danger, they sent a crier through the city to announce the closing of the customhouse and reduction of the alcabala to 4 per cent. The corregidor believed the rebels wanted to cut all ties with Spain, and Rafael Villanueva, a clerk, held the same opinion. When Visitador Areche was informed of the councilmen's measure, however, he protested that the authorities of La Paz had no right to rescind a royal law. He ordered the customhouse to be administered again, the 6 per cent to be collected on the alcabala, and all disturbers of the peace to be punished.[2] Meanwhile, the inhabitants of La Paz heard about José Gabriel Túpac Amaru and his assaults on the Spaniards. When they saw that little had been gained from their activities and believed that conditions were growing worse, they eagerly supported him.

Sebastián de Segurola, corregidor of the province of Larecaja, took the initiative to ward off danger. He did everything he could to protect his territory after the other corregidores had fled at the time the Inca attacked Lampa. Luckily, he had had eighteen years of military service in Spain and had helped force the Portuguese to surrender Colonia to the Viceroyalty of Peru.[3]

Now Segurola lacked money to check the Inca rebellion because one-third of the tribute had already been paid to the royal treasury. Nevertheless, he ordered supplies to be collected, pro-

---

[2] Lewin, op. cit., 55–58; Carta de Areche al corregidor de la Paz, desprobando la suspención de la aduana, Lima, July 22, 1780, AGN, Buenos Aires, Criminales, Leg. 16, exp. 26 (published in Lewin, op. cit., 432–33); Valcárcel, Rebeliones Indígenas, 89–91.

[3] Ballivián y Roxas, op. cit., 279.

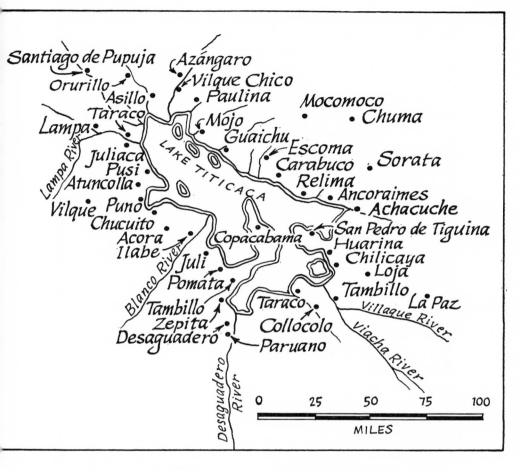

TOWNS IN THE LAKE TITICACA REGION AFFECTED BY THE REVOLT

vided firearms, organized Spanish and mestizo troops to guard the roads, drew up a plan of campaign, and summoned the people to ward off any attack. Then he took the Spaniards and mestizos to Sorata and offered a reward of 12,000 pesos for Túpac Amaru dead or alive.

On December 30, 1780, the Viceroy ordered Segurola to help Flores pacify Chayanta and the neighboring provinces, after which he was to proceed to La Paz and take charge of the defense there on January 1, 1781. Upon his arrival, he found that La Paz offered no natural defense since it was situated in a narrow valley hemmed in by steep mountains. The former corregidor had made some military preparations. With 30,000 pesos withdrawn from the treasury, he had constructed twenty-four bronze fieldpieces and lances and had bought munitions and other supplies. Only half of the money had been spent, and Segurola made good use of what was left.

Segurola noticed a general restlessness among the Indians and kept on with the military preparations even after he heard that Túpac Amaru had withdrawn to Tinta. He had a quantity of tents and cannonballs made, but money remained scarce because most of it had been sent to Tacna and Oruro. He therefore solicited funds from wealthy citizens and inhabitants of neighboring provinces. The bishop, Gregorio Francisco de Campos, sold all his possessions to aid the city during the siege. Later the King recognized his services, but would not promote him to the Archbishopric of Charcas because he considered him more useful in La Paz. The King rewarded the Bishop's brother, Andrés José de Campos, who raised and paid for a cavalry regiment, with the rank of colonel and the cross of the Order of Calatrava.

Segurola asked the higher authorities for veteran troops and more firearms, as he had only one hundred guns of inferior quality. He enclosed the principal part of the city with trenches, but the suburbs and three Indian towns were left outside. He found it difficult to collect supplies since the harvests of the preceding year had been scant. Aid could not be sent to him because the rebellion

284

in Chayanta spread so rapidly that governors and corregidores everywhere were compelled to act in their own defense.[4]

Every day the number of insurgents increased, and almost all the towns of the province of Paucarcolla were invaded. Despite the weakness of the La Paz forces, Segurola decided to send aid to places harassed by the enemy. Therefore he sent out Colonel José Pinedo and two companies of cavalry and himself went to the province of Larecaja to obtain more than two thousand men. Those forces, along with the people in the province of Omasuyos, were to work with the governor of Chucuito and with Corregidor Orellana of Puno to hinder Túpac Amaru's progress. They were also to check the enemy in Oruro, who, along with the revolutionists of the provinces of Carangas, Paria, and Chayanta, had cut off all communication with the higher government.

Segurola had already sent money and ammunition to Puno by another route. He also showed the Board of Finance the need of more financial assistance in order to gather supplies for the troops. The money was provided and some provisions were collected, although uprisings in the provinces of Sicasica and Pacajes and a large part of Chulumani cut off aid from La Paz and obliged the corregidores of the first two provinces to flee to that city. Segurola then asked for men from the neighboring regions to unite at La Paz to bolster the defense of the city, but the request was largely ignored. Only two hundred men from Pacajes, the same number from the valleys of Chulumani, and a few from Sicasica joined the troops of La Paz.

In a few days the revolt spread to La Paz, leaving its bloody traces in towns all along the way, where Spaniards and mestizos were killed. The assistant priest of Viacha, only six leagues away, came fleeing to La Paz on March 9, 1781, and told about the rebellion in his town. An expedition of nearly five hundred soldiers left at midnight, under Colonel Manuel Franco, to punish the

---

[4] Informe de Sebastián de Segurola, La Paz, July 1, 1781, in Balivián y Roxas, *op. cit.*, 2–7, 118; Temple, *op. cit.*, 107–109; Relación de los hechos mas notables acaecidos en la sublevación general . . . , 116–19. MS copy in B. L.

rebels and subjugate the neighboring communities. Arriving at Viacha at daybreak, it surprised the Indians and put three hundred of them to death, but pardoned those who fled to the church and proclaimed obedience to King Charles III. This action had a restraining effect upon the Indians in the three parishes of San Sebastián, San Pedro, and Santa Barbara, and neighboring towns. They offered a hypocritical fidelity to the sovereign, but Segurola did not trust them.

He decided to lead out some six hundred men to strike terror among the revolutionists in Laja. Then he would go to Calamarca to try to catch the rear guard of the Indians at Ventilla. When the corregidor of Omasuyos told the people of Sorata of this, they sent three hundred men to check the Indians of Achacache. As the latter had given proof of their disloyalty and had obliged their corregidor to flee to La Paz, Segurola ordered the Soratans to join him in Laja. He also ordered twelve hundred Indians of La Paz to come along, but only three hundred from the parish of San Sebastián obeyed; in this manner he learned which men were treacherous.

He left the city at midnight (March 13), sending Colonel Manuel Franco and Captain Dionisio Escauriza with separate forces to attack the Indians' farms. With the principal body he marched toward Laja. On a hill near the town he saw eight Indians hurling stones with their slings. He tried to climb the hill, but failed to do so and had to retreat. When he arrived in Laja at sunset, he found the town abandoned. As soon as the infantry and cavalry entered, they began to plunder and became insubordinate. When a small force joined Segurola, he tried again to take the hill, but was repulsed three times by the Indians, who fought with astonishing courage. After additional reinforcements arrived, the hill was captured in a fourth attempt, and more than fifty Indians were killed. Segurola said that the enemy troops showed a determination which might serve as an example to the most valiant nation, for many wounded Indians resisted desperately until they died.

The commandant then returned to Laja, where the detachments sent to the farms were waiting, having killed some sixty Indians. Most of the soldiers went to the cemetery to spend the night, but a number disobeyed orders and could not be kept from looting. Meanwhile, Colonel Antonio Pinedo reported that the Indians in Ventilla had united and now many of them approached La Paz by the heights. Segurola quickly set fire to many of the houses in Laja, and late in the afternoon marched for Larecaja. He was followed by a body of Indians, who did not dare to attack until night. One league from La Paz, Lieutenant Colonel Juan Bautista Zavala, commanding the rear guard, heard extraordinary sounds and realized that the city was being attacked. The men made the proper formation, placed two fieldpieces on the right and left, and then gave a false call. This caused the enemy to rush upon them, but the fire from four cannons put them to flight.[5]

After the moon came out, the enemy halted in a better place near a slope and, when fired upon, fled to the hill. They fought furiously and threw innumerable stones, causing the Spaniards to take another position. When it began to rain, the insurgents attacked boldly, believing the Spanish firearms would be useless, but they were wrong; these weapons proved to be quite serviceable. Fighting continued during the greater part of the night. At three o'clock in the morning the Indians tried to block the narrow pass on the Lima road below the city. Segurola hastened to prevent this and, when it grew light, dislodged the rebels from the hill. He wanted to pursue them, but could not do so, for part of his soldiers had fled to the city, leaving him unsupported and facing an Indian army of ten to twelve thousand men.

The Spaniards withdrew easily to La Paz because the insurgents had not yet noticed their weakness. When the battlefield was examined, only twenty or thirty dead Indians could be found at first since the natives were always careful to hide their dead; later in ravines along the road to Lima four or five hundred were seen. The Spaniards had lost fifty men. It was a bad night for them, as they could not restrain the native soldiers from San Sebastián, who stole cattle, and could not prevent most of them from deserting to the enemy.

[5] Ballivián y Roxas, *op. cit.*, 8–17; Relación de los hechos mas notables acaecidos en la sublevación general . . . , 120–26.

The commandant received news on March 16 that the people coming from Sorata would arrive in the afternoon and needed help to enter the city. As the Indians of the parish of San Pedro had openly favored the enemy and would oppose the entrance, Segurola went out to subdue them and killed more than fifty. The others from that parish then hastened to join the rebels on the heights. Next day the commandant marched out to help the troops coming from Larecaja, but when they did not appear, returned to the city. At three o'clock in the afternoon of the eighteenth, a combat observed on the heights gave notice that the people from Sorata had arrived. Before many soldiers could be sent from La Paz to aid them, some of the Soratans deserted the battlefield and came hurriedly into the city under the pretext of informing the inhabitants of their danger. In the midst of the great confusion the Indians fell upon the disorganized Spaniards, killed twenty-five of them, and captured ten guns, eighty loads of provisions, and the greater part of the baggage.

The commandant hurried out by the road to Lima and decided to take the heights. He ordered an attack launched at three different areas: The loyal Indians of the city aided by soldiers with firearms were to strike in one direction, but they fled just when success was within their grasp. A troop of lancers made the attack on the second area, but they also fled in great disorder. The other division was under Segurola himself, who tried to take the height with some foot soldiers and gunners, who became terrified by the stones hurled at them and also ran away. That day the Spaniards saw the enemy use a gun, which killed only a mule.

The enemy army kept increasing on the heights and tried to come down to the suburbs of La Paz to burn the houses. By March 21 the Spaniards were completely surrounded on the valley side, since a large number of Indians from the provinces of Sicasica and Chulumani had gone up the river ravine. All along the way they burned and destroyed haciendas and controlled all the entrances to the city. The Spaniards ventured out in a rainstorm next day to check the rebels, who entered the suburbs and burned a few houses. The heights might have been taken at that time if it had not been for the disorder among the Spanish forces. On the following day the Indians seized all the animals provided for the troops and killed seven men in charge of them. Three detachments were then sent against the insurgents, but the same disorder in the ranks kept them from catching the rebels.[6]

Segurola then decided to attack the enemies of Potopoto, and on the twenty-sixth made a sally with a detachment of six hundred men under Colonel Franco. As he was unable to draw the rebels back to the plain, he planned to cross the river and dislodge them from the hill of Pampajasi. The troops advanced to the middle of the river but, when they realized the difficulty of taking the hill, decided to withdraw. The Indians attacked, killed thirty men, and seized their four fieldpieces and more than twenty-five firearms. This unfortunate incident convinced the commandant that it was useless to undertake anything without the aid of veteran soldiers. Although he and the retreating Spaniards killed many insurgents, they were pursued to the city gates, and great terror resulted in the plaza. The cavalry fled through the streets not knowing where to go and the infantrymen ran to the cathedral. In the parish of Santa Barbara many persons did not have time to take cover in the trenches and became the victims of the Indians. The enemy also burned several houses in the wards of San Sebastián and San Pedro before being checked by Colonel Salvador Cardón.

A formal siege of La Paz now began from the surrounding hills and shut it in so completely that it could neither send nor receive communications. Then a mestizo from the province of Pacajes told the Spaniards that the Indians knew that aid was being sent from La Plata and Potosí and were determined to attack the city every day with all their forces. They proceeded to do so, using the guns and fieldpieces captured from the Spaniards. Even though they suffered heavy losses—350 of them were killed on March 28—they always returned during the day and withdrew to the heights at night. By the last of March, supplies were badly needed in La Paz; therefore many Indians of the city ventured out to collect food

[6] Relación de los hechos mas notables acaecidos en la sublevación general . . . , 126–31; Ballivián y Roxas, *op. cit.*, 17–24.

from the river ravine, while others guarded them and the city at the same time.

From April 1 to April 3 the Indians kept coming down to the city and shooting into the houses, burning some of them. On the third they threw a letter into the orchard of the Franciscan convent, which had been sacked because it was outside the fortifications. The letter, from José Gabriel Túpac Amaru, was dated March 29, 1781, and was similar to other documents of his concerning the redress of grievances and promising protection for ecclesiastics and favor for mestizos who joined his cause. The Bishop of La Paz answered the letter, urging the Indians to recognize their errors and repent. If they did so, he said, he would try to obtain pardon for them.

The Spaniards made two sallies on April 5—one from the parish of San Sebastián and the other from Santa Barbara. The first succeeded, but the second led to a disorderly flight in which the Indians killed thirty-six men in the rear guard, including Gregorio Farfán, a priest of La Paz who served as captain of one of the companies from Sicasica. The Indians took cover in the ruins of the burned houses outside the trenches, but lost about three hundred men. Next day Túpac Catari answered the Bishop's letter and showed either naïveté or ignorance when he said:

> I will now thank your Grace to let me know how your Grace has learned that a number of ships are coming from Buenos Aires with troops to destroy us, when your Grace knows that Charles III has resigned in favor of the Inca king, on account of the wrongs and robberies committed. . . . May God preserve your Grace many years! I, the Señor Viceroy Túpac Catari.[7]

Many Indians came down on April 7. Most of them marched on foot in two files, with those on horseback in the middle. In the afternoon they withdrew to the heights in the same formation,

---

[7] Relación de los hechos mas notables acaecidos en la sublevación general . . . , 137; Temple, *op. cit.*, II, 115; Ballivián y Roxas, *op. cit.*, 24–30; Carta de José Gabriel Túpac al prior del convento, Altos de combate, March 29, 1781, and carta de Túpac Catari á Gregorio Francisco de Campos, Altos de combate, April 3, 1781, in Ballivián y Roxas, *op. cit.*, 192–94.

leaving a red banner hanging on a wall. Fastened to the banner was a paper which read:

> Now if you Christians wish evil, tomorrow you shall see it with the favor of God. Already I consider it necessary to attack, as I have no other remedy. If you persist in your obstinacy, there is not more than three hours' work, with the help of God, for I tell you my soldiers will finish you without doubt. Notwithstanding the arms you have, you must know that, with the help of God, I will reduce you to clay and dust. You will see that God will aid us, that we are right vigorous fellows, and that it is decreed from above. It is my will, Don Julián Puma Catari, that you Creoles shall bring well secured to me those thieves, and you shall all be pardoned. You must deliver up the other European Spaniards, which will insure pardon to all. . . . If you Creoles do not unite and put to death all European Spaniards . . . take heed unto this my present warning . . . for everything will be turned into ashes and you shall not live eight days. In the meantime I hope for a speedy conclusion of this affair. I the Señor Viceroy Túpac Catari.[8]

When the Indians came down on April 8, they seemed to be friendly and called to the Spaniards. A Franciscan friar spoke to them and discovered that they were drunk. They offered to discuss the matter of making peace with their viceroy, Túpac Catari, and said that on the following day a reply would be sent. Meanwhile, the Spaniards were to suspend all hostilities. The rebels approached the city next day, bringing with them the man called their chief, along with a great number of mounted Indians. The chief spoke to the Spaniards with the Franciscan as intermediary, saying that if all arms were collected and the entrances to the city opened, the Indians would be obedient and he would make peace. On the other hand, if they did not accede to his request, he would destroy them, for he had 100,000 Indian soldiers around the city ready to demolish it. If they met his terms they would be good friends; although he would kill the Europeans and confiscate their property, the Creoles would be pardoned.

[8] Relación de los hechos mas notables acaecidos en la sublevación general . . . , 137; Carta de Túpac Catari virrey á los habitantes de la Paz, April 7, 1781, in Ballivián y Roxas, *op. cit.*, 194–95; Temple, *op. cit.*, II, 116.

The one-eyed Pedro Obaya delivered this discourse. Nothing came of the parley, for the speech of the Indian "viceroy" only showed that he was completely intoxicated. Nevertheless, a few soldiers and a Franciscan friar trusted in peace and approached the heights, but were seized by the Indians. Among them was Mariano Murillo.[9]

At daybreak on April 11, many Indians began shouting from the walls of the burned houses. When the Spanish commandant noticed that some of them were inside a house which had not been burned, near the parish of San Francisco, he took a detachment, surrounded it, and set fire to it. The rebels fought desperately and, after using all their stones, threw red-hot tiles. A number of the enemy perished in the flames, and fifty-three were taken alive. Segurola then went to the ward of San Sebastián and killed thirty Indians. The total number put to death in both places was three hundred. Next day when an Indian boy reported that the Franciscan friar Antonio Barriaga had been killed because the insurgents thought he had been the cause of their misfortunes of the day before, the Spaniards retaliated by beheading the Indian prisoners.

When the Indians came down to draw water on the fourteenth, they put up a banner in the parish of San Sebastián. On it was a letter from Túpac Catari, which said that he was waiting for a response to his proposal of surrendering arms. If the Spaniards did not reply, he would conquer the city without further ado.[10]

La Paz placed its hopes on the aid that General Flores was bringing. The delay in his arrival was due not so much to the distance he had to travel as to the fact that a number of the provinces on the route had declared in favor of the revolution.[11]

Every day the insurgents came down from the heights to annoy La Paz and gained new courage when Túpac Catari told them that the city would soon be destroyed. From seven provinces he

[9] Relación de los hechos mas notables acaecidos en la sublevación general . . . , 138–40; Ballivián y Roxas, *op. cit.*, 31–32; Carta de Túpac Catari al padre de San Francisco, Altos de combate, April 9, 1781, in Ballivián y Roxas, *op. cit.*, 195–96.
[10] Relación de los hechos mas notables acaecidos en la sublevación general . . . , 140–42; Ballivián y Roxas, *op. cit.*, 32–34; Carta de Túpac Catari á sus amigos, April 14, 1781, in Ballivián y Roxas, *op. cit.*, 196; Gutiérrez, *op. cit.*, 9.
[11] Odriozola, *Documentos,* I, 104–105.

had collected more than fifteen thousand natives. Eight thousand of the most valiant and robust of them had been picked for combat in the trenches and the other seven thousand reserved for ambushes outside the walls and for dealing with the sallies from the city. The besiegers were now using two cannons and shouting with each shot fired, but Mariano Murillo, who had been pressed into service with one cannon, usually fired high in order not to injure the royalists.

On April 21, the Augustinian friar Borda noticed a slight negligence in the Indian camp where he carried on espionage and slipped away to the city and tried to establish contact with Murillo. Whenever silence reigned on the heights, the Spaniards grew suspicious, fearing that the enemy were plotting something new. On the twenty-fifth, an unusual silence prevailed everywhere; then at midnight the people of La Paz heard a gun report on the height of Calvario. At one o'clock they heard another, which was the signal to attack the city on all sides. Some Indians carried large firebrands to set the houses on fire, others had bars to batter down the walls, and others attacked by hurling large stones and discharging guns. They kept this activity up until daylight, but lost more than three hundred men.

That same night Túpac Catari remained at the edge of the heights with the priest Borda, other ecclesiastics, and his wife. When he saw half of the city burning and the people fighting the fire, the chief said, "Already we conquer. Already we are happy, and now I must try to make war on Túpac Amaru, in order to become the only monarch in these kingdoms." Later, when conflicting reports were brought to him, some favorable and others unfavorable, he called the Spaniards demons.

Next night the besiegers came silently at two o'clock, but were more cautious in attacking the city. At daylight it was discovered that their cannon had been removed from the height of Calvario and taken to the elevated section of the road leading toward Potosí. At eleven o'clock in the morning a letter, signed "Diego Oblitas," was delivered to the Spaniards announcing the approach of the auxiliary expedition coming to their relief. Since Oblitas had died

293

three years before, the royalists immediately recognized it as a forgery and a stratagem to draw them out of the city into an ambush.

When the royalists did not appear, in the afternoon the Indians pretended to be fighting with the auxiliary forces on the summit of the road from Cuzco. Some, dressed in Spanish uniforms, were on horseback, others on foot; and the author of this scheme, Guaina Capac, looked very fine on a horse with rich trappings. Seeing that the Spaniards still did not leave the city, Guaina Capac approached, shouting and making signals as if asking aid. When his horse took him nearer than he intended and was wounded, he had to dismount close to one of the trenches, where the soldiers caught him and took him into the city.

In the afternoon another letter from Túpac Catari was put up on a banner in the ward of San Francisco. Addressed to Segurola, it said that a boy called Pedro Nogales, who claimed to be a nephew of José Gabriel Túpac Amaru, had arrived on the heights and had had the deceptive letter prepared to lure the militia out of the city. Segurola answered that if Túpac Catari's letter had been written to ask pardon for his crimes and those of his followers, he would treat them kindly and would suspend the measures he intended to take against them. The Indians did not desire peace, however, for that same afternoon when an escort went out from the parish of Santa Barbara to seek saltpeter, they attacked it.[12]

The Indians came down next day late in the afternoon and brought two additional letters. In one, Túpac Catari said that he had not written to ask pardon from the Europeans, but was moved by love for the Creoles. This love applied, however, only to good Creoles, as the evil ones would be reduced to ashes along with the Europeans who oppressed the Indians. He was determined to throw off the unbearable Spanish yoke and suppress bad government. He was ready to break into the entrenchments and over-

---

[12] Relación de los hechos mas notables acaecidos en la sublevación general . . . , 142–46, 182–84; Ballivián y Roxas, op. cit., 34–39; Carta de Diego Oblitas á Sebastián de Segurola, Callampaya, April 27, 1781; Carta de Julián Túpac Catari á Sebastián de Segurola, Altos de combate, April 27, 1781; and Carta de Sebastián de Segurola á Julián Apasa, llamado Túpac Catari, La Paz, April 28, 1781, in Ballivián y Roxas, op. cit., 197–99; Informe de Fray Matías Borda, La Paz, May 20, 1781, in Ballivián y Roxas, op. cit., 229–32.

come the people in La Paz, and no one would have the power to do anything to him. In the other letter he said that the people of all the communities in all the provinces were united in accordance with José Gabriel Túpac Amaru's command, and now were ready to fight or die to get rid of their oppressors. On the following day the rebels showed the Spaniards that they meant what they said, because greater numbers came down than before and for the first time discharged four cannons against the city. The cannonade continued until five o'clock.[13]

When the month of May arrived, every day the Indians fired on the city, and celebrated by dancing and getting drunk. But very few casualties occurred among the Spaniards. The royalists began to notice blazing fires on the heights and believed them signals to summon additional Indians. On May 9, 1781, a boy came down from the heights with another letter from Friar Borda. The messenger said there were other ecclesiastics in the enemy camp and that Murillo still had charge of the cannon. In the letter the friar asked Segurola to make every effort to advance against the Indians or the churchmen would lose their lives. He reported that Túpac Catari was going to Sicasica with soldiers and two cannons in order to suppress a rival Indian leader. A letter from Sicasica had informed Túpac Catari that the Indians of the great Ayllo did not wish to obey him because he was of low rank. Borda added that the insurgents wanted to suspend the blockade around La Paz for fear they would be ruined, as Spanish aid had already arrived in Oruro. He proposed that when Túpac Catari left for Sicasica, he himself should go down as if to place guards on the hill and thus signal an attack by the royalists.

In the afternoon of the fifteenth, an Indian arrived on horseback in the ward of San Sebastián with another letter. He threw it into a trench, and one of the soldiers took it to the commander. Priests in the rebel army had sent it when told that the chief was returning from Sicasica and that on Sunday the thirteenth a three-

---

[13] Relación de los hechos mas notables acaecidos en la sublevación general . . . , 146–49; Carta de Túpac Catari á Sebastián de Segurola, Altos de combate, April 29, 1781; and Carta de todos los comunicades de los cuarto provincias á Sebastián de Segurola, April 29, 1781, in Ballivián y Roxas, *op. cit.*, 199–200.

day festival would begin, to celebrate the letter written by José Gabriel Túpac Amaru to Visitador Areche, a copy of which had been brought to the camp. They also reported that the visitador had ten thousand men in Cuzco and the Inca seventy thousand on the heights, that troops approached to aid La Paz, and that many Indians had fled from the camp. The writers urged Segurola to free them and the other Spanish captives from the barbarian Túpac Catari. They asked him to display a black banner on a large rock as a signal for them to bring out the two cannons and as a sign that he was coming to help them. As soon as the commandant received the letter, he sent out a detachment to reconnoiter the enemy movements. Then between Monday and Thursday, while the Indians were still intoxicated from their celebration, he put up the black banner.[14]

On the following days the Spaniards made sallies from La Paz to obtain saltpeter. An Indian told them that, on the night of May 17, Túpac Catari had gone a second time toward Sicasica with many of his people, four cannons, and munitions to attack the Spanish auxiliary troops coming from that town. Then on the twenty-first, at seven o'clock in the morning, the royalists discerned a commotion on the heights and a large number of Indians coming down toward Potopoto on mules. At nine, when they noticed many more rebels following on foot, among them the chief's wife, they sent a detachment out of the city to capture her. The detachment obtained some cattle, but did not succeed in getting the woman. When the Indians received reinforcements, they killed twenty-five or thirty Spaniards.

Friar Borda made use of that occasion to enter the city. He brought along six Spanish boys with guns and said that three other captives were ready to come, but at the last moment were unable to leave the camp. They gave Segurola another letter and

[14] Relación de los hechos mas notables acaecidos en la sublevación general . . . , 149-55, 184-85; Ballivián y Roxas, *op. cit.*, 40-45; Carta de Fray Matías Borda á Sebastián de Segurola, May 8, 1781; Carta de Fray Matías Borda y Mariano Murillo á Sebastián de Segurola, May 13, 1781, in Ballivián y Roxas, *op. cit.*, 201-30; Informe de Fray Matías Borda, La Paz, May 30, 1781, *ibid.*, 232-33; Temple, *op. cit.*, II, 138.

a document, in which he was advised to make an expedition that day to Chocata, so that the Spanish soldiers in the enemy's camp might join him. As Túpac Catari was two leagues from Sicasica, not many Indians were on the heights. Then another messenger arrived, saying that the Spanish auxiliary forces had killed many Indians and that Túpac Catari was frightened. Meanwhile, the chief had left the care of the encampment to his wife, who had sent him a reinforcement of one thousand infantrymen and cavalrymen.

Borda continued to invent schemes to rescue the Spanish captives. He told Segurola that at nine o'clock he would shoot a gun as a signal for him to attack. He mentioned that Murillo had gone with the chief, hoping to join the royalists from Puno and the Collao, who were expected at any time. He declared that if no aid came, when Murillo returned, the Spaniards in the enemy camp, some of whom were under sentence of death, would try to kill Túpac Catari. He would warn the captive Spaniards to fire high or without bullets so that they might incorporate themselves with the royalists.[15]

The Indians did not fight for the next few days, but continued to shout, wave banners, and come down to the city. On May 27, the royalists noticed that many people were on mules; some wore yellow, red, and blue uniforms, and others clothing taken from dead Spaniards. On June 2, 1781, at eight o'clock in the evening, the enemy made a furious attack on all parts of the city. They kept this up until six o'clock in the morning, but did not cause much damage. When a sally was made in the afternoon of the fourth, Murillo threw another letter toward the trench of San Sebastián. It informed the commandant of the misfortunes that the Spaniards suffered in Sicasica. The inhabitants of La Paz were sad, yet consoled to know that some soldiers had tried to help them and that others were coming.

Friar Borda answered the letter next day, asking Murillo to

[15] Relación de los hechos mas notables acaecidos en la sublevación general . . . , 155–57, 185; Ballivián y Roxas, *op. cit.*, 45–48; Carta de Fray Matías de la Borda á Sebastián de Segurola, May 14, 1781, in Ballivián y Roxas, *op. cit.*, 203–204; Informe de Fray Matías Borda, La Paz, May 30, 1781, *ibid.*, 234–37; Temple, *op. cit.*, II, 139–40.

give some definite instructions. The letter was put inside a button on the clothes of an Indian servant from La Paz, but unfortunately, he was taken prisoner (June 6). Tortured, he confessed that he was carrying a message. Túpac Catari immediately ordered Murillo seized. Both his arms were cut off, and he was thrown near the trench of Santa Barbara, where somebody recognized him. Letter number sixteen was also picked up. The Indian servant soon returned with another letter. In it Túpac Catari said that he had seen the correspondence with Murillo and was convinced of the Creoles' treason; hence he had decided to ruin all of them. Since Murillo was to give a signal for Segurola to attack, he now sent Murillo to direct the fight in person.[16]

Before Murillo died, he related what had happened in Sicasica to the forces sent to aid La Paz. The Indians had completely defeated five hundred men under Gavino Quevedo and had obtained two cannons, forty guns, and much ammunition. The inefficiency of the Cochabamba force commanded by Ayarza, who did not co-operate with Quevedo, contributed substantially to the disaster. The men recovered somewhat by attacking the Indians and regaining part of the booty and some gold, but this corrupted the soldiers.[17]

The people of La Paz also learned that the enemy were determined to strike the city soon with all their troops. The Indians did attack at unexpected hours until June 11, when fifty mules loaded with chests and trunks went up to the height of Potosí from the hill of Potopoto. That night silence reigned again, but at dawn next day shots were fired at the city. At four in the afternoon Túpac Catari, accompanied by many followers, came from the height of Potopoto to the height of Puna. He was received with the ringing of bells and dances arranged to celebrate the fiesta of Corpus Christi; next morning many Indians went up there to take part in

---

16 Relación de los hechos mas notables acaecidos en la sublevación general . . . , 157–62; Balivián y Roxas, *op. cit.*, 48–52; Carta de Mariano Murillo á Sebastián Segurola, June 2, 1781; Carta de Túpac Catari al comandante, June 6, 1781; and Carta de Túpac Catari al friar Matías de la Borda, June 6, 1781, in Ballivian y Roxas, *op. cit.*, II, 117–18.

17 Odriozola, *Documentos*, I, 102–103.

the festivities and in the afternoon came down again escorting the chief to Potopoto.

When the celebration was repeated on June 14, Segurola decided to send out a detachment to take two of the enemy's cannon. Because of insubordination and the weakness of the beasts of burden, the expedition did not get started until three in the afternoon. When the soldiers attacked the hill on two sides, the Indians were forced to retreat so precipitately that they left many of their belongings and some food, but those descending the hill could not be caught. One hundred and fifty Indians were killed. For several days thereafter the enemy were more persistent in their attacks upon the city than before, and tried to tear down the walls and burn the houses within the trench encirclement. The rebels had constructed a thick wall and trenches for themselves outside the city, but when a detachment went out for water, those barricades were destroyed and more than one hundred Indians killed.

Good news came to La Paz on June 27. A boy who had been a prisoner escaped and reported that Túpac Catari had gone to attack the forces coming to aid the city. The royalists sent the boy back to the height of Puna next morning to obtain more information. He returned in the afternoon, reporting that the relief troops were near, that they had killed many Indians, and that the rebels on the heights were very anxious. Cayetano Silva, another prisoner who entered the city next day, gave the same information and added that the Indian woman called the vicereina had gone to Potopoto, taking loads of riches. He declared that aid would soon arrive. After other persons came with the same news, bells were rung in La Paz and salutes of cannon and guns given. The Indians, who were below near the city, now withdrew hastily to the heights.

Meanwhile, Commandant Flores had arrived at La Plata with 2,700 soldiers and a large escort. This expert military man had fought five bloody combats. In one of them at Calamarca, Túpac Catari had five thousand Indians, whom he personally commanded, but Flores had conquered them. Túpac Catari had lost his horse in the skirmish and had to flee on foot.

La Paz was now certain that help was coming, although the

rebels captured and hanged the messenger bringing a letter from Flores to Segurola. On the morning of June 30, many shots were heard on the heights, for the insurgents wanted to deceive the people in the city to prevent a sally. In the late afternoon, when great confusion arose among the Indians on the heights, all the people of La Paz came out to the plaza. They saw some enemies flee and others throw themselves headlong from the hills, and in a little while the King's banner appeared. When Adjutant Rodríguez went down to inform the city that the royalist troops had arrived, the joy of the people was unbounded. They had been besieged for 109 days by almost forty thousand Indians. And the cruelties to the Spaniards who fell into their hands cannot be related without horror. They chopped off their arms, legs, and heads, cut strips out of their skin, and then danced around the mutilated bodies and committed other barbarous acts.

The people of La Paz were almost starved. They had been forced to eat horses, mules, dogs, and cats. One-third of the population had perished either from hunger or illness or in battle; another three or four hundred persons had been killed when they had to go outside the trenches for food or to pasture their cattle.[18]

All the auxiliary troops except those encamped now pursued the enemy, who entirely abandoned the heights around the city. The pursuit lasted until night, when Commandant Flores returned to the camp with Reseguín, who was seriously wounded. It was believed that fifteen hundred Indians were killed.

On July 1, 1781, the people of La Paz began to experience the first joys of freedom. They went up to Flores' camp on the height, threw themselves on their knees, kissed the ground, and gave thanks to God for sending aid. As some of them were mere skeletons, Flores ordered all the cattle taken from the Indians during the march to be sent to the city. Then the Bishop and other high church functionaries distributed meat to the starving people.

The greatest care still had to be taken, for many rebels remained

[18] Relación de los hechos mas notables acaecidos en la sublevación general . . . , 157–71; Ballivián y Roxas, *op. cit.*, 48–52; Odriozola, *Documentos*, I, 106; Temple, *op. cit.*, II, 117–18.

on the height of Potopoto, the city lacked an adequate rear guard, and the generals could not prevent the people from leaving the city or make them return at night. Next day when some Indians came to seek pardon, which was granted, they brought with them Túpac Catari's wife and his chief messenger, Juan Hinojosa. Flores took them into the city to guard them better and hear their confession. Not all the people who presented themselves to Flores imploring mercy were sincere. Some merely pretended repentance in order to spy on the military preparations made by the Spaniards.

Auxiliary forces soon went out to seek food for the city and obtained about one thousand head of cattle and a large number of sheep. On July 5, Flores moved his camp one league from La Paz to the Río Seco on account of the lack of pasture and scarcity of water in the city. The camp was to serve as a rear guard for La Paz; and from it supplies could be obtained for the city, since the Indians continued to kill isolated persons in search of food and to steal the cattle brought by the auxiliary force. The revolutionists then occupied the former royalist camp and went down to the hill of Potopoto.

In three days the insurgents posted a letter on a white banner and brought it to the Spanish camp. It came from Túpac Catari's chaplain, Vicente Rojas, who said that the Indians wanted pardon on condition that the vicereina would be surrendered in exchange for the chaplain. Segurola answered that the King did not wish or intend to ruin his people and offered them pardon if they would return to their homes and live as obedient subjects. Next day the white flag reappeared with the head of an Indian hanging from its staff. The bearer delivered three letters. One was from a body of rebels who solicited pardon, another from the priest imploring his exchange for the chief's wife. The third was from Túpac Catari himself, who stated that he had sent the head of Marcelo Calle, the first revolter of Sicasica, because he had discovered that the Spanish general had been corresponding secretly with him.[19]

[19] Ballivián y Roxas, *op. cit.*, 67–73; Temple, *op. cit.*, II, 142–43; Odriozola, *Documentos*, I, 107–108; Cánovas del Castillo, *op. cit.*, V, 453; Relación de los hechos mas notables acaecidos en la sublevación general . . . , 112–13. MS copy in B. L.

Commandant Flores then decided to punish the Indians in the town of Achocalla for their unfaithfulness. On July 10 he asked Segurola to send out a detachment from La Paz. When it was posted on the hills above Potopoto, many rebels appeared on the hill of Pampajasi and some descended with a white banner. When Segurola ordered an interpreter to speak to them, they said that they came for a reply to the letter of the day before. They were told that Commandant Flores had not yet decided what he would do. They asked again for Túpac Catari's wife to be returned, promising that if this were done, they would make peace and go home. Then, noticing the scorn with which their proposal was received by the Spaniards, they left in a hurry.

In a little while more Indians rode down on mules and said that the community desired peace. They pretended to break and burn their weapons and seemed to be contented when told that they would soon be pardoned for their crimes. They embraced the Spaniards and withdrew, saying they would consult with the communities about peace and return with their decision on the following day. About an hour later another letter came from the prisoner Rojas. It appeared to have been dictated by the chief and led the Spaniards to believe that he had acquiesced to the execution of his wife and the surrender of arms. Nevertheless, they attacked Achocalla, causing the Indians to flee to the valley ravines, burned the town, and brought forty or fifty Indian men, nine women, some cattle, and some food to the Spanish camp. At that time the priest of Pucarani, Julián Bustillos, who had been taken prisoner and then appointed to guard the possessions of Túpac Catari, escaped with a group of Indians from his parish. He brought to the camp about 12,000 pesos and eighteen chests containing silver and clothing.

The skirmishes around La Paz continued, although the Indians from the near-by farms kept asking for pardon. On July 12 about eight hundred Indians put up a red banner near the trench of Santa Teresa. On it were two letters for Segurola, one from Chaplain Rojas and the other from Túpac Catari, containing the same messages as the earlier ones. The besiegers remained around the city until four o'clock in the afternoon, the chief appearing occasionally at the edge of the height on foot and on horseback, making gestures which showed clearly that he was drunk. When a party of two hundred men from Cochabamba went out to examine the camp near Ventilla, the enemy attacked them on the plain of Amachuma, when the royalists killed 150 Indians. The Spanish camp was then moved to Ventilla, four leagues from the city; and from there punitive expeditions made sorties to the near-by farms and villages.

Since the Indians did not accept their defeat as final, the royalists fought a hard battle on July 22 to dislodge three thousand of them from the hill of Pampajasi near Potopoto. During the night more than two thousand soldiers went out to surround the hill, but, since one division left later than the other two and did not arrive at dawn, military operations had to be suspended for some time. This delay aided the Indians, who showered the Spaniards with stones. When the column under Ayarza finally arrived, it did not follow orders, and the objective was not attained. Many strategies were tried to seize the height, but it could not be taken because of the steepness of the hill and the large number of insurgents. When the Indians came down to try to take possession of the six cannons and cut off the retreat of the contingent, Commandant Diego Velasco fell upon them, killed more than twenty, and forced the remainder to flee. The Spaniards then withdrew to the city with the enemy in pursuit, yet about 150 Indians had been killed.[20]

One of the principal problems confronting the Spaniards was desertion in their army, especially among the Cochabambinos. Segurola tried to put a stop to it, but did not succeed because of insubordination among the soldiers. The city also needed supplies and munitions badly. Three hundred soldiers were ill, many mules had died, and money was lacking. To make matters worse, Túpac Catari showed himself constantly with his followers and word came that Andrés Túpac Amaru was approaching Loxa and Pau-

---

[20] Ballivián y Roxas, *op. cit.*, 72–81; Odriozola, *Documentos*, I, 108; Relación de los hechos mas notables acaecidos en la sublevación general . . . , 114. MS copy in B. L.

carani, near the city, with his troops. It was then decided to send three hundred men from Cochabamba home to get food and to hasten the coming of the detachment from Tucumán and the other soldiers waiting in Oruro.

Commandant Flores finally decided to withdraw from La Paz himself since he could not keep the Cochabamba soldiers there. He proposed to take all the people able to bear arms so that the city food supply would last longer. At first Segurola told him that he would not remain in the city with his small force; however, he finally consented to stay. Flores left a garrison of eighty veteran soldiers and four companies of militia to reinforce the troops of La Paz, and, promising to return in two months with fresh troops, raised his camp on August 4, 1781.[21]

After Flores and his troops left La Paz great silence prevailed among the insurgents. A sally was made the next day from the ward of Santa Barbara to put up on a pole, as a warning, the head of the one-eyed Pedro Obaya, who had been executed the day before. Afterwards an Indian came near the trench of Santa Barbara and hoisted a banner containing a letter from Chaplain Rojas asking again for the release of the wife of Túpac Catari. On the eighth the Spaniards discovered the chief, dressed like an Inca, and many of his people on mules on the height. Shortly they commenced firing upon the city.

The priest Rojas, accompanied by a number of the insurgents, approached the trench of Santa Teresa on August 13. They reported that the Indians had united and were only five leagues from the city. Three colonels of Túpac Amaru commanded them, but all three were subject to Andrés Túpac Amaru's orders. Rojas said that Túpac Catari had gone with many people to visit the three colonels, but a report that he had been imprisoned by them proved to be false. He added that the forces of the four leaders had now united for a more vigorous siege of La Paz and that they had three cannons.

---

[21] Ballivián y Roxas, *op. cit.*, 81–86; Odriozola, *Documentos,* I, 108; Relación de los hechos mas notable acaecidos en la sublevación general . . . , 113–15. MS copy in B. L.

At this time Tito Atauchi, an Indian, came to the camp of Pampajasi with twelve men. He went to the height of Puna and freed Rojas and another priest called Silva. In the afternoon another cleric who had been freed by the same chief arrived and reported that the Indians were again surrounding La Paz.

This new siege was similar to the first, with the Indians annoying the city as much as possible every day. On August 24, they came down to a small plantation near the orchard of San Francisco, where some men on mules appeared who were believed to be chiefs. Túpac Catari was with them. They wore yellow and red uniforms and fired repeatedly at the Spaniards without causing the least injury. The royalists returned the firing and forced the rebels to hasten to the heights.[22]

About twenty Indians on mules then escorted the priest, Eustaquio Caravedo, as an ambassador, toward the little plaza of San Sebastián on the twenty-seventh. They brought three letters from Andrés Túpac Amaru. Two were for the Bishop and the other for the community. A fourth, signed by some Spanish gunners, was sent to the Creoles.[23] One letter, dated July 1, 1781, was a copy of the proclamation of José Gabriel Túpac Amaru, and the others were similar to it. Since the Inca had already been put to death (on May 18 of that year), the document must have been a forgery, no doubt by Andrés Túpac Amaru. The letters claimed that King Charles III approved of all that José Gabriel did and, as a reward, had designated him viceroy of Lima.

Andrés said that the same powers had been transferred to him by right of primogeniture and that he intended to use them and appoint officials. He pitied the Creoles, who defended the corregidores without knowing that they were their adversaries and persecutors. As he desired peace, he asked that all arms in La Paz should be surrendered and that the people put themselves under his banners. They were to hand over to him corregidores, chapetones, and customs collectors. He warned them that if they refused, they should remember what had happened at Sorata. The

---

[22] Ballivián y Roxas, *op. cit.*, 87–93; Odriozola, *Documentos*, I, 110.
[23] Ballivián y Roxas, *op. cit.*, 94.

Bishop was to confer with the ecclesiastical and secular cabildos and other officials concerning the matter and communicate their decision to him, so that he might arrange for peace or to continue the war that Julián Túpac Catari carried on, as a brother of the other dead commissioner, Tomás Catari.[24]

The people of La Paz did not receive definite news of Túpac Amaru's death until August 28. Then Juan Alliaga, a captured mestizo revolutionist, reported that Andrés Túpac Amaru was the commander now and that troops were coming from Lima to punish the Indians. As soon as he made these statements, he was hanged.

September came, and the Spaniards were still holding out. From Indian women entering the city they learned that the rebels were anxious because they knew that aid would come again. On the ninth, they were seen to bring loaded mules down toward the road to Lima. Next day, from their ambush among the walls of the burned houses outside the trenches, they made a lively attack, set fire to the Franciscan convent, sacked it, and took two friars as prisoners. Nothing could be saved except the church. A captured Indian related that the rebels had written a letter to members of the order in which they ordered them to tell the Creoles to join the natives. They said that there were already a number of Creoles in Andrés Túpac Amaru's army who spoke well of him. The Creoles were quoted as saying:

> With the coming of the Marquis we have obtained and enjoy all his protection and clemency, since we have surrendered to him. He has pardoned us and received us into his . . . true love, as the best father or dearest mother. The Marquis takes care of our needs, quenches our hunger . . . and has clothed us with the best clothes, without permitting us to suffer need. With this intelligence, you who see or know the contents of this letter can decide to ask for the same mercy that we enjoy, for at the hour you wish it, you

[24] Carta de Andrés Túpac Amaru, Inca, á Dr. Gregorio Francisco de Campos, Cruz Pata, August 27, 1781; Bando de José Gabriel Túpac Amaru, Inca, Tinta, July 1, 1781; Copia de original certificado por Andrés Túpac Amaru, Inca; Bando de Andrés Túpac Amaru, Cruz Pata, August 27, 1781; Carta de los habitantes de Real de Cruz Pata á los de la Paz, August, 1781. All these items are in Ballivián y Roxas, op. cit., 238–48.

Balsa boat used for navigation and to construct pontoon
bridges on Lake Titicaca.

From *The Incas of Pedro de Ciezo de León*
(ed. by Victor Wolfgang von Hagen)
(Norman, 1959)

Inca suspension bridge over the Apurímac River
as E. G. Squier pictured it in his *Peru* (1877).

shall receive it as soon as possible, or when you reply to this letter and show submission.

The two captured Franciscans entered La Paz with another letter on September 12. They said that the Indians believed the Spanish troops would come from Oruro in three days and that the forces uniting in Cuzco and Arequipa had defeated the insurgents under Diego Túpac Amaru in the province of Azángaro. Other messengers kept coming with the same news.

In the afternoon of the seventeenth, Túpac Catari had a banner put up outside a trench with two letters on it. The first asked for the pardon of his wife and threatened to burn La Paz if she was not freed. The second was supposed to have been written by the madman Bernardo Gallo, who had run away from the Spanish camp. It was full of incoherencies and signed Andrés Laura, the Inca governor. Gallo asked the royalists to surrender their arms to avoid suffering, and declared that the Indians were not guilty of destruction since they had often asked for peace. He said that if the people of La Paz did not give up their arms, the Marquis of Alcalises would enter the city with four thousand men and eight cannon and reduce it to ashes.[25]

A mestizo woman who arrived in La Paz on September 24 reported that Andrés Túpac Amaru had marched with all the whites, mestizos, and Negro gunners to oppose the troops coming from Oruro. She also reported that the Indians were working on the river at the upper part of the city and had made the water muddy. When the Spaniards went to see what was going on, they found that the rebels were building an aqueduct to turn the water against the ward of San Sebastián and in that way enter the city, as the Indians had done at Sorata. The workmen were soon chased away.

Three days later a number of Indians dressed as Spaniards and others in their own dress fought a sham battle on the heights. They carried a large white banner with a coat of arms on it, saluted the

[25] Ballivián y Roxas, *op. cit.*, 95–106; Carta de los habitantes de Tejar, September 11, 1781; Carta de Julián Túpac Catari, Inca, al cabildo de La Paz, September 17, 1781; Carta de Andrés Laura, Inca gobernador, á Dr. Gregorio Francisco de Campos, obispo de La Paz, Quiabaya, September 12, 1781, all in Ballivián y Roxas, *op. cit.*, 255–61.

city with it, shouted, fired guns, and made all kinds of maneuvers. Some men went up to the heights as if trying to oppose the royalists, while others threw themselves into the ravines and pretended to be pursued. Those garbed as Spaniards then came down near the walls of the burned houses and began new demonstrations of feigned attacks. When the people in the city would not come out, the insurgents laughed and finally returned to their encampment.

When October came, the besiegers seemed more friendly than before. Certain priests therefore went out of La Paz with a written pardon from Segurola to entice them to make peace. The commander also permitted the gates of San Sebastián and Recogidas to be opened so that the people could buy supplies in the Indian market of San Pedro. However, the Indians soon showed their evil intentions. Orders were then given that no persons should go outside of the trenches except women to bring water and other necessities. Many women ventured forth to obtain the badly needed food and brought back news of the approaching aid and of the rebels' defeat.

In the afternoon of October 5, many Indians drew near the trench of Santa Barbara. They explained that they wished to ask for pardon and wanted it to be conveyed to them by Túpac Catari's imprisoned wife. Suspecting a trap to get her back, Segurola decided to turn the tables and seize Túpac Catari. He ordered the woman to be taken from prison and stationed in a visible place outside the trenches. At the same time troops were to be placed in ambush to attack the Indians when they came near to speak to her. Although Túpac Catari sent several men to talk to his wife, there was no place to put her where they could see her, and the plan failed.[26] Later, when peace was almost certain, Diego Túpac Amaru promised to persuade the commandant to permit her to return to her husband.[27]

One of the priests detained by the Indians returned on October 6 with a letter from Miguel Túpac Amaru for the Creoles. Miguel

[26] *Ibid.*, 107–16; Carta de Juan de Dios al marquis Don Miguel de las Didas, Yaco, October 2, 1781, *ibid.*, 261–62; Temple, *op. cit.*, II, 160–61.

[27] Carta de Diego Cristóval Túpac Amaru á Miguel Bastidas, Azángaro, November 7, 1781, in Odriozola, *Documentos*, I, 334.

308

said that the insurgents wanted them to put themselves under his banner, where they would be appreciated. He wrote the letter not because of lack of forces, but through pity for the Spaniards. He warned that 100,000 soldiers were going to punish the Spaniards, and he did not want the Creoles to die.[28]

An Indian from the doctrina of Chincha then arrived to ask pardon. He said that all the people in his province of Chulumani wanted to be pardoned so that they could return to their homes. A proclamation of pardon was given to him to take back to his fellows, but the proclamation also offered a reward of more than 2,000 pesos for each of the principal chiefs.

Two days later an Indian entered the city bringing a letter for the Bishop and one for Segurola from Miguel Túpac Amaru. Miguel asked the prelate to use his influence to promote peace, asserting that he desired to prevent the evil consequences of continuous wars for the Spaniards as well as for the natives. He was sorry that the city had suffered because of the need to reform the government. In the letter to the commandant he said that he would treat with the Spaniards when they surrendered their arms and would let them go back to their land, but if his offer was ignored, he would attack the city on all sides that night. Segurola answered that a treaty would have to be drafted, and that he would send Andrés Coasaca, the bearer of his letter, to confer with Miguel at the well at three o'clock in the afternoon.[29]

The Indians came down at the time designated to the ward of San Sebastián and put up a large white banner outside of the burned houses. Then emissaries asked the Spaniards to come out to hold a parley. When they did not appear, the insurgents came nearer to the little plaza of San Sebastián and showed their bad faith by firing the many guns which they had concealed. But as news of the approach of the second Spanish relief expedition reached the heights, the besiegers became less militant. On Oc-

[28] Carta de Miguel Túpac Amaru á los creoles de la ciudad de La Paz, Tejar, October 6, 1781, in Ballivián y Roxas, *op. cit.*, 262–63.

[29] *Ibid.*, 116–18; Carta de Miguel Túpac Amaru, Inca, á Dr. Gregorio Francisco de Campos, Tejar, October 8, 1781, and Carta de Miguel Túpac Amaru á Sebastián de Segurola, Tejar, October 8, 1781, *ibid.*, 263–65.

tober 9, two more letters were brought to the trenches. One was from Túpac Catari for the Creoles of the city, whom he was still trying to win over, and stated that he expected his wife to be released "tomorrow" because she was not guilty of any crime. The other, from one of his captains, Martín Chuquicallota, asked for an audience with Segurola.[30]

Some Spaniards among the rebels now formed a small company, escaped, and brought into La Paz early next day twelve guns, two small pieces of ordnance, and a brace of pistols. Other Spanish stragglers came later and assured the people that aid would arrive in a few days. It was noticed that the Indians had withdrawn from Tejar with their possessions and were on the road leading to Lima. In the afternoon the royalists made a sally, killed a number of Indians on the plain of Potopoto, crossed the river, and came to Túpac Catari's lodging. They put Catari to flight, took the height of Pampajasi, and obtained many supplies, which somewhat relieved the distress in the city. Next day another letter was received from Andrés Túpac Amaru asking the people to surrender and obey the King's order.[31]

People who left the city to collect herbs and food were still attacked by the enemy, and Padre Juan Sainz was killed. His death caused much grief because he had served from the beginning of the siege. On the night of October 12, the sound of rushing water was heard in the river bed. The torrent reached a height of twenty rods, damaging many houses near the banks. Fortunately, after an hour, the water began to recede gradually. The Indians had dammed up the Choqueyapu River in a narrow pass three leagues from La Paz, hoping to flood the city and enter it, but the plan failed again. Later, when Commander Reseguín saw on the height of Achachicala the huge depression, which was fifty rods deep, he estimated that it had taken ten thousand Indians to construct it. He ordered the walls of this great hydraulic work to be destroyed.

Meanwhile, Reseguín was already at Mojo, where he had fought

[30] *Ibid.*, 118–20; Carta de Túpac Catari a los creoles de La Paz, and Carta de Martín Chuquicallata á Sebastián de Segurola, October 10, 1781, *ibid.*, 265–66.

[31] *Ibid.*, 120–22; Carta de Andrés Túpac Amaru al cabildo de La Paz, October 11, 1781, *ibid.*, 267.

with the insurgents and opened the way to La Paz. In La Paz the food situation had become desperate again, and two mounted men were sent to the height of Puna on October 16 to reconnoiter. Finding the height deserted by the enemy, they signaled to the people to come up and collect the food, flour, and sheep left behind. Next morning a drove of llamas, laden with provisions, descended to the city by the road from Potosí. The people immediately made use of the supplies and of the animals carrying them. At noon people began to appear on the height of Puna who were believed to be Spaniards. Soon the slopes were covered with royalists, who saluted the city with their artillery. The joy in La Paz was unbounded when Commander Reseguín sent word that he was there with more than seven thousand soldiers and plenty of food. The second relief expedition thus arrived, finally saving the besieged and starving city. The siege had cost the lives of twenty thousand whites and mestizos and forty thousand Indians.

The insurgents had fled La Paz, but much remained to be done elsewhere.[32] Andrés Túpac Amaru had hastened with his Indians to the sanctuary of Las Peñas, where he gave up his command as highest chief to his cousin, Miguel Bastidas. He then journeyed to Azángaro probably to take part in the deliberations for peace and pardon.[33]

The siege of La Paz was the longest of the Inca Revolt. It revealed remarkable inventiveness on the part of the Indians, yet the lack of discipline and training among the peasant levies weakened it. Early in the campaign the Indians were armed only with slings and stones and attacked most fiercely during rainy weather, since they believed that European firearms would be rendered ineffective. At this stage Indian morale was high, as the dead were concealed and buried and the few prisoners preferred suicide to captivity. Soon the natives extended the siege by burning surrounding communities, taking all livestock, and placing ambushes on the roads over which reinforcements might come. Then they produced

[32] *Ibid.*, 120–28; Temple, *op. cit.*, II, 161–63; Gutiérrez, *op. cit.*, I, 83, 106; Santa Cruz, *op. cit.*, 121–23, 127.

[33] Correspondencia Vertíz-Gálvez, 1782, num. 590, AGN, Buenos Aires. Cited by Lewin, *op. cit.*, 273.

firearms, which snipers, sheltered within the ruins of the burned houses, aimed at the royalists. They forced captive Spaniards to serve the newly acquired artillery and augmented the rebel army by mestizo deserters from La Paz. Their files of foot soldiers attacked while moving behind the cover of horses and pack animals. They used cannon and hand grenades, mortars, muskets, and explosive sling missiles, rockets, and incendiary arrows that caused much damage. The artillery, however, did little harm, for the captives fired it unwillingly and thus inaccurately. The Indians tried the ruse of impersonating Spanish soldiers and of damming up the headwaters of the river to flood the city. The Spanish commandant, Segurola, was efficient and persistent and managed to hold out until the second aiding expedition finally broke the siege of 184 days. While the lifting of the siege of La Paz did not end the revolt, yet it did much to weaken it; moreover, the ability of the Spaniards to succeed in the face of overwhelming numbers of enemy troops demonstrated conclusively the superiority of Spanish arms. La Paz did not fall.

CHAPTER XIV

End of the Uprising

THE BACKBONE OF THE REBELLION was broken with the recovery of the heights of La Paz, but the fighting was not over. The Indians in the region around Cuzco were also hostile, but they did not cause as much trouble now as those near La Paz. The rebels had been defeated, yet their important leaders had not been captured and they did not consider themselves crushed. For two years longer fighting was to continue in many parts of South America.

The situation around Cuzco was soon taken care of. On November 17, 1781, the rebels came down from three posts to the bridge of Pisac, evidently to destroy it, but withdrew when they saw the royalist troops stationed there. Then when the priest of Lamay asked aid, a detachment hurried out of Cuzco to help him and also freed some soldiers of Huamanga, about to surrender. The Spaniards tried to pursue the Indians, but, when the latter made an ambush, the royalists threw down their arms and fled, leaving the town of Taray in great danger. The Indians of Lamay now joined the rebels and returned to burn the town. Unfortunately, the commander could not lend aid because night was approaching and he was helping the faithful people who came from along the river.[1]

About a week later priests began to send word that the Indians around Cuzco desired pardon. When Father Josef de la Sota of the Order of Mercy said that the natives of San Salvador and Pisac sought pardon so that they might obtain passports to go to Cuzco, it was granted. La Sota reported also that already, on October 20, the rebels had sent a woman to the commandant of Taray to ask if pardon was certain. After he assured her that it was, she said that the Indians would come the following day. One man arrived

[1] Carta de Josef del Valle á Dn. Agustín de Jáuregui, Cuzco, November 18, 1781. MS copy in B. L.

313

on foot at Pisac. The commander called to him, but he withdrew again to the heights. La Sota was then sent to try to persuade the Indians to seek pardon, but none of them came as they had offered. After a skirmish at Cusipata, they did ask pardon; therefore the commander let them approach. They deposited their arms at a distance, but as soon as they were trusted, killed eighteen men, seized a number of weapons, and withdrew because of fear of the recruits being sent by the commander of Quiquijana.[2] This incident, however, was the last disturbance in the Cuzco area.

Expeditions also went out from La Paz to pacify the regions still in rebellion. On October 7, 1781, Commandant Reseguín marched from that city with his troops to attack the rebels remaining in Potopoto. He found only women there, who said that the Indians had abandoned the place as soon as they caught sight of the royal troops. The commander then withdrew and placed his encampment on the heights, an advantageous position for sending out troops to collect cattle and supplies as well as to check enemy movements.[3]

Commandant Flores helped Reseguín's troops at La Paz twice with provisions, mules, and munitions of war, so that he could advance toward the most distant provinces. Moreover, Flores asked Baltasar Sematnat, corregidor of Arequipa, to send to Reseguín 200 or 300 guns, since his army had only 250 and was using 4,000 cudgels and a number of lances.[4] Later the Viceroy of Peru told Sematnat to send 400 guns with the expedition from Arequipa. Sematnat answered that he had already ordered weapons to be made, but he was anxious because time for manufacturing the required number of guns was short and it was difficult to obtain mules to transport arms and supplies for the troops.[5]

2 Ibid., October 26, 1781. MS copy in B. L.

3 Relación de los hechos mas notables acaecidos en la sublevación general . . . , 217. MS copy in B. L.

4 Ignacio Flores á Dn. Baltasar Sematnat, Oruro, October 25, 1781, MS copy in B. L.

5 Carta de Dn. Baltasar Sematnat á Ramón Arias, Arequipa, November 26, 1781; Carta de Agustín de Jáuregui á Dn. Ramón de Arias, Lima, December 11, 1781; Carta de Baltasar Sematnat á Dn. Agustín de Jáuregui, Arequipa, November 26, 1781; Carta de Agustín de Jáuregui á Baltsar Sematnat, Lima, December 14, 1781.

General Ramón Arias, commander of the troops from Arequipa, also tried to help and kept insisting that more arms and supplies should be delivered from that town. He had heard that the Indians under Diego Túpac Amaru, his nephew, and Colonel Ingaricona were still armed with three hundred guns and twelve cannon.[6]

Meanwhile, Reseguín received several letters from Miguel Bastidas, who had accompanied Diego and Túpac Catari to the sanctuary of Las Peñas and still had a considerable number of Indians under him. He proposed that the royalists should either meet the Indians in battle or agree to terms of peace. Reseguín answered that he needed to confer personally with him before any peace could be made.[7]

As Bastidas did not reply immediately, the army started for the sanctuary of Las Peñas. On October 31, 1781, the troops advanced to Patamanta, where they met Licenciado Manchego y Loayza, who brought with him two Indian insurgents. They said that Bastidas and all the natives were sincere in asking pardon, but the officers opposed it because the men from Cochabamba had sacked and burned estates. They also reported that Túpac Catari had gone to the sanctuary of Our Lady of Copacabana to calm certain rebels.

Reseguín did not trust Bastidas. In a letter of November 2 to Segurola, he said that next day Miguel Bastidas would be in the camp with his captains to confer about peace—"a subject of great seriousness, since pardon must be treated for men who had been criminals of state." In his letters to Miguel, he said, he had never definitely promised pardon in the King's name, only insisting that he must speak personally with him before sealing the bargain. Segurola advised Reseguín to make peace with Miguel on the basis of re-establishment of the old relations between the Indians and the Spaniards and not to issue a definite statement about a general pardon.

Copies of these letters were obtained from the National Archives of Peru, and are in the Bancroft Library.

[6] Carta de Ramón Arias á Sor. gral. Dn. Baltr. Sematnat, Campo de Río Blanco, November 23, 1781. MS copy in B. L.

[7] Relación de los hechos mas notables acaecidos en la sublevación general . . . , 217–18; Carta num. 1 de José de Reseguín al teniente colonel Sebastián Segurola, Patamanta, November 2, 1781, in Odriozola, *Documentos*, I, 226; Cánovas del Castillo, *op. cit.*, V, 456.

On November 3, Bastidas, showing no fear, appeared with a number of his colonels in the camp at Patamanta. Although Reseguín was sick in bed, he received him in his tent, embraced him, and showed him every attention. Miguel declared that Diego Túpac Amaru and all his officers were ready to receive pardon. He then confessed before the king's clerk that he and his followers had fought a civil war with the Spaniards, Europeans, and Americans, and had incited robberies and murders.

Reseguín was willing to pardon the rebel general and his captains on the following conditions. They must hand over all the weapons in their camp within twenty-four hours. They should go to the provinces, make known to the people the King's pardon, persuade them to obey the sovereign, and stop the uprisings. Within twenty-four hours they should take the natives out of their troops and send them to their provinces. They should warn them not to take up arms again against the King, the Spaniards, or mestizos if they did not want to incur severe penalties. The Indians must furnish the royal army with supplies and cattle when it was in their provinces and provide competent persons, whom the commandant favored and the Viceroy or the King finally approved, to govern the provinces. Justices in turn should appoint caciques and commanders who would be obedient to the King and co-operate with his higher officials. The Indians also should go to La Paz to supply the inhabitants with all the cattle and food needed at fair prices, leave the roads open, and aid post office administrators with guides and mules at prices provided by the royal regulations. Finally, they were to influence Diego Túpac Amaru to appear before the commandant general to ask pardon and promise to obey the King.[8]

To receive pardon, Bastidas went to the camp at Las Peñas in company with Captain Mariano Ybáñez and Mateo Tagle. Rese-

[8] Tratado con Miguel Túpac Amaru, Patamanta, November 3, 1781; Carta num. 3 de José Reseguín al comandante Sebastián de Segurola, Patamanta, November 3, 1781, in Odriozola, *Documentos*, I, 226–30; Cánovas del Castillo, *op. cit.*, V, 457–58; Oficio del comandante D. Ignacio Flores al virrey de Buenos Aires . . . José de Vertíz, La Paz, August 6, 1782, in Odriozola, *Documentos*, I, 265–66; Angelis, *Documentos*, 127–28, 173–74.

guín had to be carried, since he was still ill. He was well received by the 22,000 Indians on the heights, who repeatedly acclaimed King Charles III. On November 7, Miguel and more than 15,000 Indians attended divine services. Afterwards, at the church door, in the presence of the military officials and the veteran troops, they asked pardon, offered obedience to the King, accepted the terms of surrender, and laid down their arms. When Bastidas and his colonels swore that they would fulfill all the provisions of the agreement, the witnesses promptly signed the document. The insurgents very likely did not realize that the treaty contained only the old obligations of the Indians to the Spaniards. The Indians of the provinces of Sicasica, Pacajes, Omasuyos, and Larecaja and of the parishes of La Paz thus received pardon, but it was noticed that the natives of Azángaro, Carabaya, and Lampa were absent that night.[9] Bastidas and some of his colonels were then conducted to La Paz, where he was free and well treated.

As Túpac Catari still roamed around, it was necessary to deal with him. When the Spanish army had approached the heights of La Paz, he had taken refuge on the hill of Potopoto. Reseguín waited only three days before going against him. The enemy obstinately disputed the march from the craggiest mountain, but the commander overcame all obstacles. Túpac Catari then hastened to the sanctuary of Las Peñas to increase his forces and unite them with those of Bastidas. On the afternoon (November 3) that Bastidas and his followers accepted pardon, he went to the town of Hachacachi with Juan de Dios Mullapuraca and Tomás Inga Lipe to urge the natives to continue the revolt. He still counted on his five thousand men to win a victory and did not wish to accept any pardon. When he learned that Bastidas had done so, he fled toward Azángaro.

He had a friend called Inga Lipe, the good, with whom Reseguín carried on secret negotiations. This false friend agreed to lay a trap for Túpac Catari. Reseguín sent out a party of veteran soldiers under Captain Ybáñez and guided by Inga Lipe. They marched day and night until they reached a place twelve leagues

[9] Cánovas del Castillo, *op. cit.*, V, 458–59; Angelis, *Documentos*, 130–32.

from Achacache, where Inga Lipe entertained Túpac Catari at a great feast. In the meantime Captain Ybáñez appeared with one hundred men. When the false friend believed the chief had fallen asleep from his pleasures, he told the other diners to withdraw since Bastidas was coming. At the end of the meal, Ybáñez entered the room, easily seized Túpac Catari, and took him to the Spanish encampment to await trial.

The capture of the rebel chieftain caused great rejoicing in La Paz. In the name of the city, the corregidor girded on Reseguín a short gold sword and presented him with a staff with a gold point.

Many of the pardoned Indians now considered Túpac Catari the author of the calamities suffered in La Paz and other towns, and asked that he be severely punished. Tadeo de Medina, a judge of the Audiencia of Chile, tried him. Túpac Catari lacked fortitude and did not defend his actions. He tried to gain the good will of his enemies by putting the blame for his deeds on the Inca leaders. He confessed to all his crimes, declaring that he had summoned the Indians of the provinces and was guilty of high treason. He admitted that he had besieged La Paz for 109 days until Flores came, and for 75 days after he had left—until Reseguín arrived with another expedition. He said that he had cut off the food supplies from the city, burned the greater part of it, and assassinated many innocent people—even priests. He had taken the title of viceroy, appointed many officers, and usurped ecclesiastical jurisdiction. He declared that he deserved any penalty and exhorted the gathering to take warning from him and desert the insurgents.

The Chilean judge proved to be as inexorable as Areche. The sentence which he pronounced on November 13, 1781, was indeed severe. The chief was to be taken out of prison, with a hemp rope around his neck and a crown of pasteboard on his head, and tied to the tail of a horse. The town crier would call out his crime, and the Indians of the province would be summoned to witness his execution. Túpac Catari would then be torn to pieces by four horses, as José Gabriel Túpac Amaru had been. His head would be put up on the gallows in La Paz; his limbs would be displayed in the places where he had caused the greatest injuries. The rest

318

of his body would be burned and the ashes scattered in the air. His possessions would be confiscated for the treasury. This penalty was carried out on the same heights that he had held so long near La Paz.[10]

Túpac Catari's wife was sentenced to death later (September 5, 1782) by the same judge. Wearing a leather crown with plumes and carrying a cross in her hand, she was taken out of prison, tied to the tail of a horse, and dragged to the place of execution. A crier made known her crimes. Then the executioner hanged her and dismembered her body so that it could be dealt with as her husband's had been.[11]

The other rebels taken at Las Peñas and punished after Túpac Catari's death were also important. Miguel Puiocava from Azángaro, a man who had influenced José Gabriel, a relative and ambassador of Diego Túpac Amaru's, and a minor judge of Túpac Catari's, was among them. There were six Indian colonels and half-bloods from the provinces of Azángaro, Chumbivilcas, Carabaya, Larecaja, and Omasuyos. Two women, Gregoria Apasa, a sister of Túpac Catari who was called vicereina and said to be very bloodthirsty, and María Lupiza Amasia, a sister of Gregoria, were executed. Among the condemned were Chief Sergeant Gerónimo Gutiérrez, clerks, confidants, and dependents of the criminals, amounting in all to thirty-seven individuals.[12]

Later the royalists learned that Miguel Bastidas and his colonels had not been sincere in receiving pardon. They discovered hidden arms and a document telling Túpac Catari not to surrender, but to appear friendly until the troops withdrew. Then he was to attack La Paz again. Miguel had also ordered him to steal all the

[10] Relación de los hechos mas notables acaecidos en la sublevación general . . . , 218–19; Carta de Ignacio Flores á Dn. Agustín de Jáuregui, Oruro, December 3, 1781, MS copy in B. L. Odriozola, *Documentos*, I, 112–14; Cánovas del Castillo, *op. cit.*, V, 456, 459; Carta de Josef Reseguín á Dn. Agustín de Jáuregui, Sanctuario de Nra. Sa. de la Peñas, November 15, 1781. MS copy in B. L. Causa criminal de Julián Apasa, alias Túpa Catari, Sanctuario de Nuestra Señora de las Peñas, November 14, 1781. MS copy in B. L.

[11] AGN, Buenos Aires, Criminales, Leg. 18, exp. 7, in Lewin, *op. cit.*, 276.

[12] Causa criminal de Julián Apasa, alias Tupa Catari, Sanctuario de Nuestra Señora del las Peñas, November 14, 1781. MS copy in B. L.

mules in the city. When all of this chicanery was exposed, the Spaniards imprisoned Bastidas and his colonels in La Paz.[13]

Diego Túpac Amaru was terrified when he heard of the punishment of Túpac Catari and the arrest of Bastidas. He united his followers to continue the rebellion. If he had acted promptly when Reseguín was dealing with Bastidas, when the commandant was ill, and when the royalist army had been greatly decreased by desertion, he might have been successful. Instead of acting, however, on November 14, 1781, the Inca wrote to the commandant rejecting the pardon offered by the Viceroy of Peru, although by that time thirty thousand persons had been pardoned. Mariano Túpac Amaru favored this act and worked with him, yet at the same time pretended that he was going to publish the general pardon. Diego made truce with the forces which garrisoned Arequipa, while Mariano broke his agreement with the Spaniards and again collected fifteen thousand Indians and five cannon for the purpose of besieging La Paz for the third time. In Azángaro many people were loyal to Diego and Mariano, but in the town of Guaqui and many other places the inhabitants asked Segurola for aid, which he could not send because he had to defend La Paz.[14]

The Spanish army in La Paz was now obliged to reorganize and enlist more men. Expeditions had been made to put down the disorders of the internal provinces, but the leaders were hindered by scarcity of provisions and the renewed clamor of the Cochabambinos to go home. When their captains tried to restrain them, they deserted. Of the 7,300 men brought to La Paz to break the second siege, only 1,800 remained. All these things made Reseguín so ill that he asked to be relieved of his command.

[13] Carta de Ignacio Flores á Dn. Agustín de Jáuregui, Oruro, December 3, 1781; Carta de Josef Reseguín á Dn. Agustín de Jáuregui, Sanctuario de Nra. Sa. de las Peñas, November 15, 1781; Carta de Don Agustín de Jáuregui á Josef del Valle, Lima, December 15, 1781; Carta de Don Agustín de Jáuregui al Señor obispo del Cuzco, Lima, December 15, 1781 (MS copies in B. L.); Carta de Vertíz á José de Gálvez, Montevideo, February 20, 1782, AGN, Buenos Aires (published in Lewin, op. cit., 484–85); Cánovas del Castillo, op. cit., V, 459–60.

[14] Odriozola, Documentos, I, 114; Carta de Josef Reseguín á Don Agustín de Jáuregui, Sanctuario de Nra. Sa. de las Peñas, November 15, 1781. MS copy in B. L. Cánovas del Castillo, op. cit., V, 452–63.

Segurola, who had withstood the two long sieges of La Paz, became the new commander. Using kindness, he persuaded the soldiers to continue their service for the King and sent Captain Pasqual Borje with his company to Pucarani to guard it and subdue the enemies in that region. As soon as the captain arrived at his destination, he sent a detachment of fifty soldiers to the ravine of Alcacollo, where the Indians were put to rout so soundly that they did not stop fleeing until they reached the mountain ridges.[15]

Segurola then decided to encamp in the town of Guarina to check the enemy. He entered the town on December 14, but since he was forced to go to many other places, he had to abandon it. After placing a force under Ybáñez and ordering him to take Achacache, the capital of Omasuyos, he returned to La Paz. On the twenty-third, he sent out of La Paz three thousand soldiers who marched to Obejuyo along the river below the city, put the enemy to flight, and killed many. When the Spanish forces were about to withdraw, the Indians attacked fiercely and killed more than three hundred royalists. Contributing to the disaster were the deep ravines, the ruggedness of the land, and the bad management of the royalist commander, Manuel Franco.

La Paz rejoiced to see the encampment of the faithful Manuel Chuquimaca on the height on December 26, 1781. In it were three thousand volunteers who had subjugated towns in the province of Pacajes and forced the inhabitants to obey the King. They had also defeated the rebels in the province of Chucuito and had brought supplies into La Paz. Now they greatly encouraged the recently defeated Spaniards and urged Segurola to make another expedition. This he did on the twenty-ninth, camping on the heights of Mecapaca.[16]

General del Valle and the authorities in Cuzco believed that the best way to pacify the provinces was to send a large army to La Paz. Captain Arias therefore brought there from Arequipa a force of two thousand men. After their arrival most of the people

[15] Relación de los hechos mas notables acaecidos en la sublevación general . . . , 219–22. MS copy in B. L.

[16] *Ibid.*, 222–23; Carta de Ignacio Flores á Dn. Agustín de Jáuregui, Oruro, December 3, 1781. MS copy in B. L.

in the provinces of Omasuyos and Larecaja showed great submission, and those of Chucuito were entirely pacified. Only the
rebels from the ravine of Río-abajo, in the province of Sicasica,
were stubborn and obstructed the roads communicating with
Oruro and Cochabamba. Segurola then held a council of war in
which it was decided to send fifteen hundred chosen armed men
against them. After an expedition of eight days, the soldiers returned to La Paz victorious. A few days later, however, it was
necessary to send Chuquimaca with his Indians to punish the
people of Cooni, who attacked the Spaniards from the hills. He
defeated them with some loss.

While this was going on, the troops in Achacache were not idle.
They sent out Indians who seemed loyal to pacify the towns in
the interior of Larecaja, but most of them soon joined the rebels.
Many persons perished at their hands and from the hostility of
the Ingas faction in Mocomoco. The Indians of the town of Italaque
killed all the women who fell into their power. Captain Ybáñez
therefore left Achacache in January, 1782, with 3 officers, 150 veteran soldiers, and a number of loyal Indians to aid Mocomoco,
twenty-five leagues away.

Along the way the natives of Ancoraimes, Carabuco, and Escoma made demonstrations of fidelity, but soon committed in those
towns the same bloody crimes committed in Italaque and Mocomoco.[17] Andrés Guachalla, a pardoned rebel, turned traitor and
stirred up the Indians. He and his four sons and a woman, said to
be his wife, were taken prisoner and put to death. The royalists
also defeated the enemy on the heights of Italaque.[18]

Mariano Túpac Amaru, who had left Achacache before Ybáñez
entered it, now sent word that he was ready to confer with him
concerning pardon. Ybáñez met with him and believed that his

[17] Relación de los hechos mas notables acaecidos en la sublevación general . . . ,
223–24; Informe de Sebastián de Segurola, La Paz, June, 1782, in Ballivián y
Roxas, *op. cit.*, 130–32.
[18] Relación de los hechos mas notables acaecidos en la sublevación general . . . ,
224–25. MS copy in B. L.

request was sincere when he surrendered two cannon, thirty-two guns, and a quantity of ammunition.[19]

Then Ybáñez hastened to Mocomoco and routed the Indians in a few hours. He rescued more than five hundred women and some old men. He began to march with them, but as the people were tired and the mules in bad condition, it became necessary to spend the night near the enemy on the hills. Next morning, while preparations were being made to continue the journey, the enemy attacked so fiercely that the baggage was lost. All day the Indians pursued the troops, and at night, when the soldiers pitched camp on a little plain, threatened to destroy everyone. The officers then held a consultation and decided to raise the camp as silently as possible to elude the enemy.

The royalists placed the women and defenseless persons in the middle of the troop, abandoned the cattle, and marched until daylight. In the darkness of midnight the rear guard got separated from the vanguard, and a bell had to be rung to unite them. The Indians heard the bell and shouted so loud that the terrified women began to run, not knowing where they were going. In the confusion some people entered ravines without outlets, where the Indians killed them cruelly.

At that time Ramón de Arias had gone to La Paz with his troop, and a reinforcement of eight hundred Cochabambinos under Josef Ignacio Sivirche had also arrived. Commandant Segurola decided to go with them to Achacache on an inspection trip. On February 23, 1782, he camped four leagues from the town, where Ybáñez and the few men who followed him united with the new recruits. Segurola hurried out next day to punish the rebels and rescue the rest of the Spanish women they held captive. On the twenty-fifth, he camped near the town of Ancoraimes and surprised the Indians on their farms, killing five hundred.

Fifty musketeers reinforced the Cochabambinos, who remained

---

[19] Carta de Vertíz á José de Gálvez, Montevideo, February 20, 1782, AGN, Buenos Aires, Correspondencia Vertíz-Gálvez, 1782 (published in Lewin, *op. cit.*, 485–86).

in the ravine while the rest of the army advanced on the heights over the road from Carabuco. The divisions were to be united in Churimani. When the Spaniards had advanced one league, they found on the bank of a lake many Indians, shouting and playing musical instruments. The site was advantageous, on a hill with walls and precipices that led down to the lake. Eighty veteran soldiers and a group of volunteers fired upon the hill, discovering that scarcely eighty people bravely defended it. As the royalists ascended, many·of the women jumped into the lake rather than be captured, leaving a number of infants, whom the Spaniards killed.[20]

On March 3, 1782, Segurola again sent Ybáñez, with a detachment of fifty veterans and two hundred Cochabambinos, to Mocomoco. He ordered them to punish the Guarcas Indians and destroy part of the town, but they did not find the Guarcas or the Ingas. The latter sent a priest to say that they wished to be loyal and had fled to a hill on account of fear of the soldiers. They soon came bringing gifts for the troops and also the Spanish women, whom they had freed from the Guarcas and hidden. They offered to obey the King and hand over the chiefs' heads. Unfortunately, the Cochabambinos could not be restrained; they killed about twenty-five Indians and robbed the church.

The great number of women, children, and other persons who accompanied the army hindered the march. On March 6, near the town of Escoma, they noticed parties of Indians on the heights and a band across the river. From a high hill the natives began to insult and fire upon the Spaniards, who dislodged them, killed fifty, and took their guns. Then the Cochabambinos forded the river and put to death fifty Indians. As a result, in the afternoon many people from Carabuco offered to aid the Spaniards and surrendered a musket. At night the inhabitants of Escoma also surrendered, but Segurola sent them back to bring the heads of the rebels.

[20] Relación de los hechos mas notables acaecidos en la sublevación general . . . , 225; Ballivián y Roxas, *op. cit.* 133–39; Carta de Ramón de Arias á Josef del Valle, Sepita, February 27, 1782. MS copy in B. L.

Next day as the army advanced, three to four thousand shouting Indians carrying four large banners were seen in the same place as the day before. Segurola arranged an attack at once with three divisions. He led out the first group, Ybáñez the second, and Sivirche the Cochabamba column. As the third division did not arrive on time, the enemy escaped on that side of the river. The Spaniards pursued them over the plains but could not keep them from taking a rugged hill; however, when Segurola received reinforcements, he drove them from the hill and many threw themselves into the river and perished. The camp was covered with about eight hundred dead Indians. When the rebels on the other bank of the river saw what had happened, they fled hurriedly.

The army took the route back to Achacache on March 10, arriving there at a critical time. The Indians had not kept faith with Segurola because the insurgents on the mountains had told them that they had killed the Spanish commander with all his men and ordered them to join their force or perish. One faction in the town vascillated, but another was loyal. The people of Achacache were greatly agitated when they saw a detachment of Indians coming. They finally united, drove them out, and captured three of their officers.[21]

The people of the Río-abajo region were still hostile and pursued the royalists even to La Paz. Commandant Flores urged the Arequipa troops in La Paz to punish them; therefore Segurola decided to embark on another expedition. Meanwhile, when the pardon that the Viceroy of Buenos Aires had issued on January 21, 1782, arrived in La Paz, Segurola published it at once, sent emissaries to the enemy, and wrote letters urging the rebels to seek pardon. The Viceroy of Peru had also issued a general pardon, but the Indians of the above-mentioned regions disregarded it entirely and kept on killing and robbing.

A good-sized expedition under Segurola left La Paz on April 18, 1782. He camped at Calacoto, where the insurgents shouted insults at him and at night fired upon the camp. The following day they repeated their insults and prevented the Indians of Chucuito

[21] Ballivián y Roxas, *op. cit.*, 139–51.

and Copacabana from joining the Spaniards on time. On the next day those reinforcements met Segurola at Obejuyo and told him that on the road over the height of Ánimas and at the right on the hills more than five thousand armed warriors awaited him. Even though the enemy had an advantageous position, the commandant planned to attack. He placed a company of musketeers from Arequipa and a cannon on a hill from which they could fire upon another elevation covered with Indians and could check any action on the royal road. Segurola then led the attack on the road with a company of foot soldiers from Lima and other forces. The rebels did not wait for him, but withdrew to a position believed to be impregnable. There was a long entrenchment with a high, wide stone wall, but four companies of soldiers attacked so violently that more than one hundred rebels were killed and the rest fled.

Segurola sent a detachment, on April 21, to punish the people of Palca, but it found the town and near-by farms deserted. As terrible cruelties had been committed here earlier, the Spaniards burned the Indians' houses. Next day between two and three thousand angry natives assembled near Collana and discharged guns to cut off the march of the royalists. Segurola, however, ousted them from their advantageous position. The Spaniards followed them to Mecapaca and then to Collana, where a party of Indian women on a hill threw stones at the soldiers without regard for the shooting. Despite their fatigue, the royalists attacked the hill, killed six hundred men and women, collected some provisions, and burned the whole town except for the church.

No other serious encounters occurred until April 27. Near Cohoni at the base of the celebrated Mount Illimini, more than three thousand Indians took their stand, believing the mountain was inaccessible for the Spaniards. When soldiers attacked the rebels, they killed one hundred of them. As the Spaniards pursued those who fled, they faced them again in another place very favorable for the Indians. The enemies were dislodged, however, and pursued for more than a league.[22] News now arrived at the Spanish camp at Cohoni that the Indians of Puno had tried to attack the

[22] *Ibid.*, 152–65.

district of Achacache and that Ybáñez had repulsed them, killing more than three hundred.

Segurola remained at Cohoni two days longer, as the horde of women and idle men hindered his march. He now ordered them to go to La Paz. On the thirtieth, when the march was resumed, four Indian men of Cohoni and some women appeared with a white banner. They said that if pardon was granted, three hundred of their friends would also come down. They were pardoned and told to go home quietly to care for their farms and families. Next day, more Indians arrived with their families to be pardoned and were treated kindly. Segurola sent written messages to others about the advantages of pardon and waited vainly in the camp for a reply.

When the camp was raised on May 3, 1782, a mestizo who had delivered one of the messages returned with the information that many of the rebels wanted pardon and were trying to persuade their companions to seek it also. Then the Indians who had delivered the first message appeared and reported that the insurgents favored pardon, but could not answer because nobody knew how to write. The rebels offered to collect their people and come as soon as possible to obtain pardon. Soon 150 Indians went to the Spanish camp on the hacienda of Santiago near Táca with a white banner and a document asking pardon. It was granted.

News arrived on May 11 that Tomás Arancivia, who was stationed on the heights of Húsi, had been attacked the day before by more than two thousand Indians of Legue, Luribay, and Araca. Although the fight lasted from dawn until midday, he had succeeded in overthrowing them and had killed three hundred, including the principal chief, Silvestre Choquetiglla, and had captured another chief, Marcos Copa, who was called colonel general.

On the seventeenth, the Spaniards followed the route by the river ravine to La Paz and camped at Guara. As the Indians in the towns along the way now seemed friendly, Segurola appointed caciques, alcaldes, and other officials. Letters came from Suri and Circota, which were in the other ravine on the side of Cochabamba, saying that the natives were obedient and had accepted the pardon. Three days later Segurola took the route to Chulumani, where the

327

inhabitants received him well and sought pardon. He then wrote to the people of Coripata, charging them with insolence and urging them to make use of the pardon, so that they might return to their homes. If they did not do so, they would be severely punished. He repeated this order in gentler terms to the Indians of Coroico, Pacallo, Chupe, and Yanacachi.

He remained in Chulumani on the twenty-second to rest and appoint officials. While he was there, Indians from the hacienda of San Cristóbal brought him a message sent to them by the people of Coripata urging them to unite and resist the Spaniards. They said that many of the people in Coroico were under the power of a brother of Túpac Catari, named Tomás, who favored continued resistance. Next day the Indians of Coripata sent an answer to Segurola's letter in which they asked pardon and blamed other people for their errors. Shortly they sent him another letter saying that they feared Túpac Catari's brother in Coroico and advising him not to go to the other bank of the Tamampaya River. He replied that they would be freed from such enemies if they served the King.[23]

All the night of May 24 the shouting enemy remained on the heights of the opposite bank of the Tamampaya River. Early in the morning Segurola received another letter from the people of Coripata urging him to remain where he was. He marched on, despite the rough roads and the necessity of fording the river. He advanced as far as Coripata without opposition, but saw on the highest parts of the transit mounds of stones which had been collected to throw on the Spaniards. The commandant was well received in the town, where the people blamed the Indians on the hacienda of Peri, and especially Mateo Flores, for their resistance.

Next day the army marched to Peri and saw plenty of evidence that the Indians intended to resist. On the heights was a gallows, which Segurola ordered torn down. As soon as the Spaniards arrived, many people from the hacienda and near by, including Mateo Flores, who had hidden Segurola's letter and the document from the Viceroy, started down to seek pardon. At the last minute

[23] *Ibid.*, 166–80.

328

the chief disappeared. Through the influence of Father Marcos Aliaga the Indians of Peri, who had beheaded in the church 575 persons, expressed willingness to obey the king again and sent many of their leaders to La Paz to be pardoned.

The troops arrived at Coroico on May 27, where they were well received, but were depressed by the memory of the outrages committed by the inhabitants. The latter asked for pardon, which was granted; and Segurola appointed officials for Coroico and Pacallo and afterwards sent the army to Peri, where the natives brought Mateo Flores as prisoner. They said that he did not want to be pardoned and was influencing other men to continue the rebellion. Gradually the ravine was pacified. And on August 31, in the commune of Millahuaya, the commandant received a letter from Del Valle reporting that he had taken Carlos Puma Catari, an important chief. Del Valle said that the Indians of the ravine continued to ask pardon and that Blas Choque, a chief, was in the neighborhood with Marcos Copa, whom some people had believed to be dead.

The troops united with those from Arequipa under General Arias in the town of Palca on June 6. Then Segurola sent certain peaceful Indians to search for Choque and Copa and to show the Indians of the ravine the benefits of pardon. In twenty-two days the total pacification of Yungas was accomplished without bloodshed. Later word came from Del Valle that the famous chief, Alejandro Calisaya, his companion, Felipe Niña, and other refugees had been imprisoned and that the province of Larecaja was completely pacified. The two chiefs, Blas Choque and Copa, were still free. When Isidro Calisaya and his followers sought pardon on the fifteenth, it was granted. Next day the army returned to La Paz and was received with great joy, after having pacified two of the most important ravines—the Río-abajo and Tungas. To make the victory complete, word came on May 17 that Copa and Choque had also been pardoned.[24]

The revolution was practically over, although Melchor Laura still held out in Chucuito, but he soon lost the province because his moves were badly planned. General Arias entered the Chucuito

[24] *Ibid.*, 180–91.

329

and Puno regions and overthrew Laura in two encounters, which subdued the last of the provinces and caused the people of Pomata to surrender Laura.

When Ignacio Flores was promoted to the presidency of Charcas for his services, he completed the pacification of the vice-royalty of La Plata. He sent Reseguín out again with a considerable army to contend with the indomitable people of the ravine of Tapa-carí, in the province of Cochabamba. It reduced the town of Caravi to ashes and won a hard-fought victory at Hucamarini, where the Indians hurled huge rocks upon their opponents. The royalists finally gained the eminence and killed eight hundred enemies; the terrified Indians now believed that the Spaniards fought under a magic spell. Reseguín then marched to the strong, entrenched camp of the Baquerías, surprised and conquered them, and paci-fied the province.[25]

Work also had to be done in the viceroyalty of New Granada. There the people had heard of Túpac Amaru's cause and held rev-olutionary juntas, called communes. In that northern viceroyalty the regent visitador, Juan Francisco Gutiérrez de Piñares, a man of firm character, had been granted power to regulate the treasury and increase the revenues. As his measures were very imprudent, the Viceroy disapproved of them; but, despite the protests of the executive, the King permitted the visitador to have his way con-cerning the treasury. Prices of monopolies were raised and dues im-posed upon all industries; the alcabala and tax for the Armada of the Windward Islands *(Barlovento)* were increased; new contribu-tions were levied upon the people; and guards were appointed to watch for contraband trade and to collect the taxes. The measure caused disturbances immediately in the towns of Barichara, Sima-cota, and Mogate, which were easily repressed, but the inhabitants of Charolá resisted more violently. These incidents were the pre-lude to the revolution of the comuneros.[26]

[25] Odriozola, *Documentos*, I, 115–17.

[26] José Manuel Groot, *Historia ecclesiástica y civil de Nueva Granada*, II, 187; Briceño, *op. cit.*, 10; José Manuel Restrepo, *Historia de la revolución de la república de Colombia*, II, 12–13.

Piñares appointed as his assistant in the Audiencia of Quito Antonio Solano de la Sala. At the beginning of 1780, La Sala raised the alcabala and established the aguardiente monopoly. It was an inopportune time to introduce such measures, and the people resisted them. In the parish of Pelileo in the district of Ambato, on February 10, 1780, the inhabitants threw sticks and stones at the clerk of the new monopoly and took away from him the proclamation for its establishment. On the same date the Indians of Quizapincha rose because jugs of aguardiente were sold for the government. They assembled in large numbers, threw sticks at the petty officials, and for three days threatened them with war cries. Finally the visitador's assistant sent out a force to scatter them.

The Indians then withdrew to the ravine of Alhajuna, between Quizapincha and Pasa, where they rolled down stones and fired with slings at the soldiers. They attacked and overthrew an armed party coming from the heights west of Ambato, between Quizapincha and Santa Rosa. As soon as La Sala heard about this, he dispatched two columns of soldiers under Pedro Cevallos and Baltazar Carriedo to punish the rebels. After five hours' resistance the Indians scattered, leaving behind two dead and three prisoners. The latter the Spaniards soon hanged.

At the same time the inhabitants of Pillaro rebelled for the same reason. They killed the alcabala collector, cut off the bridge of Culapachan, and camped on the hill to control the river pass. La Sala ordered Francisco Lalama and Francisco Ripalda to attack the revolters, but the royalists had to retreat. A reinforcement under Carriedo and Diego Melo fought for seven hours, finally defeated the insurgents, and took many prisoners, who were hanged and quartered.

Echoes of the insurrection were heard in Baños, Patate, Izamba, Pasa, and Santa Rosa. Attempts at revolt were unsuccessful, however, and the people decided to obey the government when an order was issued that the Indians need not pay any tax except the tribute. Four women rebels of Baños were whipped through the

331

streets; a number of persons found guilty in Pelileo had their hair and eyebrows cut off and others were hanged.[27]

To make matters worse, the fiscal, Francisco Moreno, also caused trouble. He arranged for people of small towns to be added to other municipalities, where they would be given land, and their own land in their former towns would be sold for the King. This procedure caused great excitement and ill feeling among the natives just at the time when news of Túpac Amaru's uprising came from Peru.[28]

Efforts were made in Quito to communicate with the Inca of Peru. Agustín Martín Blas, the visitador's secretary, learned at the end of 1781 about the proposals of Miguel Tovar de Ugarte, a clerk in one of the judicial courts, to send a letter to José Gabriel Túpac Amaru.[29] The author of the revolutionary plan, who had dictated the letter to Tovar, was Mariano Ortega, a Franciscan friar. The friar urged Túpac Amaru to continue his work and told him that the provinces around Quito were ready to co-operate with him. The letter was to be carried to Peru by Jacinto Fajardo, a scribe, hidden between the soles of his shoes, but Fajardo turned traitor and informed the authorities of the conspiracy. They arrested Tovar, took the documents away from him, and condemned him to ten years in the presidio of Chagre. During the questioning the condemned man denounced Father Ortega as an accomplice, yet nothing was done to the friar.[30]

Melchor de Guzmán, a Peruvian and possibly a confidential agent of José Gabriel Túpac Amaru, inspired the Indians of New Granada to rebel. Guzmán appeared mysteriously in Santa Fe and cultivated the friendship of the people. He was a famous silversmith and a poet and knew Túpac Amaru. His friends in Peru informed him of what was occurring in the viceroyalty. Soon after

[27] Pedro Fermin Cevallos, *Resumen de la historia del Ecuador desde su origen hasta 1845*, II, 105–107.

[28] Briceño, *op. cit.*, 7–8.

[29] Pedro Torres Lanzas, *Independencia de América, fuentes para su estudio; cátalogo de documentos conservados en el Archivo General de Indias de Sevilla*, Segunda serie, I, 2–3.

[30] Federico González Suárez, *Historia general de la república del Ecuador*, V, 303; Torres Lanzas, *op. cit.*, 7.

Guzmán arrived in the northern region, the spark of revolution was kindled in Socorro.

The town of Socorro was the most populous parish in the archbishopric. Since it had many industries, it felt the visitador's measures most and soon became the center of an uprising, which spread through the district of San Gil to Pinchote, Simacota, Tunja, and Sogamose. On March 16, 1780, a market day, many men led by José Delgadillo, who beat a drum, appeared in the plaza of Socorro. They stopped in front of the home of the alcalde ordinario, José de Angulo y Olarte, and shouted that they would not pay the new taxes. The alcalde came out on the balcony and tried to calm them. He was supported by Salvador Plata, an influential citizen, who told the people that they should obey the orders of the audiencia because they came from the legitimate authority. This caused cries of indignation and threats from the crowd.

An old woman, Manuela Beltrán, then went to the door where the visitador's edict was posted on a board and, crying, "Long live the King and death to bad government!" she furiously tore down the edict and broke the board into pieces. She then beat a drum to summon the people to take up arms against the hated measures of the visitador and fiscal. While the terrified alcalde hid, the mob surged through the streets. The revolt thus began, and prisoners were set free, revenues seized, alcabalas and all kinds of burdens declared abolished, and four chiefs appointed to lead the insurrection. One of them was Salvador Plata. He gave as the cause of the uprising the harshness and rudeness of tax collectors:

> Their abominable conduct makes the name of guard so hated that the people regard collectors as barbarous enemies of the human race. . . . They abuse the confidence entrusted to them. . . . They deny the judges' authority, trample individuals under foot, and are supported by higher officials.[31]

As the authorities did not have sufficient forces to suppress the uprising, the cabildo and audiencia decided to yield to the people,

[31] Briceño, *op. cit.*, 7–8, 13; Groot, *op. cit.*, II, 188–89; Restrepo, *op. cit.*, II, 15; Loayza, *op. cit.*, Serie I, Vol. XIII, 132–33n.

who declared they were not hostile to the King. On March 16 the cabildo suspended the collection of the new taxes and gave account to the audiencia. Their action calmed the insurrection somewhat. The audiencia met on the twenty-third and commissioned the alcalde and collector of the alcabala, Angulo y Olarte, to imprison the instigators of the revolt and send them to the capital. He was to continue the tax gathering and post a new edict stating that the right to collect taxes had existed since 1635. On the same day that the measure was carried out by the alcalde, the inhabitants of Socorro broke down the edict and attacked the guards and the alcabala administrator, Diego Berenguer. They also poured out the brandy, burned the tobacco, and destroyed everything else in the monopoly offices. Finally Lorenzo Alcantuz threw down the royal arms and trampled on them. He instructed the revolutionists to meet in Socorro on April 15 in order to burn the building of the monopolies and the archives. The flame of revolt also spread to La Rabada and Guadalupe.[32]

Before the meeting on April 15, the people had obtained a revolutionary hymn, which attracted the multitude. Poetically it was of no great value, and nobody knew who wrote it. Some people attributed it to Friar Ciriaco de Archila, a Dominican of Santa Fe and a friend of Jorge Lorenzo y Peralta, the marquis of San Jorge. The hymn arrived in Socorro on March 30 in a bundle of papers which the friar had sent from the capital of the viceroyalty. The package of letters was opened in the presence of influential people in the house of Juan Manuel Ortiz, the doorkeeper of the cabildo. Ortiz read some verses which caused great exultation among the persons present. When someone rang an alarm bell, more than four thousand persons hastened to obey the summons. The verses were then read by a crier. Inspired by the hymn, the crowd stormed the monopolies building, broke open the doors, tore the royal shield in pieces, poured out the aguardiente, and destroyed the cards, stamped paper, and tobacco.[33]

The people then chose Francisco Berbeo, Salvador Plata, Fran-

[32] Briceño, op. cit., 14–15.
[33] Ibid., 17–18, 23–24.

334

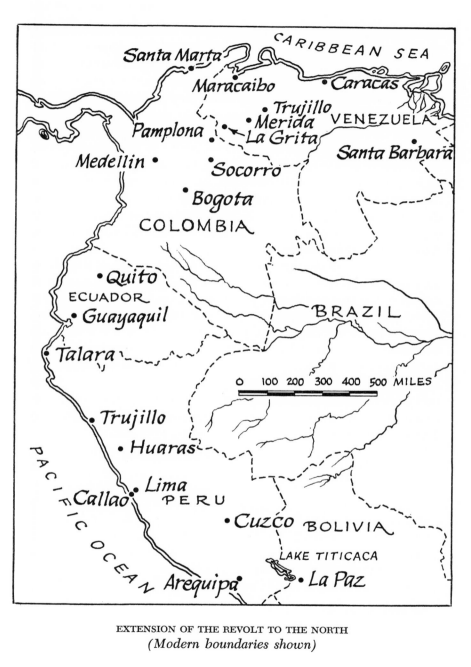

EXTENSION OF THE REVOLT TO THE NORTH
(Modern boundaries shown)

cisco Rosillo, and José Antonio Monsalve as their chiefs and gave them the title of captains general. They were to have equal authority, and when they met, they would constitute a supreme council of war. Other towns followed the example of Socorro, deposed all their officials, and chose captains general and minor officers. All the captains subjected themselves to the higher generals of Socorro in order to unify their movement. The purpose of each town was to abolish the tobacco monopoly, so that every person could freely cultivate tobacco plants; to lower the tax on aguardiente; and to reduce the alcabala by 2 per cent. Furthermore, the people intended to suppress the excise on food and liquor, the dues for the Armada of the Windward Islands, for stamped paper, for customs receipts, for certificates of lading and destination (*guias*), and other burdensome taxes.[34]

The revolt became general, spreading to Pamplona, the plains, and all through the large viceroyalty. Everywhere the insurgents appropriated treasury funds, persecuted administrators, abolished hated taxes, and assigned the accumulations from them to their cause. Despite the passions of people throwing off the yoke of the authorities, nowhere did assassination or serious crimes result.[35]

News of the triumph of the Inca in Peru was often exaggerated to stir up the Indians. As a result, in the town of Silos the people proclaimed Túpac Amaru king of the Indies. The letter of the commune of Cocuy to the captains and lieutenants of the people of Támara, Ten, and Manare, dated May 23, 1781, said:

> Let us participate [in the revolt], since the new Inca king of the Indies is crowned. He is powerful and is called Don José Francisco Túpac Amaru, and, they say, he comes to remove all taxes. . . . [Therefore] breaking earthen jars of aguardiente and burning tobacco, we have taken the money away from the administrators of salt and have returned it to the owners. We advise that if the governor collects the arrears, you shall not pay it. If he wants to punish you for this [refusal], rise up against him. If you do not rise up, we shall go to Santa Fe and make war on the people there and if,

34 Restrepo, *op. cit.*, II, 15–17.
35 *Ibid.*, II, 18.

336

when we return, you have not done [what we advised], we shall make war on you. Let us inform you that many places have risen, among them the city of Vélez, the town of San Gil, Cocuy, Mogotes, Santa Rosa, and many other places.[36]

Rapid communication existed between the people of New Granada and Túpac Amaru. Luis Vidalle said in his report to the English government that it took only sixty days to send a letter and receive a reply from him.[37] When Intendant Abalos of Caracas favored the resolution to suspend the new constitution, he maintained that the disturbance was due to the notice sent from Lima about the success of Túpac Amaru, "who is supposed to have united . . . with the discontented people of Santa Fe."[38] Salvador Plata reported that in Socorro the parish priest, Francisco Vargas, spread the news of Túpac Amaru's movement, after Manuel García, administrator of the revenue from the post office, provided it for him. This news, which spread even to Cartagena and other places, encouraged the people to rebel against their king.[39]

In Nieva, when the governor ordered the rebels to lay down arms, the leader answered that he had orders from Túpac Amaru.[40] The uprising had great success on the plains of Casanare, where a Creole, Javier Mendoza, incited the Indians of Pore, Támara, and Ten to rebel in the name of the Inca of Peru. The revolt started in the first town (May 19, 1781) the day after the Inca's death. Mendoza assumed the governorship of the province, made the people swear allegiance to Túpac Amaru, informed the comuneros of the events, and put himself at their service. On the plains the Indians directed their fury against priests who had exploited them. They shut the priest of Ten in his house for eight days, letting him go out only for a bottle of water.[41] Mendoza ordered the

---

[36] Briceño, *op. cit.*, 46–47.

[37] *Ibid.*, Documento XXXVI, pp. 231, 237.

[38] Informe del 23 de Septiembre de 1781, *Boletín del Archivo Nacional* (Caracas, Venezuela), Xol. XXV, No. 99 (1940), 303–304 (cited by Lewin, *op. cit.*, 376).

[39] A. M. Galán, "Vida de José Antonio Galán en los comuneros," *Biblioteca de historia nacional*, Vol. IV, pp. 229–30 (cited by Lewin, *op. cit.*, 377).

[40] Germán Arciniegas, *Los comuneros*, 277.

[41] *Ibid.*, 254–55.

churches closed, although Túpac Amaru had never given such a command.[42]

When all efforts to pacify the people failed, the audiencia decided to subjugate them by force. In Santa Fe very few soldiers knew how to handle arms, and only two hundred old guns could be found. One hundred men finally assembled under the command of Joaquín de la Barrera and marched toward Socorro, taking the guns with them to arm people along the way. Judge José Osorio of the audiencia went with them as a peace commissioner.[43] The royalists arrived at Puente Real on May 22, where the judge decided to fortify himself and finish the recruiting of volunteers. He had little success, for the total number of the audiencia's soldiers scarcely exceeded two hundred.

He then received discouraging news from Estévez, the priest of Oriba, who said that Socorro had about four thousand courageous men. He warned that the King's troops would all perish if they attacked Socorro, and that they would not be safe even in the churches.[44] As the four thousand men were armed with lances, machetes, sticks, and slings, the royalists had slight hope of defending themselves against the large number of the comuneros. In addition, the insurgents had friends even among the soldiers recruited by Osorio. In the first encounter some of the royalists threw the people guns from the balconies of houses which had been turned into fortresses.[45]

At Puente Real, four hundred comuneros attacked the soldiers, who fled in every direction, leaving their arms for the enemy. The judge, the commander, and the adjutant, Francisco Ponce, were taken prisoner, but the latter escaped disguised as a Franciscan friar and took the news to Santa Fe.[46] Elated with victory, the comuneros advanced along roads full of people and made the countryside resound with their shouts as each new recruit was gained.

[42] Restrepo, *op. cit.*, II, 19.
[43] Groot, *op. cit.*, II, 189–90; Restrepo, *op. cit.*, II, 20.
[44] Arciniegas, *op. cit.*, 157.
[45] Briceño, *op. cit.*, 28–30.
[46] Groot, *op. cit.*, II, 190–91; Restrepo, *op. cit.*, 21.

General Berbeo, their highest chief, rode among them. He received many letters brought from neighboring towns by Indian runners and, when with difficulty he read the messages aloud, the people listened attentively to each word.[47] At the beginning of the revolt, Berbeo, Plata, Monsalve, and Rosillo had tried to play safe by signing before the Socorro notary on April 18, 1781, a document affirming their fidelity to the king and stating that they had accepted the positions of captain general because of the people's threats, that they feared for their lives and those of their families if they refused.[48]

The people in the capital were terrified because there was no reserve force to defend it. Furthermore, Ponce had announced that it would be invaded immediately. The comuneros had published an edict sentencing the regent visitador and Fiscal Moreno to death, and threatened to enter Santa Fe and stir up all the kingdom. This declaration caused panic among the judges and alcaldes. Visitador Piñares ordered a junta of the tribunals to be held on May 12. The members decided to take the hated visitador to Honda, collect militias to guard the royal interests, and send a commission, composed of Judge Joaquín Vasco, the alcalde ordinario, Eustaquio Galavís, and Archbishop Antonio Góngora, to treat with the revolutionists. Piñares, angered at the decision of the junta, fled hurriedly toward the coast. By other action taken by the junta, the alcabala was decreased 2 per cent, dues on aguardiente were rebated two reales on each measure *(azumbre)*, the tax for the Armada de Barlovento was suspended, and the formalities of customs receipts and certificates of lading were abolished.

The junta broke up at two o'clock on the morning of the thirteenth. That same day the commission started for Zipaquirá, four leagues distant and already occupied by about twenty thousand comuneros under Berbeo. Meanwhile, the tobacco storehouse, the administrator's house, and the homes of many people were robbed. When the commissioners arrived at Zipaquirá on May 14, 1781, they sent a letter to the chief of the comuneros, saying:

[47] Arciniegas, *op. cit.*, 167–68.
[48] Galán, "Vida de José Antonio Galán en los comuneros," *Biblioteca de historia nacional,* Vol. IV, p. 247 (cited by Lewin, *op. cit.*, 372).

For the purpose of re-establishing public tranquility in this kingdom and to reconcile the towns of San Gil and Socorro and their parishes, we came to this town last night, having been given ample powers from the real *acuerdo* [viceregal council], the general junta of tribunals, and the cabildo, to inform you, the principal chiefs, that your people shall come to this town to confer. . . . The judges shall propose what is fitting for the benefit of the King and all the people.[49]

Berbeo received the note while he was in Raquirá. He did not pay much attention to it and, at the head of the comuneros, continued his march to Nemocón. He arrived there on May 26 and took part in the negotiations, but the results were not what had been expected. The comuneros feared treason from their chief, because of his intimacy with the Archbishop, and demanded that he continue the march to Santa Fe. To satisfy them, on May 27, Berbeo, who had sixteen to eighteen thousand men under him, moved his camp to the plains of El Mortiño, halfway between Nemocón and Zipaquirá. Here the conference began again and lasted more than a week. The rebel leader, however, ordered the commissioners to come to his camp and proposed his own terms.

The capitulations contained thirty-six articles which were nothing more than the program of the comuneros. The first article, directed against Visitador Piñares, abolished his position; the second confirmed the leaders of the uprising in their offices, which they were to keep. Article twenty-one gave Creoles privileges and denied them to Europeans. Another diminished the King's authority; others treated economic matters, getting rid of the hated taxes, the defense of the Indians, abuses by corregidores and by priests, and finally a pardon for all that had happened.[50]

The commissioners, Galavís and Vasco, did not dare sign the document because it granted so much authority to the Creoles. To avoid responsibility for it, they decided to send it to the junta of tribunals. The representatives of both groups met again, although the negotiations had now lasted two weeks. The junta refused to

[49] Briceño, *op. cit.,* 106; Groot, *op. cit.,* II, 192; Restrepo, *op. cit.,* II, 24–25.
[50] Briceño, *op. cit.,* 49, 123–24, 130–33; Restrepo, *op. cit.,* II, 28–31.

approve the capitulation, for it humiliated the government. The only positive result for the royalists was the prevention of the march to Santa Fe. When the comuneros saw how things were going, they rioted and shouted, "War on Santa Fe!"[51] Through the Archbishop's influence the junta finally approved the document without modification, but in the same meeting signed a secret protest. The protest declared that approval had been given under compulsion and to prevent greater evils. Then Galavís declared the capitulation null. The commissioners, nevertheless, knelt before the prelate and swore in the King's name to fulfill the requirements of document. Afterwards most of the comuneros, satisfied that they had obtained the advantage, returned to their towns.[52] About the same time that the capitulations were accepted, news of the victory of the comuneros was reported way down in Mendoza. The inhabitants of this Andean city were filled with envy, for they wanted to obtain similar advantages.[53]

José Antonio Galán, the standard bearer and the boldest chief, and his faction were dissatisfied with the capitulation. As they wanted the war to continue in order to rob the people and strike Santa Fe a blow, they separated from the bulk of the revolutionists, marched through the towns of the district of Sabana in the province of Mariquita, committed many depredations, and even stirred up the slaves. At the same time the Archbishop, Berbeo, other comunero leaders, and three Capuchin friars from Santa Fe —Joaquín de Finestrad, Féliz de Goyanes, and Miguel de Villajoyosa—made an excursion through the towns of the north. They urged peace and obedience to the King and had a good response. Berbeo went to Pamplona, where he established peace by banishing the Spaniards Antonio Pásos and Joaquín de Molina. He called a junta to be held on Juan José García's hacienda. When it met, the chiefs of the insurrection tried to get in touch with Luis Vidalle, who served in the English navy. Apparently they wanted to ask the British for protection if they obtained their independence.

---

[51] Briceño, *op. cit.*, 64.
[52] Restrepo, *op. cit.*, II, 32–33.
[53] Testimonio de Martín Cavallos, AGN, Buenos Aires, División colonía, Sección gobierno, Mendoza, 1759–82, VI–III–I–I (cited by Lewin, *op. cit.*, 378).

Berbeo escaped to Curaçao, where he continued the revolt and assumed the name of Aguiar. In May, 1784, three men—Vidalle, Pita, and Moreles—said in London that they had been sent by Aguiar and a certain Contreras of Santa Fe, who were chiefs of the comuneros in New Granada. They maintained that they were allies of Túpac Amaru to obtain aid for the independence of South America; they promised liberty of worship and commerce in return for help, but England paid no attention to them. Spanish agents drove them to France, but Count Aranda sent them to Spain.

At the first outbreak in Socorro the authorities had asked Viceroy Flores for aid. Unfortunately, he could not help the capital since he had only one regiment in Cartagena to protect the coasts from the English. Later he managed to send five hundred militiamen under Colonel José Bernet and at the same time asked the governor of Havana for men and money. Bernet's force arrived in Santa Fe just in time to prevent a new uprising under Galán, who was now terrifying the people. The inhabitants of the towns armed themselves against Galán, and finally the people of Onzaga captured him and took him to Santa Fe with three of his companions. When Plata handed him over to the authorities, he said, "I present to your Excellencies the Túpac Amaru of our kingdom."

The Viceroy disapproved of the capitulations, for one of the articles excluded Spaniards from public offices and would have caused his own removal. When the comuneros learned of the Viceroy's displeasure, they wanted to take up arms again; however, they soon realized that with a force at hand to subdue them, they could do nothing. Galán and his three companions were hanged in February, 1782, and some of his accomplices sent to the presidios of Africa. On March 18 the audiencia revoked the capitulations, suspended the title of corregidor given to Berbeo, and tried to blot out all traces of the uprising. In the same year the revolt flared up again in the south of Colombia, when Governor Peredo of Popayán went to Pasto and established the hated monopolies of tobacco and aguardiente. The people rose and assassinated him, but the popular movement was soon checked and the instigators punished.

The comuneros no doubt desired independence and a republic, yet the King pardoned them and even their leaders and permitted them to hold high offices again. The imprisoned revolutionists were ordered to be set free. The limbs of Galán and his accomplices were taken down from the public places where they had been displayed as a warning, and the rebel was given a funeral according to church rites.[54] After being pardoned, Berbeo lived in obscurity, and was perhaps the only chief who had made war against the Spanish king to survive in his dominions.[55]

The captaincy general of Venezuela also felt the revolutionary disturbances. In his report of August 23, 1781, the intendant of the royal treasury, Abalos, said that there was the same spirit of dissatisfaction in Venezuela as elsewhere, and because of it he found it necessary to decrease certain taxes and suppress others. He accused the Marquis of Toro, the chief alcalde, and José Cocho of being the principal instigators of the movement, which extended toward the capital of the captaincy general.[56] Open rebellion, however, occurred only in the provinces of Maracaibo, San Cristóbal, and Mérida, near Columbia. Arciniegas maintains that only two men, Silvestre Carnero and Miguel Suárez, were active in the uprising in Venezuela. Some two thousand comuneros marched toward Rosario, but only two very courageous men crossed the frontier, deposed the alcalde in San Cristóbal, and then went on to La Grita.[57]

Later, on July 10 or 11, some two hundred men of Lobatera entered La Grita with their captains. When several of the leading citizens talked to them, no damage was done. Next day, however, the uninvited guests put the treasury administrator, José Trinidad Noguera, his brothers, and his sons in chains. They kept them prisoners for five days, while they took the revenues and papers

[54] Groot, *op. cit.*, II, 193–98; Del Solar, *op. cit.*, 156–57; Briceño, *op. cit.*, 67–76, 85; Lewin, *op. cit.*, 375, 389; Restrepo, *op. cit.*, II, 35–39, 41–42; Carlos Navarro y Lamarca, *Compendio de la historia general de América*, II, 539–40.

[55] Restrepo, *op. cit.*, II, 44.

[56] Oficio al ministro de Indias José de Gálvez, *Boletín del Archivo Nacional* (Caracas, Venezuela), Vol. XXV, No. 99 (1940), 303–304 (cited by Lewin, *op. cit.*, 383).

[57] Arciniegas, *op. cit.*, 259.

in the royal treasury. Then they went to the hacienda of Estanques. They sent long letters to García de Hevia and the people of La Grita inviting them to join the insurrection. They appointed Pedro Urrea captain general, but he would not accept the position, and García de Helvia replaced him. Other officials were also chosen. Salvador Contreras asked to have the province of Mérida united to the captaincy general, since it had belonged to it from the time of the Conquest until 1777, but the proposal was not favored. The people demonstrated against the monarchy not only in La Grita but also in Lagunillas, where they proclaimed Túpac Amaru their leader.[58] The bonds between the comuneros of these places and Túpac Amaru are unknown. Likely certain malcontents had heard about his uprising in Peru and decided to imitate him; no doubt the towns were influenced more by the comuneros of Colombia than by events in Peru.

The revolt soon spread through the province of Maracaibo to Mérida, and in the latter place only the clergy opposed it. Even the cabildo sympathized with the insurrectionists and did not resist them. Baliadores, a poor tailor, was appointed ambassador of the comuneros, and the capitulations of Zipaquirá were read by the public crier in the main plaza. Two thousand rebels came to the city, where four ambassadors, with unfurled banners, met them. The flags were then crossed to form an arch for the entrance of the comuneros, who forced the administrator of the royal treasury to hand his documents over to them.[59] After the commune of Mérida was formed, captains were appointed, and militias, consisting of two thousand men, organized. Then the comuneros marched to Timotes, which divided their province from Trujillo. From there they sent a message to Trujillo, saying that the people of Venezuela were oppressed like the Israelites under Pharaoh. They mentioned the success of Socorro and other towns in Colombia and added:

[58] Vicente Dávila, "Los comuneros de Mérida," *Investigaciones históricos*, II, 241–43 (cited by Lewin, *op. cit.*, 383–84).
[59] Arciniegas, *op. cit.*, 260.

We live deceived by the commands of cruel ministers. . . . Seeing our parents, wives, children, and families die of hunger, we do
not hesitate to receive and obey the capitulations which the Audiencia of Santa Fe accepted and swore to obey. . . . Long live
Charles III and death to the bad government of his ministers![60]

As a result of the message, the people of Trujillo assembled
in Mesa Esmujaque, sent an evasive answer to the comuneros on
August 4, 1781, and finally decided not to join them. When the
authorities recovered from their fright, they began a cruel perse-
cution of the Venezuelan rebels; then the captains of Mérida
claimed that they had been forced to lead the rebels.[61] A military
expedition, which the governor of Maracaibo equipped, soon pacified Mérida and the country as far as Cúcuta. When the soldiers
sent from Santa Fe killed some Indians in the revolting town of
Enemocón and put their heads on pikes at the entrance of the
town, the revolt ended.[62]

A document of September 15, 1781, found in Buenos Aires, im-
plies that even distant Panamá was influenced indirectly by the
Túpac Amaru revolt. When the people of Panamá heard about
events in Peru, the movement in Quito, and the capitulations in
Santa Fe, they rose, complaining about their many taxes and their
customhouse. When they burned the building of the tobacco monopoly, the fire destroyed two blocks. Since there were no repartimientos in Panamá, the movement was likely not the work of the
natives.[63] The disturbance may therefore be attributed to the Creoles, and had little connection with the trouble in Peru.

Some writers believe that Chile, too, was involved in the last
Inca revolt. The economic measures to increase the royal revenues
were received with great hostility when Jáuregui, the future viceroy of Peru, was serving there as president. Later, in 1781, two
Frenchmen, Antonio Gramusset, a farmer and miner, and Antonio

[60] Dávila, "Los comuneros de Mérida," *loc. cit.*, 207–11 (cited by Lewin, *op. cit.*, 387).
[61] *Ibid.*, 217–18 (cited by Lewin, *op. cit.*, 288).
[62] Restrepo, *op. cit.*, II, 39–40.
[63] AGN, Buenos Aires, VI–XVI–9–12 (cited by Lewin, *op. cit.*, 389).

Alejandro Berney, a professor of Latin and mathematics, conspired to throw off Spanish domination and establish an independent government. Their chief accomplices were the rich Chilean aristocrat, Josef Antonio Rojas, and the Peruvian Manuel José Orejuela. Rojas had been in France and returned to America as a rebel, with new ideas and many forbidden books, whereas Orejuela seemed to have obtained his advanced ideas through commerce. The time chosen for the uprising was the moment when Spain was involved in war with Great Britain, and would begin through the spreading of false news that English ships had appeared. Then the insurgents would attack the Spanish authorities. Berney even prepared a constitution for the new state, but lost his manuscript on the way to Santiago. The authorities learned of the plot when the document was found. Both Frenchmen were caught, tried in a process that lasted four years, and sent to Spain in 1784 on the ships bearing the people sentenced to banishment in the Túpac Amaru rebellion. Gramusset reached Cádiz and died in prison, while Berney perished in a shipwreck. The Chilean conspiracy appears to have been a separate movement from the Inca revolt, although it, no doubt, had some of the same causes.[64]

The comuneros in the north were finally calmed, yet the people of Upper Peru were never again satisfied with Spanish rule. In 1809 they formed an independent government, which they called *Institutión de Gobierno* (Institution of Government), but they could not hold out long against superior arms. Some people, however, seized that occasion for beginning an insurrection in Cuzco, the leader of which was a very old man, Mateo García Pumacagua, cacique of Chinceros. He had earlier, in January, 1781, intended to join Túpac Amaru with his Indians when the Inca had occupied the heights of Picchu, but had changed his mind on hearing that a large Spanish army was advancing from Lima. He then fought against his countrymen with such energy that the Viceroy rewarded him by making him a brigadier in the Spanish army. On August 3, 1814, this Indian and his three brothers declared for independence in Cuzco, where the whole population heartily joined the

[64] Valcárcel, *La rebelión de Túpac Amaru*, 142–44.

insurrection because they had never become reconciled to Spanish rule after the suppression of the Inca revolt.[65]

In the Inca revolt the Indians were always as courageous and determined as their Spanish oppressors, and at times their strategy was excellent. The royalist commanders recognized their bravery and spoke highly of it. Ignacio Flores wrote to José de Gálvez on May 6, 1781, saying that in their attacks and defenses the Indians showed an uncommon valor. Other Spanish soldiers declared that their bravery could well serve as an example for the most valiant nation.[66] Commandant Segurola said, "We have seen them fight with ardor and it excites our admiration. If their cause were just, they would deserve the most glorious name."[67]

The Indians, fighting against oppression and political corruption, really had a just cause. They were protesting their exclusion from their own government and their inability to initiate social and economic legislation. Unfortunately, their great leader, José Gabriel Túpac Amaru, was more of an idealist than a military man. The Spaniards, however, derived little profit and honor from their victory, for the Indians remained hostile and always ready to join their enemies. The King evidently realized this, for he tried to prevent unnecessary offense to the natives and was willing to make some important concessions. He removed the hated repartimientos and the corregidores, since they seemed to be the root of the trouble; but even this measure could not win back the confidence of people who had suffered so much.

[65] Markham, *Travels in Peru and India,* 170.

[66] Carta de Flores á Gálvez del 6 de Mayo de 1781, Biblioteca Nacional, Buenos Aires, Sección manuscritos, num. 2158 (cited by Lewin, *op. cit.,* 214); Ballivián y Roxas, *op. cit.,* 14.

[67] Correspondencia Vertíz-Gálvez 1782, Informe de Segurola del 14 de Marzo de 1782, AGN, Buenos Aires, VI–XVI–9–12, in Lewin, *op. cit.,* 400.

CHAPTER XV

Annihilation

Diego Túpac Amaru held out courageously under rapidly worsening adverse conditions. When he saw the final suppression of the revolt in Upper Peru by Flores, Reseguín, and Segurola, however, he began to think more favorably of the proffered amnesty.

At first General del Valle thought that Diego and Mariano Túpac Amaru and Túpac Catari should be excluded from the pardon because of the seriousness of their crimes, and he wrote Viceroy Jáuregui of Peru on August 8 expressing that opinion.[1] Visitador Areche, on the other hand, believed that the principal chiefs should be pardoned because the rebels wanted their lives spared even more than their own. He said that there were millions of people, not really rebels, who wanted peace, but hesitated to seek pardon because these leaders were not included.[2]

Viceroy Jáuregui finally heeded Areche's advice and included everybody in the pardon, issued on September 12, 1781. At the same time he said that even though the leaders did not deserve it, they might now return to their homes without fear of reprisals. If any official dared to harm them, he would be deprived of his office forever. On the other hand, if the Indians persisted in hostilities, they would be punished severely.[3] Viceroy Vertíz of Buenos Aires was not so liberal, and in November he advised that the chiefs of the rebellion should not be pardoned. Finally, through the in-

[1] Carta de Josef del Valle al virrey Agustín de Jáuregui, Cuzco, August 8, 1781; Carta del fiscal, Castilla, al virrey, Agustín de Jáuregui, Lima. September 3, 1781; Carta de Agustín de Jáuregui al visitador Antonio de Areche, Lima, September 7, 1781. Copies of these MSS in B. L.

[2] Josef Antonio de Areche al virrey Agustín de Jáuregui, Lima, September 7, 1781, MS copy in B. L.

[3] Bando de Jáuregui, September 12, 1781, in Angelis, *Documentos*, 111–12; Bando de Agustín de Jáuregui, Lima, September 3, 1781. MS copy in B. L.

fluence of the Peruvian viceroy, on January 21, 1782, Vertíz issued a pardon similar to that proclaimed by his colleague.[4]

Evidently Diego Túpac Amaru did not learn for some time that the pardon was extended to him. On October 1, 1781, Del Valle told him that he and his nephews, Mariano and Andrés, and Túpac Catari were responsible for the rebellion and did not deserve pardon. He said that they were all in danger of suffering the same fate as José Gabriel Túpac Amaru unless they truly repented of their crimes and obeyed the King's orders.

Diego's reply, on October 18, did not show repentance, but, instead, constituted a defense of his actions. He declared that he had received the Viceroy's proclamation of pardon and that he was serving the King, whose infallible word had been violated by his own ministers. He maintained that he was showing his loyalty by enforcing the law and putting a stop to the thievery by corregidores and chapetones. Furthermore, his brother, José Gabriel, should have been sent to Lima or to Spain so that the King could have learned the truth about the iniquity of the chapetones.[5] Diego had published the text of Viceroy Jáuregui's pardon in the form of a proclamation on October 14, the next day after he had received it. At the same time he had learned of other, conflicting edicts offering rewards for his apprehension, dead or alive. He did not know, he told Del Valle, what to believe.[6] On November 16, Del Valle wrote the Viceroy of Peru that the rebels of Quispicanchis remained obstinate because Túpac Amaru was not sure of his admission to pardon.[7]

Father Antonio Valdés, priest of Sicuani, was accordingly sent to Azángaro to convince Diego of his inclusion and to persuade

---

[4] Correspondencia Vertíz-Gálvez 1782, Oficio 590, fechado el 20 de Febrero de 1782 en Montevideo, AGN, Buenos Aires, VI–XVI–9–12, in Lewin, *op. cit.*, 398–99.

[5] The proclamation is published in C. A. Mackehenie, *Un inédito sobre Diego Cristóbal Túpac Amaru*, Vol. I, No. 6 (cited by Lewin, *op. cit.*, 330–31).

[6] Informe de Diego Túpac Amaru, Azángaro, October 18, 1781, in Odriozola, *Documentos*, I, 216–17.

[7] Carta de Agustín de Jáuregui á Jph. del Valle, Lima, November 16, 1781. MS copy in B. L.

him to surrender and accept pardon. The two men discussed the matter while walking on the riverbank, where Diego's general, Vilca Apasa, overheard their conversation and remonstrated strongly because he did not think a Spaniard's word could be trusted. The priest Antonio Martínez also used his influence to try to remove Diego's suspicions of the Viceroy. He asked, "Do you not know that if the executive failed to keep his word, he would fail the King, God, the world, his conscience, and the right of the people?" Martínez offered to accompany Diego to Lima if he wanted to go there to seek peace, but assured him that he could safely accept the pardon, even with his eyes closed.[8]

General Arias also took a hand in persuading Diego to accept pardon. He told him that, if he truly repented, he should give thanks for the goodness of the Viceroy, who had blotted out his crimes in the general pardon. He said that José Gabriel's aims had been absurd and that, if Diego continued to work for them, he would suffer a fate similar to his brother's. If he surrendered his arms, he would receive pardon and live happy. If he persisted in his obstinacy, six thousand soldiers were ready to inflict severe reprisal.[9] When the beautiful Angelina Sevilla added her persuasion to that of the priests and other persons, Diego yielded.

Vilca Apasa, Alejandro Calisaya, and a number of other chiefs refused to submit. They held out for some time in the provinces of Carabaya and Azángaro, sacked the towns of Calamarca and Ayoayo, and fiercely attacked and burned Achacache. Vilca Apasa finally suffered defeat at the hands of General del Valle. He was captured in his native village of Tapa-tapa, eighteen miles east of Azángaro, and torn to pieces by horses in the plaza of the latter place. Carlos Choquetiglla, Calisaya, and many other rebels were

[8] Copia de carta que responde Dn. Diego Túpac Amaru al Dr. Dn. Antonio Martínez cura de Sicuani, Azángaro, November 6, 1781; Carta de Dr. Antonio Martínez á Diego Cristóbal Túpac Amaru, Sicuani, November 14, 1781. MS copies in B. L.

[9] Copia de carta de Ramón de Arias á Diego Túpac Amaru, Campa de Cabanilla, December 1, 1781, in Odriozola, *Documentos*, I, 235–37; Angelis, *Documentos*, 137–40.

hanged,[10] but it was not until August 3, 1782, that Flores could announce the total pacification of the viceroyalty of La Plata.[11]

To return to Diego's dilemma, at first the Bishop of Cuzco believed that Diego's promises to surrender were mere pretense. Convinced that the insurgents still carried on correspondence with the Inca and took orders from him, he feared that the Inca intended to strike a mortal blow against the crown under the cloak of pardon. Yet he received word that Diego and the Indians of Azángaro, Asillo, and Orurillo had given proof of their good intentions by keeping priests with them, that they had shown the churchmen due respect and had asked that other priests be sent to the towns where there were none. Diego had written the Bishop on November 5, 1781, that the native uprising had been caused by the cruelties and greed of corregidores, caciques, and other domineering officials who considered nothing but their own interests. He said that he had been influenced to take part in the revolt by their cruelties and by José Gabriel's upholding of the royal decrees, although he himself did not favor violence. He pointed out that the Bishop had censured and excommunicated the miserable Indians, causing greater injuries than before, yet no harm had befallen him and his property was protected. Diego continued:

> My particular attention has been to calm the disturbed spirits of the natives, even at the risk of my own life, and to check in the most expeditious manner their excesses, robberies, and other proceedings, in order that they may keep united ... with the Spaniards and other inhabitants of these countries. Although I have not been able to control the Spanish troops, and, because of this, no crime should be attributed to me, since any quarrel . . . which I have caused has been only to preserve my life and that of my family.

[10] Markham, *A History of Peru,* 211; Markham, *Travels in Peru and India,* 163–64; Oficio del inspector D. José del Valle al virrey de Buenos Aires, Juan José de Vertíz, Ayaviri, July 14, 1782, in Odriozola, *Documentos,* I, 249; Angelis, *Documentos,* 154–55.

[11] El virrey de la Plata continua la relación de los sucesos del Peru, Montevideo, September 30, 1782, AGN, Buenos Aires, Correspondencia Vertíz-Gálvez, 1782 (published in Lewin, *op. cit.,* 481–82).

Stating that he had not committed crimes against the church or the King, Diego asked the prelate to use his influence to keep him from being punished for treason if he accepted pardon. He promised to show in the future affection for the Roman Catholic religion and blind obedience to King Charles III. He would also work for peace by calming the natives and persuading them to be submissive. He pointed out that abuses were being committed contrary to the general pardon since Spanish soldiers from Arequipa and other provinces had gone to the camp of Coporaque to arrest the natives. A letter from Puno had informed him that corregidores intended to behead all the natives except those under seven years of age, yet many Indians had already been pacified by his influence.[12] In this manner rumors of atrocities were spread at that time.

Diego was willing to promote the safe return of priests to their parishes, although certain individuals should be excepted because their return would cause disturbances in the towns. Others would be especially welcomed because of their excellent services to the natives—for example, Josef Calisto de Castro in Pucará, who loved the Indians. Manuel Salazar also was to come directly to Azángaro, where his house and a good position awaited him,[13] and the people wanted Father Maruri to return to Asillo and Josef de Escobar to Azángaro.

In another letter, dated December 9, 1781, Diego told the Bishop that the towns of Azángaro, Orurillo, and Asillo wanted to surrender. He also said that he would willingly give his life for the King and was ready to surrender. He asked the prelate's help.[14]

[12] Carta num. 1 de Diego Xal, Túpac Amaru al obispo del Cuzco, Azángaro, November 5, 1781. MS copy in B. L.

[13] Memoria por Diego Xal, Túpac Amaru y razón de los S. S. curas del obispado del Cuzco, á q.nes no quieren admitir las comunidades de naturales de los pueblos que se van a referir, por justas causas que para ello expresan tener, num. 4, Azángaro, November 6, 1781; Carta de Diego Xal. Túpac Amaru á Señores curas y vicarios Dn. Juan de Dios Adrian, D. Manuel Salazar, D. Francisco Aragón y Ochoa, D. Vicente Otazú, y Juan Bautista Moran, Azángaro, November 7, 1781; Carta de Antonio Martínez á Juan Manuel de Moscoso y Peralta, Sicuani, November 14, 1781, num. 7. Copies of all these MSS are in B. L.

[14] Carta num. 2 de Diego Xal, Túpac Amaru al obispo del Cuzco, Azángaro, December 9, 1781. MS copy in B. L.

The Bishop replied that he was happy to learn that Diego had abandoned his criminal ways to become a Christian and a faithful vassal. He assured him that his sins were already blotted out and that he loved him. He also pointed out to him the many benefits of peace and urged him to have faith in the amnesty. Del Valle had acted discreetly as a Christian and had been prompt to pardon the insurgents.

The prelate also informed Diego that Indian hostilities had not ceased after the Viceroy's proclamation was sent to him. In Cusipata the rebels had killed eighty soldiers and carried off their arms. On the road to Paucartambo and in Caycay there had been similar incidents. Some three thousand Indians had gone to Checacupe, where a skirmish had occurred in which a number of persons were killed, and in the mountain towns of Tinta, Coporaque, Checa, Yauri, and Pichigua hostilities had taken place. Priests had been carried off, as in the case of Estebán Bustamante, who was seized and taken to the hill of Tocto, where the Indians established themselves again and threatened the province of Chumbivilcas and the chief justice. The Bishop related that the rebels had imprisoned in Checa the Recollect friar Andrés Carrasco, ordering him not to leave, but a Christian woman had shown him how to escape. In Coporaque the Indians had stolen some brandy, and in capturing four of the thieves a soldier had lost his life. Furthermore, the natives had stolen many cattle and cut off food supplies. The Bishop reminded Diego that when the troops were used, it was only to punish such offenders.

Francisco de Rivera and the Inspector General also corroborated his statements. Del Valle reported to the Viceroy the disaster to the troop of Taray, in which some soldiers, boys, and women died, and said that the Indians had burned the town of Lamay. Although the Viceroy thought that these acts had been committed by a group of plunderers whose chief interest was robbery, yet he said that the incidents "gave a sufficient idea of the little confidence one should have in his [Diego's] promises."

The Bishop told Diego that the rumor about the soldiers' intending to behead Indians over seven years of age was absolutely false. He would swear by the cross that it was safe for the natives to return to their towns. He asked Diego, Mariano Túpac Amaru, and other chiefs to come to Quiquijana for the passports that the Inspector General had sent. The prelate would go there also, although he was not well. He promised to let the desired priests return to their doctrinas and to order them to treat the Indians kindly.[15]

At the same time the Bishop wrote letters to the inhabitants of Azángaro, Orurillo, and Asillo. He told them that he was happy to see them restored to obedience and only wanted their repentance to be permanent:

> My sons, make use of this opportunity to return to your repose.
> . . . Are you not already satisfied with the measures of the higher
> government? Have not the repartimientos been removed? The
> Viceroy and the Visitador General, Josef Antonio de Areche, rec-
> ognize your cause and have arranged that the unwise measures of
> the corregidores shall never be seen again. . . . Give thanks to God
> that he still maintains in your souls some sentiments of religion.

He also asked them to show respect to their priests and not to mistreat them in any way.[16]

After a conference with the Inspector General, the authorities decided to impress upon Diego and his followers the importance of surrender and pacification. They wrote Diego to go on urging the Indians not to take up arms again, as they were doing in Paucartambo, Cacay, Checacupe, and the mountain towns of Checa, Coporaque, Yauri, and Pichigua in the province of Tinta. And the inspector ordered the postponement of an expedition to those places until he received a reply.[17]

[15] Carta de Juan Manuel obispo del Cuzco á Diego Túpac Amaru, Cuzco, November 17, 1781, num. 3; Carta de Francisco de Rivera á Juan Manuel Moscoso y Peralta, Sicuani, November 9, 1781, num. 5; Carta de Agustín de Jáuregui á Sor. inspr. gral. Dn. Jph. del Valle, Lima, December 10, 1781; Carta de Tomás Machado á Dn. Baltazar Sematnat, Caylloma, November 13, 1781; Carta de Beltazar Sematnat á Tomás Machado, Arequipa, November 19, 1781. MS copies in B. L.

[16] Carta de Juan Manuel obispo del Cuzco á los Indios de las comunidades de Azángaro, Orurillo, y Asillo, Cuzco, November 17, 1781. MS copy in B. L.

[17] Carta de Juan Ml. obispo del Cuzco á Exmo. Sor. Dn. Agustín de Jáuregui, Cuzco, November 18, 1781, MS copy in B. L.

The corregidor of Tinta reported that Diego had grave fears that treason would be committed against him by some minor officer.[18] The Bishop therefore suggested that the Viceroy issue a decree to assure the Indians that the proclamation of pardon guaranteed their safety. The executive, however, did not consider it necessary to do so since inferiors must obey his orders. The military expedition had been organized to repel those people who were still in rebellion and to guard the faithful. The Viceroy hoped that Diego would soon calm the Indians who were still hostile. Moreover, he and his people should be grateful for the benefit granted them after they had been so disloyal and had caused so much expense to the royal treasury.[19]

Diego finally accepted the pardon. He published it in Azángaro and other places and tried to send the rebels to their towns and prevent injuries to the Spaniards. But the Viceroy was still suspicious and did not recall the expedition of 23,000 men prepared in Arequipa. Rather, he hastened the departure of the troop in order that the rebels might know that he had not granted them pardon from necessity, but on account of his humanity and pity, and that it would be withheld from obstinate individuals.[20] He told the Bishop of Cuzco to travel with all possible caution and learn whether his pardon was accepted in good faith by the 30,000 Indians.[21]

Apparently Del Valle now began to believe the Indians sincere in their repentance since they had opened the roads for the priests, detained in Sicuani, to go to their parishes. He suggested that Diego Túpac Amaru be summoned to Quiquijana or Sicuani, where the Bishop would also go on the assigned day, so that peace might be concluded with the greatest solemnities. A safe-conduct

[18] Carta de Don Josef del Valle á Don Agustín de Jáuregui, Cuzco, November 24, 1781, MS copy in B. L.

[19] Carta de Dn. Agustín de Jáuregui al obispo del Cuzco, Lima, November 30, 1781, MS copy in B. L.

[20] Carta de Agustín de Jáuregui á Señor Josef Reseguín, Lima, December 15, 1781; Carta de Agustín de Jáuregui á Josef del Valle. Lima, December 15, 1781. MS copies in B. L.

[21] Carta de Agustín de Jáuregui al Señor obispo del Cuzco, Lima, December 15, 1781. MS copy in B. L.

should be given to the Inca to remove any doubt which he still might have.[22]

Diego really wanted peace. In a letter to Friar Rafael Ponce he had said that he had rejoiced greatly when the pardon from the Viceroy of Lima arrived in Arequipa, and he hoped it would soon pacify the country.[23] When the priests, Father Valdés, Francisco Rivera, Manuel Mora, Pedro Ledesema, and Friar Padilla, arrived in Azángaro on November 28, Diego Túpac Amaru received them kindly. They reported that he was anxious for peace and the security of his family and that he was grateful for what the Bishop had done.[24] The churchmen carefully explained to Diego, Mariano, and Andrés the security that they, their families, and their followers would have under the general pardon.[25]

The Viceroy approved of either Sicuani or Quiquijana as the meeting place of Diego and the military authorities. But he was still suspicious because of

> the inconsistent minds of those natives and the little confidence which one should have in their promises, on account of what has already begun to be experienced in those pretending to surrender. As they have made use of arms, surprised our men, and killed some of them, it is necessary now more than in other circumstances that one must proceed with the greatest care and vigilance. One must be very watchful of their operations, connect their movements with their offers, and take the precautions which prudence dictates in these occurrences. Neither shall the execution of my orders . . . be delayed.

He asked Inspector del Valle to tell Túpac Amaru again that Spanish troops never failed people who surrendered. As proof of their

[22] Carta de Marcos Palomino á Juan Manuel Moscoso y Peralta, Sicuani, November 14, 1781, num. 6; Carta de Josef del Valle á Agustín de Jáuregui, Cuzco, November 18, 1781; Copia de carta que responde Dn. Diego Túpac Amaru al Dr. Dn. Antonio Martínez cura de Sicuani, Azángaro, November 6, 1781. MS copies in B. L.

[23] Carta de Diego Xal, Túpac Amaru á Fr. Rafael Ponce, Azángaro, November 14, 1781. MS copy in B. L.

[24] Carta de Antonio de Valdés al obispo del Cuzco, Azángaro, November 28, 1781. MS copy in B. L.

[25] Representación de los curas y demas religiosos en el pueblo de Azángaro, Azángaro, December 2, 1781. MS copy in B. L.

submission the Indians were to surrender their cannon and munitions in the time required and must return to their towns. If they
went to the hills, they would be treated as enemies.

Del Valle was to see that Diego came to Sicuani or Quiquijana
without armed escort. He was also to proceed with the greatest
caution to prevent treason. He was to keep as many soldiers on hand
as possible to protect the city and the province and to notify the
corregidor of Tinta to take similar care. If the Inca refused to hand
over his arms, Del Valle should hold him as hostage or prisoner.[26]
The Viceroy was much concerned because of Diego's contradictory
actions. On the one hand, the Inca had promised to obey his proclamation and said that he had made it known in Azángaro, while
on the other, he had issued an edict on October 17 detailing oppressions under the repartimiento, a copy of which had been received
by the Viceroy. Believing that Diego sought to stir up the natives
again, the Viceroy told Del Valle to be cautious and Francisco de
Salcedo to delay the expedition from Azángaro in order that troops
might be available if they were needed.[27] In fact, he advised Salcedo to take every precaution until the rebel arms were surrendered
and Diego had parted from his followers.[28]

The Viceroy did not need to be alarmed. Diego was being careful to maintain peace while at the same time guarding against
treachery on the part of the Spaniards. On November 7, 1781, the
Inca had urged Miguel Bastidas to take such measures that contro-
versy on both sides would cease. If the Spaniards came to Larecaja
or other places, they were to be protected from injury and favored
as much as possible. Miguel was to make the capitulations with the
help of Juan de Dios Mullapuraca and other reasonable persons.
He was to be prudent and to take great precaution to avoid treason.

[26] Carta de Agustín de Jáuregui al Sor. inspr. gral. Dn. José del Valle, Lima,
December 5, 1781; Carta de Agustín de Jáuregui á Josef del Valle, Lima, December 6, 1781. MS copies in B. L.

[27] Carta de Diego Xal, Túpac Amaru al Señor Francisco Salcedo, Azángaro,
November 13, 1781; Carta de Agustín de Jáuregui á Francisco Suárez de Salcedo,
Lima, December 5, 1781, reservada; Auto de Diego Xal, Túpac Amaru, Azángaro,
October 17, 1781. MS copies in B. L.

[28] Carta de Agustín de Jáuregui á Francisco de Salcedo, Lima, January 5,
1782, MS copy in B. L.

But Diego also ordered him to provide the Indians with sufficient arms since the Spaniards would be well provided with them.[29] At the same time he wrote to Julián Túpac Amaru to take orders from Miguel in the observance of peace.[30]

Meanwhile, General del Valle was waiting to go to the conference as soon as Diego agreed to the place. The officer proposed to the Viceroy that if, after disarming, the Indians did not keep their promise, they must be punished for all the crimes that had been committed. He pointed out that Mariano Túpac Amaru might claim the caciqueship of Tungasuca held by his father, although to do so was contrary to Visitador Areche's provisions; the stolen possessions and cattle might also cause controversies. There might be trouble if corregidores returned to their former provinces because some people hated even the word corregidor.

The Indians of the three provinces of Lampa, Azángaro, and Carabaya especially resisted the return of corregidores. The people of Azángaro were filled with so much despair when they heard that the corregidores were returning that they were ready to retreat to the Andes of Carabaya and Apolo, where they believed their lives would be safe from Spanish hostilities. Many families had already left for the interior of Carabaya with their cattle and other belongings. That province was one of the most mountainous in the kingdom; if the Indians took it, reconquest would be very dangerous and expensive. Since Del Valle did not want to make the Indians hostile, he suspended the return of all the corregidores until the Viceroy should determine what to do.

The Peruvian executive was willing to compensate the Indians if they returned stolen jewels and cattle, and he would treat the matter of the corregidores later.[31] Since some of the provinces be-

[29] Carta de Diego Cristóbal Túpac Amaru á Miguel Bastidas, Azángaro, November 7, 1781, in Odriozola, Documentos, I, 232–33; Angelis, Documentos, 134–36.

[30] Carta de Diego Cristóbal Túpac Amaru á Julián Túpac Amaru, Azángaro, November 7, 1781, in Odriozola, Documentos, I, 234; Angelis, Documentos, 136–37.

[31] Carta de José del Valle á Agustín de Jáuregui, Cuzco, December 4, 1781; Representación de los curas y demas religiosos en el pueblo de Azángaro, Azángaro, December 2, 1781; Carta de Agustín de Jáuregui al Señor inspector general José del Valle, Lima, January 5, 1782; Representación de los naturales del Peru al rey, December 4, 1781; Carta de Manuel obispo del Cuzco á Agustín de Jáuregui, Cuzco,

longed to the viceroyalty of Buenos Aires, he had no authority regarding them. Therefore he sent Colonel Flores a copy of the resolutions drawn up by the council of war to inform him what was being done to conclude the pacification of the country. If a peace was not ratified at Sicuani and force had to be used, he asked that Flores or Reseguín start for Azángaro with troops.[32]

Diego Túpac Amaru finally chose Sicuani for the conference. He wanted to take the people of Azángaro and other places with him, saying that the Indians feared what the soldiers of Chuquisaca might do. Indeed, the Indians would not permit him to go there unaccompanied because they knew what had happened to Túpac Catari and Bastidas after peace had been made with the natives of La Paz. The Spaniards did not want Diego to bring so many people, but they believed that if this right should be denied him, he might stir up new revolts.

On his part, Diego did not favor the coming of the Spanish troops from the coast. He feared that they would destroy the cattle needed by the Indians, that minor officers might violate the Viceroy's promises, and that, if the people thought the forces came to harm them or their haciendas, the desired peace could not be made. The Inca therefore asked for the withdrawal of the Arequipa soldiers, who were in Cabanilla, on the grounds that they would burden the treasury, it was a violation of the law to send them there, and they might incite trouble. He decided to go in person to Cabanilla to see if something could be done since the soldiers had gone there after all the Indians had surrendered and there was no need for them. He proposed that the natives should be free to travel anywhere on the roads without molestation or injury, that the same right be extended also to Spaniards, and that trade be carried on freely again. As soon as terms were made with Bastidas and other chiefs, he declared, the natives would be withdrawn from the blockade of La Paz and other cities. He objected to Gen-

December 10, 1781; Carta de Antonio de Valdés al obispo del Cuzco, Azángaro, December 6, 1781; Carta de Diego Xal, Túpac Amaru a Juan Manuel Moscoso y Peralta, num. 1, Azángaro, December 15, 1781. MS copies in B. L.

[32] Agustín de Jáuregui al Señor inspector general José del Valle, Lima, January 5, 1782, MS copy in B. L.

eral Flores' having any part in the negotiations since he had irritated and injured the natives. He was alarmed to hear that Commander Reseguín had issued orders to capture him, but happy that the Bishop of Cuzco would be in Sicuani.[33]

Bishop Moscoso answered the objections stated by Diego in a letter of December 10, 1781. Saying that he was his defender who had endeavored to influence the Viceroy and Inspector General in his behalf, he reported that those officials were displeased by pamphlets from Arequipa in which the Inca had expressed himself in a manner inconsistent with the gratitude he should have shown for the pardon. The Bishop went on to say that if Diego brought all his people (whose number he estimated at forty thousand) to Sicuani, then the Inspector General would feel compelled to summon a large force so that the two parties would be equal. Having, in effect, two armies facing each other would create an explosive situation. Certainly, if disputes arose, the pardon might be withdrawn. Moreover, the people of Sicuani would find it difficult to supply a great number of troops, and the Indians were sure to cause more damage to the haciendas of the area than the Spaniards since the latter would be supplied with money to buy necessary provisions. Finally, since peace would be the subject of discusion, a large number of troops was unnecessary.

The Bishop proposed a compromise. The cabildos and leaders of the towns could accompany Diego to Sicuani to witness the treaty ratification and see for themselves the kind treatment he would receive. If he desired, he could send Mariano Túpac Amaru

[33] Carta de Juan Manuel obispo del Cuzco á Agustín de Jáuregui, Cuzco, December 10, 1781; Carta de Diego Xal, Túpac Amaru á Juan Manuel obispo del Cuzco, Azángaro, November 29, 1781; Carta de Diego Xal, Túpac Amaru al obispo del Cuzco, Azángaro, December 5, 1781; Carta de Diego Xal, Túpac Amaru al Señor inspector general Josef del Valle, Azángaro, November 28, 1781; Carta de Josef del Valle á Agustín de Jáuregui, Cuzco, December 13, 1781; Carta de Josef del Valle á Diego Cristóbal Túpac Amaru, Cuzco, December 10, 1781; Carta de Diego Xal, Túpac Amaru á Agustín de Jáuregui, Azángaro, December 5, 1781. Copies of the above letters in B. L. Carta de Diego Cristóbal Túpac Amaru al comandante José Reseguín, Azángaro, November 5, 1781, in Odriozola, *Documentos*, I, 231–32; Angelis, *Documentos*, 133–34; Repuesta de Diego Cristóbal Túpac Amaru á comandante Ramón Arias, Azángaro, December 4, 1781, in Odriozola, *Documentos*, I, 238–39; Angelis, *Documentos*, 141–42.

ahead to see that everything was all right. When his nephew returned, he could enter the town with his attendants and have equal security. He could also take with him the priests whom the Bishop had sent. If Diego insisted on coming with all his people, however, the prelate said, he would not be there.

The Bishop assured Diego that he need not fear the troops in Cabanilla, who would aid him and check the evil designs of people who still persisted in rebelling. What had happened at La Paz and the tragic end of Túpac Catari had no bearing on Diego's case.[34]

On December 12, Commandant Arias, along with certain priests and two officials of higher rank, went to see Diego, who was on the heights of Lampa with Fathers Valdés and Francisco de Rivera, to arrange the terms of the treaties of reconciliation. Diego saluted the Spaniards humbly, declaring that he had never intended to disobey the sovereign, but had tried only to remove the oppression suffered by the natives. He asked that the Spanish troops be withdrawn when he went to Sicuani to avoid a feeling of mistrust among the Indians. Commandant Arias replied that the soldiers would be sent to Vilque to await the inspector's orders; but the troops from Arequipa were not disbanded, as Diego had hoped.[35]

In the conclusion of the treaty Diego made certain representations:

> I, the said Túpac Amaru, offer to surrender, and I command and will not permit any native to offend the Spaniards. At the same time they shall be assembled in their towns and live with the Spaniards in peace and union, as God commands and our Catholic monarch wishes. After hostilities have ceased and precautions are taken to prevent future injuries, everything will be peaceful and

[34] Carta de Juan Manuel obispo de Cuzco á Diego Túpac Amaru, Cuzco, December 10, 1781; Carta de Agustín de Jáuregui al obispo del Cuzco, Lima, December 30, 1781; Relación de Juan Manuel de Moscoso obispo del Cuzco, Cuzco, December 8, 1781; Relación del obispo del Cuzco, Cuzco, December 10, 1781; Carta de Juan Manuel obispo del Cuzco á Agustín de Jáuregui, Cuzco, December 12, 1781; Carta de Juan Manuel obispo del Cuzco á Diego Cristóbal Túpac Amaru, Cuzco, December 12, 1781; Carta de Josef del Valle á Diego Cristóbal Túpac Amaru, Cuzco, December 10, 1781. MS copies in B. L.

[35] Carta de Francisco de Rivera á Juan Manuel Moscoso y Peralta, Azángaro, December 15, 1781, num. 2; Carta del obispo del Cuzco á Francisco Rivera, Cuzco, December 21, 1781. MS copies in B. L.

there will be harmony between the Spaniards and the Indians, so that commerce may be carried on, the farms repopulated, the mines worked, the Indians instructed by their respective priests, and finally we shall live as true vassals of the Catholic king of Spain.[36]

When the preliminary meeting was finished, Arias told Diego to come another time to sign the document.

Prisoners were exchanged, and Diego proposed that he or his nephew accompany Commandant Arias to help subdue the towns not yet pacified. He promised to be in Sicuani at the designated time and to send his troops from Lampa to Puno to help repopulate that town. The Inspector General then guaranteed complete safety to the Inca, his nephews, and the followers he might bring to Sicuani.

The good results of the meeting were felt at once. The natives seemed calmer and no longer blockaded the roads. When sugar and brandy from Arequipa were sold in Azángaro as a result of the restoration of commerce between the two places, the Viceroy was pleased. He still insisted, however, upon keeping troops near the conference town or in Puno in case the former rebels did not act in good faith. Commandant Arias did not trust Diego completely either, for he proposed that, when peace was definitely established, the Inca and his nephews should be sent to Spain so that no new sedition might arise.[37]

Diego, Del Valle, and the Bishop awaited the day for the final conference. The Inca asked the prelate to fix the day when he could come to see him in order to receive the King's favor and public exoneration. He promised not to fail in his loyalty even though

---

[36] Tratado entre Túpac Amaru y Ramón de Arias, Lampa, December 11, 1781. MS copy in B. L.

[37] Carta de Antonio de Valdés al obispo del Cuzco, Azángaro, December 6, 1781; Carta de Josef del Valle á Agustín de Jáuregui, Cuzco, December 13, 1781; Carta de Josef del Valle á Diego Cristóbal Túpac Amaru, Cuzco, December 10, 1781; Orden de Josef Antonio del Valle del pasaporte de Diego Cristóbal Túpac Amaru, Cuzco, December 8, 1781; Carta de Josef del Valle á Agustín de Jáuregui, Cuzco, December 22, 1781; Carta de Diego Cristóbal Túpac Amaru á Josef del Valle, Azángaro, December 15, 1781; Carta de Agustín de Jáuregui al Señor inspector general José del Valle, Lima, January 5, 1781. MS copies in B. L.

he saw troops come out against his people. He asked the Bishop to use his influence with the Viceroy so that he, who had the most illustrious blood of the country in his veins, should not be forced to live the miserable life of an exile. He said that he worked constantly to keep the Indians from assaulting the Spaniards, although this was a very difficult task since they had become accustomed to killing.[38]

Diego wrote a similar letter to the Viceroy. He said that he had committed many errors in the rebellion because he loved José Gabriel like a father, but declared that neither one of them had aspired to the crown which justly belonged to the King, despite any claims to the contrary. They had wanted only to stop the corregidores' misdeeds which could not be remedied in any other way. It grieved him to be accused of the abominable crime of conspiring against the crown. He had made peace with Commandant Arias and was now awaiting the day to conclude it.[39] He reminded the Viceroy that he had asked him to consider his case in the highest court without the intervention of minor ministers, who did not know how to observe great orders.[40]

The fiscal claimed that it would be illegal for Diego to be judged only by the Viceroy. Therefore, he sent measures to the territorial judges for the protection of the Inca under the pardon granted. Since not all the desired results had been obtained or suspicion removed, the fiscal suggested summoning a junta to deal with the matter.[41]

The Bishop answered first on December 21, 1781. He reminded Diego of the good treatment he had received on the heights of

[38] Carta de Diego Xal, Túpac Amaru á Francisco de Salcedo, Azángaro, December 15, 1781; Carta de Juan Manuel obispo del Cuzco á Agustín de Jáuragui, Cuzco, December 22, 1781; Carta de Diego Xal, Túpac Amaru á Juan Manuel Moscoso y Peralta, num. 1, Azángaro, December 15, 1781; Carta de Diego Xal, Túpac Amaru á Agustín de Jáuregui, Azángaro, December 5, 1781. MS copies in B. L.

[39] Carta de Diego Xal, Túpac Amaru á Agustin de Jáuregui, Azángaro, December 15, 1781. MS copy in B. L.

[40] Carta de Diego Xal, Túpac Amaru á Agustín de Jáuregui, Azángaro, December 5, 1781. MS copy in B. L.

[41] Carta del fiscal, Moreno, á Agustín de Jáuregui, Lima, December 31, 1781. MS copy in B. L.

Lampa from Commandant Arias and that the troops had been withdrawn toward Puno. The manner in which military officials had respected the Viceroy's proclamations should leave no doubts in the Inca's mind. He should also remember that the pardon provided that he and his family could live in their home, that their possessions would be safe, and that he would be protected.[42]

The Viceroy answered, too, and tried to relieve Diego's apprehensions. He told him to go to the place appointed by the Inspector General and enjoy the pardon granted in his proclamation. He promised:

> You, your nephews, and dependents shall be entirely free from cares, since you are admitted under the royal protection. The pardon shall be kept in good faith, if you remain faithful and obedient to the King and to the judges and ministers who govern in his name.

He added that Commandant Reseguín had dealt harshly with Túpac Catari because that chief had not asked for pardon, and that the men who were arrested had conspired after they had promised fidelity.[43]

In a general junta held on January 3, 1782, the Viceroy decided that the terms of the pardon should be defined and put into effect as soon as possible by the Inspector General. This should be done when Túpac Amaru came with his family and followers to the place assigned for the surrender of his person and arms as a sign of obedience. After arms had been surrendered, the Inspector was to make known to the natives the measures adopted for the extinction of the repartimientos. If the terms were not accepted, the commandant of the Arequipa troops should be ordered to advance with his soldiers.[44]

Areche was not as sympathetic toward Diego as were the Viceroy and the military authorities. He said that the chief made

[42] Carta de Manuel obispo del Cuzco á Diego Cristóbal Túpac Amaru, Cuzco, December 21, 1781, num. 3. MS copy in B. L.

[43] Carta de Agustín de Jáuregui á Diego Cristóbal Túpac Amaru, Lima, January 5, 1782. MS copy in B. L.

[44] Carta de Agustín de Jáuregui al obispo del Cuzco, Lima, January 5, 1782; Auto de la junta general de guerra, Lima, January 3, 1782. MS copies in B. L.

scandalous demands and seemed to value them more than his life: "To ask that the corregidores should not return was arrogance, and, when he requested that the troops should not enter the Basin of Lake Titicaca, he intended the rebels to take up arms in a few days." The Visitador contended that Diego should be given only a brief time to accept the pardon and lay down arms.[45]

The Inspector General finally set the conference date, and the Bishop and Diego Túpac Amaru started for Sicuani at the beginning of January, 1782. Diego sent ahead three hundred sheep and thirty cows for the Spanish troops, asked Commandant Arias to free Melchor Niña Laura, and promised that he would do the same with any imprisoned Spaniards when peace was ratified.[46]

Although continual rain and snow delayed Diego on the journey, he arrived in the town of Maranganí on the afternoon of January 26 with an escort of two hundred Indians. The corregidor of the province, Francisco de Salcedo, went out to receive him and made the greatest efforts to overcome his suspicions. At the same time Del Valle published a proclamation threatening to impose the death penalty upon any soldier who dared to insult the Inca.

Diego entered the Spanish camp with fifty armed Indians. The others accompanying him remained on the mountains near by to observe their chief's fate. Three banners were surrendered when Diego dismounted in front of Del Valle's tent. Then the Inspector General received him in his tent. Diego knelt at his feet so agitated that he could not utter a word. Del Valle helped him up, supported him with his arm, and assured him that he had the protection of the King's arms. He then asked about his nephews, his wife, and his mother. The Inca finally answered that they would come later, although he feared they might be delayed by the weather. He put a paper into Del Valle's hands, which was received without being read. The Inspector General then asked him to go into Sicuani to offer submission to the Bishop of Cuzco. All the delegation was now escorted to the church by the provincial dragoons of Lima

[45] Carta de Josef Antonio de Areche á Agustín de Jáuregui, Lima, January 2, 1782, num. 383. MS copy in B. L.

[46] Carta de Diego Cristóbal Túpac Amaru al comandante Ramón Arias, Azángaro, January 19, 1782, in Odriozola, *Documentos*, I, 242; Angelis, *Documentos*, 146.

and Carabaya. The Bishop had come out of the sanctuary situated in the great plaza. When the Inca saw him, he prostrated himself at his feet and, weeping, implored mercy and protection.[47]

In the church the royal standard bearer of Cuzco read the paper that Diego had presented. It began:

> In this illustrious council . . . I, my family, and all other erring vassals are now going to receive that most generous pardon, which in future ages will be regarded with astonishment. Behold, Sir, prostrate at your feet, that scandal of Peru, he whose conduct and excesses have proved him a conspicuous leader in the innumerable calamities which have befallen this kingdom. It is I, Diego Cristóbal Túpac Amaru, brother of that unfortunate José Gabriel, the principal promoter of the rebellion, whose steps I followed and whose commissions I executed, not from ambition or selfish motives, much less with disposition to rebel against my king and Lord, however much appearances may seem to the contrary. I was, in fact, totally ignorant of my brother's intentions; he never communicated to me his plans or projects, although he called me his son, and as such he always treated me. When he committed his first crime at Tungasuca by putting the corregidor to death, he enjoined me, at the peril of my life, to pursue the line of conduct which he was to point out. I punctually executed his commands, mastered and excited the Indians.[48]

Diego acknowledged his guilt and did not try to diminish his crimes. He said that he would always be proud that the blood of José Gabriel Túpac Amaru circulated in his veins, but it had caused him to sink into deep disgrace. He then surrendered arms, saying:

> These are the arms with which I have offended my sovereign. I now surrender them with the serious intention to use them never again, not even in defense of my own life. At Azángaro I left several pieces of cannon, which I did not bring with me lest the Indians should think I was preparing for a new revolt. You may dispose of them for the best service of my king and Lord. Do also the same with me and my family. I only pray you not to reduce me to

[47] Carta de Josef del Valle á Agustín de Jáuregui, Sicuani, January 27, 1782. MS copy in B. L.
[48] Papel de Diego Túpac Amaru, Sicuani, January 26, 1782. MS copy in B. L. Temple, *op. cit.*, II, 163–66; Odriozola, *Documentos*, I, 242–44.

366

so hard a fate as to deprive me of my liberty and honor; rather than that, I am ready to sacrifice a thousand lives, if it is possible, to appease my offended sovereign. If I am allowed, I will endeavor to restore my name and reputation and blot out the stain which my conduct has cast upon my family.

If pardon had been offered sooner, he said, he would have accepted it, but when he saw his life threatened daily, he had delayed his submission.[49] Del Valle then agreed that the petition of surrender should be accepted.

Next the ban of excommunication had to be removed from Diego and his followers. The dean of the Cuzco Cathedral, Manuel de Mendieta, absolved from ecclesiastical censure the Inca and all his followers who asked absolution as penitents. More than three hundred of the former rebels took advantage of the occasion to be forgiven.[50]

Afterwards Colonel Gaspar de Ugarte, auditor of war and the royal ensign bearer of Cuzco, read the pardon to the assembly. Ugarte warned that, although Diego had surrendered the arms brought with him, proper measures must be taken to collect weapons, caps, and other military insignia in distant places, where they were to be handed over within twelve days. Within the same time Andrés and Mariano Túpac Amaru and the rest of the family had to come personally to take the oath of fidelity, although Mariano had surrendered at La Paz to Commandant Segurola. Diego was asked to aid in the pacification of the people still rebelling, to swear to subject himself to the King's wise laws and the orders of the magistrates, and to treat the Spaniards and mestizos with brotherly kindness.

Diego heard all these conditions while standing in front of the royal standard of Cuzco and the two banners of his army. He swore to fulfill every provision faithfully. He then repeated the same oath in the name of his relatives, Mariano and Andrés, and all his family.

[49] Decreto de Josef del Valle, Sicuani, January 26, 1782; Decreto del Yltmo, Señor obispo, Sicuani, January 26, 1782; Notificación y absolución de Diego Cristóbal Túpac Amaru, Sicuani, January 26, 1782. MS copies in B. L.

[50] Notificación de Josef del Valle, Sicuani, January 26, 1782, in Odriozola, *Documentos*, I, 245–47; Angelis, *Documentos*, 150–52.

He took off his sword, which he had been allowed to wear, and, as a sign of obedience, handed it to the Inspector General. Del Valle immediately returned it to him and told him to conquer with it the towns still in revolt. Next Diego was conducted to the chancel of the main altar, where he knelt at the feet of the officiating minister. Colonel Ugarte saluted him three times with the royal standard used in the conquest of Peru and waved it over his head. During the artillery salutes that followed the standard bearer of the veteran troops and militias in the plaza waved their banners. In this way Diego was assured that none of the subordinate officials would harm him, his family, or his followers.[51]

Next morning when Diego took the oath of eternal fidelity and a pontifical mass of thanks was said, all the surrounding mountains were crowned by Indians. They had journeyed not only from the neighboring provinces but also from Larecaja, La Paz, Pacajes, and even the Andes to see the sight. When they learned of the good treatment that their chief received, they came down in numerous troops to ask absolution from excommunication and to offer obedience to the King. More than thirty thousand insurgents sought absolution, which the Bishop granted.

Diego wrote his wife, his mother, and his nephews to hasten there without delay, bringing the cannon and arms left in Azángaro. He promised to send messengers to all the provinces of the viceroyalty of Buenos Aires still in rebellion ordering the caciques and other leaders to come and receive assurance of his sincere repentance and obedience to the King. Some authorities believed that Diego was sincere. Del Valle declared that in everything he did Diego showed undeniable repentance for his past crimes, that he had discernment and talents uncommon to Indians, but found it difficult to express his thoughts on account of his crude education.[52]

51 Carta de Josef del Valle á Agustín de Jáuregui, Sicuani, January 27, 1782; Carta de Juan Manuel Moscoso, obispo del Cuzco, al obispo de La Paz, Dr. Gregorio Francisco del Campo, Huayallabamba, July 20, 1782, in Odriozola, *Documentos*, I, 261.

52 Copia de carta escrita á un Sor. ministro de Madrid por un vecino del Cuzco, Cuzco, September 1, 1782, signed "B. L. M." MS copy in B. L.

Diego was honored by being lodged in the room next to the Bishop's in the house of a priest and by being seated at Moscoso's table. Both the prelate and the Inspector General treated him kindly. When the Bishop came out under the canopy at a pontifical mass of thanks, Del Valle stood on the right and Diego on the left. The former rebel was permitted to appoint caciques in Tinta and other provinces and was granted an annual pension of one thousand pesos; each of his nephews was to receive six hundred.[53]

Diego seemed to be very grateful for the treatment he received at Sicuani. He wrote to the Viceroy on January 29, 1782, that he had done everything to show his sincerity and had surrendered his arms. He had ratified the treaty and promised to be a most faithful servant, even to shed his blood if necessary, but he realized that his new life and happiness depended entirely upon the executive's wishes.[54]

Meanwhile, Melchor Laura started a new uprising in Chucuito, but was unsuccessful. On February 4, the Indians of Pomara handed him over to the Spaniards. When Commandant Arias asked Laura whether he had received notice of the general pardon, he said he had, but the love he professed for Túpac Amaru and his desire to conquer the province for him did not permit him to accept it.[55] For a wonder, the royalists did not hold this attempted revolt against Diego.

In February and March, 1782, a number of priests and Corregidor Salcedo reported the good results of the pardon. They said that the Indians were happy to return to their towns, that priests were well received, and that the natives took part in church services. Father Valdés reported that in Tungasuca the people had obtained possession of their houses and lands, had elected their officials, and that there was great calmness everywhere.

[53] Carta de Diego Xal, Túpac Amaru á Agustín Jáuregui, Sicuani, January 29, 1782. M.S. copy in B. L.

[54] AGN, Buenos Aires, Criminales, Leg. 21, in Lewin, *op. cit.*, 400.

[55] Carta de Salcedo á Juan Manuel de Moscoso y Peralta, Pitamarca, February 26, 1782; Carta de Dr. Antonio de Valdés al obispo del Cuzco, Checacupe, February 26, 1782; Carta de Juan Manuel obispo del Cuzco á Agustín de Jáuregui, Cuzco, March 4, 1782; Carta de Josef del Valle á Agustín de Jáuregui, Sicuani, March 2, 1782; Carta de Josef del Valle á virrey, Agustín de Jáuregui, Cuzco, August 8, 1781. MS copies in B. L.

Diego Túpac Amaru seemed to live an exemplary life. When he desired to resume his dead brother's government because he had always been accustomed to command, Del Valle pointed out the danger and advised him to forego public affairs completely, and Diego gave up the idea. He accompanied Valdés and Salcedo to Combapata, about which they were anxious because of rumors of Indian disturbances. After the Indians had come to mass and chosen their caciques and officers, Diego persuaded them to return the booty collected in the early stages of the revolt. The three men then journeyed to Checacupe, where the people had haughtily refused pardon in order to prolong their robberies. There, and also in Pitamarca, Diego helped to restore peace.[56]

Meanwhile, Andrés Mendagure, who had remained in Azángaro, went to Sicuani on March 1 and presented himself to Del Valle. As he seemed to be very repentant, Father José Gallegos absolved him from excommunication. Then he took an oath of fidelity. Mendagure explained that he was unable to bring his grandmother, Marcela Puyocagua, on account of her age and illness. Neither could he bring the three cannons because they were so heavy that the strongest mules could not carry them. He had ordered, however, that the twenty guns which he still had and all others in possession of the Indians should be brought as soon as possible. Del Valle then sent for mules from Cuzco to go into the Lake Titicaca Basin to bring the cannons and arms mentioned.

The country was rapidly being calmed. Even the provinces of Lampa, Azángaro, and Carabaya were quiet. Suspicion, too, seemed to slumber. When Mariano Túpac Amaru asked Del Valle's permission to go to Azángaro on business, the request was granted. Afterwards it was reported that he went in another direction.[57]

After the general pardon, the authorities freed Juan Bautista Túpac Amaru and permitted him to return to his home. He was so weak from his long imprisonment in Cuzco that he could scarcely walk the fourteen leagues from there to his home. His life was

---

[56] Carta de Josef del Valle á Agustín de Jáuregui, Sicuani, March 1, 1782; Carta de Josef del Valle á Agustín de Jáuregui, Sicuani, March 2, 1782. MS copies in B. L.

[57] Loayza, *op. cit.*, Serie I, Vol. I, 28–29.

hard now because he had lost all his possessions. For a year he and his wife struggled to find enough to eat and to clothe themselves. They were regarded with contempt in spite of the security that King Charles III had promised. The corregidor of Urcos humiliated the family and inflicted new cruelties upon the Indians.[58]

Some individuals distrusted Diego Túpac Amaru and his nephews even after they had received pardon. The day following the preliminary signing of the peace treaty the corregidores of Lampa, Chucuito, and Azángaro had sent Commandant Arias a letter demanding the arrest of the Inca during his stay in the royalist camp, since they thought that his repentance was not genuine and that his followers despised the pardon.[59] Next day Arias told the corregidores that he could not proceed violently against Diego, his nephews, or the natives because of the orders from the Viceroy and the Inspector General. Later, however, in a letter of February 13, 1782, Arias indicated that he wanted to take vengeance upon the Inca's followers.[60]

Then, on March 14, 1782, a lampoon appeared on the corner of the Episcopal Palace in La Paz. When it was taken to Commandant Segurola, he found it hard to read because it was badly written with poor ink. It seemed to be a notice to summon the Indians, and was signed Andrés Túpac Amaru, but the Inspector General did not think that Andrés or Diego Túpac Amaru or any of the family had anything to do with it.[61]

The faithful Indian Chuquicallata became suspicious of Diego no doubt because he was prejudiced against him. He said that in October of 1781, Diego had issued a proclamation commanding all males above seven years of age to arm, put themselves under his command, and make ready for war. In November he had sent out new summons for the Indians to make another attack on La Paz

[58] Oficio de los corregidores de Chucuito, Lampa, y Azángaro de 12 de Diciembre de 1781, pidiendo la detención de Diego Cristóbal Túpac Amaru, AGN, Buenos Aires, VI–XVI–9–12, in Lewin, *op. cit.,* 483.

[59] AGN, Buenos Aires, VI–XVI–9–12, *ibid.,* 398.

[60] Carta de Josef del Valle á Agustín de Jáuregui, Sicuani, March 12, 1782; Testimonio de Ramón de Arias dirigido á Josef del Valle, La Paz, February 14, 1782. MS copies in B. L.

[61] Carta de Diego Chuquicallota á Agustín de Jáuregui, Cuzco, February 18, 1782. MS copy in B. L.

and to destroy the troops coming from Buenos Aires under Rese-guín. Afterwards he intended to go to Cuzco. Meantime, he was writing deceitful letters asking pardon, but was acting with the same despotism as before. Chuquicallata said that at the beginning of January, 1782, five or six mules loaded with trunks containing treasure arrived at Diego's house in Azángaro. A few days before January 21, when he started for Sicuani to ask pardon, Diego summoned him and told him that there was nothing with which to pay him in those trunks. Chuquicallata was to accompany Diego to Sicuani and then return to Azángaro with the Inca's wife. She was to give him a chest full of wrought silver in Santa Rosa, but he received only a few coins. Because of these incidents Chuquicallata could not be convinced that Diego had accepted pardon in good faith.[62]

A certain inhabitant of Cuzco, whose name is unknown, wrote a minister in Madrid that the former rebel had been treated too leniently. He reported that the Inca had appointed the most rebellious Indians to the caciqueships, among them Juan Antonio Camaque, who, as chief justice of Pichigua, Yauri, and Coporaque, had instigated many robberies in those places. The hacendados complained to the president of Charcas, who asked Corregidor Salcedo of Tinta to have Camaque removed and arrested. Del Valle, however, had confidence in Diego and took him along to La Paz, which greatly increased his pride. The writer declared that on one occasion Diego had claimed to be the true Túpac Amaru and had asked who Areche was to deprive him of his legitimate title.

During the rebellion Diego had married Manuela Titu Condori, an Indian woman in Azángaro, although he was still under excommunication. The clergy excused this defect; and it was reported that Del Valle, his major general, Joaquín Valcárcel, and Salcedo crowned themselves with flowers and danced *cashicas* (country dances) in the public plaza of Sicuani with the couple. The In-

[62] Copia de carta escrita á un Sor. ministro de Madrid por un vecino del Cuzco, Cuzco, September 1, 1782, signed "B. L. M." MS copy in B. L. Markham, *Travels in Peru and India,* 164.

spector General paid respect to Diego's wife as to a lady of great merit. After Cecilia, Diego's sister who had been in the royal prison, was freed by the pardon, the Bishop and Del Valle seated her at the table in a place higher than that of the dean of the cathedral. This was a bad mistake which a pure-blood European could not overlook.

When Diego's wife gave birth to a son, Salcedo permitted a salute of twenty-four cannons to be made in her honor by the artillery of the fort at Sicuani and presented her with a costly gift. The same Salcedo carefully delayed the child's baptism until November 4, so as to name him Carlos after the King and himself since he was the godfather. When the child died a few days later, the corregidor showed the tenderest sentiments and arranged for him to be buried in the church of Sicuani.

This same Cuzco citizen complained that Del Valle even incorporated Diego and Mariano Túpac Amaru into his army. In August, 1782, he entered Cuzco with his army, with the two Incas marching in it. This was shortly after the Inspector General had forced Diego to witness the execution of his old friends, Vilca Apasa and Calisaya. The Cuzco citizen also said that Diego was so proud and insolent that he excited the anger of the greater part of the people. He rode on a well-caparisoned horse, wore the uniform of a colonel, and was very close to Del Valle and the cabildo members of the city.

When the Inspector General died in Cuzco on September 4, 1782, Diego lost a good friend, the command devolving upon General Avilés.

The fact that Diego and his nephews had been given the greatest freedom at Sicuani, led to suspicion that they were plotting new revolts. It was reported that Diego held nocturnal juntas with persons of questionable character in the home of Dr. Ysunsa. On August 26, Diego provided the money for great honor to be accorded in the convent to José Gabriel Túpac Amaru, which was strictly against the law for a person as infamous as the Inca leader —indeed, against the law to the fourth generation descended from the Inca.

373

It was also believed that Diego was hoarding money. He was said to have exchanged for stamped silver 20,000 pesos in gold gained from his robberies. After his surrender he gave the Bishop a flock of sheep with five hundred lambs, the greater part of which had been stolen in the provinces of the Collao. To avoid any appearance of evil, the prelate handed the gift over to the royal treasury. Since the Inca refused to reveal the hiding place of his brother's treasure, it looked as though he had disposed of it.

Certain Spaniards thought that Diego's nephews had too many privileges. They did not like it when Andrés Mendagure (Túpac Amaru) was entertained in the Episcopal Palace at Cuzco. No church authority seemed to remember that his father, Pedro Mendagure, had been executed at the time of José Gabriel Túpac Amaru's death and was buried in a criminal's grave. Andrés succeeded in getting the Bishop to allow him to move his father's remains to a vault in the church used for dignitaries. In August, Mariano Túpac Amaru wanted to marry a chola, who was forthwith sent to a convent in Cuzco. Aided by friends, with drawn saber, on September 9, Mariano rescued her from the cloister, but was not censured or punished.[63]

All these charges reveal the prejudice of some people against the Túpac Amaru family. They also indicate that the attitude of the authorities had changed markedly after Del Valle's death.[64] According to Sir Clements Markham, Diego was permitted to retire to Tungasuca, while Mariano and Andrés resided at Sicuani. Cánovas del Castillo, on the other hand, says that Diego remained in Cuzco but did nothing to check the fickleness and forays of his nephews, so the three men were ordered to go to Lima. The two young men obeyed and entered the College of Caciques to receive instruction, but Diego obstinately refused and went to places which caused suspicion.[65]

It seems obvious that the Spaniards never intended to deal

---

[63] Valcárcel, *Rebeliones indígenes*, 131.

[64] Markham, *Travels in Peru and India*, 166; Cánovas del Castillo, *op. cit.*, V, 465; Lorente, *Historia del Peru bajo los Borbones*, 208–209; Del Solar, *op. cit.*, 108–109.

[65] Markham, *Travels in Peru and India*, 165; Del Solar, *op. cit.*, 110.

fairly with the Incas, and were only looking for an excuse to get rid of the whole family. A pretext was soon found in an uprising of the Indians at Marcapata and Lauramarca in January, 1783. The corregidor of Quispicanchis, Ramundo Necochea, reported a suspicious junta on the heights of Marcapata. When a Spanish force under Necochea approached, the Indians withdrew to the lofty heights of Hapo and Ampatuni. In February, their leader, Santos Huayhua, was finally captured with his family and was torn to pieces by horses.[66]

Miguel Bastidas, imprisoned earlier, was ordered (January 28) to be sent to Spain. Evidently he did not go at that time, for on March 17 another decree demanded compliance with the former order. He was told to sail for Spain with his wife and small son on the frigate *La Venus*. Whether he went or not is unknown, for there is no further trace of him.[67]

The Viceroy of Buenos Aires also received alarming news from Peru concerning Inca plots. General Avilés, Bishop Moscoso, and various priests verified these reports, and a plot was reported near Lima. All things taken together seemed to prove that Diego had violated his pardon. Viceroy Jáuregui of Peru believed he had sufficient evidence to arrest him.

The corregidor of Quispicanchis dealt treacherously with Diego while pretending friendship for him. Appearing unexpectedly at his home on March 14, 1783, he refused Diego's invitation to dine, saying that he wanted to take him to see a glutton in the neighborhood. Diego was unsuspicious and went along with his visitor, who arrested him and on April 15 imprisoned him in Sicuani, at the same time that the insurgents of Marcapata and other persons were apprehended. In the same manner the corregidor arrested Diego's mother, Marcela Castro. He also arrested Cecilia Túpac Amaru in

[66] AGN, Buenos Aires, Criminales Leg. 20, exp. 15, in Lewin, *op. cit.*, 343.

[67] Lorente, *Historia del Peru bajo los Borbones*, 209; Markham, *Travels in Peru and India*, 165; Del Solar, *op. cit.*, 109; Oficio del comandante D. Gabriel de Avilés al corregidor de Azángaro, Cuzco, March 14, 1783, in Odriozola, *Documentos*, I, 267; Angelis, *Documentos*, 174–75; Oficio de D. Gabriel de Avilés al D. Sebastián de Segurola, Cuzco, March 31, 1783, in *Odriozola, Documentos*, I, 270; Angelis, *Documentos*, 179; Valcárcel, *La rebelión de Túpac Amaru*, 159–60; Loayza, *Cuarenta años de cautiverio, op. cit.*, Serie I, Vol. I, 31–34.

Sicuani and Mariano and Fernando Túpac Amaru and Andrés Mendagure in Lima. One hundred people, among them sixty-three of the immediate Túpac Amaru family, were arrested without the least resistance. Mariano and Andrés were confined to prison in Lima, where their case was entrusted to one of the leading judges of the audiencia. Viceroy Jáuregui ordered that all the kingdom be notified of the arrests. General Avilés reported that in some provinces dissatisfaction was shown on account of them, but no new uprisings occurred.[68]

The charges brought against the prisoners were trifling, and evidence to support them was lacking. Diego was accused of being deceitful, of corresponding with the natives, of giving them titles of governor and chief justice, and of urging them to keep the land they had taken. Further, he called the Indians his sons, and they treated him like an Inca governor and father. It was said that he had concealed arms and funds, that he wanted to keep his ancestral name, Túpac Amaru, that he lived in a manner unbecoming to a pardoned rebel, and that he had conducted funeral rites for his brother.

Mariano was charged with rescuing his lady-love from the nunnery of Santa Clara. Andrés Mendagure was accused of conducting himself in a suspicious manner, and Diego's mother of prolonging dissatisfaction among the Indians. Lorenzo and Simón Condori, brothers-in-law of Diego, were charged with aiding the rebels in Marcapata and with carrying Mariano's banner as messengers. Certain other members of the family were accused only of being Diego's relatives.[69]

Viceroy Jáuregui tried to justify the arrests. He said that the fear of past calamities and the need to protect the worship of God and fidelity to the King had finally obliged him to arrest the Túpac Amaru family. He believed they had evil designs and had abused

[68] Copia del Bando original de Agustín de Jáuregui, virrey del Peru, Lima, March 29, 1783, in Odriozola, Documentos, I, 271–73; Angelis, Documentos, 180–83; Sentencia contra el reo Diego Cristóbal Túpac Amaru y demás cómplices, pronunciado por Gabriel de Avilés y Señor Benito de la Mata Linares, in Odriozola, Documentos, I, 275; Angelis, Documentos, 184ff.

[69] Copia de bando original de Agustín de Jáuregui, virrey del Peru, Lima, March 29, 1783, in Odriozola, Documentos, I, 271–73.

the clemency granted them. He said that at first they seemed to repent, but many suspicions had arisen concerning them and certain influential persons clamored for the arrest of the principal members of the family. The Viceroy of Buenos Aires thought they were hiding arms; and the Bishop, the attorney-general, and other persons in that city had always doubted their loyalty.[70]

Mata Linares arrived in Cuzco from Lima on April 20. He was granted the same extraordinary judicial power as had been given to Areche, but he admitted that in regard to Diego and his family he could not find substantial misconduct that might incite a new uprising.[71]

However, one member of the family, who had escaped arrest, did start an uprising while the trial was in progress. Cacique Felipe Velasco, cousin of the Inca, took the name Túpac Inca Yupanqui and made a final effort to help his relatives through the revolt which began in Huarochirí on June 1. He declared that José Gabriel was still ruling in Gran Paytiti, a fabulous region supposed to exist to the east of the Andes. He knew perfectly well that his cousin had been executed, and no doubt used this ruse to gain a following. He appointed his principal collaborators, made Ciriaco Flores captain general, and found accomplices. He summoned the Indians, saying that God wanted them to take up arms and that he would give them a new order from the Inca. His movement, however, extended only to the towns of Ascención and Carampora. The Indians of those towns soon betrayed him; and Felipe Carrera, corregidor of Parinacocha, captured him and started for Lima.

Carrera had scarcely gone six leagues when fifteen hundred armed Indians surrounded him. They tried to rescue the prisoner and kill the official. For almost four hours the corregidor defended himself on a hill. He then broke through the enemy's line without their knowledge, returned to the town he had left, obtained rein-

---

[70] Valcárcel, *La rebelión de Túpac Amaru*, 160.

[71] Markham, *Travels in Peru and India*, 166–67; Copia de carta de Felipe Velasco Túpac Amaru á sus caciques, Ascención, May 31, 1783, in Odriozola, *Documentos*, I, 274; Angelis, *Documentos*, 183–84; Oficio de D. Felipe Carrera, corregidor de Parinacochas al virrey de Buenos Aires, Juan José de Vertíz, Santa Inéz, July 12, 1783, in Odriozola, *Documentos*, I, 281–82; Angelis, *Documentos*, 191–94; Del Solar, *op. cit.*, 112; Valcárcel, *Rebeliones indígenes*, 133–37.

377

forcements, and finally reached Lima safely with the prisoner on June 6. Carrera believed that Felipe was bolder than José Gabriel, for he even tried to stir up Lima and the near-by provinces, took measures to block the roads and bridges, and intended to put all Spaniards to death. In a short time troops from Lima pacified Huarochirí and captured sixteen more leading rebels. To prevent other revolts, they established a military government in the province, which later became an intendancy.[72]

The Viceroy took severe measures against Felipe, who was condemned to death on July 4, 1783. The Viceroy ordered that he was to be tortured only on the head in an effort to discover his accomplices. Then he would be taken from the prison in a hamper with his hands and feet tied, dragged through the streets fastened to the tail of a beast of burden, and conducted to the chief plaza, where a crier would make known his crimes. He was to be hanged and quartered; his head would be placed in an iron cage at the gate of Maravillas, and his limbs would be put up along the roads. Ciriaco Flores was to suffer the same penalty. Eight accomplices, six men and two women, after witnessing the death of Felipe and Flores, were to be passed under the gallows, given two hundred lashes, and sent to the presidios of Africa for ten years. This awful penalty was carried out on July 7, 1783.[73]

On July 17, Linares sentenced Diego Túpac Amaru. He was to be brought to the place of execution in the plaza of Cuzco in the usual manner. There he would be hanged and quartered; his body and limbs would be distributed among the towns of Tungasuca, Lauramarca, Paucartambo, and Calca; his possessions would be confiscated and his houses destroyed. His mother, Marcela Castro, was to be hanged and quartered, and her body burned in the plaza before Diego's eyes. Lorenzo and Simón Condori were to be hanged

[72] Sentencia dada por el virrey de Lima contra los reos que señala el oficio de D. Felipe Carrera, in Odriozola, Documentos, I, 284–88; Angelis, Documentos, 194–98; Valcárcel, Rebeliones indígenes, 133–37.

[73] Sentencia contra el reo Diego Cristóbal Túpac Amaru y demás cómplices, pronunciado por Gabriel de Avilés y Señor Benito de la Mata Linares, in Odriozola, Documentos, 275–80; Angelis, Documentos, 185–90; Markham, A History of Peru, 212–13; Lorente, Historia del Peru bajo los Borbones, 210; Del Solar, op. cit. 111.

378

and quartered; and Manuela Titu Condori, Diego's wife, was to be banished for life. Other relatives were to be strangled to death.

Diego was tortured before being killed by having pieces of his flesh torn off with red hot tongs. His mother's tongue was cut out because she had heard the conversation relative to the uprising of Marcapata and did not report it.

These judicial murders were committed on July 19, 1783. Father Valdés must have felt tortured, too, since he was forced to view the execution of his friends, who had trusted him and whom he had persuaded to accept the Viceroy's pardon.

Andrés and Mariano were condemned to banishment to a presidio for life. Their ultimate fate remains a mystery. It was later reported that they were placed on board a ship headed for Spain and killed at sea. When news of Andrés' fate was received, his beloved Angelina died of a broken heart.[74] However, there is a slight possibility that Andrés and Mariano escaped, since two documents found in the Archives of the Indies ask the governor of Guiana to investigate whether they were among a group of fugitives in Surinam.[75] Other refugees had fled to Surinam, and the two young men might have been among them, but nothing has ever been definitely proved. The most widely accepted belief is that Mariano died at Rio de Janeiro on his way to Spain and Andrés was drowned in a shipwreck off the coast of Portugal.[76]

A son of Diego Túpac Amaru, only eleven years old, was sent to Spain, where he shortly died a natural death.

The Viceroy tried to wipe out the whole Inca family. Even persons connected by marriage did not escape. Francisco Tadeo Díaz de Medina reported: "Neither the King nor the state thought it fitting that a seed or branch of that family should remain, or the commotion and impression that the wicked name of Túpac Amaru caused among the natives."[77] Ninety members of the famous family

[74] Torres Lanzas, *op. cit.*, primer serie, num. 256, Estado-Caracas, Leg. 8; *ibid.*, num. 258, estante 131, cajon 1, Leg. 27 (cited by Lewin, *op. cit.*, 406).

[75] Valcárcel, *Rebeliones indígenes*, 132.

[76] AGN, Buenos Aires, Criminales, Leg. 18, exp. 7, in Lewin, *op. cit.*, 341.

[77] Markham, *Travels in Peru and India*, 167–68; Markham, *A History of Peru*, 213; Loayza, *Martires y heroinas, op. cit.*, Serie I, Vol. IX, 20 n.; *ibid.*, Serie I, Vol. I, 34–40.

were therefore taken to Lima in chains. Their conductor, Juan González, refused to give them water or food for two or three days so that they suffered untold misery in the forty days it took to reach Lima. Among them were Bartolomé Túpac Amaru, great-uncle of the Inca; Marcela Pollocahua, his mother-in-law; Manuela Titu Condori, Diego's wife; Pedro Venero and his wife; and Bartola Escobedo, sister of José Gabriel Túpac Amaru. The first was an aged prince who had led a life of great activity and temperance. The horrors of prison life in Lima finally killed him at the unusual age of 125.

From Callao the unfortunate survivors sailed in two ships, *El Peruana* and the *San Pedro*, to Cádiz. They were treated so cruelly on the voyage that half of them died before reaching Rio de Janeiro. Food was so scarce that they were always hungry; and only once during the two months did Captain José Córdova let them wash their tattered clothes. He treated them like dogs and did not remove their fetters, although he had promised to do so.[78]

Among the prisoners were Juan Bautista Túpac Amaru and his wife, Susana Guerra. He had been whipped through the streets of Cuzco in 1781, saved in the general pardon, and sentenced again in 1783 to six years of exile. He had to travel first from Huamanga to Cuzco and then from there to Lima. Only one Indian of the six thousand whom he saw on the way showed any kindness. This one recognized him and presented him with a horse. This gift freed him from the suffering which his companions could hardly bear. On the first part of the journey the Inca's mother died from thirst because the merciless guards refused to give her water.

Juan Bautista entered Lima in November, 1783, and was imprisoned there for five months until he boarded the ship that was to take him to Spain. The prisoners had to stay in Rio de Janeiro for four months because Spain and England were at war and there were no boats. In Brazil the unfortunate people were also mistreated and suffered greatly. Just before they reached Cádiz, the

[78] Loayza, *op. cit.*, Serie I, Vol. I, 34ff.; Valcárcel, *La rebelión de Túpac Amaru*, 81 n. and 168–71; Miller, *op. cit.*, I, 70; Markham, *Travels in Peru and India*, 168; Memorias relativas á la sublevación del cacique de Tungasuca, José Gabriel Túpac Amaru . . . en el año 1780. MS copy in B. L.

Inca's wife died, but he could not get near her because his chain was too short. In all, the journey from Lima to Cádiz took ten months and one day. When the boat arrived in Spain, Juan Bautista could hardly walk and had to be supported by two soldiers. In Cádiz he was imprisoned in the fortress of San Sebastián among assassins and thieves, where he remained three years and three months. King Charles III then had the Indian prisoners separated and distributed among prisons in the interior of Spain; many remained there until they died.

Juan Bautista was sent to Ceuta to live in the home of a silversmith, where he suffered greatly. He appealed to the authorities to let him live alone. His plea was granted, but he found it difficult to live. He cultivated a small orchard, and in the thirtieth year of his banishment became acquainted with Marcos Durán Martel, an Augustinian friar who had been exiled in 1812 for taking part in a revolt in Huánuco led by Crespo y Castillo. The friar helped the Inca work the land and took care of his health. In the 1820 revolution in Spain, the surviving Americans imprisoned there for political crimes were finally freed. Juan Bautista and the friar then went to Algeciras, obtained money, and arrived in Buenos Aires in August, 1822, after traveling for seventy days. The Inca's banishment had lasted forty years; he was now eighty years old. A friend obtained government support for him. He received a pension of thirty pesos a month and a house to live in for the rest of his life on condition that he write his memoirs, which he did. He lived in Argentina until he died, on September 2, 1827, at the age of eighty-five. Pedro de Angelis considered him an impostor who wanted to obtain a pension from the Argentine government, but Loayza says that Angelis is wrong, that Juan Bautista was the son of Ventura Monjaras and Miguel Túpac Amaru and therefore the last survivor of the Inca dynasty.[79]

Fernando, the youngest son of José Gabriel Túpac Amaru, attended the College of Caciques and Noble Indians in Lima for

[79] Del Solar, *op. cit.*, 105; Carta de Fernando Túpac Amaru al rey, Castillo de Santa Catalina, September 7, 1787, AGN, Leg. 1049, Audiencia de Lima, in Loayza, *op. cit.*, Series I, Vol. I, 72–75.

a short time until Areche took him to Spain,[80] where he was imprisoned in the castle of San Sebastián at Cádiz for four years. Luis Ocampo, a citizen of Cuzco, in 1783 managed to get into the fort somehow, perhaps by bribing the guards, and talked with Fernando through the iron grating of his cell. He learned that the government allowed him six reales a day for maintenance and that the soldiers guarding him stole half of it. Ocampo therefore gave the boy the equivalent of three dollars a week during his visit in Cádiz.

In September, 1787, Fernando wrote to the King and implored mercy. He said that he had been declared a criminal because he happened to be the son of José Gabriel Túpac Amaru. The letter showed that the boy was intelligent and extraordinarily precocious. A year afterwards, when the prisoners were scattered in different cities of Spain, Fernando, who now received a pension from the state, entered the College of Pia de Getafe. The last notice of him is a medical certificate dated June 15, 1798, issued by a certified doctor, Francisco Rivas y Peralta, to the effect that Fernando was suffering from melancholia. He was so poor that he could not afford to buy medicine. He died shortly at the age of twenty-six.

In 1828, a person who called himself Fernando Túpac Amaru appeared in Buenos Aires and from there journeyed to Lima. He became a monk at San Pedro, where he died, but he was an imposter.

It is obvious that the royal court wanted to rid Peru of the Túpac Amaru family in order to destroy the root of dangerous uprisings. The pardon was extended to them to get them to lay down their arms. They accepted in good faith the assurances of the Viceroy, high military authorities, and the Bishop that this pardon would protect them and their families, and they kept their promises to serve the King. Apparently they did not foresee that after the death of Del Valle charges would be brought against them by

[80] Memorandum escrito en el Cuzco, Februaro 15 de 1835, Valle de Paucartambo, August 5, 1835. MS copy in B. L. Valcárcel, *La rebelión de Túpac Amaru*, 168; Markham, *A History of Peru*, 213–14; Mendiburu, *Diccionario*, VIII, 144.

distrustful and hostile persons determined to ruin them. It was to the detriment of Peru and of Spain that these people, descended from the splendid culture of the Incas, who were patient, long suffering, and remarkably industrious, were killed and exiled. The qualities which they possessed would have made them excellent citizens under an enlightened government and would have added strength to the nation.

CHAPTER XVI

Aftermath of Rebellion

THE EXTENT AND DURATION of the Inca revolt aroused the Spanish authorities, and they dealt severely with everybody connected with it. No one directly or indirectly involved—neither Spanish officials nor churchmen—escaped censure.

Even Bishop Moscoso of Cuzco felt the force of Spanish wrath. Although he had assisted the government and was a member of the junta in which Areche pronounced sentence on José Gabriel Túpac Amaru, he was nevertheless accused of sympathy for the Inca. In all, twenty-two charges were brought against him. He was accused of protecting the Indians, of laying the ban of the church on a priest for betraying the natives' confidences given under the seal of the confession, and of trying to save the lives of a number of Indian rebels. Even worse, he had asked for a general pardon after the Inca's death and had permitted Mariano Túpac Amaru to conduct funeral rites for his father. The Bishop was obliged to go to Lima to give account of his conduct, and he answered the charges in detail in a work published later in Madrid. The King imposed upon him perpetual silence concerning matters in Peru, but appointed him archbishop of Granada because of his services to the crown.

Visitador Areche also was removed from his position and was summoned to Spain in 1782.[1] The King deprived him of his honors and income, for provoking the insurgents by his exactions and severity. The charges against Areche were many. Inspector General del Valle before his death had complained of Areche's inefficiency in conducting military operations against the Incas. The

[1] Sentencia dada contra el visitador Don José Antonio de Areche en la que este dío en la causa del alazamiento de los Túpac Amaru el año de 1781 en el Cuzco, August 27, 1789. MS copy in B. L. See also Lorente, *Historia del Peru bajo los Borbones*, 211; Markham, *Travels in Peru and India*, 164.

Visitador did not furnish aid to him or provide sufficient supplies for the troops. Money was always lacking. For example, when Francisco Celorio was sustaining the second siege of Paucartambo for seventeen days against Diego Tupac Amaru, he had to get money from his friends to support his troops. Del Valle's predecessor, General Aviles, had lacked money for the Cuzco garrison and had had to summon a junta to urge the inhabitants to supply necessary funds. Areche gave neither the women of Langui, who helped to capture José Gabriel Túpac Amaru, nor the officials of the Cochabamba troop, who took the rebels Paruma and Bermúdez, the promised rewards. Mules lost in the campaign were not paid for. Further, reported Del Valle, Areche had tried to weaken his military command during his absence and to impose upon the Indians the diezmos, which they had never paid before. The Visitador was also accused of sending to the cabildo of Cuzco a plan for exacting taxes on maize, meat, coca, sugar, and other articles, and of ordering the cabildo to try certain inhabitants who dared to protest. Such actions naturally caused dissatisfaction.[2]

At Areche's trial his judges found him guilty of misconduct, malicious, lacking in the propriety which the laws demanded, and no longer fit to serve the King. They pronounced a number of his charges against Viceroy Guirior false and suggested that he should make recompense for the injuries he had inflicted upon the former viceroy. Fourteen men who were judged to have sworn falsely against Guirior were fined 10,000 pesos each and practically ruined. The King fined Areche one-third of his salary as a member of the Council of the Indies, 200,000 pesos, refused to grant the audience he asked, and ordered him to withdraw twenty leagues from the royal palace. This harsh sentence implied that he was among the persons held responsible for the Inca rebellion.

The case was considered closed in 1789. Areche, nevertheless, tried three times after that to have the charges against him revoked.

---

[2] El mariscal del campo D. José del Valle escribió y firmó en Cuzco en 30 de Sete. de 1781 un manifesto que no sé si se imprimió y que acredita el desacuerdo y enmistad en que se hallaba con el visitador Areche. MS copy in B. L.

On two occasions the audiencia denied him the right to reopen the case; however, the King showed more leniency than the judges and finally permitted a fourth appeal.

Areche was not without support. The Duke of Alcudia believed that he had been following orders in giving the confidential information about Viceroy Guirior, that he had proceeded officially, and that he had not criticized conditions in Peru more severely than other visitadors had. The Duke said that viceroys and visitadors never got along well, and no doubt many falsehoods were told about Areche. The governor of the Council of the Indies and Léon Pizarro also defended the deposed visitador.

After five years, certain members of the Council of the Indies advised the King to permit Areche to enter the royal service again.[3] Guirior's widow said that she held no grudge against Areche, that she had wanted only to vindicate her husband's honor.[4]

Areche asked to be granted a position in which he might serve the King again. The sovereign submitted the petition to the Council of the Indies with instructions to take whatever action it thought best. That body finally recommended that banishment be rescinded and Areche be restored to his position or given another.[5] Areche was restored to royal favor, but he never returned to the New World.

The last Inca revolt was not in vain, even though the Indians were defeated. Important reforms were made on account of it.

[3] Consulta del consejo á su Majestad, sobre Areche, Acompaña la repuesta fiscal, Madrid, May 23, 1794, and February 6, 1794, num. 4 and 5, AGI, 111-1-8, Audiencia de Lima; Cargos formados á el virrey que fue del Peru Don Manuel Guirior conforme á la instrución dada por el visitador Don Josef Areche, que el consejo ha estimado por falsos, December 28, 1787, and January 14, 1788, AGI, 111-1-8, Audiencia de Lima. For the charges against Guirior and a discussion of them, see El consejo de Indias en el pleno de tres salas, Madrid, April 1, 1789, AGI, 111-1-8, Audiencia de Lima; Sentencia dada contra el visitador Don José Antonio Areche en la que este dió en la causa del alzamiento de los Túpac Amarus el año 1781 en el Cuzco, August 27, 1789; Acaecimientos sucedidos al mismo Areche después de la sentencia dada por el consejo. Copies of the above MSS in B. L.

[4] Carta de Josef Antonio de Areche al Señor Pedro Acuña, Bilboa, July 28, 1792, AGI, 111-1-8, Audiencia de Lima. MS copy in B. L.

[5] Carta de Don Pedro de Acuña al Señor marqués de Bejamar, San Ildefonso, September 7, 1793, AGI, 111-1-8, Audiencia de Lima; Carta de Silvestre Collar al Señor Don Pedro de Acuña, Madrid, October 15, 1793, AGI, 111-1-8, Audiencia de Lima. MS copies in B. L.

For example, during the insurrection the hated repartimientos were abolished and the Indians relieved from the payment of tribute for one year provided they returned to their homes. The Viceroy did not think that this measure would injure the treasury because more revenue could be obtained if the rebels were working.[6] Areche had not favored this provision, for he believed it would have a more harmful effect on the faithful Indians than any good will it might engender in the rebels. The former would realize that they were excused from paying tribute on account of the uprising and that it would be collected from them if the rebellion did not continue. Areche believed that it would have been better to impose tribute upon the rebels and give the peaceful Indians money to build their houses and re-establish their industries.[7]

Because of the revolt Viceroy Jáuregui recommended fair treatment for the natives, equal justice, and more moderate demands on labor. As a result, the mita was modified so that workers were sent only to the mines and to cultivate the fields.[8] Service in the mines was also subject to restrictions. Only a specified number of Indian laborers, not to exceed one-seventh of the inhabitants, might be taken from any one place and could be retained in the mines only for six months. As the workers received four reales a day, they were not likely to be transported from the warm lowland climate to the cold mountain regions. The natives might now be employed in occupations that contributed more directly to the welfare of society, such as raising grain and cattle and constructing bridges, roads, and edifices for public use.[9]

Areche's successor as visitador general, Jorge Escobedo y Alarcón, a councilor of the Indies, found the Peruvian treasury empty and faced with huge debts. He also found a scarcity of food. He advised re-establishment of the repartimientos under the *consulado* in order to raise money, reporting that while the hostility

[6] Carta de Agustín de Jáuregui á José Antonio de Areche, Lima, September 7, 1781, MS copy in B. L. Bando de Jáuregui, September 12, 1781, in Angelis, *Documentos*, 111–12.

[7] Carta de Josef Antonio de Areche al virrey Agustín de Jáuregui, Lima, September 7, 1781. MS copy in B. L.

[8] Markham, *A History of Peru*, 215.

[9] Moses, *op. cit.*, 217.

between classes and races had not decreased, the Indians did show an exaggerated humility and seemed sincerely religious. The King wisely did not accept his recommendation.[10]

Some of the reforms for which Túpac Amaru had given his life were inaugurated under Teodoro de Croix, Jáuregui's successor as viceroy. Croix immediately undertook to establish the intendant system in Peru and Chile in 1785, and thereby did away with the hated corregidores. Eight intendancies, headed by intendants, were created in Peru and divided into fifty-seven districts or *partidos,* over which sub-delegates were placed. Other intendancies were established in the viceroyalty of La Plata.[11]

The new intendants, or governors, were expected to improve conditions for the Indians in the war-ravaged provinces. They were to do everything possible to promote peace and prosperity and to keep the natives satisfied. They were to see that justice was administered for the good of the people and that local officials did not tyrannize over them as the corregidores and alcaldes had done. Part of their task was to supervise all construction work in the towns, to inspect their intendancies frequently to discover how they might promote agriculture, industry, commerce, and mining, and to check corruption of any kind. The King ordered them to observe the proceedings of municipal juntas of finance to prevent abuses, to regulate currency, and to see that no dishonesty arose in tribute collection or in making tax lists. In fact, the department of finance was their special and most urgent care. Most of the reforms along other lines were expected to come by more efficient tax collection; through it colonial administration was to be invigorated and great benefits brought to all the people. Under such a reform system as the intendancies the Indians no longer suffered the abuses endured before Túpac Amaru's revolt.[12]

10 Valcárcel, *La rebelión de Tupac Amaru,* 174–75.

11 Lillian Estelle Fisher, "Teodoro de Croix," *Hispanic American Historical Review,* Vol. IX, No. 4 (November, 1929), 491–92. Twelve intendancies and three provinces were established in New Spain in 1786.

12 For the reforms under the intendancies see Lillian Estelle Fisher, *The Intendant System in Spanish America,* 33–65; *Real ordenanza para el establecimiento é introducción de intendentes de ejército y provincia en el virreinato de Buenos Aires.*

The new governors were generally higher types of men than the corregidores had been. Men like Ignacio Flores and Sebastián de Segurola were appointed intendants, the latter in La Paz, which he had defended so bravely.[13] The Indians found no fault with them.

The intendant system, however, did not prove to be as successful as was expected, for abuses gradually crept into the administration again. After the system had been tried for several years, the very man who had inaugurated it in Peru denounced it. Some progress occurred, yet there was nowhere visible any appreciation of the need of evolving self-government or greater well-being through an evolutionary process of placing responsibility upon the colonial himself.

An audiencia in Cuzco, another of Túpac Amaru's goals, also became a reality. In 1787, Viceroy Croix established this audiencia, which served as a court of appeals for the natives. The first regent, José de la Portilla, a judge from Lima, arrived at Cuzco, in June, 1787. When a tribunal of accounts was also located there, Cuzco, the old capital of the Inca Empire, was thus fittingly honored for the many insults suffered so long.[14] Croix also caused the Acobamba and Vitoc valleys to be repopulated and tried to wipe out the effects of the revolt in those regions.[15]

Peru was aided economically by the regulation for free trade. As the beneficial measure, an important reform of King Charles III in 1778, had not yet been put into effect in Peru when Viceroy Croix arrived, he was commissioned to inaugurate the reform. He was a great champion of free trade and intervened when anything interfered with it.[16]

Free trade soon proved to be profitable to Peru. During the five years of Croix's administration exports amounted to 36,000,000 crowns and imports to 42,000,000. The revenues of the country averaged 4,500,000 crowns. Surprisingly, expenditures did not ex-

[13] Relación de los hechos mas notables acaecidos en la sublevación general . . . , 229–30. MS copy in B. L.
[14] *Memorias de los virreyes que han gobernado el Peru*, V, 73–74.
[15] *Ibid.*, V, 165–71.
[16] *Ibid.*, V, 146–51.

ceed this amount; thus for the first time in a number of years the budget was balanced.[17]

Without doubt Croix was an able administrator, who helped Peru recover from the disastrous Inca revolt. If there had been such a just executive before the insurrection, it might have been prevented and thousands of lives spared. Croix was determined to correct abuses; therefore he made subordinate officials perform their duties properly. He removed from office Francisco Hurtado, an intendant who had committed abuses. He did the same with Gonzáles, the military governor of the island of Juan Fernández because he had aided an American boat from Boston with Gray and Kendrick on board. Even ecclesiastics did not escape his watchfulness. He removed Gaspar de Ugarte from the province of Jauja, José de Hoya from Tarma, and Pedro Escobar from Huarochirí because they tyrannized over their Indian parishioners and did not instruct them sufficiently in the faith.[18]

All together, the Inca revolt thoroughly alarmed the Spaniards. As a result, certain badly needed reforms were inaugurated at last, making it possible for Spain to hold its vast American possessions for another half-century. The energetic Viceroy Croix and the wise reforms of King Charles III did much to remove the worst abuses in Peru. The social and economic life of the Indians changed after the rebellion. The mining enterprises of Upper Peru were gradually abandoned, not to be revived until the nineteenth century, but the yield had been dwindling before the revolt. The insurrection hastened the disintegration of the labor service and thus created a situation favorable to the later wars for independence. In spite of reforms, it did not take much urging later on by the Creoles, who had also been dissatisfied with the political, economic, and social regime, to turn the Indians into champions of the movement for independence.

[17] Charles François Croix, *Correspondance du marquis de Croix, capitaine general des armés de S. M. C., viceroi du Méxique,* 249–50.

[18] Fisher, "Teodoro de Croix." *Hispanic American Historical Review,* Vol. IX, No. 4 (November 1929), 439–500.

Bibliography

Unfortunately, the person who copied the manuscripts in the National Library and the National Archives of Peru omitted the *expediente* and *legajo* numbers. Because of a fire in the National Library of Lima in 1943, many of the original manuscripts have been lost; therefore it has been impossible for the author to obtain these numbers. Copies of the manuscripts from Peru and of the Areche papers from Spain used in this work are in the Bancroft Library of the University of California. The Areche papers were copied for the Bancroft Library by the late Arthur Aiton from the originals in the Archives of the Indies at Seville, while the old *expediente* and *legajo* numbers were still used.

In this listing, the abbreviation AGI is used for Archivo General de Indies, IGN for Archivo General de la Nación, and B. L. for Bancroft Library.

I. Manuscripts

Acuña, Pedro de
    Carta de Don Pedro de Acuña al Señor marqués de Bejamar. San Ildefonso, September 7, 1793, AGI, 111–1–8. Audiencia de Lima.

Apasa, Julián
    Causa criminal de Julián Apasa, alias Túpac Catari. Sanctuario de Nuestra Señor de las Peñas, November 14, 1781.

Areche, Josef Antonio de
    Acaecimientos sucedidos al mismo Areche después de la sentencia dada por el consejo.

    Cargos formados á el virrey que fue del Peru Don Manuel Guirior conforme a la instrucción dada por el visitador Don Josef Areche, que el consejo ha estimado por falsos. December 28, 1787, and January 14, 1788, AGI, 111–1–8. Audiencia de Lima.

    Carta de Don Josef Antonio de Areche á Agustín de Jáuregui. Lima, January 2, 1782, num. 383, AGI, 111–1–8. Audiencia de Lima.

Carta de Don Josef Antonio de Areche á Don Fernando Márquez de la Plata. Lima, February 1, 1783, AGI, 111–1–8. Audiencia de Lima.

Carta de Don Josef Antonio de Areche á Don Josef de Gálvez. Lima, February 5, 1783, num. 485, AGI, 111–1–8. Audiencia de Lima.

Carta de Josef Antonio de Areche al marqués de Sonora sobre el asunto con Guirior. Madrid, March 17, 1787, AGI, 111–1–8. Audiencia de Lima.

Carta de Josef Antonio de Areche al Señor Don Pedro Acuña. Bilboa, July 28, 1792, AGI, 111–1–8. Audiencia de Lima.

Carta de José Antonio de Areche al virrey Agustín de Jáuregui. Lima, September 7, 1781, AGI, 111–1–8. Audiencia de Lima.

Consulta del consejo á su Majestad, sobre Areche Acompaña la repuesta fiscal. Madrid, May 23, 1794, and February 6, 1794, numeros 4 and 5, AGI, 111–1–8. Audiencia de Lima.

Contestación de José Antonio de Areche á José Gabriel de Túpac Amaru. Cuzco, March 12, 1781, AGI, 111–1–8. Audiencia de Lima.

Representación última de José Antonio de Areche á Don Antonio Porlier. Madrid, April 7, 1789, AGI, 111–1–8. Audiencia de Lima.

Sentencia dada contra el visitador Don José Antonio de Areche en la que dió en la causa del alzamiento de los Túpac Amaros el año de 1781 en el Cuzco. August 27, 1789, AGI, 111–1–8. Audiencia de Lima.

Sentencia dada por el Sor. Visitador D. José Antonio de Areche al rebelde José Gabriel Túpac Amaru en la ciudad del Cuzco, May 15, 1781, AGI, 111–1–8. Audiencia de Lima.

Su propria defensa por Don Josef Antonio de Areche. Madrid, March 17, 1787, AGI, 111–1–8. Audiencia de Lima.

Arias, Ramón

Carta de Ramón Arias á Josef del Valle. Sepita, February 27, 1782.

Carta de Ramón Arias á Sor. Gral. Dn. Baltr. Sematnat. Campo de Río Blanco, November 23, 1781.

Testimonio de Ramón de Arias dirigido á Josef del Valle. La Paz, February 14, 1782.

Auto de la junta general de guerra. Lima, January 3, 1782.

Castilla (a fiscal)

Carta del fiscal, Castilla, al virrey. Lima, September 3, 1781.

Chuquicallata, Diego

Carta de Diego Chuquicallata á Agustín de Jáuregui. Cuzco, February 18, 1782.

Bibliography

Collar, Silvestre

    Carta de Silvestre Collar al Señor Don Pedro de Acuña. Madrid, October 15, 1793, AGI, 111–1–8. Audiencia de Lima.

Consultas del consejo de Indias. February 18, 23, and December 16, 1741, AGI, legajo 104. Audiencia de Quito.

Copia de carta escrita á un Sor. ministro de Madrid por un vecino del Cuzco. Cuzco, September 1, 1782, signed "B. L. M."

Copia de una carta escrita por un sugeto residente en Lima con referencia á las noticias que se hacen comunicado del Cuzco. Lima, December 23, 1780.

Decada 4.ª de la escena en la rebelión de José Gabriel Túpac Amaru. Cuzco, May 22, 1781.

Del Valle, Joseph

    Carta de Josef del Valle á Agustín de Jáuregui. Cuzco, November 18, 1781.

    Carta de Josef del Valle á Agustín de Jáuregui. Cuzco, November 24, 1781.

    Carta de Josef del Valle á Agustín de Jáuregui. Cuzco, December 4, 1781.

    Carta de Josef del Valle á Agustín de Jáuregui. Cuzco, December 13, 1781.

    Carta de Josef del Valle á Agustín de Jáuregui. Cuzco, December 22, 1781.

    Carta de Josef del Valle á Agustín de Jáuregui. Sicuani, January 27, 1782.

    Carta de Josef Del Valle á Augustín de Jáuregui. Sicuani, March 1, 1782.

    Carta de Josef del Valle á Agustín de Jáuregui. Sicuani, March 2, 1782.

    Carta de Josef del Valle á Agustín de Jáuregui. Sicuani, March 12, 1782.

    Carta de Josef del Valle á Diego Cristóbal Túpac Amaru. Cuzco, December 10, 1781.

    Carta de Josef del Valle á Dn. Agustín de Jáuregui. Cuzco, October 26, 1781.

    Carta de Josef del Valle al virrey Agustín de Jáuregui. Cuzco, August 8, 1781.

    Decreto de Josef del Valle. Sicuani, January 26, 1782.

    El mariscal del campo D. José del Valle escribió y firmó en el Cuzco

en 30 de Sete. de 1781 un manifesto que no sé si se imprimió y
que acredita el desacuerdo y enmistad en que se hallaba con el
visitador Areche.

Orden de Josef Antonio del Valle del pasaporte de Diego Cristóbal
Túpac Amaru. Cuzco, December 8, 1781.

Providencia de Josef del Valle. Sicuani, January 26, 1782.

El consejo de Indias en el pleno de tres salas. Madrid, April 1, 1789,
AGI, 111-1-8. Audiencia de Lima.

Flores, Ignacio

Carta de Ignacio Flores á Baltasar Sematnat. Oruro, October 25, 1781.

Carta de Ignacio Flores á Dn. Agustín Jáuregui. Oruro, December
3, 1781.

Jáuregui, Agustín de

Bando de Dn. Agustín de Jáuregui. Lima, September 3, 1781.

Bando por el Sor. Virrey Agustín de Jáuregui. Ciudad de los reyes
del Peru, December 12, 1780.

Carta de Agustín de Jáuregui á Baltasar Sematnat. Lima, December 14, 1781.

Carta de Agustín de Jáuregui á Diego Cristóbal Túpac Amaru. Lima,
January 5, 1782.

Carta de Agustín de Jáuregui á Dn. Ramón de Arias. Lima, December 11, 1781.

Carta de Agustín de Jáuregui á Francisco de Salcedo. Lima, January 5, 1782.

Carta de Agustín de Jáuregui á Francisco Suárez de Salcedo. Lima,
December 5, 1781, reservada.

Carta de Agustín de Jáuregui á José del Valle. Lima, December 6,
1781.

Carta de Agustín de Jáuregui á Josef del Valle. Lima, December 5,
1781.

Carta de Agustín de Jáuregui á Josef del Valle. Lima, December 15,
1781.

Carta de Agustín de Jáuregui á Señor Josef Reseguín. Lima, December 15, 1781.

Carta de Agustín de Jáuregui á Sor. inspr. gral. Dn. Jph. del Valle.
Lima, December 10, 1781.

Carta de Agustín de Jáuregui al obispo del Cuzco. Lima, November
30, 1781.

Carta de Agustín de Jáuregui al obispo del Cuzco. Lima, December 30, 1781.

Carta de Agustín de Jáuregui al obispo del Cuzco. Lima, January 5, 1782.

Carta de Agustín de Jáuregui al Señor inspector general Don José del Valle. Lima, January 5, 1782.

Carta de Agustín de Jáuregui al Señor obispo del Cuzco. Lima, December 15, 1781.

Carta de Agustín de Jáuregui al Sor. inspr. gral. Dn. Josef del Valle, Lima, December 1, 1781.

Carta del virrey Agustín Jáuregui á Baltazar de Sematnat. Lima, December 14, 1781.

Carta del virrey Jáuregui á Jph. del Valle. Lima, November 16, 1781.

Copia de carta de Agustín de Jáuregui á José Antonio de Areche. Lima, September 7, 1781.

La Plata, Fernando, Marqués de

Informe del alcalde de corte de la audiencia de Lima, Don Fernando, Marqués de la Plata. Lima, December 22, 1783, AGI, 111–1–9. Audiencia de Lima.

Machado, Tomás

Carta de Tomás Machado á Baltazar Sematnat. Caylloma, November 13, 1781.

Martínez, Antonio

Carta de Antonio Martínez á Juan Manuel de Moscoso y Peralta. Sicuani, November 14, 1781, num. 7.

Carta de Dr. Antonio Martínez á Diego Cristóbal Túpac Amaru. Sicuani, November 14, 1781.

Memorándum escrito en Cuzco, Febrero 15 de 1835. Valle de Paucartambo, August 5, 1835.

Memorias relativas á la sublevación del cacique de Tungasuca, José Gabriel Túpac Amaru, sus consecuensias y fin esta extraordinario suceso cuyo acaecimiento emplezó el año de 1780.

Moreno (a fiscal)

El fiscal Moreno á Don Agustín de Jáuregui. Lima, December 31, 1781.

Moscoso y Peralta, Juan Manuel

Carta de Juan Manuel obispo del Cuzco á Agustín de Jáuregui. Cuzco, December 10, 1781.

Carta de Juan Manuel obispo del Cuzco á Agustín de Jáuregui. Cuzco, December 22, 1781.

395

Carta de Juan Manuel obispo del Cuzco á Agustín de Jáuregui. Cuzco, March 4, 1782.

Carta de Juan Manuel obispo del Cuzco á Diego Túpac Amaru. Cuzco, November 17, 1781, num. 3.

Carta de Juan Manuel obispo del Cuzco á Diego Túpac Amaru. Cuzco, December 10, 1781.

Carta de Juan Manuel obispo del Cuzco á Diego Cristóbal Túpac Amaru. Cuzco, December 12, 1781.

Carta de Juan Manuel obispo del Cuzco á Francisco Rivera. Cuzco, December 21, 1781.

Carta de Juan Manuel obispo del Cuzco á los Indios de las comunidades de Azángaro, Orurillo, y Asillo. Cuzco, November 17, 1781.

Carta de Juan Ml. obispo del Cuzco á Exmo. Sor. Dn. Agustín de Jáuregui. Cuzco, November 18, 1781.

Decreto del Yltmo. Señor obispo. Sicuani, January 26, 1782.

Relación de Juan Manuel de Moscoso obispo del Cuzco. Cuzco, December 8, 1781.

Relación del obispo. Cuzco, December 10, 1781.

Palomino, Marcos

Carta de Marcos Palomino á Juan Manuel Moscoso y Peralta. Sicuani, November 14, 1781, num. 6.

Pasquines puestos en Juyjuy. 1780. AGN, Peru. MS copy in B. L.

Relación de los hechos mas notables acaecidos en la sublevación general fraguada en los reynos del Peru, por el Indio José Gabriel Túpac Amaru, gobr. del pueblo de Tungasuca en la prova. de Tinta, que asociado de otros sus saquaces, causó horrorosos estragos desde el año 1780, hasta el de 1782 en que se reprimió el orgullo de la conjuración. (This is a long, bound manuscript.)

Relación de los pasages acaedidos en esta ciudad del Cuzco con motivo de la rebelión causada por el Indio José Gabriel Túpac Amaru cacique del pueblo de Tungasuca anexo de la doctrina de Pampamarca sita en la provincia de Tinta. Cuzco, December 3, 1780.

Representación de los curas y demas religiosos en el pueblo de Azángaro. Azángaro, December 2, 1781.

Representación de los naturales del Peru al rey. December 4, 1781.

Reseguín, Josef

Carta de Josef Reseguín á Agustín Jáuregui. Sanctuario de Nra. Sa. de las Peñas, November 15, 1781.

Bibliography

Rivera, Francisco de
    Carta de Francisco de Rivera á Juan Manuel de Moscoso y Peralta.
    Sicuani, November 9, 1781, num. 5.
    Carta de Francisco de Rivera á Juan Manuel de Moscoso y Peralta.
    Azángaro, December 15, 1781, num. 2.
Salcedo, Francisco de
    Carta de Francisco de Salcedo á Juan Manuel de Moscoso y Peralta.
    Pitamarca, February 26, 1782.
Sematnat, Baltazar
    Carta de Baltazar Sematnat á Agustín de Jáuregui. Arequipa, November 26, 1781.
    Carta de Baltazar Sematnat al Exmo. Sor. Dn. Agustín de Jáuregui. Arequipa, November 23, 1781.
    Carta de Baltazar Sematnat á Ramón Arias. Arequipa, November 26, 1781.
    Carta de Baltazar Sematnat á Tomás Machado. Arequipa, November 19, 1781.
Tratado entre Túpac Amaru y Ramón de Arias. Lima, December 11, 1781.
Túpac Amaru, Diego Cristóbal
    Auto de Xal. Túpac Amaru, Azángaro, October 17, 1781.
    Carta de Diego Cristóbal Túpac Amaru á Josef del Valle. Azángaro, December 15, 1781.
    Carta de Diego Xal. Túpac Amaru á Agustín de Jáuregui. Azángaro, December 5, 1781.
    Carta de Diego Xal. Túpac Amaru á Agustín de Jáuregui. Azángaro, December 15, 1781.
    Carta de Diego Xal. Túpac Amaru á Agustín Jáuregui. Sicuani, January 29, 1782.
    Carta de Diego Xal. Túpac Amaru á Francisco de Salcedo. Azángaro, December 15, 1781.
    Carta de Diego Xal. Túpac Amaru á Fr. Rafael Ponze. Azángaro, November 14, 1781.
    Carta de Diego Xal. Túpac Amaru á Juan Manuel Moscoso y Peralta. Azángaro, December 15, 1781, num. 1.
    Carta de Diego Xal. Túpac Amaru á Juan Manuel obispo del Cuzco. Azángaro, November 29, 1781.
    Carta de Diego Xal. Túpac Amaru al obispo del Cuzco. Azángaro, November 5, 1781, num. 1.

Carta de Diego Xal. Túpac Amaru al obispo del Cuzco. Azángaro, December 5, 1781.

Carta de Diego Xal. Túpac Amaru al obispo del Cuzco. Azángaro, December 9, 1781, num. 2.

Carta de Diego Xal. Túpac Amaru al Señor Don Francisco Salcedo. Azángaro, November 13, 1781.

Carta de Diego Xal. Túpac Amaru al Señor inspector general Josef del Valle. Azángaro, November 28, 1781.

Carta de Diego Xal. Túpac Amaru á Señores curas y vicarios D. Juan de Dios Adrián, D. Manuel Salazar, D. Francisco Aragón y Ochoa, D. Vicente Otazú, y D. Juan Bautista Moran. Azángaro, November 7, 1781.

Copia de carta que responde Dn. Diego Túpac Amaru al Dor. Dn. Antonio Martínez cura de Sicuani, en repuesta de la que escribió á Andrés Guaranca colonel de Sta. Rosa encargandole se la remitiese á dho. Dn. Diego, y Dn. Mariano Túpac Amaru. Azángaro, November 6, 1781.

Memoria y razón de los S. S. curas del obispado del Cuzco á q. nes no quieren omitir las comunidades de naturales de los pueblos que se van a referir, por justas causas que ello expresan tener, Azángaro, November 6, 1781, num. 4.

Papel de Diego Túpac Amaru. Sicuani, January 26, 1782.

Túpac Amaru, José Gabriel

Bando por José Gabriel Túpac Amaru. November 29, 1780.

Carta de José Gabriel Túpac Amaru al Sor. D. D. Juan Manuel Moscoso y Peralta. Tungasuca, November 21, 1780.

Carta escrita del Inca Túpac Amaru al Illmo. obispo del Cuzco. No date.

Carta escrita por D. Gabriel Túpac Amaru al visitador D. José Antonio Areche antes de ser tomado prisionero. Tinta, March 5, 1781.

Extorto y requirimento por José Gabriel Túpac Amaru. Tungasuca, November 21 de 1780.

Valdés, Antonio de

Carta de Antonio de Valdés al obispo del Cuzco. Azángaro, November 28, 1781.

Carta de Antonio de Valdés al obispo del Cuzco. Azángaro, December 6, 1781.

Carta de Dr. Antonio de Valdés al obispo del Cuzco. Checacupe, February 26, 1782.

Bibliography

Vertíz, Juan José de
    Correspondencia Vertíz-Gálvez 1781. Archivo de la Nación. Buenos
    Aires.

II. Printed Documents

Alós Joaquín
    "Decreto de Alós de 12 de Junio de 1779 ordenando la prisión de
    Tomás Catari." Archivo General de la Nación. Buenos Aires.
    Criminales. Legajo 181, expediente 28. In Boleslao Lewin, *Tupac
    Amaru el rebelde su época, sus luchas y su influencia en el con-
    tinente*, Appendix, p. 459.
    "Informe de Alós á la audiencia de 7 de Septiembre de 1779." AGN.
    Buenos Aires. Tribunales. Leg. 181, exp. 29. *Ibid.*, Appendix,
    pp. 460–61.
    "Informe de Alós al presidente de la audiencia de 29 de Junio de
    1779." AGN. Buenos Aires. Tribunales. Leg. 171, exp. 29. *Ibid.*,
    Appendix, pp. 459–60.
    "Informe de Alós al presidente de la audiencia de 20 de Junio de
    1780." AGN. Buenos Aires. Tribunales. Leg. 181, exp. 79. *Ibid.*,
    Appendix, p. 463.

Abellafuertes, José
    "El corregidor de Pasco, José Abellafuertes á Don José Antonio de
    Areche. Pasco, March 22, 1780." In Francisco A Loayza, ed., *Los
    pequeños grandes libros de historia Americana*, Serie I, Vol. XIII.
    Lima, 1947.

Angelis, Pedro de
    *Colección de obras y documentos para la historia antigua y moderna
    de las provincias del Río de la Plata.* 6 vols. Buenos Aires, 1836.
    *Documentos para la historia de la sublevación de José Gabriel Túpac
    Amaru, cacique de la provincia de Tinta, en el Peru.* Primera
    edición. Buenos Aires, 1836.

Angulo, Valentín de
    "Carta á Don José Antonio de Areche. Caja de Real de Pasco, March
    8, 1780." In Loayza, *op. cit.*, Serie I, Vol. XIII. Lima, 1947.

Areche, José Antonio de
    "Carta de José Antonio de Areche al Antonio de Arriaga. Lima, June
    28, 1780." In Loayza, *op. cit.*, Serie I, Vol. III. Lima, 1948.
    "Carta de Areche el corregidor de la Paz desaprobando la suspención

399

de la aduana." Lima, July 22, 1780. AGN. Buenos Aires. Criminales. Leg. 16, exp. 26. In Lewin, *op. cit.*, Appendix, pp. 432–33.

Arriaga, Antonio de
  "Carta de Antonio de Arriaga al visitador José Antonio de Areche. Cuzco, July 22, 1780." In Loayza, *op. cit.*, Serie I, Vol. III. Lima, 1948.

Arriaga, Miguel de
  "Representación diriguda al rey por Don Miguel de Arriaga y Don Eusebio Balza de Verganza con fecha de 24 de Diciembre de 1780." In Loayza, *op. cit.*, Serie I, Vol. III. Lima, 1948.

Ballivián y Roxas, Vicente de
  Archivo Boliviano. Colección de documentos relativos a la historia de Bolivia, durante le época colonial. Paris, 1782. (This work contains an abundance of printed source material on the uprising of Túpac Amaru.)

Beltrán y Rózpide, Ricardo
  Colección de las memorias ó relaciones que escribieron los virreyes del Peru acerca del estado en que dejaban las cosas generales del reino. Madrid, 1921.

Balza, Eusebio
  "Representación de Don Eusebio Balza dirigida desde el Cuzco al supremo consejo de Indias en 8 de Septiembre de 1781." In Loayza, *op. cit.*, Serie I, Vol. III. Lima, 1948.

Casa Hermosa, Marqués de
  "El marqués de Casa Hermosa á Don José Antonio de Areche. Huaráz, February 9, 1780." In Loayza, *op. cit.*, Serie I, Vol. XIII. Lima, 1947.

Catari, Tomás
  "Carta de Tomás Catari al fiscal protector general de la primera mitad de Junio de 1779." AGN. Buenos Aires. Tribunales. Leg. 181, exp. 29. In Lewin, *op. cit.*, Appendix, pp. 457–58.
  "Catari y otros Indios denuncian (en Mayo o Junio de 1779) las violencias de Bernal." AGN. Buenos Aires. Criminales. Leg. 181, exp. 29. In Lewin, *op. cit.*, Appendix, p. 456.
  "Petición de Tomás Catari al virrey de los primeros días de Enero de 1779." AGN. Buenos Aires. División colonia. Sección gobierno. Tribunales. Leg. 181, exp. 29. In Lewin, *op. cit.*, Appendix, pp. 452–53.

Bibliography

"Petición de Tomás Catari. Dirigida al presidente de la audiencia el 12 de Diciembre de 1779." AGN. Buenos Aires. Tribunales. Leg. 181, exp. 29. In Lewin, *op. cit.*, Appendix, p. 461.

"Representación de Tomás Catari al virrey del 12 de Noviembre de 1780." AGN. Buenos Aires. División colonia. Sección gobierno. Tribunales. Leg. 124, exp. 3. In Lewin, *op. cit.*, Appendix, pp. 465–69.

Colección de documentos inéditos relativos al descubrimiento, conquista organización de las antiguas posesiones españoles de América y Oceanía. 42 vols. Madrid, 1864–84.

Colección de memorias y documentos para la historia y geografía de los publos del Río de la Plata. Montevideo, 1849.

Croix, Charles François
  Correspondance du marquis de Croix, capitaine general des armés de S. M. C., viceroi du Méxique. Nantes, 1891.

"Dictamen del fiscal de la audiencia de Charcas del 15 de Abril de 1779." AGN. Buenos Aires. Tribunales. In Lewin, *op. cit.*, Appendix, pp. 455–56.

Documents from Early Peru: The Pizarros and the Almagros, 1531–78. Harkness Collection, Library of Congress. Washington, 1936.

"El cabildo de Córdoba dictamina sobre los motivos de la sublevación. Córdoba, June 8, 1781." AGN. Montevideo. Colección de documentos copiados por Mario Falcao Espalter del Archivo General de Indias en Sevilla. Años 1781–83. In Lewin, *op. cit.*, Appendix, pp. 479–81.

"El virrey del Río de la Plata continua la relación de los sucesos del Perú. Montevideo, September 30, 1782." AGN. Buenos Aires. Correspondencia Vertíz-Gálvez, 1782. In Lewin, *op. cit.*, Appendix, pp. 481–82.

Falcón, Francisco
  "Representación hecha por el licenciado Francisco Falcón en concilio provincial sobre los daños y molestias que se hacen a los Indios." In Loayza, *op. cit.*, Serie I, Vol. X. Lima, 1946.

Flores, Ignacio
  "Carta de Ignacio Flores á Juan Josef de Vertíz. La Paz, August 4, 1782." AGN. Montevideo. Fondo documental. Ex-Archivo y Museo Histórico Nacional. In Lewin, *op. cit.*, Appendix, p. 417.
  "Carta de Ignacio Flores á Vertíz sobre la prisión de Catari sin orden suya ni del virrey. La Plata, April 15, 1781." AGN. Montevideo.

Fondo documental. Ex-Archivo y Museo Histórico Nacional. In Lewin, *op. cit.*, Appendix, p. 469.

"Informe de Flores sobre los oidores de la audiencia. La Plata, April 14, 1783." AGN. Buenos Aires. Correspondencia Vertíz-Gálvez 1783. In Lewin, *op. cit.*, Appendix, pp. 439–40.

González Pavón, Antonio

"Causas de la sublevación indígena (Documento inédito del año 1788)." In Loayza, *op. cit.*, Serie I, Vol. X. Lima, 1946.

Gutiérrez, Rozendo José

Documentos para la historia antigua de Bolivia. La Paz, 1879.

"Informe de los oficiales de Potosí del 13 de Noviembre de 1780." AGN. Buenos Aires. División colonia. Sección gobierno. Tribunales. Leg. 124. exp. 4. In Lewin, *op. cit.*, Appendix, p. 464.

"Informe del procurador general de Salta sobre los motivos de la subla-vación. Salta, June 9, 1781." AGN. Montevideo. Colección de docu-mentos copiados por M. Falcao Espalter en el Archivo General de Indias en Sevilla. Años 1781–83. In Lewin, *op. cit.*, Appendix, pp. 477–79.

Instrucción que los virreyes de Nueva España dejaron a sus sucesores. Mexico, 1867.

Jiménez Villalba, Simón

"Carta de Simón Jiménez Villalba al Señor Don Benito de la Mata Linares, Cuzco, June 18, 1784." In Loayza, *op. cit.*, Serie I, Vol. III. Lima, 1948.

Juan, Jorge, and Antonio de Ulloa

Noticias secretas de America sobre el estado naval, militar, y político de los reynos del Peru y provincias de Quito, costas de Nueva Granada y Chile: gobierno y regimen particular de los pueblos de Indios: cruel opresión y extorsiones de sus corregidores y curas; abusos escandalosos introducidos entre estos habitantes por los misioneros: causas de su origin y motives de su continuación por el especio de tres siglos. Escritos fielmente segun las instrucciones del excelentísimo Señor marqués de la Ensenada, primer secretario de estado, presentadas en informe secreto á S. M. C. el Señor Don Fernando VI. London, 1826. (Juan and Ulloa made a scientific expedition to South America from 1736 to 1744, carefully observ-ing conditions, and from 1758 to 1763, Ulloa was governor of Guancavelica. The *Noticias secretas* was written in 1749 as a confidential report for the Spanish court, but in 1826 an English merchant, Davis Barry of Cádiz, obtained a copy and had it published in London.)

Lamas, Andrés
Colleción de memorias y documentos para la historia y geografía de los pueblos del Río de la Plata. 2 vols. Montevideo, 1949.

"La prisión del hijo de Túpac Catari. La Paz, April 8, 1783." Biblioteca Nacional. Buenos Aires. Sección manuscritos. Num. 6139. In Lewin, *op. cit.,* Appendix, p. 476.

Loasa, Friar Rodrigo de
Memorial de las cosas del Peru tocante á los Indios. Madrid, 1889.

Loayza, Francisco A., ed.
Cuarenta años de cautiverio (Memorias del Inka Juan Bautista Túpac Amaru). In *Los pequeños grandes libros de historia Americana.* Serie I, Vol. I. Lima, 1941.

Estado del Peru. Ibid., Serie I, Vol. V. Lima, 1944.

Juan Santos, el invencible (Manuscritos del año 1742 al año de 1755). Ibid., Serie I, Vol. II. Lima, 1942.

La verdad desnuda o dos faces de un obispo. Ibid., Serie I, Vol. III. Lima, 1948.

Martires y Heroínas (Documentos del año de 1780 á 1782). Ibid., Serie I, Vol. IX. Lima, 1945.

Preliminarios del incendio. Documentos del año de 1776 á 1780 en su mayoría inéditos, anteriores y sobre la revolución libertadora que engendró y dió vida José Gabriel Túpac Amaru, en 1780. Ibid., Serie I, Vol. XIII. Lima, 1947. (All of Loayza's works contain many hitherto unedited and unpublished letters and documents.)

Lupa, Florencio
"Documento anónimo sobre el papel desempeñado por Florencio Lupa." Biblioteca Nacional. Buenos Aires. Sección manuscritos 2158. In Lewin, *op. cit.,* Appendix, p. 470.

Mackehenie, C. A.
Un inédito sobre Diego Cristóbal Túpac Amaru. Vol. I, No. 6 (Peru, 1924).

"Manifesto. Cuzco, November 11, 1782." In Loayza, *op. cit.,* Serie I, Vol. III. Lima, 1943.

Memorias de los virreyes que han gobernado el Peru. 6 vols. Lima, 1859.

Merlos, Gregorio
"Oficio de Merlos á Vertíz, de 14 de Noviembre de 1780." AGN.

Buenos Aires. División colonia. Sección gobierno. Tribunales. Leg. 124. In Lewin, *op. cit.*, Appendix, pp. 424–26.

"Oficio de Merlos á Vertíz del 15 de 1781. La Plata, February 15, 1781." AGN. Buenos Aires. In Lewin, *op. cit.*, Appendix, pp. 427–29.

Miller, John

    Memorias del General Miller al servicio de la república del Peru. Traducidas al castellano por el General Torrejos. 3 vols. Santiago de Chile, 1912. (While in Peru, General Miller collected many documents and interviewed people who had taken part in the Inca revolt.)

Moscoso, Juan Manuel

    "Carta de Juan Manuel [Moscoso] obispo del Cuzco al Señor Don Agustín de Jáuregui, Cuzco, January 5, 1780." In Loayza, *op. cit.*, Serie I, Vol. V. Lima, 1944.

Odriozola, Manuel de

    Documentos históricos del Peru en las épocas del coloniaje después de la conquista y de la independencia hasta la presente. 10 vols. in 6. Lima, 1863–77. (This work contains an abundance of printed source material on the uprising of Túpac Amaru.)

"Oficio de los corregidores de Chucuito, Lampa y Azángaro del 12 de Diciembre de 1781, pidiendo la detención de Diego Cristóbal Túpac Amaru." AGN. Buenos Aires. VI–XVI–9–12. In Lewin, *op. cit.*, Appendix, p. 483.

"Pasquín fijada en Santiago del Estero. Acuerdo del cabildo del 31 de Mayo de 1782." AGN. Buenos Aires. División colonia. Sección gobierno. VI–VII–7–5. In Lewin, *op. cit.*, Appendix, p. 451.

"Petición del protector de naturales, del 4 de Diciembre de 1778." AGN. Buenos Aires. División colonia. Sección gobierno. Tribunales. Leg. 181, exp. 29. In Lewin, *op. cit.*, Appendix, p. 462.

Real ordenanza para el establicimiento é introducción de intendentes de ejército y provincia en el virreinato de Buenos Aires. Madrid, 1782.

Revista de archivos y bibliotecas nacionales. Peruanas. Año 1900. Vol. IV.

Revista del Archivo General de Buenos Aires. 4 vols. Buenos Aires, 1869–72.

Santos, Andrés

    "Carta de Andrés Santos al rey. La Plata, April 25, 1778." In Loayza, *op cit.*, Serie I, Vol. III. Lima, 1948.

Bibliography

Torres Lanzas, Pedro
Independencia de America, fuentes para su estudio; cátalogo de documentos conservados en el Archivo General de Indias de Sevilla. Segunda serie. Seville, 1924.
Túpac Amaru, Andrés
"Carta de Andrés Túpac Amaru al rector Don Francisco de Miranda y Montoya. La Paz, September 5, 1781." AGN. Buenos Aires. División colonia. Sección gobierno. VI–VIII–5–6. In Lewin, *op. cit.*, Appendix, pp. 475–76.
Túpac Amaru, Diego
"Bando de Diego Túpac Amaru. Azángaro, August 29, 1781." AGN. Buenos Aires, VI–XVI–9–12. In Lewin, *op. cit.*, Appendix, pp. 471–74.
Túpac Amaru, José Gabriel
"Carta de José Gabriel Túpac Amaru al corregidor Don Antonio de Arriaga. Tungasuca, March 15, 1780." In Loayza, *op. cit.*, Serie I, Vol. III. Lima, 1948.
"Carta de José Gabriel Túpac Amaru á Don Antonio de Arriaga. Tungasuca, March 22, 1780." In Loayza, *op. cit.*, Serie I, Vol. III. Lima, 1948.
"Genealogía de Túpac Amaru por José Gabriel Túpac Amaru (Documento inédito del año de 1777)." In Loayza, *op. cit.*, Serie I, Vol. X. Lima, 1946.
Vertíz, Juan Josef de
"Carta de Juan Josef de Vertíz al José de Gálvez. March 15, 1781, num. 458 reservada." AGN. Buenos Aires. Correspondencia Vertíz-Gálvez, 1781. In Lewin, *op. cit.*, Appendix, pp. 434–37.
"Carta de Vertíz á Gálvez sobre la conducta de Merlos y Ormachea. May 31, 1783." AGN. Buenos Aires. Correspondencia Vertíz-Gálvez, 1783. In Lewin, *op. cit.*, Appendix, pp. 429–30.
"Carta de Vertíz á José de Gálvez. Montevideo, February 20, 1782." AGN. Buenos Aires. Correspondencia Vertíz-Gálvez, 1782. In Lewin, *op. cit.*, Appendix, pp. 484–86.
"Orden de Vertíz sobre la aparición de pasquines en Buenos Aires. Buenos Aires, August 23, 1779." AGN. Buenos Aires. Criminales. Leg. 15, exp. 20. In Lewin, *op. cit.*, Appendix, p. 432.
"Vertíz informe á Gálvez que el corregidor de Chananta Joaquín Alós, resultó indemne de los cargos que se le formaron." AGN.

Buenos Aires. Correspondencia Vertíz-Gálvez, 1783. In Lewin, *op. cit.*, Appendix, p. 484.

"Visita fiscal del 15 de junio de 1781, respectiva al informe de Maestre de 26 de Mayo de 1781." AGN. Buenos Aires. Tribunales. Leg. 127, exp. 13. In Lewin, *op. cit.*, Appendix, p. 440.

III. OTHER SOURCES

Abecia, Valentín
  Historia de Chuquisaca. Sucre, 1934.
Arciniegas, Germán
  Los comuneros. 2nd. ed. Bogotá, 1939.
Barreda Laos, Felipe
  Vida intelectual del virreinato del Peru. Buenos Aires, 1937.
Briceño, Manuel
  Los comuneros. Historia de la insurrección de 1781. Bogotá, 1880.
Bromley, Juan
  Virreyes, cabildantes y oidores. Lima, 1944.
Cánovas del Castillo, Antonio de
  Historia general de España. 6 vols. Madrid, 1890–96.
Carrió, V. M.
  Crónicas Americanas. La Paz, 1910.
Cevallos, Pedro Fermin
  Resumen de la historia del Ecuador su origin hasta 1845. 5 vols. Guayaquil, 1886.
Colección de libros españoles raros ó curiosos, XIII. Madrid, 1879.
Dávila, Vicente
  "Los comuneros de Mérida," *Investigaciones históricos,* Vol. II (Caracas, 1927), 241–43.
Del Campillo y Cosio, Josef
  Nueva sistema de gobierno económico para la América. Madrid, 1789.
Del Solar, Emilio
  Insurección de Túpac Amaru, sus antecedentes y efectos. Lima, 1926.
Eguiguren, Luis Antonio
  Guerra separatista del Peru 1777–1780. Lima, 1942.
Eguren de Larrea, D. F.
  Cuzco. Lima, 1929.
Fisher, Lillian Estelle
  "Teodoro de Croix," *Hispanic American Historical Review,* Vol. IX, No. 4 (November 1929).

Bibliography

The Intendant System in the Spanish Americas. Berkeley, 1929.
Viceregal Administration in the Spanish American Colonies. Berkeley,
1926.
Funes, Gregorio
Ensayo de la historia civil de Buenos Aires: Tucumán y Paraguay.
2 vols. in 1. Buenos Aires, 1856.
Galán, Angel
"Vida de José Antonio Galán en los comuneros," Biblioteca de his-
toria nacional, Vol. IV (Bogotá, 1905), 229–30.
Gamarra, Manuel Jesús
La ciudad de los Incas. Cuzco, 1922.
García Naranjo, Joaquín
Sublevación de Túpac-Amaru en el Peru. Seville, 1912.
Gibson, Charles
The Inca Concept of Sovereignty and the Spanish Administration in
Peru. Austin, 1948.
González, Suárez, Federico
Historia general de la república del Ecuador. 6 vols. Quito, 1890–1903.
Groot, José Manuel
Historia ecclesiástica y civil de Nueva Granada. 2nd. ed. 5 vols.,
Bogotá, 1889–93.
Hakluyt Society
History of the Incas. Publications, Ser. II, No. XXII. Cambridge, 1907.
Humboldt, Alexander von
Ensayo político sobre Nueva España. Paris, 1836.
Kubler, George
"The Quecha in the Colonial World," Handbook of South American
Indians (ed. by Julian Steward, 6 vols., Washington, 1946–50),
II, 331–409.
Lewin, Boleslao
Túpac Amaru el rebelde su época, sus luchas y su influencia en el
continente. Buenos Aires, 1943.
Lorente, Sebastián
Historia de la conquista del Peru. Lima, 1861.
Historia del Peru bajo los Borbones, 1700–1821. Lima, 1871.
Luna, Carlos Correa
Don Baltasar de Arandia. Buenos Aires, 1918.
Markham, Sir Clements R.
A History of Peru. Chicago, 1892.

Travels in Peru and India. London, 1862.

The Incas of Peru. New York, 1910.

Matienzo, Juan

Gobierno del Perú: Obra escrita en el siglo XVI. Buenos Aires, 1910.

Means, Philip Ainsworth

Ciertos aspectos de la rebelión de Túpac Amaru II, 1780–1781. Lima, 1920.

Fall of the Inca Empire and the Spanish Rule in Peru: 1530–1780. New York, 1932.

"The Rebellion of Túpac Amaru II, 1780–1781," *Hispanic American Historical Review,* Vol. II, No. 1 (February, 1919).

Mendiburu, Manuel de

Diccionario histórico-biográfico del Peru. 8 vols. Lima, 1847–90.

Moses, Bernard

South America on the Eve of Independence. New York, 1908.

Navarro y Lamarca, Carlos

Compendio de la historia general de America. 2 vols. Buenos Aires, 1910–13.

Ordóñez López, Manuel de, and Crespo, Luis S.

Bosquejo de la historia de Bolivia. La Paz, 1912.

Palma, Ricardo

Tradiciones Peruanas. 4 vols. Barcelona, 1893–96.

Paz Soldán, Mariano Felipe

Diccionario geográfico estadístico del Peru. Lima, 1877.

Pereyra, Carlos

Historia de la América Española. 7 vols. Madrid, 1925.

Prado, Javier

Estado social del Peru durante la dominación Española. Lima, 1941.

Radin, Paul

Indians of South America, New York, 1942.

Restrepo, José Manuel

Historia de la revolución de la república de Colombia. 10 vols. Paris, 1827.

Rowe, John Howland

Colonial Portraits of Inca Nobles. Reprint from *Proceedings* of the 29th International Congress of Americanists, I. Chicago, 1951.

Santa Cruz, Victor

Historia colonial de la Paz. La Paz, 1942.

Bibliography

Temple, Edmond
    Travels in Various Parts of Peru, including a Year's Residence in Potosí. 2 vols. London, 1830.
Valcárcel, Daniel
    La rebelión de Túpac Amaru. Mexico, 1947.
    Rebeliones indígenes. Lima, 1946.
Valega, José M.
    El virreinato del Perú; historia crítica de la época colonial, en todo sus aspectos. Lima, 1939.
Vargas Ugarte, Ruben, S. J.
    Historia del Peru Virreinato (1551–1590). Lima, 1942.
Vidaurre, Manuel de
    Plan del Peru, defectos del gobierno español antigua, necessarias reformas. Filadelfia, 1823.
Villanueva, Carlos A.
    Napoleón y la independencia de América. Paris, n.d.
Wiesse, Carlos
    Historia del Peru. Lima, 1914.
Whitaker, Arthur P.
    "Antonio de Ulloa," *Hispanic American Historical Review,* May, 1935.
Zimmerman, Arthur Franklin
    Francisco de Toledo, Fifth Viceroy of Peru, 1569–1581. Caldwell, Idaho, 1938.

Index

Index

413

419